Constructivist Epistemology and Pedagogy

Insight into Teaching Learning and Knowing

Arbind Kumar Jha

ATLANTIC
PUBLISHERS & DISTRIBUTORS (P) LTD

ATLANTIC
PUBLISHERS & DISTRIBUTORS (P) LTD

7/22, Ansari Road, Darya Ganj, New Delhi
Tel.: +91-11-4077 5252, 2327 3880
E-mail: orders@atlanticbooks.com
Web: www.atlanticbooks.com

Reprint 2025, 2026

Published by Atlantic Publishers & Distributors (P) Ltd.

Printed & bound in India by Atlantic Print Services

Preface

Today's mutable world is generally recognized as the multi-cultural and multi-perspectival in which we all are bound to live with our own multi-coloured realities of the so-called ultimate reality. The production of realities—the production of viable ways of 'world-making and meaning-making' in the sense of both knowing and known—is a process of construction by the people themselves.

Constructivism, in general, is perceived as the philosophical position which propounds that any reality is, in most immediate and concrete sense, the mental construction of those who believe that the knowing and the known are the processes of construction by the people themselves and that they have discovered and investigated on the basis of their own experiences in a given set of culture. Constructivism is a holistic realistic philosophy which advocates a kind of epistemology which talks about knowing rather than knowledge as such. It is an epistemology, a learning or meaning-making theory, which offers an explanation of the nature of knowing and how human beings learn.

Constructivist education, with all its strength and limitation, proclaims to be a tool in hand that not only meets the pragmatic needs of education, but also extends the operational boundaries of teaching, learning and above all, knowing to register qualitative advance on run-of-the-mill function of education at different levels. The book in hand is a small contribution like a drop of water in the ocean of constructivist education.

I am one of those fortunate enough to be blessed with that positive and refurbishing energy which is the cause of creation of everything in this cosmic drama of the world. This very energy has always been motivating and propelling me to do some constructive and challenging work. This work is also the creation of the same cosmic energy where I have played merely a role of an agent. Thanks to that energy.

No work is a unitary work and I have no hesitation to say that the present work is also a synergetic work as there are many people behind this—directly or indirectly. Thus, first of all I would like to express my deep and sincere gratitude to all those thinkers and writers, whose works I have consulted for the completion of the book.

I feel privileged to express my heartfelt thanks to Prof. R.P. Sharma and Prof. Giriswar Misra who have been generous in extending all help and guidance from time to time. Their timely and prudent interventions have indeed helped me immensely.

I am grateful to my parents for their tireless efforts to make me what I am. Thanks to my brothers—Dharmendra and Birendra—sisters-in-law and all kith and kin. Also thanks are due to my parents-in-law. Many thanks to my wife, Sangeeta for all her love and care that she has been bestowing upon me. I must acknowledge my son, Advait, for his unconditional love, spontaneous inquisitiveness and wonderful joy that he brings to us by his cute naughty little acts.

Last but not least, I am thankful to Atlantic Publishers & Distributors (P) Ltd., New Delhi, for giving this book its present shape.

Arbind Kumar Jha

Contents

Acknowledgements *iii*

Preface *v*

1. **Introduction** **1-11**

2. **Constructivism: Thinkers, Theories and Theorists 12-131**

 2.1 Concept and Perspectives 12

 2.2 Constructivist Thinkers, Theories and Theorists 17

  2.2.1 Giambattista Vico 21

  2.2.2 Immanuel Kant 28

  2.2.3 John Dewey 33

  2.2.4 Jean Piaget 46

  2.2.5 Lev Semyonovich Vygotsky 59

  2.2.6 Jerome Seymour Bruner 68

  2.2.7 Ernst von Glasersfeld 80

  2.2.8 Kenneth J. Gergen 90

 2.3 What is Constructivism 99

 2.4 Types of Constructivism 111

 2.5 Implications of Constructivism 123

3. **Constructivist Epistemology** **132-170**

 3.1 Epistemic Aspect of Constructivism 132

 3.2 Epistemological Aspect of Constructivism 138

 3.3 Constructivist Learning: A New Approach to Learning 144

  3.3.1 Constructivist Learning Principles 154

  3.3.2 Constructivist Learning Theory 160

 3.4 Constructing Knowledge of Constructivism 166

4. Constructivist Pedagogy 171-249

4.1 Constructivist Teaching: Nature and Processes 171

4.2 Constructivist Principles of Teaching 179

4.3 Constructivist Notion of a Teacher 182

4.4 Designing the Classroom in a Constructivist Setting 186

4.5 Becoming a Constructivist Teacher 202

4.6 Constructivist Teaching Strategies 211

4.7 Assessment from a Constructivist Perspective 231

5. Constructivism and Teacher Education 250-311

5.1 Foundations of Teacher Education 251

5.2 A New Approach to Teacher Education 258

5.3 The Issue of Preservice Teacher Education 271

5.4 Teacher-Educator Paradigm Revisited 286

5.5 Bringing Change in Teachers' Thinking 296

5.6 Redesigning Teacher Preparation Programme 301

6. Constructivism and Distance Education 312-336

6.1 Issues in Instructional Design in Distance Education 312

6.2 Constructivism in Instructional Design in Distance Education 325

7. Constructivism and Instructional Technology 337-384

7.1 Enriching the Practices of Instructional Technology 337

7.2 Instructional Design Revisited 347

7.3 Traditional Instruction vs. Constructivism 360

7.4 What Role can Technology play in a Constructivist Setting? 366

7.5 The Constructivism-Computer Connection 373

8. Constructivism and Curriculum 385-400

9. Constructivism in Mathematics and Science Education 401-433

9.1 Constructivist Mathematics Education 401

9.2 Constructivist Science Education 417

10. Constructivist Research 434-450

11. Constructivism: Potentials and Problems 451-466

Bibliography 467-477

Index 478

1

Introduction

Calling a society a 'knowledge society' has virtually become a fashionable paradigm for speaking about the future society in every nation of the world. This phrase has attracted almost every intellectual irrespective of fields of study to inquire into the realms of its various layers which have remained confined to the domain of either philosophers or psychologists. Today, from educationists to policymakers, researchers, etc. are found interested to unearth the various seethes of knowledge which if excavated properly may bring unlimited source of intellectual mites to equip one to discover the mysteries of the nature and human potentialities. But, ironically every good thing carries, to some extent, some bad things, too. The way every one is projecting the importance of knowledge it seems that it has created the illusion that we know what we are talking about when we talk about knowledge. On the contrary, the hard fact is that we do not know what we are talking about particularly knowledge due to narrowed and coloured perspective. In spite of stupendous progress in every field, the discourse of the knowledge society suffers from major deficiencies such as it does not take a critical enough view of what knowledge means and of the fundamental changes that the concept of knowledge has undergone. Also, the discourse on knowledge and the knowledge society fails to recognize that the debate on the concept and the production of knowledge has a major global and universal dimension.

It was Machlup (1962) who for the first time introduced the notion of a knowledge society by analyzing the growth of the knowledge producing industries such as education, research and development, media and communications and information machinery. Bell (1974) observed that information and knowledge has become key resources in the post-industrial society, in much the same way that labour and capital are central resources of industrial societies. Since then the concept of knowledge has undergone profound changes and has been at the centre of major controversies so much so that it will not be incorrect to speak of a deepening sense of crisis in the modern knowledge system. These changes have to do with the epistemological foundations of our understanding of knowledge, but also with the way in which we assess different processes and institutional forms of knowledge production. The central issues are both the criteria for judging the validity and adequacy of knowledge and the structural arrangements under which knowledge is being produced. In substantial terms, this process of transformation is diverse; it involves, among other things—both the questioning of the epistemological tradition of a unified science and the de-monopolization of a concept of knowledge that has its roots in the natural sciences as well as the emergence of new ways of knowing. What all of them have in common is the fact that they question the notion of a homogenous and uniform concept of knowledge that can be applied equally to every conceivable object. This notion originated in the epistemology of the classical natural sciences and its extension to the social and behavioural sciences.

Now the moot point is what is valid and what is not valid. To call something valid or invalid it is important to ascertain first what is validity itself? Is there something like universal valid or is validity universal? After thorough examining of validity we will be in a position to answer questions like what is valid knowledge. And finally is valid knowledge knowable? The perceived knowledge tells us that the whole concept of validity and valid knowledge, at least from the positivists' points of view, is based on simple cause effect relationships. On the contrary, the demand of the time, at least in the paradigm of changed concept of knowledge and validity of knowledge, is that a context-dependent is more desirable instead of simple cause effect relationships (Mishra, 1996).

A study is valid if its measures actually measure what they claim to, and if there are no logical errors in drawing conclusions from the data. There are a great many labels for different types of validity, but they all have to do with threats and biases which would undermine the meaningfulness of educational research. The traditional criteria for 'validity' find their roots in a positivist tradition, and to an extent, positivism has been defined by and bolstered along by a systematic theory of 'validity'. Within the positivist terminology, 'validity' resided amongst, and was the result and culmination of other empirical conceptions: universal laws, evidence, objectivity, truth, actuality, deduction, reason, fact and mathematical data to name just a few. It is within this tradition and terminology that our educational affair is traditionally defined. Recently, in India, new education process, arising out of the post-positivist rejection of a single, static or objective truth, has concerned itself with the meanings and personal experience of individuals, groups and sub-cultures. Thus, reality is now more concerned with the negotiation of 'truths' through a series of subjective accounts.

Thus, unquestionably reliability and validity are tools of an essentially positivist epistemology. While they may have undoubtedly proved useful in providing checks and balances for objectivist and behaviourist paradigm of education, they sit uncomfortably in that kind of education which is better concerned by questions about equity and equality, power and influence, adequacy and efficiency, suitability and accountability, etc. On the other hand constructivist epistemology takes completely opposite view due to dynamicity of change which has always affected every aspect of human life and knowledge. This change is explicitly evident in epistemology too where the trend has been to move from a static, passive view of knowledge towards a more adaptive and active view (Heylighen, 1993). Each theory emphasized knowledge as being awareness of objects that exist independent of any subject. According to this objectivist view, objects have intrinsic meaning and knowledge is a reflection of a correspondence to reality. In this tradition, knowledge should represent a real world that is thought of as existing, separate and independent of the knower, and this knowledge should be considered true only if it correctly reflects that independent world. In contrast, the Constructivists argue that knowledge and reality do not have an objective or absolute value or at the least, that we have no way of knowing this reality. von Glasersfeld (1995) indicates in relation to the concept of reality: "It is made up of the network of things and relationships that we rely on in our living, and on which, we believe, others rely on, too." The knower interprets and constructs a reality based on his experiences and interactions with his environment. Rather than thinking of truth in terms of a match to reality, von Glasersfeld focuses instead on the notion of viability: "To the Constructivist, concepts, models, theories, and so on are viable if they prove adequate in the contexts in which they were created."

In short, it can be asserted on the basis of above stated facts that 'validity' is not a single, fixed or universal concept, but rather a contingent construct, inescapably grounded in the processes and intentions of particular theory of knowledge. There is no single form, construct or concept that can universally be claimed to define or encompass the term. Neither, however, can validity be said to be a discretely identifiable element. This way we find that the concept of validity is in constant flux as two differing paradigms of education such as Objectivist and Constructivist look at it from the different perspectives and suggest different measures to find the validity of knowledge. There is indeed a need to have differing realms of reality and validity as today's world is mostly depicted as multi-perspective or multi-reality world in terms of socio-political and socio-cultural settings in which we are bound to live with differing and divergent notions and opinions. In the latest paradigm of reality, knowledge and learning, it is no more perceived as fixed or absolute rather it has been accepted that it is constructed one on the basis of acquired and perceived experiences in a particular context.

Unfortunately our formal education has traditionally relied on the objectivist view of knowledge too much. This view of learning and knowledge assumes that knowledge can be imparted from teacher to learner through instruction, lecture and practice. This view of traditional adult education assumes true reality can be determined by "a large accumulation of facts"

(Kelly, 1970). Teaching and research driven by this philosophy discourage different views and understandings, disregarding different contexts, and experiences of individuals, and regard individuals as passive recipients of knowledge. Although lectures and information giving techniques may be affective in some contexts and for some individual learning styles, their continued use as a dominant pedagogy has allowed limited recognition to diverse preferences of learning. Limited learner participation and interaction in the objectivist view has also disallowed pedagogues to realise the need for learner control during the process of learning. Learning in this context rather places emphasis on teacher-control and learner compliance (Gulati, 2004).

In recent times, educators and institutional discourses have begun to challenge the objectivist view, with an increasing appreciation of different ways of knowing the world. Constructivist writers in education have described varied versions of constructivism, but commonly acknowledged the active role of the learner in interpretation of reality (Larochell & Bednarz, 1998). They challenge the objectivist view that suggests "facts speak for themselves" and that "knowledge is the reflection of ontological reality, and that language objectively refers to this reality" (Larochell & Bednarz, 1998). The constructivism alternativism philosophy, described by George Kelly (1970) instead suggests that our constructions and views of the world are not stable, but are in continuous change as we build on past experiences. This change signifies learning and supports the understanding that as human beings, we are always construing and learning, and we are never inert (Kelly, 1970).

Constructivist education with all its strength and limitation, proclaims a tool in hand that not only meets the pragmatic needs of education, but also extends the operational boundaries of teaching and learning to register qualitative advance on run-of-the-mill function of education at different levels.

There may be the difference of perception in viewing the relationship between the teaching and learning and accordingly they may be adopting the approaches. Also, teachers use different method to impart contents of the curriculum, but, there is no doubt that they all use the same method or technique to reinforce and extend the learning by situating the entire context in behaviouristic paradigm which denies the multiperspectivity on behalf of learners. On the other hand there is constructivism which advocates the multiperspectivity in widest sense. Now, the question of constructivist education brings in its train a host of many other contentious issues. What is constructivism?, what are types of constructivism?, what constructivism does advocate regarding teaching, learning and knowing? etc.—these are question which have evoked multiple response from the people engaged in constructivist education. These are the problems, which need to be studied in terms of aspects that are theoretical as well as practical in nature. Therefore, this is an attempt to revisit Constructivist Education to see its import and implications for modern education.

The debate over constructivist education must be redirected. To increase students' buy-in, it's time to rethink how to make constructivism a more valued part of the pedagogic process. In addition to promoting academic achievement in holistic sense, constructivist education can inculcate habits of self-discovery and independent study along with cooperative learning where one learns how to value others view. We must find ways to make constructivist educational practices an interesting and challenging educational experience for students, instead of the uniform, seat-bound, memorization focused solo exercise it has been. Otherwise, all our talk about high standards and improving student achievement will run up against the same roadblock that has stymied the pursuit of educational excellence in the past.

Apart from above stated facts, a sincere attempt has been made to highlight some of the cultural myths that are prevalent in today's education systems and have made a deep impact in the psyche of all the stakeholders of education in general and teachers in particular. Taylor (1996) has explicated beautifully about the myths in education in following words:

- The rationalist myth of cold reason—where knowledge is seen as discovery of an external truth. This can lead to the picture of the teacher in a central role as transmitter of objective truths to students. This philosophy does not promote clarifying relevance to the lives of students, but instead promotes a curriculum to be delivered.

- The myth of hard control—which renders the teacher's classroom role as controller, and "locks teachers and students into grossly asymmetrical poor relationships designed to reproduce, rather than challenge, the established culture".

Together these myths produce a culture that portrays classroom teaching and learning as "a journey through a pre-constructed landscape". There is a dire need to modify such entrenched environments to reduce these myths and promote constructivism. The main ideas underpinning constructivism learning theories are not new. They began with the insights of Socrates who claimed that there are basic conditions for learning that are in the cognition of the individual (Kanuka & Anderson, 1998). But it was Piaget's theory of intellectual growth that had the primary influence on the development of current positions. Specifically, Piaget first emphasized the processes of conceptual change as interactions between existing cognitive structures and new experience. The book is an endeavour to expose these cultural myths and to make and establish constructivism as one of the most potent philosophies on which entire gamut of art and science of educational affairs in general and method of teaching and learning in any form of educational set up in particular may be structured and organized. A sincere attempt has been made to convince all the stakeholders of education that constructivism is one of the most powerful tools of learning experience. The method of this book is to present basic theoretical understanding and methodological ideas about constructivist epistemology and pedagogy, which are essential to the investigation and solution of learning problems faced by students, teachers and researchers. A second and more important reason for the method of the book is that at the very outset it provides some necessary ideas for teaching and learning processes that take place in every classroom. Stemming from the emphasis upon a sound practical and theoretical basis as the perquisite for solutions to practical problems, this book has been organized in such a way as to present relevant conceptual understanding of constructivism before discussing some problems and its solution faced on the part of teachers, students and teacher educators. In short, the style is interactive-cum-suggestive.

This book in hand has been organized systematically in eleven chapters. Chapter 2 describes various ideas propounded by various constructivist thinkers and theories. In this chapter the author has sketched the ideas of different theorists in capsule form. Prominent theorists are Vico, Kant, Dewey, Piaget, Vygotsky, Glasersfeld and Gergen. This chapter also deals with implications of constructivism in detail. The highlight of this chapter is an in-depth analysis of what is constructivism on the basis of its typology.

Chapter 3 outlines the fundamental assumptions of epistemic and epistemological aspects of constructivism. According to Driscoll (1994), the study of learning is essentially derived from two sources. The first concerns the nature of knowledge or how we come about to know things, and the other is how that knowledge is acquired and represented in the mind. Here comes the importance of epistemology which not only gives us conceptual inputs about knowledge but also about learning. Thus, this chapter also deals with the constructivist learning principle stating that learning is neither understanding the true nature of things, nor is it remembering dimly perceived perfect ideas, but rather a personal and social construction of meaning out of the bewildering array of sensations which have no order or structure besides the explanations which we fabricate for them.

Chapter 4 spotlights the latest trend and understanding of constructivist pedagogy in educational practice with an assertion that a key notion in constructivist teaching is the importance of matching teaching style to student learning style. This chapter also deals with various aspects of constructivist teacher and teaching. Practical measures have been suggested how a lesson should be designed by the teacher to teach in constructivist settings. From the perspective of all practical purposes, constructivist teaching strategies are most exciting subunits of this chapter.

In chapter 5 which is entitled as "Constructivism and Teacher Education", and attempt has been made to have a new foundation for teacher education in the light of constructivism. The issues of pre-service and in-service teacher education have been explicated conceptually by suggesting some sound practical measures how to bring change in teachers' thinking.

Chapter 6 depicts and highlights the need of having a new paradigm of distance education in a constructivist perspective. This chapter will help all those who are engaged in distance learning programme to realize that through utilizing the virtual learning scaffolding model, teachers can incorporate multiple instructional routes to include all learners, fostering active and social learning.

In chapter 7, 'Constructivism and Instructional Technology', a depiction has been made to show the difference between the traditional and constructivist instruction by highlighting the role of computer in general and internet in particular.

In chapter 8, it has been shown that there is a dire need to make our existing curriculum a real thinking curriculum by incorporating constructivist education in our education system as we have evidenced that India is in a process of curriculum reform involving a change of paradigm of education. The shift is from a rather "pure" behaviourist to an eclectic constructivist approach and this has wide-reaching implications throughout the educational system.

Constructivism has been facing a biggest challenge by the mathematics and science teachers. In chapter-9, an attempt has been made to help science and mathematics teachers how to situate mathematics and science teaching in constructivist paradigm of teaching and learning as much of the old curriculum approach to mathematics teaching is counter-productive. The instructivist approach has led to feelings of shame and inadequacy in learners (Peter de Lisle, 1997). Also, there is evidence that students taught by constructivist methods learn science concepts better than those taught even by talented lecturers (Hake, 1998).

In chapter 10, the role of research in improving constructivist practices has been highlighted. Also, it has been established how the research outcome has helped the stakeholders of education to develop and implement constructivist policies and practices in the schools to help students to achieve better achievements and goals in education and life. Different researches conducted in the area of constructivist policies and practices have been described to assist teachers, parents and students for better performance. Some researchers have urged the schools to take a fresh look at constructivist pedagogy and its potential for engaging students and improving student performance. It has been shown how research findings have provided a sound theoretical insights and pragmatic ideas regarding constructivism to be implemented effectively in our education system.

In this chapter, some suggestions have been given regarding what kind of further researches are required which may be helpful for the potential researchers who are going to conduct research in the field of constructivist education as a whole.

In the last chapter, entitled as "Constructivism: Potentials and Problems" along with potentials some problems have also been discussed in detail so that the readers may have a holistic picture of constructivism.

In short, the writer has tried to traverse the whole terrain of constructivist education. Without presuming to be encyclopedic or thesaurus, an attempt has been made to take cognizance of the predominant elements, concepts and assumptions that have characterized constructivism as one of the most powerful alternatives to behaviourism in education in general and teaching and learning in particular. The specific features of various facets of constructivist ideas and practices have been highlighted keeping the child in centre of teaching, learning and evaluative processes. With all conviction the assertion is this that constructivist education is fully capable to provide basic learning needs to all the learners as we know that the satisfaction of basic learning needs empowers individuals in any society and confers upon them a responsibility to respect and build upon their collective cultural, linguistic and spiritual heritage. Also, to promote the education of others, to further the cause of social justice, to achieve environmental protection, to be tolerant towards social, political, and religious systems which differ from their own, ensuring that commonly accepted humanistic values and human rights are upheld, and to work for international peace and solidarity in an interdependent world.

2

Constructivism: Thinkers, Theories and Theorists

2.1 CONCEPT AND PERSPECTIVES

In comparing constructivism to both behaviourism and cognitivism; Cooper summarizes: "The constructivist...sees reality as determined by the experiences of the knower. The move from behaviourism through cognitivism to constructivism represents shifts in emphasis away from an external view to an internal view. To the behaviourist, the internal processing is of no interest; to the cognitivist, an internal processing is only of importance to the extent to which it explains how external reality is understood. In contrast, the constructivist views the mind as a builder of symbols—the tools used to represent the knower's reality. External phenomena are meaningless except as the mind perceives them.... Constructivist view reality as personally constructed, and state that personal experience determine reality, not the other way round" (Cooper, 1993).

Piaget's approach also went counter to well established ideas in philosophy. Most philosophers considered knowledge as a static entity. Knowledge, for them, was *there*, ready to be *discovered*. The notion that individuals could *generate* knowledge, and that one could specify the processes involved in its production, was not a notion that fitted the traditional pattern. How something arises and comes to be what it is, its evolution was not to be considered a justification or valid explanation. Indeed, philosophers had formulated a ban against 'genetic fallacies'. Einstein explained this in 1938 with the help of a striking metaphor: Physical concepts are free creations of the human mind, and are not, however it may seem, uniquely determined by the external world.

In our endeavour to understand reality we are somewhat like a man trying to understand the mechanism of a closed watch. He sees the face and the moving hands, even hears its ticking, but he has no way of opening the case. If he is ingenious he may form some picture of a mechanism which could be responsible for all the things he observes, but he may never be quite sure his picture is the only one which could explain his observations. He will never be able to compare his picture with the real mechanism and he cannot even imagine the possibility or the meaning of such a comparison (Einstein & Infeld, 1967).

There is a great deal of resistance against this view of knowledge, and of scientific knowledge in particular. The philosophical tradition has for more than two thousand five hundred years perpetuated the notion of human knowledge as the more or less 'true' representation of a real world. This view has dominated absolutely and it is no wonder that people find it difficult to change their perspective. No matter how often Piaget has reiterated that our knowledge is not and cannot be a picture of the world as it might be in itself, his theory is nevertheless taken as a description of reality. This is a colossal distortion and leads to contradictions that cannot be resolved.

The two views of science and the cognitive processes that produce it are incompatible. On the one side, there are the realists, for whom the essence of science lies in the collecting of 'objective' data which, they believe, speak for themselves and automatically provide true explanations. Knowledge, for them, is the result of discovery. On the other side is Piaget's constructivism, for which all science is the product of a thinking mind's conceptualization. From this perspective, knowledge does not 'represent' or depict an independent reality but is a collection of inventions that happen to fit the world as it is experienced.

This dichotomy, of course, did not begin in our time. In fact, it goes back all the way to the Pre-Socratics five or six centuries before the birth of Christ. "Thought and being are one and the same", said Parmenides—and then he proceeded to think up a metaphysics that might explain how the world could exist in itself, without a thinker. And the whole of Western philosophy followed his lead.

From Plato to Whitehead and most contemporary philosophers, the fundamental problem was twofold: on the one hand, the task was to provide rational knowledge of the real world; on the other, it was to provide an explanation of how we could attain such knowledge. Although the sceptics had demonstrated quite irrefutably that the senses are fallible, the philosophical tradition did not relinquish the faith, and implicitly continued to trust observation. Seeing was still believing, because what you see must have been there before you saw it—that is, it must *exist*.

In one way or another, philosophers escaped into metaphysics. The prime example is Descartes, who, at the end of all his doubting, simply asserted that God could not have been so mischievous as to equip us with deceptive senses. At some point even physicists tend to turn to metaphysics. Einstein did it by stating a simple act of faith: "God does not play dice." This was a playful way of stating his faith that God was rational and his reason had to be accessible to us. We could, therefore, assume that He had arranged His creation so that the human mind could invent laws that actually turn out to be laws of nature.

Some other thinkers made their move into metaphysics more elaborate. George Berkeley, for instance, stated quite clearly that the only form of 'being' his rational thought could grasp was a being which his senses could substantiate with repeatable evidence. In order to 'exist' in itself, which is without a human observer, the world required faith in a God who could keep it constant by His divine perception. But Berkeley's logic was generally misunderstood—and so was his metaphysics. He did not claim that our picture of the world is ultimately like God's reality, he merely posited God's world as an independent substrate that allowed the human mind to construct its own.

The deliberate separation between rational thinking and metaphysics as the domain of mystical intuitions was not understood by Berkeley's contemporaries nor by most of his later readers. Consequently, in much of the literature, he is condescendingly referred to as 'Bishop Berkeley'—as though he might be important to religion, but irrelevant to philosophy.

In this back drop, let's again turn back to constructivism. The verb 'to construct' comes from the Latin '*construere*', which means to arrange or give structure. Ongoing structuring processes are the conceptual heart of constructivism. Among the earlier recorded proponents of some form of constructivism are Lao Tzu, Buddha, and the philosopher of endless change, Heraclitus. In western cultures, constructivists often trace their intellectual genealogy to Vico, Kant, Schopenhauer and Vaihinger. Vico had emphasised the role of fantasy and myth in human adoption. Kant emphasised the power of patterns in our thinking and he regarded ideas as regulative principles in our experiencing. His categories were predecessors of what are now called "constructs" and "schema" (Mahoney, 1995).

Vaihinger (1876) in Philosophy of "As If" has argued that the primary purpose of mind and mental processes is not to portray or mirror reality, but to serve individuals in their navigations through life circumstances. Vaihinger (1876) said that we live our lives by means of "functional fictions". Piaget developed a model of cognitive development in which balance was central. Piaget described knowing as a quest for a dynamic balance between what is familiar and what is novel. He noted that we organize our worlds by organizing ourselves. This theme of developmental self-organization pervades constructive views of human experience.

Constructivism has grown like wild-fire throughout the world in academic parlance. Many thinkers have contributed tirelessly in the development of constructivist ideas—theoretically and practically both. Much of the impetus for constructivism as an educational movement stems from a reaction to the over-reliance in classrooms on rote memorization, which is regarded as a serious problem in education (Lipman, 1991). Many critics of education insist that the most important goal of school is to teach children how to think and solve problems. Also, many critics and researchers lament the fact that students who can answer complex questions and solve problems are unable to explain the underlying reasons or methods they use to reach their conclusions (Stever, 1989 & Swamy, 1987). Regardless of how well concepts and ideas are presented to children in a classroom, they will not really learn them unless they make personal use of them through some process.

The constructivist movement has grown essentially from dissatisfaction with educational methods where rote memorisation, regurgitation of facts and the division of knowledge into different subjects, led to a situation where learners were not necessarily able to apply what they have learned in real life (Dixon-Kraus, 1996). As early as 1929, A.N. Whitehead argued that the way students learn many things in school produces inert knowledge—knowledge that can be used to answer items on a school test but which is not available to the student when he or she is trying to solve a problem that requires that knowledge (Flavell and Piaget, 1963).

Furthermore, in traditional rationalist and behaviourist approaches, instruction is focused on covering an extensive subject area, reducing the amount of time for problem-solving and thinking beyond the facts, thus minimising independent and autonomous learning. It also encourages didactic lecture formats rather than active student learning (Holt and Willard-Holt, 2000). This fundamental problem led to the viewpoint that instructors should only provide appropriate learning situations that will allow students to develop their own knowledge, meaning and truth that will be useful in later life. Providing a problem-solving context for actively engaging students in the thoughtful application of knowledge is an important variable in increasing learning (McMahon, 1997). This educational viewpoint is called cognitive constructivism and was derived from the work of Piaget (Flavell and Piaget, 1963). It defines learning as an internal process of accommodation, assimilation, and equilibration (Flavell and Piaget, 1963). Piaget thus saw learning as a process where an individual constructs his or her own meaning through cognitive processes. The main underlying assumption of constructivism is that individuals are actively involved right from birth in constructing personal meaning that is their own personal understanding from their experiences (Flavell and

Piaget, 1963). This action-based theory is thus more concerned with the process of learning than with what is learned (McMahon, 1997). Constructivism thus goes beyond the study of how the brain stores and retrieves information to examine the ways in which learners make meaning from experience (Savery, 1994). Rather than the transmission of knowledge, learning is an internal process of interpretation: learners do not transfer knowledge from the external world into their memories, rather, they create interpretations of the world based upon their past experiences and their interactions in the world. How someone construes the world, their existing metaphors, is at least as powerful a factor influencing what is learned as any characteristic of that world (McMahon, 1997). Most cognitive theories, and the constructivist approaches that have grown out of these, argue that learning should be durable, transferable and self-regulated (Di Vesta, 1987). Mechanisms need to be in place to promote the deeper internal processing required for such learning to occur.

2.2 CONSTRUCTIVIST THINKERS, THEORIES AND THEORISTS

There is a strong correlation between the thinkers and theories. They are the thinkers who provide us theories at the same time theories also have given us the most sophisticated theorists. Without good thinkers there is no possibility to have good theories. What is a theory? In simple terms a theory is an explanation of behavioural or physical events. The more powerful a theory is, the more events can be explained by it. Constructivist theory is considered by some educationist to be powerful because it provides an explanation for a vast range of educational issues in general and teaching and learning in particular. Theories consist of generalizations and constructs (Brog and Gall, 1979). Also, to many people the term theory suggests an ivory tower, something unreal and of little practical value. On the contrary, a theory establishes a cause and effect relationship between variables with the purpose of explaining and predicting phenomena. Those who engage in pure research devote their energies to the formulation and reformulation of theories and may not be concerned with their practical applications. However, when a theory has been established, it may suggest many applications of practical value. John Dewey has rightly said that there is nothing more practical than a good theory (Best and Kahn, 1989).

Piaget's (one of the pioneer constructivists) theory of cognitive development is a good example of a theory that has been developed with little or no concern for application. Only one of Piaget's many books discussed education in any great detail (Piaget, 1970), and even this book does not deal with the specifics that most teachers need. However, innumerable books, chapters and articles written by followers of Piaget have explicated the usefulness of his theory for teaching practices from preschool to high school. So although Piaget's aim was to understand the cognitive structures and functioning of children and adults, his theory has been embraced by educators and psychologists who have investigated ways in which this theory could be used to improve educational practice. Despite above mentioned facts, today we have got a clear cut definition in well worded statements such as a theory is an attempt to develop a general explanation for some phenomenon. In other words, a theory is primarily concerned with explanation and therefore focuses on determining cause-effect relationships (Best and Kahn, 1989). Thus, in short what is a theory?:

- A theory provides a general explanation for observations made overtime.
- A theory explains and predicts behaviour.
- A theory may be modified.
- Theories seldom have to be thrown out completely if thoroughly tested but sometimes a theory may be widely accepted for a long time and later disproved (Dori, Demmin & Gabel, 1990).

Although constructivist theory has reached high popularity in recent years, the idea of constructivism is not new. Aspects of the constructivist theory can be found among the works of Socrates, Plato, and Aristotle, all of which speak of the formation of knowledge. Saint Augustine taught that in the search for truth people must depend upon sensory experience. Philosophers such as John Locke taught that no man's knowledge can go beyond his experience. Kant explained that the "logical analysis of actions and objects lead to the growth of knowledge and the view that one's individual experiences generate new knowledge" (Brooks & Brooks, 1993). Although the main philosophy of constructivism is generally credited to Jean Piaget, Henrich Pestalozzi, also from Switzerland, came to many similar conclusions over a century earlier.

Pestalozzi maintained that the educational process should be based on the natural development of the child and his or her sensory influences.... Pestalozzi's basic pedagogical innovation was his insistence that children learn through the senses rather than with words. He labelled rote learning as mindless, and he emphasized instead linking the curriculum to children's experiences in their homes and family lives (Ornstein & Hunkins, 1993).

However, Piaget is regarded as the father of constructivism and provided the foundation for modern day constructivism. In Piaget's view, intelligence consists of two interrelated processes, organization and adaption. People organize their thoughts so that they make sense, separating the more important thoughts from the less important ones as well as connecting one idea to another. At the same time, people adapt their thinking to include new ideas, as new experiences provide additional information. This adaptation occurs in two ways, through assimilation and accommodation. In the former process, new information is simply added to the cognitive organization already there. In the latter, the intellectual organization has to change somewhat to adjust to the new idea (Berger, 1978).

Constructivist theory in education actually is a branch of neo-Piagetian thought which is rooted in Personal Constructivism (Novak, 1977; von Glasersfeld, 1989). Soloman (1987), Millar (1989), and Cobern (1993) have taken Personal Constructivism and have paved a way for Contextual Constructivism. Contextual Constructivism is defined by how the learner interprets phenomena and internalizes these interpretations in terms of their previous experience and culture. Cobern (1991) explains: "One must not suppose that cultural identification is limited to such conspicuous group identifiers as race, language or ethnicity...each of these no more identifies a homogeneous cultural group than does the term American.... In addition to race and language, other significant factors influence the construction of meaning and therefore are part of cultural identity. These include economic and education levels, occupation, geographic location, gender, religion, and philosophy. Thus, one can expect to find considerable variation among students. A student constructs knowledge so that the knowledge is meaningful in the student's life situation" (Cobern, 1991).

Constructivism or a constructivist view puts the students, their interests, and previous experiences and knowledge as paramount parts of understanding in designing curriculum. This has a particular impact when exploring the implications of pedagogy and teacher education programme. von Glasersfeld (1990) said, "Knowledge is not a commodity which can be communicated."

Five major themes can be identified throughout the variety of constructivist theories:

1. Human experience involves "continuous active agency".
2. Human activity focuses on organizing.
3. This organizing is fundamentally related to the self. This "makes the body a fulcrum of experiencing, honours deep phenomenological sense of selfhood or personal identity".
4. Although the self is central, social interaction is important. "Persons exist and grow in living webs of relationships" and they cannot be understood "apart from their organic embeddedness in social and symbolic systems".
5. Development is a lifelong as each person continues to construct new knowledge based on their own experiences. "Order and disorder co-exist in lifelong quests for a dynamic balance that is never quite achieved."

Among the thinkers who have contributed in the development of constructivism, prominent are Heraclitus, Kant, Vico, John Dewey, Jean Piaget, Lev Vygotsky, Jerome Bruner, Ernst von Glasersfeld, K.J. Gergen, etc. In the pages to come an elaborate discussion has been made about the ideas propounded by the various constructivist theorists.

2.2.1 Giambattista Vico

Giambattista Vico was an adversary of the thinking of Descartes, and may be considered as the spark behind Thomas Kuhn's idea 'paradigms'. Vico relates common sense knowledge to experience. For Ernst von Glasersfeld, **Giambattista Vico** is "the first true constructivist" (in *An Introduction to Radical Constructivism*). He is at present described as: one of the first modern thinkers to formulate in "New Science" a philosophy of mythology and to base both philosophical and historical knowledge on a conception of narration. Vico observed that the mind body split by Descartes led to a neglection of mind affairs. He was proven right. In his own words, (that 'explain' the rocksteady trust in 'reason'): "...that the world of civil society has certainly been made by men, and that its principles are therefore to be found within the modifications of our own human mind. Whoever reflects on this cannot but marvel that the philosophers should have bent all their energies to the study of the world of nature, which, since God made it, He alone knows; and that they should have neglected the study of the world of nations, or civil world, which, since men had made it, men could come to know". ".... This aberration was a consequence of that infirmity of the human mind by which, immersed and buried in the body, it naturally inclines to take notice of bodily things, and finds the effort to attend to itself too laborious; just as the bodily eye sees all objects outside itself but needs a mirror to see itself...."

One of Vico's basic ideas was that epistemic agents can know nothing but the cognitive structures they themselves have put together. He expressed this in many ways, and the most striking is perhaps: "God is the artificer of Nature, man the god of artifacts." Over and over he stresses that "to know" means to know how to make. He substantiates this by saying that one knows a thing only when one can tell what components it consists of. Consequently, God alone can know the real world, because He knows how and of what He has created it. In contrast, the human knower can know only what the human knower has constructed.

Glasersfeld has ascribed the first outline of a consciously constructivist theory to Giambattista Vico—a theory which states: man can only know what he constructs himself: *verum ipsum factum*. Whatever a man thinks and knows can therefore never represent an ontological reality, or as the Latin original from 1710 states: *Deus naturae artifex, homo arti-ficiorum deus*. For mankind, the only things that truly exist are those which mankind itself has constructed through perception and conceptual work, something illustrated in Bishop Berkeley's principle *esse est percipi* (Glasersfeld, 1989). The Italian philosopher Giambattista Vico said this very nicely at the beginning of the 18th century: "God knows the world, because He created it, human beings can know only what they themselves have made." The treatise, from which this statement is taken, is the first constructivist manifesto. Vico has maintained that it is impossible to compare our image of reality with a reality outside. It is impossible, because in order to check whether our representation is a 'true' picture of reality we should have to have access not only to our representation but also to that outside reality before we get to know it. And because the only way in which we are supposed to get at reality is precisely the way we would like to check and verify, there is no possible escape from the dilemma (Glasersfeld, 1987).

Vico's humanism and professional concerns prompted an obvious response that he would develop throughout the course of his writings: the realms of verifiable truth and human concern share only a slight overlap, yet reasoning is required in equal measure in both spheres. One of the clearest and earliest forms of this argument is available in the De Italorum Sapientia, where Vico argues that "to introduce geometrical method into practical life is 'like trying to go mad with the rules of reason', attempting to proceed by a straight-line among the tortuosities of life, as though human affairs were not ruled by capriciousness, temerity, opportunity, and chance. Similarly, to arrange a political speech according to the precepts of geometrical method is equivalent to stripping it of any acute remarks and to uttering nothing but pedestrian lines of argument." Vico's position here and in later works is not that the Cartesian method is irrelevant, but that its application cannot be extended to the civic sphere. Instead of confining reason to a string of verifiable axioms, Vico suggests (along with the ancients) that appeals to phronesis or practical wisdom must also be made, as do appeals to the various components of persuasion that comprise rhetoric. Vico would reproduce this argument consistently throughout his works, and would use it as a central tenet of the Scienza Nuova.

The 'Inaugural Discourses' are arranged around four principal themes. The first relates to the 'aims of the appropriate study of human nature', and takes up the first three 'Inaugural Discourses'. The educator, wrote Vico, must be familiar with the natural predisposition of the human soul and must impel the student to develop this familiarity as well. The purpose of this study is to identify the path that leads from knowledge to wisdom. In the second 'Inaugural Discourse', Vico introduced the themes of virtue and wisdom. These must 'adorn the human soul' and transform learning, which is sterile and rudimentary, into knowledge. The latter is a common goal towards which every teacher and student must aim. The establishment of a communion of ends is fundamental to an education system. Vico added in the third 'Inaugural Discourse' that this complicity between master and disciple 'dispels simulated and useless learning'. These words elevate Vico from a simple repeater of common formulas to an original thinker. He was concerned with transmitting knowledge through the teaching of rhetoric, but he also wanted to start a movement of autonomous self-development in the student. The latter must rediscover his soul himself, and must seek the connection between human nature and the Divine (Maiullar, 2000).

Vico underlined the importance of learning guided by 'the common good of the citizens'. The civic feeling of belonging to a community must be stimulated in the student. That which the disciple learns must help all his fellow citizens and all humanity. The subject of the fifth 'Inaugural Discourse' was, precisely, the growth 'with literature, of the glory of arms'. Every man must act to improve himself in order to help the community of men to which he belongs. The educator and student must be aware of the importance of their own roles and the worth of their education (Maiullar, 2000).

Commenting on the theory and practice of knowledge Vico has given us a unique account. 'Knowledge of oneself', said Vico, 'is for everyone the highest encouragement to bring rapidly to a conclusion the study of the entire cycle of learning'. The educator adds that 'the body is a container, or, so to speak, a receptacle of the soul'. All that we do is done, in reality, from the soul. The capabilities of the soul are unimaginable; to know it perfectly is a divine undertaking, and it is only to God that its creation can be attributed. Through application and study we can seek to discover the potential of our soul and attempt to exploit it in order to examine our own consciousness. At the moment of his entry into the academic world, Vico confronted one of the most important themes of philosophical and educational thought (Maiullar, 2000).

Human nature is senseless and completely incoherent to its own interests, wrote Vico. Consequently, the interest and the primary aim for every man must be to achieve a balance between his own nature and his own actions, between theory and action. The essence of true learning lies in modesty. The student must learn rules and ideas, but must be able to go beyond the simple accumulation of names and dates, of sterile book learning. He must think of his cultural heritage, and use it well for the collective good. 'Culture distinguishes the wise man from the common man', said Vico. 'Neither the former nor the latter knows. But the common man believes he knows, while the wise man knows he does not know.' Learning and knowledge are not true and complete if they ignore consideration of others. All humankind has a natural predisposition towards knowledge. This inclination must be individualized by the educator, a person with the task of making his student discover it. The best educational method is that based on interdisciplinary approaches.

Sensitivity of language, as a way of communication and of transmission of knowledge, pervades all of Vico's work. It is through language that one can easily arrive at full knowledge of the components of the human sciences. He did not propose a universal system of knowledge that can be applied with pre-established rules and mechanisms. Vico confirms the opinion that to bring human wisdom to perfection, new arts and new sciences are necessary. The educator must assist the student, but in so doing he must favour the latter's natural predisposition towards knowledge. Vico is not simply an inveterate opponent of the Cartesian method. He is the real creator of an education and of a complete cultural formation that, following the natural predisposition of each student, can create a group of men able to carry out their roles in society.

Vico's deduction...was quite original and had the profoundest effect. If the objects of our knowledge, as far as the natural sciences are concerned, exist as part of divine creation, the objects of our historical knowledge are more "knowable", since they are made by man in the first place. History must, therefore, be a more proper object of scientific investigation than physical nature.... Yet...Vico was not a determinist; he did not think that one can "situate" oneself in a point and time and see how the cycles [of gods, heroes, and men] will "inevitably" develop. On the contrary, he saw the basic structure of the cyclic development of nations, tribes, and individuals constantly buffeted and modified by accident so as to produce an infinitely varied account of history.

Giambattista Vico published a treatise on the construction of knowledge in 1710. This treatise illuminated (rather than invented) the idea that knowledge is something that is constructed by the knower. Vico's concepts deal mostly with the relationship between truth, knowledge and the origins of language and the desire of the human mind to create knowledge (Lo, 1996).

Vico believed that the human reason can only know what the human mind has made. Because of this philosophy, Vico is credited with being the original constructivist. Believing that there is nothing that is true or real other than what the experiencer creates within the mind. Returning to Vico's slogan, "the human mind can know only what the human mind has made", we can easily see why this view of knowledge acquisition could have a great impact on the way we see children learn. Vico consciously develops his notion of *scienza* (science or knowledge) in opposition to the then dominant philosophy of Descartes with its emphasis on clear and distinct ideas, the most simple elements of thought from which all knowledge, the Cartesians held, could be derived *a priori* by way of deductive rules. As Vico had already argued, one consequence and drawback of this hypothetico-deductive method is that it renders phenomena which cannot be expressed logically or mathematically as illusions of one sort or another. This applies not only most obviously to the data of sense and psychological experience, but also to the non-quantifiable evidence that makes up the human sciences. Drawing on the *verum factum* principle first described in *De Antiquissima*, Vico argues against Cartesian philosophy that full knowledge of any thing involves discovering *how* it came to be what it is as a product of human action and the "principal property" of human beings, viz., "of being social". The reduction of all facts to the ostensibly paradigmatic form of mathematical knowledge is a form of "conceit", Vico maintains, which arises from the fact that "man makes himself the measure of all things" and that "whenever men can form no idea of distant and unknown things, they judge them by what is familiar and at hand". Recognizing this limitation, Vico argues, is at once to grasp that phenomena can only be known via their origins, or *per caussas* (through causes). For "Doctrines must take their beginning from that of the matters of which they treat", he says, and it is one "great labour of...Science to recover...[the] grounds of truth—truth which, with the passage of years and the changes in language and customs, has come down to us enveloped in falsehood". Unveiling this falsehood leads to "wisdom", which is "nothing but the science of making such use of things as their nature dictates". Given that *verum ipsum factum*—"the true is the made", or something is true *because* it is made-*scienzia* both sets knowledge *per caussas* as its task and as the method for attaining it; or, expressed in other terms, the content of *scienza* is identical with the development of that *scienza* itself.

The challenge, however, is to develop this science in such a way as to understand the facts of the human world without either reducing them to mere contingency or explaining their order by way of speculative principles of the sort generated by traditional metaphysics. They must be rendered intelligible, that is, without reducing them, as did the Cartesians, to the status of ephemera. Vico satisfies this demand by distinguishing at the outset of *The New Science* between *il vero* and *il certo*, "the true" and "the certain". The former is the object of knowledge (*scienzia*) since it is universal and eternal, whereas the latter, related as it is to human consciousness (*coscienza*), is particular and individuated.

Vico's Quotes:

".... The principles of physics which are put forward as truths on the strength of the geometrical method are not really truths, but wears a semblance of probability."

"In the past, all arts and disciplines were interconnected and rested in the lap of philosophy; subsequently, they were sundered apart. Those responsible for this separation can be compared to a tyrannical rule who, having seized mastery of a great, populous, and opulent city, should, in order top secure his own safety, destroy the city and scatter its inhabitants into a number of widely strewn villages."

"Man, having within himself an imagined World of lines and numbers, operates in it with abstractions, just as God, in the universe, did with reality."

"It is true that men themselves made this world of nations... but this world without doubt has issued from a mind often diverse, at times quite contrary, and always superior to the particular ends that men had proposed to themselves."

"...it is an error to apply the prudent conduct of life the abstract criterion of reasoning that obtains in the domain of science. A correct judgment deems that men—who are, for the most part, but fools—are ruled, not by forethought, but by whim or chance. The doctrinaires judge human actions as they ought to be, not as they actually are...."

"The systematization in preceptive form of many subjects that depend on common sense does harm rather than benefit to our study methods. In those subjects in which discretion and practical common sense are supreme, a great number of preceptive treatments is no more helpful than their absence."

"Humans are human because they are conscious of living within a community. When the sense of fellowship is lost humanity is lost."

"The order of ideas follows the order of things (completely opposed to the Enlightenment credo: 'Reason dictates Nature')."

"Common sense is judgment without reflection, shared by an entire class, an entire nation, or the entire human race."

2.2.2 Immanuel Kant

Constructivism refers to the notion according to which knowledge results from a process based on mental operations or judgments or the capacity of judgment. Kant proposed that the theoretic or pure capacity of judgment be based on a priori synthetic judgments of space and time. Since then there is a controversy about the reality of those judgments and about its explicative power. Immanuel Kant explained that "logical analysis of actions and objects lead to the growth of knowledge and the view that one's individual experiences generate new knowledge" (Brooks & Brooks, 1993). He wrote in the Introduction to his famous Critique of pure reason: "Human reason can grasp only what she herself has produced according to her own design" (Kant, 1787).

Kant emphasised the power of patterns in our thinking and he regarded ideas as regulative principles in our experiencing. His categories were predecessors of what are now called "constructs" and "schema". Some of his important quotations indicate clearly that there was clear germ of constructivism in his thinking and thoughts. For example, "It is beyond a doubt that all our knowledge begins with experience", shows us that experience is one of the most important components of knowledge. Thus, it will not be an exaggeration to say that Kant had perhaps represented the initial formulation of constructivism as an educational philosophy. Now, it is an open and established fact that Piaget is credited for establishing constructivism as educational pedagogy, and that constructivism as a philosophy goes back to Socrates. But, it is sure that the strands of thought that separate constructivism from rationalism can be found throughout the history of thought, but, undoubtedly, it is interesting to consider Kant's role in the relationship between philosophy of science and the pedagogy of constructivism.

Here are some other quotes from Kant:

"All our knowledge begins with the senses, proceeds then to the understanding, and ends with reason. There is nothing higher than reason."

"All thought must, directly or indirectly, by way of certain characters, relate ultimately to intuitions, and therefore, with us, to sensibility, because in no other way can an object be given to us."

"Experience without theory is blind, but theory without experience is mere intellectual play."

"Immaturity is the incapacity to use one's intelligence without the guidance of another."

"Intuition and concepts constitute...the elements of all our knowledge, so that neither concepts without an intuition in some way corresponding to them, nor intuition without concepts, can yield knowledge."

"To be is to do."

This one reminds a bit of Descartes. Here are some quotes from Descartes:

"Except our own thoughts, there is nothing absolutely in our power."

"Each problem that I solved became a rule which served afterwards to solve other problems."

"If you would be a real seeker after truth, it is necessary that at least once in your life you doubt, as far as possible, all things."

"There is no knowledge or experience without a synthesis of perception."

Kant defines his theory of perception in his influential work *The Critique of Pure Reason*, which has often been cited as the most significant volume of metaphysics and epistemology in modern philosophy. Kant maintains that our understanding of the external world has its foundations not merely in experience, but in both experience and *a priori* knowledge—thus offering a non-empiricist critique of rationalist philosophy. Before discussing his theory it is necessary to explain Kant's distinction between analytic and synthetic propositions. Analytic proposition: a proposition whose predicate concept is contained in its subject concept. Synthetic proposition: a proposition whose predicate concept is not contained in its subject concept. Analytic propositions are true by nature of the meaning of the words involved in the sentence—we require no further knowledge than a grasp of the language to understand this proposition. On the other hand, synthetic statements are those that tell us something about the world. Synthetic statements are true or false because their meaning transcends the content of the language used. Before Kant's first critique, empiricists and rationalists assumed that all synthetic statements required experiènce in order to be known.

Kant, however, contests this: he claims that elementary mathematics, like arithmetic, is synthetic *a priori*. Here Kant includes *a priori* and *a posteriori* concepts into his argument, and posits that it is in fact possible to have knowledge of the world that is not derived from empirical experience. Thus does Kant develop his arguments for transcendental idealism, basically contending that the world conforms to our understanding, rather than the *vice versa*. He justifies this by arguing that experience depends on certain necessary conditions—which he calls *a priori* forms—and that these conditions hold true for the world. In so doing, his main claims are that mathematic judgments are synthetic *a priori* and in addition, space and time are transcendentally ideal and at the same time are necessary conditions for experience.

Kant asserts that perception is based both upon experience of external objects and *a priori* knowledge. The external world, he writes, provides those things which we sense. It is our mind, though, that processes this information about the world and gives it order, allowing us to comprehend it. Those things which we perceive are apparently unknowable as they themselves are mere concepts. It is our mind that supplies the conditions of space and time to these things. According to the "transcendental unity of apperception", the concepts of the mind (Understanding) and the intuitions which garner information from phenomena (Sensibility) are synthesized by comprehension. Without the concepts, intuitions are nondescript; without the intuitions, concepts are meaningless—thus the famous quotation, "Intuitions without concepts are blind; concepts without intuitions are empty."

Kant states that all of "our cognition begins with experience", but experience is a composite of both matter and form, with the matter being "what we receive through impressions" and the form being "what our own cognitive power supplies from itself". Since we do not want to consider the matter of experience, but only the form, we need to derive a cognition without taking it directly from experience. Such cognitions derives their conclusions from a universal rule and is called an *a priori* cognition, opposed to the cognitions directly from experience which are *a posteriori* cognitions. A *pure* cognition is a cognition that is derived *exclusively* from a universal and not from experience. Hence, pure cognitions are the types of cognitions that we are interested in to look at the form of experience. Notice that this does not to imply that the critique of pure reason is merely concerned with pure cognitions and has nothing to say about experience. Instead, pure cognitions as leads us to the form of experience without involving the matter, so that it allows us to talk about experience.

Kant divides our higher (i.e., not including intuition) cognitive powers into three different faculties with each faculty having its own essential principle function of thought. These are the faculties of understanding, (power of) judgment, and reason, whose respective functions deal with the doctrines of concepts, of judgments, and of inferences. *Concepts* are representations that refer indirectly to a universal. The matter of concepts is their intentional objects and the form of concepts is their universality. General logic concerning concepts involves such issues as the formal generation of concepts (by comparison, reflection, and abstraction) and the parts of concepts (i.e., content and extension). Judgments are the representation of a unity of several representations. Roughly, this is the same thing as a proposition but is more general (i.e., does not necessarily have to be in propositional form). The matter of judgments is the component representations (e.g., the terms in a proposition). The form of judgments is how these component representations are connected by the four principle moments of judgment: quantity, quality, relation, and modality. *Inferences* are the functions of thought that derive a judgment from other judgments. There are three types of inferences: inference of the understanding, inferences of reason, and inferences of (the power of) judgment. *Inferences of the understanding* are inferences that alter the form of the judgment without changing the matter. For instance, the inference from all men are mortal to some men are mortal. *Inferences of reason* are the logical inferences such as the demonstrative syllogisms, hypothetical inferences, and disjunctive inference of traditional logic but with a twist (see below). *Inferences of the judgment* are not strict inferences of reason, but are logical presumptions that do not have the necessity associated with them that inferences of reason do. Induction, analogies, sorites, fallacy, and sophisms are all types of inferences of judgment. The matter of inferences is made of the judgments in the inference and the form is the logical structure of the inference.

Inferences of reason will turn out to be quite important when we attempt to flesh out the analogy between general logic and transcendental philosophy. Kant defines an inference of reason as "the cognition of the necessity of a proposition through the subsumption of its condition under a given universal rule". That is, the conclusion of an inference of reason is a proposition that is true by applying the major premise on the minor premise as if the first premise were a *formal condition* on the *matter* of the second premises. Inferences of reason make up a triad of *form* (*consequentia*), *matter* (*ground of proof*), and *form applied to matter* (*conclusion*).

Kant's Quotes:

"It is beyond a doubt that all our knowledge begins with experience."

"Experience without theory is blind, but theory without experience is mere intellectual play."

"Our understanding of the external world has its foundations not merely in experience, but in both experience and *a priori* knowledge."

"Our cognition begins with experience", but experience is a composite of both matter and form, with the matter being "what we receive through impressions" and the form being "what our own cognitive power supplies from itself".

2.2.3 John Dewey

Among all the great intellectual giants, Dewey should be viewed as unorthodox realist, with respect to both general metaphysical debates about realism and with respect to debates about human knowledge and knowing. Dewey's epistemology, metaphysics and logic have opened a new door for all those who are committed to understand the problem of knowledge and knowing in holistic-realistic perspective. Some readings take Dewey to be an early exemplar of "social constructivist" views (Hacking, 1985). Dewey is a philosopher of reconstruction who reconstructed his own thinking several times in the course of his life (Jim Garrison, 1999). He has recognized the importance of the subjective experience of individual people in introducing revolutionary new ideas. For Dewey, it was vitally important that education not be the teaching of mere dead fact, but that the skills and knowledge which students learned be integrated fully into their lives as persons, citizens and human beings. The most basic idea of John Dewey's with regard to education was that greater emphasis should be placed on the broadening of intellect and development of problem-solving and critical thinking skills, rather than simply on the memorization of lessons. Dewey saw the human mind as a meaning-making organ, relentlessly driven to make sense of its world—an idea that predates today's notions of constructivism and active learning (Teets & Starnes, 1997). Dewey considered reflection central to all learning experiences, enabling us to act in a deliberate and intentional fashion to convert action that is merely blind and impulsive into intelligent action. In calling for educational experiences that open possibilities for all, Dewey recognized the need for building experiences upon a form understanding of what they need to know and how they come to know.

It is generally viewed that the central focus of Dewey's philosophical interests throughout his career was what has been traditionally called epistemology or the theory of knowledge. It is evident, however, of Dewey's critical stance toward past efforts in this area that he expressly rejected the term epistemology preferring the "theory of inquiry" or epistemological logic as more representative of his own approach. Dewey found himself uneasy to accept the stand taken by traditional epistemologists—rationalists or empiricists. Traditional epistemologies had drawn too stark a distinction between thought, the domain of knowledge, and the world of fact to which thought purportedly referred: thought was believed to exist apart from the world, epistemically as the object of immediate awareness, ontologically as the unique aspect of the self (Richard Field, 2006). The commitment of modern rationalism, starting from Descartes, to a doctrine of innate ideas, ideas constituted from birth in the very nature of the mind itself, had effected this dichotomy; but the modern empiricists, beginning with Locke, had done the same just as markedly by their commitment to an introspective methodology and a representational theory of ideas. The resulting view makes a mystery of the relevance of thought to the world: if thought constitutes a domain that stands apart from the world, how can its accuracy as an account of the world ever be established? Dewey felt a need to have a new model and consequently he not only developed the one but also continuously refined it throughout his career. He successfully presented a unique solution to the issues, which were partly epistemic and partly epistemological, mainly along the lines of his initial adherence to Hegelian idealism: the world of fact does not stand apart from thought, but is itself defined within thought as its objective manifestation. Later he was found to reject this charging it as unnecessary and insufficient.

Dewey came to believe that a productive, naturalistic approach to the theory of knowledge must begin with a consideration of the development of knowledge as an adaptive human response to environing conditions aimed at an active restructuring of these conditions. Thus, it can be stated that Dewey's approaches understood thought genetically, as the product of the interaction between organism and environment, and knowledge as having practical instrumentality in the guidance and control of that interaction. In this way, he adopted the term *instrumentalism* as a descriptive appellation for his new approach. For Dewey, ideas are instruments in the solution of human problems. In *How We Think*, Dewey showed how ideas can be used as instruments in the solution of real problems. He described his view in five stages: (a) *a felt difficulty* that occurs because of a conflict in our experience or a hitch or block to ongoing experiences; (b) *its location and definition*, establishing the limits or characteristics of the problem in precise terms; (c) *suggestions of possible solutions*, formulating a wide range of hypotheses; (d) *development by reasoning of the bearings of the suggestions*, reflecting on the possible outcomes of acting on these suggestions—in short, mulling things over; and (e) *further observation and experiment leading to its acceptance or rejection*, testing the hypotheses to see if they really yield the desired results (Ozman and Craver, 1990). Although these five steps are presented in an orderly sequence, this does not mean that they are independent in a given situation or occur in any special order. They can occur together in such ways that the various steps interact with each other or become fused.

A detailed genetic analysis of the process of enquiry is Dewey's unique contribution. Deliberating at the phases of the process, he has stated that it begins with the problematic situation, a situation where instinctive or habitual responses of the human organism to the environment are inadequate for the continuation of ongoing activity in pursuit of the fulfilment of needs and desires. He has categorically asserted that the uncertainty of the problematic situation is not inherently cognitive, but practical and existential. Cognitive elements enter into the process as a response to precognitive maladjustment. The second phase of the process involves the isolation of the data or subject matter which defines the parameters within which the reconstruction of the initiating situation must be addressed. In the third, reflective phase of the process, the cognitive elements of inquiry (ideas, suppositions, theories, etc.) are entertained as hypothetical solutions to the originating impediment of the problematic situation, the implementations of which are pursued in the abstract. The final test of the adequacy of these solutions comes with their employment in action. If a reconstruction of the antecedent situation conducive to fluid activity is achieved, then the solution no longer retains the character of the hypothetical that marks cognitive thought; rather, it becomes a part of the existential circumstances of human life (Richard Field, 2006).

The basis of Dewey's discussion in the logic is the continuity of intelligent enquiry with the adaptive responses of pre-human organisms to their environments in circumstances that check efficient activity in the fulfilment of organic needs. What is distinctive about intelligent enquiry is that it is facilitated by the use of language, which allows, by its symbolic meanings and implicatory relationships, the hypothetical rehearsal of adaptive behaviours before their employment under actual, prevailing conditions for the purpose of resolving problematic situations. Dewey's aim has been to offer functional analysis of logical principles and techniques that exhibit their operative utility in the process of enquiry. The resolution of a problematic situation may involve transforming the inquirer, the environment, and often both. The emphasis is on transformation. Further in his book *Reconstruction in Philosophy* (1957), he says that knowledge is power and knowledge is achieved by sending the mind to school of nature to learn her processes of change. In his book, *Democracy and Education: An Introduction to the Philosophy of Education* (1916), he says, "Knowledge is a perception of those connections of an object which determine its applicability in a given situation. Our beliefs are only hypothesis, theories, suggestions, and guesses and are to be entertained tentatively and to be utilized as indications of experiments to be tried." In summary, all of human knowledge consists of actions and products of acts in which men and women participate with other human beings, with animals and plants, as well as objects of all types, in any environment. Men and women have, are and will present their acts of knowing and known in language. Generic man, and specific men and women are known to be vulnerable to error. Consequently, all knowledge (knowing and known) whether commonsensical or scientific; past, present and future; is subject to further inquiry, examination, review and revision. Knowing is no process of registration or representation, but one of intervention. Knowledge does not refer to an external, independent and objective reality, but always participates in the action. Dewey's argument about the function of knowledge and reflection—to ensure the continuity of action—brings the crucial role of time to the fore (Raf Vanderstraeten & Gert Biesta, 1998). "Knowing consists of operations that give experienced objects a form in which the relations, upon which the onward course of events depends, are securely experienced." Knowledge is not concerned with experienced objects as such, but with future experiences which might ensue from the present situation. To make inferences from present situations creates at the same time uncertainty. "Inferences bring...truth and falsity in the world" as Dewey has underlined. Thus truth does not refer to the correspondence between statement and reality at the same moment, but to the correspondence of expected and realized meaning, to coherence in the course of time. Transaction does not consist of a subject who deals with an external universe. Every organism participates entirely in his life-world. There is no reality without experience. And there is no reality which is not affected by this experience. Every act (also an act of knowing) creates a new reality.

For Dewey, experience is not just an isolated happenstance—it has depth and reaches into nature. Experience and nature are not two different things separated from each other, but rather experience itself is of nature. People do not experience "experiences" but the world in which they live, a world of things, ideas, hopes, fears and aspirations, all rooted in nature. He has stressed the priority of experience over theory. He has said that we only think when we are confronted with problems. Since the problems are constantly changing, the instruments for dealing with them must also change. We learn to think and reason by thinking and reasoning, by tackling real problems which arise in our experience. When we think, we become conscious of a problem or obstacle to our development; we compare the implications of the different solutions and select the best course of action; we implement this in practice. In more general terms the practical importance of the result of thinking is subsidiary to the process of thinking. According to Dewey, solving a problem is making an incoherent situation coherent and integrated. When we solve a problem we take a selection of apparently incompatible experiences and transform them into a unified whole—the unified whole is the solution to the problem.

Dewey has observed that the world as we experience it both individually and collectively is an admixture of the precarious, the transitory and contingent aspect of things, and the stable, the patterned regularity of natural processes that allows for prediction and human intervention. Any sincere metaphysical description must take into account both of these elements of experience.

Dewey has also addressed the social aspect of human experience facilitated by symbolic activity, particularly that of language. For Dewey the question of the nature of social relationships is a significant matter not only for social theory, but metaphysics as well, for it is from collective human activity and specifically the development of shared meanings that govern this activity, which the mind arises. Thus, rather than understanding the mind as a primitive and individual human endowment, and a precondition of conscious and intentional action, as was typical in the philosophical tradition since Descartes, Dewey offers a genetic analysis of mind as an emerging aspect of cooperative activity mediated by linguistic communication. For Dewey, mind is a means of transforming, reorganizing, reshaping accepted meanings and values, a means of attending to "the lived situations of life". He kept telling his readers, "mind is active, a verb and not a noun" (Fosnot, 1996). Consciousness in turn, is not to be understood as a domain of private awareness, but rather as the fulcrum point of the organism's readjustment to the challenge of novel conditions where the meanings and attitudes that formulate habitual behavioural responses to the environment fail to be adequate. Thus, Dewey offers in the better part of a number of chapters of *Experience and Nature* a response to the traditional mind-body problem of the metaphysical tradition, a response that understands the mind as an emergent issue of natural processes, more particularly the web of interactive relationships between human beings and the world in which they live.

For Dewey, to have a mind is to participate in the socio-linguistic practices and institutions of the community that express the most important norms, ideas and actions central to the construction of mind. Language is crucial to Dewey's naturalized account of the emergence of mind: "Through speech a person dramatically identifies himself of life but in a contemporaneously enacted drama. Thus mind emerges." One acquires a mind by entering the social drama of society, recognizing the roles other play and playing roles others can recognize. Dewey makes a distinction between "individual minds" and "just individuals with minds". The latter are simply docile and conforming reproductions of the existing social order. Because of conformity to existing social institutions, they have failed to recognize their unique individual potential. Hence, they are unable to make their unique contribution to the realization of some community as indicated by the ethical postulate.

Dewey's ideas on education can lead us to have some insight into his approaches which may be labelled as constructivists. According to him, education is a necessity of life and it depends on action. It renews people so that they are able to face the problems encountered by their interaction with the environment. He has stated categorically that all living educates, but social living helps us to extract the net meaning from our education. In fact all genuine education comes through experience. Recognizing its complexity, Dewey advised using those cases in which we find there is a real development of desirable (experiences)...to find out how this development took place and using this new understanding to guide our efforts at teaching and learning. He advocated placing the learner at the centre of experiences and defined the teacher as the learner's co-partner and guide in a common enterprise—the child's education as an independent learner and thinker. Dewey, like Plato, believed people need society as a necessary part of their learning experiences, and we must guard against schools treating subject matter as if it were a thing apart from life itself (Ozman and Craver, 1990). In *My Pedagogical Creed*, Dewey set forth the belief that education has two fundamental sides: the psychological and the sociological. One could not be subordinate to the other because the child's own instincts and powers provide the material and starting point of all education, and the educator's knowledge of social conditions is necessary to interpret the child's powers. The educator does not know what these powers and instincts are until he/she can translate them into their social equivalents and project them into the future for insight into their consequences. In sum, Dewey believed that individuals should be educated as social beings capable of participating in and directing their own social affairs. According to Dewey, aims should (a) grow out of existing conditions. They should (b) be tentative, at least in the beginning, and maintain flexibility. Perhaps most important of all, the aim must (c) always be directed toward a freeing of activities, an "end in view". For Dewey, the aim of education is growth: "since growth is the characteristic of life, education is all one with growing; it has no end beyond itself". In this regard, he was speaking of growth as an enlargement of the capacity to learn from experience and to direct future experience in a meaningful way.

Dewey stressed the importance of having a student's knowledge grow from experience. Knowledge and ideas came only from a situation where learners had to draw them out of experiences that had meaning and importance to them. These situations have to occur in a social environment, when students could come together to analyze materials and to create a community of learners who built their knowledge together.

Dewey criticized the limitations of the objectivist view of formal education, particularly for its limitations in enabling students to draw from their past experiences in constructing new meaning. He called for the need for formal education to realize the importance of freedom and flexibility in education by allowing the "expression of even immature feelings and fancies to enable learning" (Dewey, 1966). He held that genuine thought begins with a "problematic situation", a block or hitch to the ongoing stream of experience. In encountering these blocks, consciousness is brought to focus, and one is made more acutely aware of the situation. It is in dealing with these real problems; Dewey argued that creative intelligence is capable of development. He argued that each situation be looked upon as unique and dealt with experimentally by investigating the probable consequences of behaving in particular ways. This approach shows Dewey's position that the world—experience and nature—cannot be understood in a monolithic way.

Dewey argued that if one accepts the hypotheses of the open-ended universe and a pluralistic reality, it becomes less important to develop abstract explanations and more important to examine the nature of thinking processes. He felt that most human difficulties result from faulty thinking.

In *The Child and the Curriculum*, Dewey has maintained that the result of fragmentation has usually been to focus primary attention upon subject matter rather than on the contents of the child's own experience. According to Dewey, there are two major concerns in such cases: the logical and the psychological. The first emphasizes "discipline" and the second "interest". The error is to see a gap between a child's interest and necessary subject matter, for appropriate subject matter is not something fixed and ready-made outside a child's interest. The problem resides in how subject matter is organized and presented to students. When we look upon what a child learns as fixed and ready-made, attention is directed too much upon outcome and too little upon process. Dewey wants to focus at least some attention on process, because ends should not be divorced from means.

Further in his book *The Child and the Curriculum,* he says, "Learning is active. It involves reaching out of the mind. It involves organic assimilation starting from within. Literally, we must take our stand with the child and our departure from him. It is he and not the subject-matter which determines both quality and quantity of learning." In his book, *Democracy and Education* (1924), he says, "...learning means something which the individual does when he studies. He learns in consequence of his direct activities. Thinking is the method of intelligent learning, of learning that employs and rewards the mind."

Dewey was convinced that the ordinary contacts of day-to-day community life, be they social, economic cultural or political, provided real and significant learning situations. He believed that school should prepare the child for active participation in the life of the community. He believed that education must break down, rather reinforce, the gap between the experience of schooling and the needs of a truly participatory democracy: "The school is primarily a social institution. Education being a social process, the school is simply that form of community life in which all those agencies are concentrated that will be most effective in bringing the child to share in the inherited resources of the race, and to use his own powers for social ends...education, therefore, is a process of living and not a preparation for future living" (Frank M. Flanagan, 1994). Conclusively, for Dewey, education is a social function. Until we know what sort of society is best, we do not know what sort of education is best.

Dewey's approach was not a matter of whim or of arbitrary convictions about school design but a central feature of his philosophy. He wanted the laboratory school to provide learners with the opportunity to create their own experience: to experiment, to enquire, to create. He wanted a classroom where children could move about, form groups, plan and execute activities, in short, learn for themselves under the direction and guidance of the teacher. In Dewey's pedagogy the teacher has two main functions. The teacher must guide the young through the complexities of life and give them opportunities to learn in the natural way, that is, by solving relevant problems. The teacher must also enable the young to cope adequately with contemporary conditions and to cope with the new tasks which an unpredictable future will bring. He states, "the teacher is not in the school to impose certain ideas or to form certain habits in the child, but is there as a member of the community to select the influences which shall affect the child and to assist him in properly responding to these influences...the teacher's business is simply to determine, on the basis of larger experience and riper wisdom, how the discipline of life shall come to the child". Dewey's understanding of the functioning of habit is not mechanical and rationalistic. He writes, "rationality...is not a force to evoke against impulse and habit. It is the attainment of a working harmony among diverse desires. 'Reason' as a noun signifies the happy cooperation of a multitude of dispositions." For Dewey, 'Reason' is not an antecedent force which serves as a panacea. It is a laborious achievement of habit needing to be continually worked over. Besides habit, Dewey has emphasized on action, need, desire and interest. The relation of the individual to her or his world is functional, we may separate them to methodological purposes, but we cannot understand what motivates someone without understanding them as active functional unity of organism and environment. That is the clue to understanding Dewey's definition of interest: "Any concrete case of the union of the self in action with an object and end is called an interest." Organic functional interdependence is also the key to understanding Dewey's theory of internal motivation: "Because an interest or motive is the union of a need, desire of a self, with a chosen object, the object itself may, in a secondary and derived sense, be said to be the motive of action.... It is true enough when we take the whole situation into account that an object moves a person; for that object as a moving force includes the self within it. Error arises when we think of the object as if it were something wholly external to the make-up of the self, when it operates to move the foreign self." The transactional unity of the self (organism, knower, subject and mind) and the world (environment, known, object and body) is Dewey's full solution to Cartesian dualism. It is also an original contribution to understanding educational motivation (Jim Garrison, 1999).

The goal of Dewey's philosophy as education is to release the human potential for growth. Growth through freedom, creativity and dialogue is, for him, the all-inclusive ideal, the greatest good. For example, in Democracy and Education he asserts, "since growth is the characteristic of life, education is all one with growing; it has no end beyond itself". For Dewey, the capacity to cultivate growth is the criterion for evaluating the quality of all social institutions. Dewey clearly states, "The subject matter of the learner is not...identical with the formulated, the crystallized, and systematized subject matter of the adult." The same holds for any pedagogical situation. That is, "the teacher should be occupied not with subject matter in itself but in its interaction with the pupils' present needs and capacities. Hence simple scholarship is not enough". Subject matter knowledge alone does not make a good teacher. Teachers teach subject matter to students. It is a triangle enclosing a pedagogical space. Just teaching the subject matter does not mean one is teaching well. To teach well, the teacher must connect the subject matter to the needs, desires, interests, stage of cognitive development, etc. of the student within the physical, social and political context that the students and teachers find themselves.

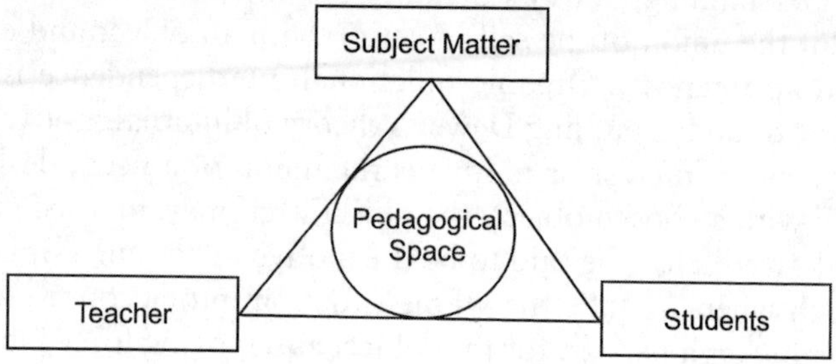

Figure

In his book, *The Child and the Curriculum* (1902), he says, "As a teacher he is concerned with the subject matter of the science as representing a given stage and phase of the development of experience. His problem is that of inducing a vital and personal experiencing. Hence, what concerns him, as teacher, is the ways in which that subject may become a part of experience."

In his another book, *Democracy and Education* (1924), he says, "This does not mean the teacher is to stand off and look on; the alternative to furnishing ready-made subject matter and listening to the accuracy with which it is reproduced is not quiescence, but participation, sharing, in a activity." In his another book, *My Pedagogic Creed*, he says, "every teacher should realize the dignity of his calling; that he is the social servant set apart for the maintenance of proper social order and the securing of the right social growth...the question of method is ultimately reducible to the question of order or development of the child's powers and interests". In the words of Frank M. Flanagan (1994), Dewey's contribution to the development of education in the 20th century has been incalculable if not without its controversies. His greatest contribution has been to liberate the education of children from the dead hand of tradition and from what he himself has called the 'static cold-storage ideal of knowledge'.

Dewey's Quotes:

"Anyone who has begun to think, places some portion of the world in jeopardy."

"Arriving at one goal is the starting point to another."

"Conflict is the gadfly of thought. It stirs us to observation and memory. It instigates to invention. It shocks us out of sheep like passivity, and sets us at noting and contriving."

"Man is not logical and his intellectual history is a record of mental reserves and compromises. He hangs on to what he can in his old beliefs even when he is compelled to surrender their logical basis."

"Such happiness as life is capable of comes from the full participation of all our powers in the endeavour to wrest from each changing situations of experience its own full and unique meaning."

"The belief that all genuine education comes about through experience does not mean that all experiences are genuinely or equally educative."

"The self is not something ready-made, but something in continuous formation through choice of action."

"We only think when we are confronted with problems."

"Education is not preparation for life; education is life itself."

"Education, therefore, is a process of living and not a preparation for future living."

2.2.4 Jean Piaget

The most influential thinker in the development of constructivist ideas was Jean Piaget. He provided much of the basis for the theoretical foundation of cognitive constructivism. He believed that individuals build understandings by a process of active interaction with their environment and that human beings are developing organisms "not only in a physical, biological sense, but also in a cognitive sense". For Piaget, equilibration was the mechanism by which changes in cognition and understanding occurred. According to his theory, equilibration consisted of two polar behaviours: assimilation and accommodation. In assimilation, individuals arrange experiences within their current structure of understandings. They view the world through familiar constructs in an effort to preserve autonomy within a personal system of meaning. As they confront new information and experiences, they modify and adjust existing structures to create new mental images to organize data. They reconstitute previous behaviour to accommodate new experiences and stimuli. This process often fosters contradictions to previous understandings that have to be addressed and resolved. The back and forth activity between assimilation and accommodation is not an invariant, step-by-step operation, however. There is no sequential process of assimilation, then conflict, then accommodation. Rather, it is a "dynamic dance" of equilibria, adaptation, growth and change. As students assert themselves to integrate new experiences and information they sometimes exhibit a type of behaviour which simply assimilates data, but at other times, they are "reflective, integrative and accommodating". In Piaget's paradigm of development, rather than knowing an objective reality, individuals only construct a version of it for themselves. As students engage in the process of equilibration, they build their knowledge through experiences and create schemata, or structures of mental images, that define their current reality.

It is also generally believed that formalization of the theory of constructivism is generally attributed to Piaget who articulated mechanisms by which knowledge is internalized by learners. He was keenly interested in the way that children think. Piaget insisted that children—even quite young—are quite sophisticated and active thinkers and theorists. If there are qualitative differences in knowledge, then thinking at the earlier developmental stages is different in kind from thinking at later stages. It is not merely that we as adults think faster, or know more; we really do think differently from babies and children, and the differences can be radical. Piaget believed that children begin development by being cognitively egocentric, meaning that they do not know about conceptual, perceptual, or affective perspectives (Flavell, 1999).

His constructivism was based on his view of the psychological development of children. He believed that the fundamental basis of learning was discovery: "To understand is to discover, to reconstruct by rediscovery and such conditions must be complied with if in the future individuals are to be formed who are capable of production and creativity and not simply repetition." He was firm in his opinion that to reach an understanding of basic phenomena, children have to go through stages in which they accept ideas that may later see as not truthful. Understanding is built up step by step through active involvement (*Building an Understanding of Constructivism*, 1995). "The focus of Piaget's theory is the various reconstructions that an individual's thinking goes through in the development of logical reasoning" (Green & Gredler, 2002). Piaget's most obvious accomplishment is overcoming the dichotomy between Nature and Nurture. Development is not simply the unfolding of a pattern dictated by the genes, nor is it simply the importation of structures from the physical and social environment. Piaget's theory of cognitive development proposes that humans cannot be "given" information, which they immediately understand and use. Instead, humans must "construct" their own knowledge. They build their knowledge through experience. Experiences enable them to create schemas—mental models in their heads. These schemas are changed, enlarged, and made more sophisticated through two complimentary processes: assimilation and accommodation.

The toughest and deepest problem raised by Piaget is the problem of novelty. During the course of development, new knowledge emerges. We acquire it through equilibration and we acquire it through reflecting abstraction. We are all creative, not in the sense that the ideas we arrive at are new and specially useful to others in our culture, but in the sense that they are new to us, different in kind from what we knew before.

Piaget has given us a different kind of epistemology. We are generally used to thinking about knowledge in terms of perception first, then concepts. But Piaget considered perception static and extremely limited. He has exhibited a strong commitment to knowledge arising from action that has more than a little in common with pragmatism and its rejection of "spectator" conceptions of knowledge. We really do learn new things and acquire novel knowledge. Piaget rejected what objectivists would call "naive realist" theories of perception, and, unusually for him, he got right to the point: To know is to transform reality through action in order to understand how a certain state is brought about. By virtue of this point of view, he is found opposed to the view of knowledge as a copy, a passive copy, of reality. In point of fact, this notion is based on a vicious circle: in order to make a copy we have to know the model we are copying, but according to this theory of knowledge the only way we know the model is by copying it, until we are caught in a circle, unable to know whether our copy of the model is like the model or not. For he continued: To my way of thinking, knowing an object does not mean copying it—it means acting upon it. It means constructing systems of transformations that can be carried out on or with this object. Knowing reality means constructing systems of transformations that correspond, more or less adequately, with reality. They are more or less isomorphic to transformations of reality. The transformational structures of which knowledge consists are not copies of the transformations in reality; they are simply possible isomorphic models among which experience can enable us to choose.

Piaget preferred to identify his enterprise as *genetic epistemology*. The core insight throughout Piaget's work is that we cannot understand what knowledge is unless we understand how it is acquired. In turn, we cannot understand how knowledge is acquired unless we carry out psychological and historical investigations. We have to test our hypotheses by collecting data, not only about the thinking of human infants and children, but also about the historical development of scientific ideas. Piaget firmly rejected the idea that epistemology could be done from the armchair. Piaget believed that the development of knowledge was a biological process, a matter of adaptation by an organism to an environment. He advocated what some others have called "evolutionary epistemology". His conception of evolution was not strictly based on variation and selection. Piaget believed that knowledge is primarily operative. For Piaget, operative knowledge is knowledge of what could happen, and (sometimes) knowledge of what must happen.

How does knowledge grow? Piaget spent his life searching for the answer to this very question. His research in developmental psychology and genetic epistemology was directed at elaborating upon a theory of knowledge about cognitive development in children also known as genetic epistemology (Driscoll, 1994). His answer is that the growth of knowledge is a progressive construction of logically embedded structures superseding one another by a process of inclusion of lower, less powerful logical means into higher more powerful ones up to adulthood (Silverthorn, 1999). Therefore, children's logic and modes of thinking are initially entirely different from those of adults (http://www.piaget.org). Piaget referred to his view as "constructivism", because he believed that the acquisition of knowledge is a process of continuous self-construction. While the child is constructing this knowledge, Piaget assumed there to be an interaction between heredity and environment and also labeled his view "interactionism" (Driscoll, 1994).

Knowledge is primarily about change and transformation. When Piaget studied mathematical ability, he wasn't terribly interested in how children determine that there are exactly the same number of things. To render the matter in greater technical detail, Piaget thought that our knowledge consists of cognitive structures. These come in various flavours. The simplest cognitive structures Piaget called sensorimotor action schemes. An action scheme is a way of accomplishing some goal in some class of situations. At a much higher level of sophistication are the different cognitive structures that are involved in logical thinking. For instance, Piaget was interested in the kinds of inferences that children can make with hierarchical systems of classification. Piaget believed that children who are able to make the inference correctly, have acquired a logical structure.

Both action schemes and logical structures, it must be emphasized, are operative. There is knowledge about static things. It is not nearly as important, in Piaget's view, and development would never happen if knowledge of static things were the only kind we had. Piaget called knowledge of static things figurative knowledge. What are examples of figurative knowledge? Well, visual perception gives us figurative knowledge. Visual images are a form of figurative knowledge. And, for the most part, language is figurative. In Piaget's theory, operative knowledge is where the action is.

Piaget's particular focus was on the intellectual or cognitive development of children and on the way in which their mind's processed and progressed in knowledge. Piaget's central thesis was that children (1) develop self-centric theories about their environment, and about objects or persons in that environment, and they grow; (2) that children base these theories on their own personal experiences interacting with persons and objects in their environment; (3) that the child used "schemas" to master and gain information about the environment; and (4) that the sophistication of a child's cognitive structures increased as the child grew and developed, as did the child's "schemas". Schemas, which are the child's tool bag of actions and responses to make things happen, start with rudimentary interactions such as grabbing and mouthing objects and eventually progress to highly sophisticated skills such as scientific observation. Piaget divided the child's path of development into four stages which began with birth and culminated in the teen years. These stages are: Sensorimotor stage (0-2 yrs.), Preoperational stage (2-7 yrs.), Concrete operations (7-11 yrs.), and Formal operations (from 11-15 and up). A chief tenet of Piaget's theory is that these stages do not vary in order, cannot be skipped, and should not be rushed.

Piaget eventually realized that every stage of development includes beliefs or assumptions that are not reflectively known at that stage (consequently they are taken for granted, and, if wrong, are difficult or impossible to correct). Reflecting abstraction can make these assumptions explicit and available for examination, but when you engage in reflecting abstraction, you move to the next higher stage, which has its assumptions that are not reflectively known.... The most important idea to come out of his work was egocentrism. When Piaget said that young children were egocentric, or thought egocentrically, he did not mean this primarily in a moral sense. Egocentrism is fundamentally a cognitive limitation; children are egocentric because they fail to understand how someone else's point of view might be different from their own—or they fail to coordinate their point of view with that other person's (Campbell, 2000).

Piaget's theory supposes that people develop schemas (conceptual models) by either assimilating or accommodating new information. Jean Piaget suggested that through processes of accommodation and assimilation, individuals construct new knowledge from their experiences. Assimilation occurs when individuals' experiences are aligned with their internal representation of the world. They assimilate the new experience into an already existing framework. Accommodation is the process of reframing one's mental representation of the external world to fit new experiences. Accommodation can be understood as the mechanism by which failure leads to learning. When we act on the expectation that the world operates in one way and it violates our expectations, we often fail. By accommodating this new experience and reframing our model of the way the world works, we learn from the experience of failure.

Jean Piaget's theory is very fundamental to constructivism. It implies the process of building, creating or making mental structures instead of merely absorbing or reproducing products. To Jean Piaget, the child's mind is self-organized by a constant antagonism between internal, subjective mental states and external reality. "In Piagetian theory there is no objective ontological reality. This progression occurs because of the reciprocal effects of assimilation and accommodation, constantly forced to attain an equilibrium between subjective and objective states" (Marsh, 1992). Assimilation and Accommodation are the two complementary processes of Adaptation described by Piaget, through which awareness of the outside world is internalised. Although one may predominate at any one moment, they are inseparable and exist in a dialectical relationship. In Assimilation, what is perceived in the outside world is incorporated into the internal world, without changing the structure of that internal world, but potentially at the cost of "squeezing" the external perceptions to fit. In Accommodation, the internal world has to accommodate itself to the evidence with which it is confronted and thus adapt to it, which can be a more difficult and painful process. In the database analogy, it is like what happens when you try to put in information which does not fit the pre-existent fields and categories. You have to develop new ones to accommodate the new information. In reality, both are going on at the same time, although most of the time we are assimilating familiar material in the world around us, nevertheless, our minds are also having to adjust to accommodate it.

Piaget's theory is based on the idea that the developing child builds cognitive structures—in other words, mental maps, schemes or networked concepts for understanding and responding to physical experiences within his or her environment. He further attested that a child's cognitive structure increases in sophistication with development, moving from a few innate reflexes such as crying and sucking to highly complex mental activities.

Jean Piaget concluded that children engage in qualitatively different kinds of thinking as they pass through various stages of development, meaning they do not learn by practicing adult knowledge. Piaget discounted the relative importance of maturation and was interested in the processes that emerge as children discard previous ways of thinking for new ones. Intellectual growth results from attempts of the child to solve problems, which in turn causes the child to continually reconstruct the external world through personal experiences as internal representations. According to Piaget, the starting point of a child's intellectual growth is his/her own action. As the child actively engages with the people and objects around him/her, he/she begins to form mental constructs about what the world is like. It's the child's own experimentation that leads him/her to certain conclusion, and to the creation of a "schema". A schema is the mental construct from which behaviour flows. A young child may construct a schema for a particular object or an animal. As children grow older, their schemas become more numerous and differentiated. Piaget was especially interested in schemas concerning the child's understanding of objects and their properties, such as shape and size. Ultimately he concluded that children's reasoning power was in no way flawed—on the contrary it was often as good as many adult scientists! However, children's limited life experience meant that they had not amassed and processed enough information about the natural and social world (nor imbibed the same biases) to come to the same conclusions that adults did. But Piaget did not conclude that children should, ergo, be force-fed more facts at an earlier age. In fact he believed quite the opposite: that such force-feeding would condition children to expect the answers to come from outside themselves, robbing them of creative initiative. He also believed that adults must exercise caution about correcting children's "mistaken notions". If done too harshly, or in a condescending manner, such correcting shamed them into intellectual passivity, causing them to abandon their innate urge to figure things out for themselves, and to come up with new and creative ideas.

Although Piaget followed a purely biological way of thinking, it led him to a theory of knowing that is perfectly compatible with that of modern physicists. Both biologists and physicists acknowledge that the conceptual structures that we consider to be 'knowledge' are the products of active knowers who shape their thinking to fit the constraints they experience (Glasersfeld, 1997). Piaget was the first methodically to employ this notion in psychology and to proceed on the assumption that our ideas are individual creations (and that their mutual compatibility with those of others has to be achieved by social interaction). The essential functions of the mind consist in understanding and in inventing, in other words, in building up structures by structuring reality (Piaget, 1971).

To grasp the full extent of this epistemological shift, one needs to be clear about what precisely 'adaptation' means and how it works. There is a widespread notion that adaptation is an activity carried out by living organisms when they are being pressed by the environment. To put it generally, an organism must *fit*, i.e. be *viable* within the constraints of the environment. In this context, to fit means to be adapted—and adaptedness, as Piaget has said explicitly, is tantamount to the ability to survive (Piaget, 1976). This perspective brings with it an important insight: If the constraints of the environment can be avoided at all, there is not only one way of doing it, but an unspecifiable number of ways. This is the reason why adaptedness does not reflect the structure of the environment—it merely shows one way of not coming into fatal conflict with it (Glasersfeld, 1997). In Piaget's theory of cognition there are two levels of adaptation. On the practical level of survival, it is a matter of devising schemes of action that circumvent the obstacles and perturbations the environment places in the organism's path. On the conceptual level of theories and explanations it is a matter of achieving a coherent balance that avoids internal contradictions (Glasersfeld, 1997).

Time and again Piaget has reiterated that our knowledge is not and cannot be a picture of the world as it might be in itself. In Piaget's model, knowledge has to be seen as a collection of schemes of action and models of thinking that allow us to live and move in the world as we experience it. For Piaget, all science is the product of a thinking mind's conceptualization. From this perspective, knowledge does not 'represent' or depict an independent reality but is a collection of inventions that happen to fit the world as it is experienced. For Piaget, there is no iconic correspondence, but knowledge fits functionally into the real world because it is an evolutionary adaptation. Adaptation is, in fact, a *negative* concept. It does not require any knowledge of what really exists—it merely implies that whatever is functionally successful will live and reproduce itself. It is the result of trial and the elimination of what does not work. The fact that an organism is 'adapted' only shows that it has found a way of coping with the world in which it lives—it does not show what a world might be like before it has been perceived and conceived by a particular living organism. The focus is on knowledge as an instrument of adaptation that enables the organism to steer clear of external perturbations and internal contradictions. Knowledge thus turns into a tool in the pursuit of equilibrium, and its purpose is no longer the representation of a 'real' world.

Piaget's work with children made him realize that all sentient living things engage in what we might call a feedback loop when interacting with their environment. The individual performs an action and observes a response. If the response was interesting or otherwise positive, the individual will repeat the behaviour. Organisms which are capable of higher intelligence will generate cognitive structures, a kind of mental map, of actions and responses that grow in complexity as the individual has more and varied experiences.

Piaget divided the course of human development into four major stages. Major stages beyond the fourth were also considered possible, and each stage could be divided into substages. We begin at birth with the sensorimotor period. Our primary means of knowing during the six substages of the sensorimotor period is our sensorimotor action schemes. We are limited, during this stage, to "thinking in action". That is, we can't contemplate the consequences of applying one of our schemes; we just have to apply it. Many important accomplishments take place by the end of the sensorimotor period, most notably a full understanding of permanent objects, and the ability to imitate someone else's action on the basis of memory alone. Around two years of age, we enter the preoperational period. The preoperational period is marked by the ability to anticipate—that is, to think about some possibilities before acting on them. It is also characterized by the appearance of the semiotic function, which embraces speaking and understanding language as well as pretend play.

However, many elementary forms of logical reasoning are not yet available.

Around six or seven years of age, we see the onset of concrete operations. During this stage, logical structures for hierarchical classification become available, as do structures for serration (putting things in order in terms of length or some other dimension), conservation of physical quantities, and mathematical operations on numbers. But children are still quite limited in their ability to generate possibilities systematically or to test hypotheses which require keeping track of multiple possibilities.

From age twelve or so, we move into formal operations. Formal thinking is marked by the ability to systematically generate and work with larger spaces of possibilities, including possibilities that are quite abstract. Inhelder and Piaget tested for formal thinking by asking children and adolescents to design and conduct scientific experiments—for instance, experiments to determine what determines the period of a pendulum, or what factors affect the bending of rods that vary in shape, length, size, material, and so on. But thinking explicitly about our values and our course in life, and comparing them with other possible values, and other possible courses in life, also qualifies as formal thinking.

In his "Sociological Studies", Piaget analyzes the processes of social interaction in far greater detail than any of the authors, who focus on the social rather than the individual construction of knowledge. Piaget has presented a list of the types of knowledge whose acquisition seems to require social interaction as opposed to those that do not. In his view, the organization of immediate experience, the sensorimotor intelligence that manifests itself in simple action schemes, and the basic ability to consider one thing as the symbolic substitute for another, are cognitive functions of the child before it has any conception of other people, let alone their common social practices. Conscious reflection, on the other hand, arises for Piaget in the context of interaction or collaboration with others. This does not happen at once, but as Piaget said: The child is socialized in the same way as it adapts itself to the external physical environment (Piaget, 1965). It happens as a result of the 'decentering', i.e. the becoming aware of other points of view, which is a prerequisite for the successful interaction with other deliberate agents.

Although Piaget did not focus on how to apply his theories within education, we do know that he advocated creative learning situations, or what is now referred to as "hands on, interactive". And one could infer, based on the example of his own self-education efforts that he also favoured making information readily available to young, enquiring minds, allowing them to progress according to their inner drive to know and explore. But Piaget's significance stretched far beyond the fields of education. His cognitive theory was applicable not only to children, but to all intelligent life. For Piaget, development is what cognitive structures do. Cognitive structures are active things; they are means of interacting with our environment. Human beings are not born with a fixed set of cognitive structures, preformed and ready to go, or waiting around till some episode of maturation comes along and triggers them. For him there was no fixed limit to human development, and, wisely, he did not attempt to forecast future creative activity. Piaget did suggest that beyond formal operations, there are post-formal operations, or "operations to the nth power". Inevitably these would be of a highly specialized nature, and might be found in the thinking of professional mathematicians or experts in some other fields.

Piaget's Quotes:

"The principle goal of education is to create men who are capable of doing new things, not simply of repeating what other generations have done—men who are creative, inventive and discoverers."

"It is with children that we have the best chance of studying the development of logical knowledge, mathematical knowledge, physical knowledge, and so forth."

"Knowledge, then, is a system of transformations that become progressively adequate."

"During the earliest stages the child perceives things like a solipsist who is unaware of himself as subject and is familiar only with his own actions."

"During the earliest stages of thought, accommodation remains on the surface of physical as well as social experience."

"Every acquisition of accommodation becomes material for assimilation, but assimilation always resists new accommodations."

"The current state of knowledge is a moment in history, changing just as rapidly as the state of knowledge in the past has ever changed and, in many instances, more rapidly."

"Knowing reality means constructing systems of transformations that correspond, more or less adequately, to reality."

"The more the schemata are differentiated, the smaller the gap between the new and the familiar becomes, so that novelty, instead of constituting an annoyance avoided by the subject, becomes a problem and invites searching."

"Scientific thought, then, is not momentary; it is not a static instance; it is a process."

"Scientific knowledge is in perpetual evolution; it finds itself changed from one day to the next."

"Logical positivists have never taken psychology into account in their epistemology, but they affirm that logical beings and mathematical beings are nothing but linguistic structures."

"To express the same idea in still another way, I think that human knowledge is essentially active."

"This means that no single logic is strong enough to support the total construction of human knowledge."

"On the one hand, there are individual actions such as throwing, pushing, touching, rubbing. It is these individual actions that give rise most of the time to abstraction from objects."

"The first type of abstraction from objects I shall refer to as simple abstraction, but the second type I shall call reflective abstraction, using this term in a double sense."

"The self thus becomes aware of itself, at least in its practical action, and discovers itself as a cause among other causes and as an object subject to the same laws as other objects."

"In genetic epistemology, as in developmental psychology, too, there is never an absolute beginning."

"Reflective abstraction, however, is based not on individual actions but on coordinated actions."

2.2.5 Lev Semyonovich Vygotsky

As per the perceived perception, Piaget is generally considered as the patriarch of constructivism, the fact is that constructivists have embraced other theorists, especially the Lev Semyonovich Vygotsky. His work is varied not only in terms of kind and nature but also in content and intent. He is generally associated with the social constructivist theory or social constructivism because he emphasized the critical importance of culture and the importance of the social context for cognitive development. Vygotsky viewed cognitive developments as a result of a dialectical process, where the child learns through shared problem-solving experiences with someone else. Lev Vygotsky considered an individual's cognitive system to be a direct result of and inseparable from social life (Vygotsky, 1987). His pivotal concern is that social interaction and social context, a world full of other people, who interact with the child from birth onwards, are essential in the cognitive development. According to Vygotsky, the intellectual development of children is a function of human communities, rather than of individuals. For Vygotsky the culture gives the child the cognitive tools needed for development. He states that "every function in the child's cultural development appears twice: first, on the social level, and later, on the individual level; first between people (inter psychological) and then inside the child (intra psychological). This applies equally to voluntary attention, to logical memory, and to the formation of concepts. All the higher functions originate as actual relationships between individuals" (Vygotsky, 1978). Vygotsky differentiated between our higher and lower mental functions. Lower or elementary functions are genetically inherited; they are our natural mental abilities. In contrast, our higher mental functions develop through social interaction, being socially or culturally mediated.

The relationship between the social and the individual in the historical processes of social and individual development is one of dialectical interaction and functional unification (Liu & Matthews, 2005). The process of individual development could perhaps be summarised as 'the social internalisation through sign mediation—restructuring conceptual system—new understanding/consciousness'. In this sense, individual mastery and development must be based on history and culture; moreover, the individual should be enabling to stand above the social collective because of the ability of the mind to generate personal understandings. This has different implications for educational practices from the common perception that Vygotsky "argued that knowing is relative to the situations in which knowers find themselves" (Cobb, 1996). In Vygotsky's theory, the development of intellect and rationality beyond situations is the central aim of education. The conceptualisation of the social and the collective is not to be viewed as a mere total sum of separate, independent individuals. The philosophical establishment of the collective being always larger than the total sum of individual persons underpins a major part of Vygotsky's theoretical system. Because every individual member always brings to the group a personal contribution at their own levels, and between individuals their unique contributions interchange, the collective forever amounts larger than the total number of separate individuals (Liu & Matthews, 2005). For Vygotsky, the connection between the collective and the individual consciousness exists through the collective subjectivity, which is produced historically by joint collective enactment. The social external world is not seen as a superstructure, fixed and self-sufficient, but is given shape historically by collective participation and collaboration. The collective subjectivity with participation and contributions from its members as authentic beings now becomes not just larger than the total sum of individual beings, but also a qualitatively different existence. This conception of the social and the individual being closely interconnected, functionally unified, constantly interacting, and the change and development in one relentlessly influencing the other provides a valid explanation for both social and individual change (Liu & Matthews, 2005).

Cognitive skills and patterns of thinking are not primarily determined by innate factors, but are the products of the activities practiced in the social institutions of the culture in which the individual grows up. Consequently, the history of the society in which a child is reared and the child's personal history are crucial determinants of the way in which that individual will think.

His central theory is that the human species is distinguished from others by use of tools, deliberate teaching, and intentional learning. Tools refer both to the variety of implements created by humans and psychological tools, such as language. The mind has social origins and the cultural tools available to the individual influence the nature of the mind that is constructed. There are three ways a cultural tool can be passed from one individual to another. The first one is imitative learning, where one person tries to imitate or copy another. The second way is by instructed learning which involves remembering the instructions of the teacher and then using these instructions to self-regulate. The final way that cultural tools are passed to others is through collaborative learning, which involves a group of peers who strive to understand each other and work together to learn a specific skill (Tomasello, et al., 1993).

Signs generally carry meaning between people, which is unique to the cultural and variable within a cultural at the familial and colloquial levels. It is here that Vygotsky believed that we may understand social influences and how culture forms the basis for translating perceptions into shared meanings and individual mental constructs. Vigorously, he forwarded the notion that culture and community play a huge role in early development. For him, a child's development is a direct result of his or her culture. For Vygotsky, development applied primarily to mental development, such as thought, language, reasoning processes and mental functions. However, Vygotsky observed that these abilities developed through social interactions with significant people in a child's life particularly parents, but also other adults. Through these interactions, a child came to learn the habits of mind of his or her culture, namely speech patterns, written language and other symbolic knowledge that effected a child's construction of his or her knowledge. The specific knowledge gained by a child through these interactions also represented the shared knowledge of a culture. This process is known as internalization. Vygotsky's cultural-historical theory of development focuses on the role of the intersubjective dimension in processes of knowledge acquisition. According to him, knowledge acquisition is equal to internalization of the environment. Knowledge and concepts are not seen as constructions that are created by the single individual, but it is historical and cultural founded mental artefacts and phenomena, which the individual takes up and makes his or her own.

Language and psychological processes develop initially as social, interpersonal interactions among people. In the first instance the individual learns by imitating the immediate social environment, which is influenced in different ways by the larger culture. The individuals' psychological processes are always bound to the culture in some way because the individual uses a particular 'set' of cultural tools, thus mental constructs are delimited by one's culture.

Language development is based on word meaning. According to him, a word without a meaning is not a word. Words are structured with sense (Vygotsky, 1962). To be meaningful, a word must be part of inner speech and language. To acquire meaning, the child transforms the word as a symbol along with many kinds of contextual experiences. In his book, *Mind and Society* (1934), Vygotsky revealed his basic theory about human cognitive development: "...the most significant moment in the course of intellectual development, which gives birth to the purely human forms of practical and abstract intelligence, occurs when speech and practical activity, two previously completely independent lines of development, converge" (Vygotsky, 1978). The significance of this 'convergence' is that speech can be used to solve problems. According to Vygotsky the 'interpersonal function' of speech or the turning inward of social speech, enables children to organize their own behaviour. Signs permit cognitive construction. Also, it mediated memory, voluntary attention, and concepts are developed on the basis of internalization of external activities begun at the school level.

This process being transformed continues to exist and to change as an external form of activity for a long time before definitively turning inward. For many functions, the stage of external signs lasts forever, that is, it is their final stage of development. Other functions develop further and gradually become inner functions. However, they take on the character of inner processes only as a result of a prolonged development. This transfer inward is linked with changes in the laws governing their activity; they are incorporated into a new system with its own laws.

Vygotsky's contribution to the inter-relationship of language development and thought is unique as this has established the explicit and profound connection between oral language (speech) and the development of mental concepts. It is through speech, Vygotsky argued that thinking, thoughts and mental constructs (a child's intellectual being) are formed. A child's conscious awareness of these and their being impressed upon a child's psyche provide the underlying theoretical rationale for such truism as "if you want to learn something teach it to someone and the observations of our need to 'talk it out' and 'think out loud'". "Thought and language, which reflect reality in a way different from that of perception, are the key to the nature of human consciousness. Words play a central part not only in the development of thought but in the historical growth of human consciousness as a whole. A word is a microcosm of human consciousness." For Vygotsky consciousness is not the ability of an individual to know all the ontological answers to the universe, rather, it is the ability to perceive meaningfully (Liu & Matthews, 2005). Consciousness is nothing but an individual's general perceptual orientation. "Meaningful perception is generalised or abstracted perception"; and to perceive something from a meaningful different way enables the individual to "acquire the potential for new relationships with it" (Vygotsky, 1987). For Vygotsky, change in the functional structure of consciousness is the main and central content of the entire process of mental development. Vygotsky distinguishes consciousness, the ability to perceive meaningfully, from conscious awareness, and defines the latter as "an act of consciousness whose object is the activity of consciousness itself" (Vygotsky, 1987). Consciousness awareness is developed in the same way as consciousness is—when consciousness means being able to generate meaningful generalization and connecting relationships between objects and concepts, consciousness awareness involves the ability to interconnect processes of mental activities.

Vygotsky contended that learning and development are intertwined from the first day of life, and learning cannot be matched to stages but must be determined by assessment to two developmental levels: (i) actual developmental level and (ii) the zone of proximal development. The 'zone of proximal development' is the 'space' where teachers, parents and peers may influence the child's development. The zone of proximal development is: "...the distance between the actual development level as determined by independent problem-solving and the level of potential development as determined through problem-solving under adult guidance or in collaboration with more capable peers" (Vygotsky, 1978). He points out at the idea that the potential for cognitive development is limited to a certain time span, which is nothing but the zone of proximal development (ZPD). In addition, full development during ZPD depends upon full social interaction. In this way we find the two major principles of cognitive development: (a) Cognitive development is limited to a certain range at any given time and (b) Full cognitive development requires social interaction. The range of skill that can be developed with adult guidance or peer collaboration exceeds what can be attained alone. It is of very fact that other people play important roles in helping children to learn, providing objects and ideas to their attention, talking while playing and sharing while playing, reading stories, asking questions. In a wide range of ways, adults mediate the world for children and make it possible for them to get access to it. The ability to learn through instruction and mediation is characteristic of human intelligence. By the help of adults children can do and understand more than they can on their own (Cameron, 2002). ZPD gave a new meaning to the concept like intelligence. Instead of measuring intelligence by what a child can do alone, Vygotsky suggested that intelligence could better be measured by what a child can do with skilled help. ZPD actually relates to the gap or difference between child's existing abilities and what he or she can learn with the guidance of an adult or a more capable peer.

As learning proceeds, the child's own language comes to help as his or her primary tool of intellectual transformation. Children can eventually use their own internal speech to direct their own behaviour in much the same way that their parents' speech once directed it. This transition reflects the Vygotsky's theme of development as a process of internalization. Bodies of knowledge and tools of thought at first exist outside the child, in the culture of the environment. Development consists of gradual internalization, primarily through language, to form cultural adaptation (Rogoff, 1990).

The zone of proximal development uses two levels to gauge a child's ability and potential. A child's actual development level is when he or she can work unaided on a task or problem. This sets a baseline for the child's knowledge and is traditionally what is assessed and valued in schools. The potential developmental level is the level of competence a child can reach when he or she is guided and supported by another person. The difference between these two levels of ability consists of the ZPD. This idea of a significant adult guiding a child through the ZPD is known as scaffolding. Within the zone, the structure that enables an individual to move forward in their ability is termed as scaffolding. Scaffolding is an incremental change in information support that steps the learner up to the highest level they can achieve with support. This gain in knowledge would be an example of intermental learning, whereas, when the individual undertakes the new skill on their own, they have accomplished intramental learning. When the individual is able to transfer the newly learned skill to a different context, which may require abstract thought, the learning becomes decontextualised. This means the individual does not have to remain in the physical situation in which they learned the skill. They are also able to imagine a scenario and use hypothetico-deductive reasoning to formulate an answer to a question which is abstract in nature.

Vygotsky's fundamental principle of development is social development: "In our conception, the true direction of the development of thinking is not from the individual to the socialised but from the social to the individual" (Vygotsky, 1988). Development can be seen as internalizing from social interaction.

Vygotsky attempted to shed light on consciousness which develops as a result of socialization. While learning a language the first utterances have a communicational purpose, but once internalized they become "inner speech". Young children can often be observed talking to themselves and act as if they carry out talks or play, in what is called private speech. As children get older they gradually speak less and less loud, and differentiate between social speech for others and "inner speech", which continues to play an important role in regulating and controlling behaviour. Wertsch (1985) emphasizes that internalization for Vygotsky was not just transfer but also a transformation; being able to do it. In the internalizing process, the interpersonal, joint talk and joint activity, later becomes interpersonal, mental action by one individual.

Learning is a constructivist activity. Cognitive development is a process in which language is a crucial tool for determining how the child will learn how to think because advanced modes of thought are transmitted to the child by means of words. "Prior to mastering his or her own behaviour, the child begins to master his or her surroundings with the help of speech." Once the child realizes that everything has a name, each new object presents the child with a problem situation, and he solves the problem by naming the object. When he lacks the word for the new object, he demands it from adults. The early word meanings thus acquired will be the embryos of concept formation. "A problem must arise that cannot be solved otherwise than through the formation of new concepts." During the course of development everything occurs twice. For example, in the learning of language, our first utterances with peers or adults are for the purpose of communication, but once mastered they become internalized and allow "inner speech". "Thought undergoes many changes as it turns into speech." An essential feature of learning is that it awakens a variety of internal developmental processes that are able to operate only when the child is interacting with people in his environment. It can be asserted that according to Vygotsky, learning is a question of appropriation of the culturally created surroundings.

Vygotsky's educational theory is guided by an alternative epistemological paradigm—that of historical-dialectical-monism (Liu & Matthews, 2005). Vygotsky asserts that the most fruitful experience in a child's education is his or her collaboration with more skilled partners. Vygotsky explains that the more experienced partner provides help in the way of an intellectual scaffold, which allows the less experienced learner to accomplish more complex tasks than may be possible alone (Stone, 1995; McClellan, 1994). Vygotsky's emphasis on imitation and learning is interesting for three important reasons. First, far from being a simple mimic or mechanical process, a child can only imitate within his or her developmental range or zone of proximal development. Second, the child is incapable of learning without social interaction and cooperation of peers and adults. Third, the child internalizes processes that are limited, making learning a 'culturally organized, specifically human, psychological' function. The activities that happen in classroom create a kind of environment for teaching, and as such, offer different kinds of opportunities for language learning. Discovery model of learning as advocated by social constructivist theory, places the teacher in an active role while the students' mental abilities develop naturally through various paths of discovery. Part of teaching skill is to identify the particular opportunities of task or activity, and then to develop them into learning experiences for the children. (Cameron, 2002). Knowledge within a discipline is important, but solving problems that encourage students to go beyond their current skill and knowledge level further development of higher functions beyond the bounds of that discipline. By implication, new knowledge can be built.

Because teaching is affective when it is based on the next stage of the child's development rather than on the current stage of development, inferentially, the instructor must be knowledgeable about child development. The instructor must also provide educational materials and content which go beyond the child's current capabilities. The teacher's role is not that of simplifying the content, but of providing unfamiliar content and the setting for learners to step from their current level to a higher level of understanding. The curriculum should consider the basic principles of Vygotsky's theory: (1) Cognitive development is limited to a certain range at any given age (the area of current development surrounded by another area of future development = ZPD), (2) Full cognitive development requires social interaction, (3) Mediation.

Vygotsky's Quotes:

"The child begins to perceive the world not only through its eyes but also through its speech."

"And later it is not just seeing but acting that becomes informed by words."

"Thought is not merely expressed in words; it comes into existence through them."

"A word devoid of thought is a dead thing, and a thought unembodied in words remains a shadow."

"A word is a microcosm of human consciousness."

"We have seen that instruction and development do not coincide. They are two different processes with very complex interrelationships."

"Instruction is only useful when it moves ahead of development. When it does it impels or wakens a whole series of functions that are in a state of maturation lying in the zone of proximal development."

2.2.6 Jerome Seymour Bruner

Jerome Bruner has been one of the most modern prominent thinkers who have influenced the theory of constructivism. In the words of Gardner, "Jerome Bruner is not merely one of the foremost educational thinkers of the era; he is also an inspired learner and teacher. His infectious curiosity inspires all who are not completely jaded. Individuals of every age and background are invited to join in. Logical analyses, technical dissertations, rich and wide knowledge of diverse subject matters, asides to an ever wider orbit of information, intuitive leaps, pregnant enigmas pour forth from his indefatigable mouth and pen. In his words, 'Intellectual activity is anywhere and everywhere, whether at the frontier of knowledge or in a third-grade classroom.' To those who know him, Bruner remains the Complete Educator in the flesh..." (Gardner, 2001). His theory states that the development of human intellectual functioning from infancy to such perfection as it may reach is shaped by a series of technological advances in the use of mind. These technological advances depend on increasing language facility and exposure to systematic instruction. Moreover, the cognitive processes that are thoughts and beliefs balance what we get from outside stimuli and give us a sense of balance.

Commenting on constructivism he says, "Constructivism's basic claim is simply that knowledge is 'right' or 'wrong' in light of the perspective we have chosen to assume. Rights and wrongs of this kind—however well we can test them—do not sum to absolute truths and falsities. The best we can hope for is that we be aware of our own perspective and those of others when we make our claims of 'rightness' and 'wrongness'. Put this way, constructivism hardly seems exotic at all. It is what legal scholars refer to as 'the interpretive turn', or as one of them put it, a turning away from 'authoritative meaning'" (Bruner, 1996). He further says, "Understanding something in one way does not preclude understanding it in other ways" and "The 'reality' that we impute to the 'worlds' we inhabit is a constructed one. To paraphrase Nelson Goodman, 'reality is made, not found'. Reality construction is the product of meaning making shaped by traditions and by a culture's toolkit of ways of thought." Commenting on knowledge he says that "knowledge is justified belief" and "all knowledge has a history". "History never simply happens: it is constructed by historians." He further says, "Knowledge helps only when it descends into habits." "Knowledge and action are always local, always situated in a network of particulars" (Bruner, 1996).

Bruner has asserted that the process of constructing knowledge of the world is not done in isolation but rather within a social context. He said that the people represent knowledge in three ways and these emerge in developmental sequence—Enactive, Iconic and Symbolic. These three ways are also known as three modes of representing, or 'symbolizing', human thought. The Enactive representation includes use of motor skills and motor capacities and includes activities such as using tools. In this representation, people manipulate objects. They learn to do things like driving a motor vehicle or handling a computer. When dealing with the enactive mode, one is using some known aspects of reality without using words or imagination. It involves mainly in knowing how to do something; it involves series of actions that are right for achieving some result (Kristinsdottir, 2001). The iconic mode pertains to sensory capacities which have to do with images and things that can be altered. This mode deals with the internal imagery, where the knowledge is characterised by a set of images that stand for the concept. The iconic representation depends on visual or other sensory association and is principally defined by perceptual organization and techniques for economically transforming perceptions into meaning for the individual (Kristinsdottir, 2001). For example, we can imagine a train compartment that is empty or a compartment that is crowded with many people. We think about the differences in these two situations separately. The symbolic mode involves reasoning, and is exemplified by language, which implies using symbols to change knowledge into a code. Through life one is always adding to the resources to the symbolic mode of representation of thought. This representation is based upon an abstract, discretionary and flexible thought. It allows one to deal with what might be and what might not, and is a major tool in reflective thinking. This mode is illustrative of a person's competence to consider propositions rather than objects, to give ideas a hierarchical structure and to consider alternative possibilities in a combinatorial fashion (Spencer, 1991). For example, mathematics variables or even advanced language skills are typical here. Bruner has called it a means not only for representing experience, but also for transforming it. The association of these ideas of manipulations of actual materials as a part of developmental model and the Socraterian notion of learning as internal reorganization into a learning by discovery approach is the unique contribution of Bruner (Romiszowski, 1997). Bruner's theory would be considered constructivist because it demands that learners assign meaningful stimuli to everything based on the cognitive capabilities and experienced they have culled and gleaned.

According to Bruner, all children have natural curiosity. Further, learning is an active, social processes in which students construct new ideas or concepts based on current knowledge. The student selects information, originates hypotheses, and makes decisions in the process of integrating experiences into their existing mental constructs. The child is a social being and through social life, acquires a framework for interpreting experiences (Bruner & Haste, 1987). Bruner has also stated that, "there is no unique sequence for all learners and the optimum in any particular case will depend upon a variety of factors, including past learning, stage of development, nature of the material and individual differences" (Bruner, 1966).

Bruner's ideas about learning is that learning is an active, social process in which students construct new ideas or concepts based on their current and past knowledge. The learner chooses and permutes the knowledge, constructs hypotheses, makes decisions and while performing these he or she relies on his or her cognitive structuring. His or her cognitive structure caters for grasping the meaning and organization of the experiences, and enables him or her to go beyond the given information. The instructor should try and encourage students to discover principles by themselves. He expressed himself by saying, "the... discovery learning mode requires that the student participates in making many of the decisions about what, how and when something is to be learned and even plays a major role in making such decisions. Instead of being 'told' the content by the teacher, it is expected that the student will have to explore examples and from them 'discover' the principles or concepts which are to be learned" (Martin, 2002). Discovering a principle should be achieved through engagement of learners and teacher in an active conversation. Teacher should be able to transform the material to be learned in such a way that it suits the learners' cognitive level. The way of presenting the material should be spiral not linear so that it allows both learners to contemplate and construct gradually upon what they have learned.

Bruner (1966) states that a theory of instruction should address four major aspects: (i) predisposition towards learning, (ii) the ways in which a body of knowledge can be structured so that it can be most readily grasped by the learner, (iii) the most effective sequences in which to present material, and (iv) the nature and pacing of rewards and punishments. Good methods for structuring knowledge should result in simplifying, generating new propositions and increasing the manipulation of information. General principles that emerge are: (i) instruction must be concerned with the experiences and contexts that make the student willing and able to learn (readiness); (ii) instruction must be structured so that it can be easily grasped by the student (spiral organization), and (iii) instruction should be designed to facilitate extrapolation and/or fill in the gaps (going beyond the information given).

Bruner has expanded his theoretical framework to encompass the social and cultural aspects of learning as well as the practice of law. He notes that language is the most important tool for cognitive growth. He investigated how adult use language to mediate the world for children and help them to solve problems. Talk that supports a child in carrying out an activity, as a kind of verbal version of fine tuned help has been labelled as 'scaffolding'. Children need space for language growth. Routines and scaffolding are two types of language—using strategies that seem to be especially helped in making space for children. Mothers who used scaffolded talk made the children interested in the task, simplified the task by breaking it into smaller steps, kept the child on track onwards completing the task by reminding the child what the goal was, pointed out what was important to do or showed the child other ways of doing the parts of the tasks, controlled the child's frustration during the tasks, demonstrated an idealized version of the task. Moreover, good scaffolding was tuned to the needs of the child and adjusted as the child becomes more competent (Cameron, 2002).

Bruner focuses in The Culture of Education, Actual Minds, Possible Worlds and Acts of Meaning on narrative as a primary mode of human discourse and therefore essential to education (Speaker, 1999). Mind and culture function through narratives in the creation of the world and the recreation of culture in the individual. For him, culture is neither a neutral passive aspect of education, nor in politics; they are pervasively enmeshed in educational practice, even if "misrecognized" to use Pierre Bordieu's term. Education "is a complex pursuit of fitting a culture to the needs of its members and of fitting its members and their ways of knowing to the needs of the culture". "Although meanings are 'in the mind', they have their origins and their significance in the culture in which they are created. It is this cultural situatedness of meanings that assures their negotiability and, ultimately, their communicability.... What is important is the meaning provide the basis for cultural exchange...nobody can do it unaided by the culture's symbolic systems." It is culture that provides the tools for organizing and understanding our worlds in communicable ways. Culture and the quest for meaning within culture are the proper causes of human action. There are four universal modes of making meanings: the intersubjective, actional, normative and propositional mode. Based on these, each culture creates its own folk psychology, which is constructed and expressed in narratives.

"Educational encounters, to begin with, should result in understanding, not mere performance. Understanding consists in grasping the place of an idea or fact in some more general structure of knowledge. When we understand something, we understand it as an exemplar of a broader conceptual principle or theory. Knowledge itself, moreover, is organized in such a way that the grasp of its conceptual structure renders its particulars more self-evident, even as redundant. Acquired knowledge is most useful to a learner, moreover, when it is 'discovered' through the learner's own cognitive efforts, for it is then related to and used in reference to what one has known before." His instructional objective is depth not coverage, and there are limits on the interpretations which are based on individual's perspective within any culture's broad rules such as "rules of evidence, consistency, and coherence. Not everything goes." "Interpretations of meaning reflect not only the idiosyncrative histories of individuals, but also the culture's canonical ways of constructing reality. Nothing is 'culture free', but neither are individuals simply mirrors of their culture. It is the interaction between them that both gives a communal cast to individual thought and imposes a certain unpredictable richness on a culture's way of life, thought or feeling."

In his *The Act of Discover*, Bruner posits discover as the most important learning process. "The immediate occasion for my concern with discovery—and I do not restrict discovery to the act of finding out something that before was unknown to mankind, but rather include all forms of obtaining knowledge for oneself by the use of one's own mind.... It is rarely, on the frontier of knowledge or elsewhere, that new facts are 'discovered' in the sense of being encountered as Newton suggested in the form of islands of truth in an uncharted sea of ignorance" (1961). Hypothesis is very important to him in this discovery mode, and he classifies teaching into two broad types: expository mode and hypothetical mode.

In *The Course of Cognitive Growth*, Bruner discusses three human information processing systems (enactive representation, iconic representation and symbolic representation) and what he calls "integration"—the building of higher order units, chunks or ensembles of the three. This poses the problem of the nature of internal representation systems and structure and their interactions as processes or structures. It also leaves open the possibility that there may be many other representational systems which a learner may use with any internal function or any external tool. Language, of course, becomes one of these tools but certainly not the only one.

Based upon the idea of categorization, Bruner's theory states, "to perceive is to categorize, to conceptualize is to categorize, to learn is to form categories, to make decisions is to categorize". He maintained that people interpret the world in terms of its similarities and differences and suggested a coding system in which people have a hierarchical arrangement of related categories. Each successively higher level of categories becomes more specific. Bruner maintained that people interpret the world in terms of similarities and differences which are detected among objects and events. Objects that are viewed as similar are placed in the same category. The major variable in his theory of learning is the coding system into which the learner organizes the categories. The act of categorizing is assumed to be involved in information processing and decision-making. Bruner's theory of cognitive learning theory emphasizes the formation of these coding systems. He believed that the systems facilitate transfer, enhance retention and increase problem-solving and motivation. He advocated the discovery oriented learning methods in schools which he believed helped student discover the relationships between categories.

Jerome Bruner has made a profound contribution to our appreciation of the process of education and to the development of curriculum theory (Smith, 2002). He makes the case for education as a knowledge-getting process. In his own words, "To instruct someone...is not a matter of getting him to commit results to mind. Rather, it is to teach him to participate in the process that makes possible the establishment of knowledge. We teach a subject not to produce little living libraries on that subject, but rather to get a student to think mathematically for himself, to consider matters as an historian does, to take part in the process of knowledge-getting. Knowing is a process not a product" (Bruner, 1966). 'Thinking about thinking' has to be a principal ingredient of any empowering practice of education (Bruner, 1996). Commenting on schooling he says, "It is surely the case that schooling is only one small part of how a culture inducts the young into its canonical ways. Indeed, schooling may even be at odds with a culture's other ways of indicting the young into the requirements of communal living.... What has become increasingly clear...is that education is not just about conventional school matters like curriculum or standards or testing. What we resolve to do in school only makes sense when considered in the broader context of what the society intends to accomplish through its educational investment in the young. How one conceives of education, we have finally come to recognize, is a function of how one conceives of culture and its aims, professed and otherwise" (Bruner, 1996). The curriculum must aim at addressing three questions: (i) What is uniquely human about human beings?, (ii) How did they get the way?, and (iii) How could they be made more so? (Bruner, 1976). He has argued that schooling and curricula should be constructed to foster intuitive grasping (Smith, 2002). Effective curriculum then must provide many opportunities and choices for children. Within the multi-age setting, opportunities exist for children to make choices about their learning experiences. The curriculum should be organized in a spiral manner so that students continually build upon what they already know. In addition, the variety of teaching methods used in the multi-age classroom provides opportunities for children to construct knowledge of ways.

For the classroom settings, Wood (1998) suggested that teachers can scaffold children's learning in various ways: to attend what it is relevant, adopt useful strategies, remember the whole task and goals teachers can suggest, praise the significant, providing focusing activities, encourage rehearsal, be explicit about organization, remind, model, provide part-whole activities. Also, classroom language and routine language development. They would allow the child to actively make sense of new language from experience and provide space for language growth. Routines will open up many possibilities for developing language skills (Cameron, 2002). Emphasising on the critical role of pedagogy he has asserted, "If pedagogy is to empower human beings to go beyond their 'native' predispositions, it must transmit the 'toolkit' the culture has developed for doing so" (Bruner, 1996).

Bruner proposes the following tenets of education (Speaker, 1999):

1. The perspectival tenet—that meaning is related to the frame of reference, stance, perspective of the interpreter and its context within some content.
2. The constraints tenet—forms of meaning making are constrained by the evolution of the species and the symbolic processing systems developed by a culture.

3. The constructivism tenet—reality is constructed by the individual.
4. The interactional tenet—human exchange occurs only in an interacting subcommunity (humans have an "astonishingly well developed talent for intersubjectivity").
5. The externalization tenet—human activity results in oeuvres (works, external products) which are developed through interaction in subcommunities (he suggests class ethnographies here).
6. The instrumentalism tenet—education is an instrumental factor in later life within a culture; ergo, "the chief subject matter of school, viewed culturally, is school itself".
7. The institutional tenet—in the developed world, schooling is an institution with all the powers and constraints of such institutions of culture and government.
8. The tenet of identity and self-esteem—humans universally perceive the "self" and recognize the selfness of others with two key properties of agency and evaluation.
9. The narrative tenet—"the mode of thinking and feeling that helps children (indeed, people generally) create a version of the world in which, psychologically, they can envisage a place for themselves—a personal world".

He comes up with four simplistic views of his theory of learner mind:

1. Imitative learner, "Know-how" acquisition;
2. Didactic learner, "Propositional knowledge" acquisition;
3. Thinking learner, "Intersubjective interchange" with theories (models) of mind, metacognition and collaborative learning;
4. Knowledgeable learner, managing 'objective' knowledge [or quasi-objective knowledge].

According to Bruner, four important new ideas about the nature of schooling and how learning occurs are:

1. Agency—"taking control of your own mental activity"—metacognition;
2. Reflection—"not simply 'learning in the raw' but making what you learn make sense";
3. Collaboration—"sharing the resources of the mix of human beings.... Mind is inside the head, but it is also with others";
4. Culture—"the way of life and thought that we construct, negotiate, institutionalize...".

His comments on evaluation are trenchant:

1. "Evaluation is best looked at as a form of educational intelligence for the guidance of curriculum construction and pedagogy";
2. "Evaluation, to be effective, must at some point be combined with an effort to teach so that the child's response to a particular process of teaching can be evaluated";
3. "Evaluation can be of use only when there is a full company on board, a full curriculum-building team consisting of the scholar, the curriculum maker, the teacher, the evaluator and the students";
4. "Evaluation, in its very nature, is likely to create suspicion and concern in the conventional educational setting where it has a history that is inappropriate to present practice...";
5. "From time to time the evaluator must design instruction as a means of probing and developing general intellectual skills";
6. "A curriculum cannot be evaluated without regard to the teacher who is teaching it and the students who is learning it";
7. "Curriculum evaluation must, to be effective, contribute to a theory of education."

The interpretation of Bruner's theory of instruction may be summarised as: It has participants: students, teachers, scholars, curriculum makers and evaluators. It has content: experiences, processes, materials, manipulatives and other sensory artifacts, including language and images. It has pace: appropriate for the development of the learners. It has sequences: spirals, branchings and themes which result in artifacts of the learning—all contextualized by the content and the participants. It has a goal: producing learners with the "will to learn" and "reading critically" (Speaker, 1999).

Bruner's Quotes:

"Learners are encouraged to discover facts and relationships for themselves."

"Experience with an incongruity is effective in so far as it modifies the set of the subject to prepare him for incongruity."

"The shrewd guess, the fertile hypothesis, the courageous leap to a tentative conclusion—these are the most valuable coins of the thinker at work. But in most schools guessing is heavily penalized and is associated somehow with laziness."

"There is a deep question whether the possible meanings that emerge from an effort to explain the experience of art may not mask the real meanings of a work of art."

"Learning and thinking arc always situated in a cultural setting and always dependent upon the utilization of cultural resources."

"Education is a major embodiment of a culture's way of life, not just a preparation for it."

"Nothing is 'culture free', but neither are individuals simply mirrors of their culture. It is the interaction between them that both gives a communal cast to individual thought and imposes a certain unpredictable richness on any culture's way life, thought, or feeling."

"'Thinking about thinking' has to be a principal ingredient of any empowering practice of education."

"Education is too consequential to too many constituencies to leave to professional educators."

"Education is risky, for it fuels the sense of possibility."

"In theorizing about the practice of education in the classroom (or any other setting, for that matter), you had better take into account the folk theories that those engaged in teaching and learning already have. For any innovations that you, as a 'proper' pedagogical theorist, may wish to introduce will have to compete with, replace, or otherwise modify the folk theories that already guide both teachers and pupils."

"Knowledge, after all, is justified belief."

"For a choice of pedagogy inevitably communicates a conception of the learning process and the learner. Pedagogy is never innocent. It is a medium that carries its own message."

"The objective of skilled agency and collaboration in the study of the human condition is to achieve not unanimity, but more consciousness. And more consciousness always implies more diversity."

"Learning to be a scientist is not the same as learning science."

"Mind is an extension of the hands and tools that you use and of the jobs to which you apply them."

"Knowledge helps only when it descends into habits."

"Education must, then, be not only a transmission of culture but also a provider of alternative views of the world and a strengthener of the will to explore them."

"Good methods for structuring knowledge should result in simplifying, generating new propositions, and increasing the manipulation of information."

2.2.7 Ernst von Glasersfeld

Ernst von Glasersfeld is one of the leading apostles of radical constructivism. Radical constructivism rejects the traditional philosophical position of realism and adopts a relativist position. The traditional view of realism sees knowledge as a representation of an absolute reality—a world "out there" prior to having been experienced. Radical constructivism has been careful to stress that all action, be it physical or conceptual, is subject to constraints.

The radical constructivist sees knowledge as something that is personally constructed by individuals, in an active way, as they try to give meaning to socially accepted and shared notions. As von Glasersfeld himself says, "knowledge is the result of an individual subject's constructive activity, not a commodity that somehow resides outside the knower and can be conveyed as distilled by diligent perception or linguistic communication" (http://www.math.upatras.gr/~mbouder//articles/constr.html). Knowledge is not a transferable commodity and communication not a conveyance (Glasersfeld, 1987). He has also said that knowledge is not a commodity which can be communicated (Glasersfeld, 1990). Coming to know is a process of dynamic adaptation toward viable interpretations of experience. The knower does not necessarily construct knowledge of a 'real' world. Knowledge has to be seen as a collection of schemes of action and models of thinking that allow us to live and move in the world as we experience it. From this perspective, knowledge does not 'represent' or depict an independent reality but is a collection of inventions that happen to fit the world as it is experienced.

He has asserted that the constructivism does not claim to have made earth-shaking inventions in the area of education; it merely claims to provide a solid conceptual basis for some of the things that, until now, inspired teachers had to do without theoretical foundation (Glasersfeld, 1995). Quoting Einstein who once said that all science is the enterprise of coordinating and arranging our experiences, Glasersfeld points out that all scientific rationality can work with experiences. There is no 'going beyond'. There is no fanciful retreat into the realm of objectivity possible. Likewise, a 'phenomenon' does not connote a mind independent entity. Instead, it refers to an isolated part of the experience. A possible objection goes, experience is a common feature of common-sense and scientific reasoning. What makes science so unique is, among others, exact measurement and quantifying, which does not allow for 'subjective interpretation'. But again, to measure means to compare two phenomena with each other, one of which already assigned with a dimension. Assigning a scale or units to a phenomenon means to compare it with yet another one, etc. Therefore, the act of quantifying does not save the realists' argument either. By introducing the notion of 'functional fit', von Glasersfeld clearly defines what it means to 'know' in a radical constructivist context. It is to possess ways and means of acting and thinking that allow one to attain one's own goals, rather than to possess a true representation of 'reality'.

The radical constructivist view offers the opportunity to investigate the phylogenetic and ontogenetic emergence of system-relative representations, i.e., "meanings" for the cognitive systems (Riegler, 2001). Such insights also have impacts on communication and language. Meaning is a human construct. It does not reside somewhere else and is not independent of the person who makes it. Meaning cannot be transmitted as an entity. It is not in the words, gestures, symbols with which we express ourselves. Language, therefore, must be seen as a behavioural system which triggers orienting actions within the cognitive domain of the interlocutor. Thus language is an ongoing process of interpretation and mutual adaptation. As Glasersfeld (1999) puts it, "to find a fit simply means not to notice any discrepancies". This is in contrast to matching something against something else; there are no ways to validate a 'correct match'. For Glasersfeld, the main characteristic of a cognitive system is to say viable in the above sense of fitting, of displaying adequate behaviour.

To claim that one's theory of knowing is true, in the traditional sense of representing a state or feature of an experiencer-independent world, would be perjury for a radical constructivist. One of the central points of the theory is precisely that this kind of "truth", can never be claimed for the knowledge (or any piece of it) that human reason produces. To mark this radical departure, he has in the last few years taken to calling his orientation a theory of knowing rather than a "theory of knowledge". He agrees whole-heartedly with Noddings when she says that radical constructivism should be "offered as a post-epistemological perspective". One of the consequences of such an appraisal, however, must be that one does not persist in arguing against it as though it were or purported to be a traditional theory of knowledge.

"Knowledge" is something of which we are quite sure that we have a certain amount, and we are not prepared to relinquish it. The trouble is that throughout the occidental history of ideas and right down to our own days, two requisites have been considered fundamental in any epistemological discussion of knowledge. The first of these requisites demands that whatever we would like to call "true knowledge" has to be independent of the knowing subject. The second requisite is that knowledge is to be taken seriously only if it claims to represent a world of "things-in-themselves" in a more or less veridical fashion. In other words, it is tacitly taken for granted that a fully structured and knowable world "exists" and that it is the business of the cognizing human subject to discover what that structure is. The weakness of the sceptics' position lies in its polemical formulation. It always sounds as though the traditional epistemologists' definition of knowledge were the only possible one. Hence, when Montaigne says "la peste de l'homme c'est l'opinion de savoir" (mankind's plague is the conceit of knowing), it sounds as though we ought to give up all knowing. But he was referring to absolutistic claims of experiential knowledge and was discussing them in the context of the traditional dogmatic belief that religious revelation is unquestionable. He had in mind absolute truth, and he was castigating those who claimed that a rational interpretation of experience (of which "scientific observation" is, after all, a sophisticated form) would lead to such truth.

In short, what the sceptics failed to stress was that, though no truths about a "real" world could be derived from experience, experience nevertheless supplied a great deal of useful knowledge. The human mind can know only what the human mind has made, was his slogan and, more like Piaget than Kant, he did not assume that space and time were necessarily *a priori* categories, but suggested that they, too, were human constructs (Vico, 1858). Pursuing this way of thinking, one is led to what he has called "a reconstruction of the concept of knowledge" (von Glasersfeld, 1985). Some reconstruction is needed because, on the one hand, one can no longer maintain that the cognizing activity should or could produce a true representation of an objective world, and on the other, one does not want to end up with a solipsistic form of idealism. The only way out, then, would seem to be a drastic modification of the relation between the cognitive structures we build up and that "real" world which we are inclined to assume as "existing" beyond our perceptual interface. Instead of the illusory relation of "representation", one has to find a way of relating knowledge to reality that does not imply anything like match or correspondence.

In his view, the following basic principles of radical constructivism emerge quite clearly:

- Knowledge is not passively received either through the senses or by way of communication;
- Knowledge is actively built up by the cognizing subject;
- The function of cognition is adaptive, in the biological sense of the term, tending towards fit or viability;
- Cognition serves the subject's organization of the experiential world, not the discovery of an objective ontological reality.

One cannot adopt these principles casually. If taken seriously, they are incompatible with the traditional notions of knowledge, truth, and objectivity, and they require a radical reconstruction of one's concept of reality. Instead of an inaccessible realm beyond perception and cognition, it now becomes the experiential world we actually live in. This world is not an unchanging independent structure, but the result of distinctions that generate a physical and a social environment to which, in turn, we adapt as best we can. Consequently, one cannot adopt the constructivist principles as an absolute truth, but only as a working hypothesis that may or may not turn out to be viable. This is the main reason why the constructivist orientation is unequivocally post-epistemological.

As he has reiterated many times, radical constructivism does not suggest that we can construct anything we like, but it does claim that within the constraints that limit our construction there is room for an infinity of alternatives. It, therefore, does not seem untimely to suggest a theory of knowing that draws attention to the knower's responsibility for what the knower constructs.

Commenting on radical behaviourist he says, "Psychology was now defined as 'the science of behaviour', and for radical behaviourists, the mind, the entire world of concepts, meanings, purposes, intentions, and indeed knowledge was discarded as a bunch of pre-scientific, mentalistic superstitions" (Glasersfeld).

Basic principles of von Glasersfeld's constructivism are following (Schmidt, 2007):

- In constructivism, the subject plays the central role of the constructor.
- It is the active subject who constructs sense, meaning and reality through his thoughts and actions.
- If reality is seen as the result of human imagination—as an inductively constructed world of experience—it follows that human knowledge can no longer be expected or obliged to represent a reality which exists objectively, and that the active observer must accept responsibility for his individual construction of reality. Such considerations make it clear that one can, and should, develop a theory of knowledge without being constrained by the demands of an epistemology. Radical constructivism, understood here as a theory of knowledge, provides a model of our ability to create knowledge in the sense of ideas which work. As Jean Piaget has shown, this knowledge results solely from our actions and the operation of our minds.
- "Cognition serves to organize a subject's world of experience, and not the subject's 'insight' into an objective, ontological reality" (Glasersfeld 1996).

The constructivist Ernst von Glasersfeld does not claim, however, that objective reality does not exist. Rather, he claims that we cannot know such a reality. "I understand by 'reality' a network of concepts, which have proven themselves to be appropriate and useful—that is, 'viable'—in the perception of the subject. They have proven this by repeatedly helping the subject to overcome obstacles successfully, and by aiding the conceptual 'assimilation' of their experiences" (Glasersfeld, 1997).

von Glasersfeld's early experience of the differences between languages gave him a clear sense "that one must build a different reality with each language. [...] This is precisely the point which led me to constructivism" (Glasersfeld, 1999). This experience also led von Glasersfeld to the conclusion that meaning does not lie in a text itself, but is *actively* constructed by the listeners in their own way.

von Glasersfeld's model of communication reacted against the behaviourists' elimination of aims and objectives from language and communication theory. Instead, he developed a cognitive language and communication theory, based on the premise that any analysis of meaning must always be connected to an analysis of concepts or mental constructs. The implication of this is that a semantic analysis should be conducted in the form of a cognitive analysis which focuses on "[...] the *conceptual* items a linguistic statement invokes and the relations that are posited between them", rather than on the statement's relationship with a non-linguistic reality or a statement's truth-value (Glasersfeld, 1974). Von Glasersfeld has stated emphatically that the development of concepts in autonomous cognitive systems can occur only through social interaction and must also relate to viable experiences in a shared field of experience (von Glasersfeld, 1997). Ernst von Glasersfeld has always emphasized that constructivists must take responsibility for their own constructions, and that this responsibility is a social responsibility. This means that we must see our fellow human beings not simply as a means, but also as a purpose. We must always respect our fellow human being's cognitive autonomy. In order to achieve a reliable construction of reality, we clearly need other people. Only in this way can we construct a better, intersubjectively valid reality. In other words, we need other people not only for ethical, but also for epistemological reasons.

From the outset he made it absolutely clear that he accepted the two basic pedagogical goals of educationalists: that pupils should learn to think independently and consistently, and that those ways of thinking and acting that are currently seen as the most effective should be preserved for the next generation (Glasersfeld, 1996).

According to von Glasersfeld, students should from the outset be made aware of the reasons why certain ways of thinking and acting are preferable. The primary aim of education should not be to pass an examination, but to be intellectually more competent and successful. Since it is one of the basic tenets of constructivism that there is never only one correct way, a constructivist cannot propose a single, authoritative, didactic method. Nevertheless, he/she can explain to a student why certain attitudes and techniques are unproductive, by using the concepts of constructivism to reassess and re-conceptualize basic notions of communication, learning, knowledge, interaction and motivation. A consequence of constructivist thought is thus the idea that learning—in contrast to training—is a product of self-organization. Knowledge is only acquired through active assimilation to cognitive structures one already possesses, and is never acquired passively (Glasersfeld, 1995). Teachers must always have the confidence that their pupils can think independently. Their art resides in "encouraging pupils to formulate problems independently—problems which promote specific ways of thinking" (Glasersfeld, 1997).

Commenting specifically on education he has asserted that it is a wide-ranging concept that may comprise training and formation, coaching in specialized competencies, fostering the ability to think, promoting manners, culture, taste, and other accomplishments. Given this variety, it should be clear that the ways of teaching and learning cannot be the same in all its branches. One of the fundamental differences between them is that certain things that should be learned do not have a logical derivation, whereas others can be generated by a thinking individual. If, for example, any Indian wants to get a driving licence in continental Europe, he/she has to learn that one has to drive on the right side of the road. "Why not ride on the left?" would be a pointless question, because he/she has to conform to a social convention for which there is no further explanation. In contrast, the fact that the numbers two and two yield four when they are added, can be worked out and checked by everyone who has learned to count. It does require knowledge of the conventional number-words, but from then on it is a question of conceiving units and mentally operating with them.

This second kind of knowledge can be gained from one's own mental operations. He has categorically reiterated that the learning of anything that is considered 'correct' only because society has agreed that it should be so, is essentially a political matter. It is 'political', because it concerns knowledge that the older generation wants to instil into the younger in order to assure the continuation of its society and, in an important sense, its *status quo*. In some respects it is quite sensible to accept this kind of knowledge. Thus, to return to the banal example of the traffic rule, it is perfectly reasonable for everyone to agree to drive on the same side of the road, but the choice of the right rather than the left does not involve rational thought.

Educationalists do not often say this very clearly. But occasionally they do assert that the deeper purpose of school is to foster independent thinking. And this invokes the second sort of learning which may be called as *conceptual learning*, for it literally has to do with the activity of conceiving.

From the constructivist point of view, creating concepts is a form of construction—and construction, under all circumstances, involves reflection. In this context, reflection means to become aware of connections that it is possible to make by coordinating sensory elements or mental operations. Piaget generally speaks of "coordination". And this, obviously, is done by a mind. Many of these coordinations quickly turn into habits and are then carried out without conscious awareness.

While commenting teaching, he has said that the teacher presents a situation in which the students' network of explanatory concepts clearly turns out to be unsatisfactory. Nothing is condemned as "wrong", and no "correct" explanations are provided by the teacher. The students' thinking is merely oriented now and then by neutral questions. The main principles of constructivist didactics are implicit in this example. They are simple, but he wants to emphasize some of them.

1. Teaching does not begin with the presentation of sacred truths, but with creating opportunities to trigger the students' own thinking. One of the prerequisites for this would be that the teacher believes that students can think.

2. It is not sufficient for teachers to be familiar with the subject matter of the curriculum; they also have to have a repertoire of didactic situations in which the concepts that are to be built up can be involved. And these situations should be such that they evoke the students' spontaneous interest.

Both these requirements are often disregarded. The fundamental fact that concepts can be formed only in the experiential world of an individual remains buried under the general notion that everything conceptual is but a representation of an independent reality and can therefore be transferred to students ready-made. But this kind of realism is a poor basis for teaching.

3. Whenever students show their work, it is misguided for the teacher to say that it is 'wrong'—irrespective of how justified this judgment might be. Students rarely produce a random solution. They have worked at it, and if the result which they consider to be right at the moment is not what the teacher thinks it should be, their effort must nevertheless be acknowledged. Disregarding it, is a sure way to demolish whatever spark of motivation they had. And then it is not surprising that their willingness to tackle new tasks disappears.

4. Many words that teachers habitually associate with specialized meanings in the particular discipline, evoke very different associations in the beginning student. An understanding of the desired conceptual network (especially in scientific domains) becomes possible only when 'naive' concepts are consciously reconstructed. In order to foster such reconstruction and the formation of new conceptual relations, teachers must have at least an inkling of the students' present ideas and theories. Only if they have some model of the students' thinking, can they begin to orient trains of thought and try to preclude 'inappropriate' constructions.

5. If it is the case that the formation of concepts requires reflection, teachers must have available some means to provoke it. By far the easiest way is to get students to talk about what they are thinking. The act of verbalization requires a review of what is to be verbalized. This review is a form of reflection and

often brings to the surface inconsistencies or gaps in a train of thought. Hence it is crucial to initiate conversations whenever a problem is to be solved. It may be students explaining their thinking to the teacher or explaining it to their classmates. Both lead to reflection and are the beginning of what Ceccato called 'operational awareness'. After a while this becomes a habit for the students, and then all problem-solving can turn into a conversation with oneself.

Glasersfeld's Quotes:

"The world in which we live and perceive ourselves is the world which we create and maintain within the constraints we have hitherto experienced."

"One must build a different reality with each language. This is precisely the point which led me to constructivism."

"If we were to believe we knew both good and evil, we would be dangerous beings indeed."

"One's thought processes can become more creative and open once one accepts the provisional nature of what all too often seems, or is made to seem, final."

"Knowledge is not a commodity that can be communicated."

"Knowledge does not represent the world at all—it comprises action schemes, concepts, and thoughts, and it distinguishes the ones that are considered advantageous from those that are not. In other words, it pertains to the ways and means the cognizing subject has conceptually evolved in order to fit into the world as he or she experiences it."

2.2.8 Kenneth J. Gergen

Kenneth J. Gergen is generally associated with constructionism. "Constructionism shares constructivism's connotation of learning as 'building knowledge structures' irrespective of the circumstances of the learning" (Papert, 1990). Social constructivism (Gergen, 1985) focuses explicitly on the role of social processes in the construction of meaning. Consequently, Gergen (1982, 1985) rejected both exogenic and endogenic epistemologies. Gergen (1995) explores the use of the metaphor of dialogue to evaluate a number of educational practices. Particularly, he views knowledge as fragments of dialogue, "knowledgeable tellings" at a given time within an ongoing relationship. This relationship can be between learners, between a learner and a teacher, or between a learner and an environment experienced by the learner. Gergen describes a lecture as a conversation where, because the lecture has already set the content, the student enters part-ways through the dialogue and finds they have no voice within it (Dougiamas, 1998).

We may distinguish between views of knowledge that are primarily exogenic (or world centred) in character as opposed to those which are endogenic (or mind centered). The exogenic tradition in educational thought can be traced to empiricist philosophies of knowledge (from Locke to logical positivism), while the endogenic tradition largely owes its intelligibility to the rationalist tradition (From Descartes and Kant through Fodor and the AI movement) (Gergen). Both orientations embrace a mind/world dualism in which the existence of an external world (typically a material reality) is set against the existence of a psychological world (cognitive, subjective, symbolic). From the exogenic standpoint, however, knowledge is achieved when the inner states of the individual reflect or accurately represent (or serve as a mirror of) the existing states of the external world. Exogenic thinkers often place a strong emphasis on keen observation in the acquisition of knowledge, and tend to view emotion and personal values as potential hazards to the neutral or "evenly hovering attention" required for accurate recording of the world as it is. The endogenic tradition is similar to the exogenic in its dualist foundations, and its emphasis on value neutrality. Yet, whereas the endogenic tradition treats careful observation of the world as the key to acquiring knowledge, the endogenecist places the chief emphasis on the powers of individual reason. Where the exogenic educator is likely to focus on the arrangement of environmental inputs necessary to build up an accurate representation, the endogenic educator lays chief emphasis on the human being's intrinsic capacities for insight, logic, or conceptual development. In this sense the exogenic theorist is likely to view the external or material world as a given, and conjecture about how nature becomes accurately represented in the mind, while the endogenic thinker is likely to view the mental world as self-evident, and raise questions concerning the way in which the mind operates so as to function adequately in nature. He has emphatically asserted that from within these two perspectives, philosophers have never been able to solve the fundamental question of epistemology—how the mind comes into knowledge of a world external to it. Unable to resolve such problems, philosophers in the present century have largely abandoned dualist metaphysics in favour of the logical analysis of propositions. And, as Richard Rorty (1979) has argued, the problem of knowledge as a relationship between mind and world cannot be solved because it is ill conceived from the beginning. If we commence with a distinction between what is *outside* and *inside* the mind of the individual, we create an inherently intractable problem in determining how the former is accurately represented in the latter.

Such debates have thus rendered both exogenic and endogenic conceptions of knowledge vulnerable to the recent developments in the field of epistemology. In the light of this newly developed epistemology, knowledge is viewed as a byproduct not of individual minds but of communal relationships. Or more generally we might say that all meaningful propositions about the real and the good have their origins in relationships. This is to bring into sharp focus the site of knowledge generation: the ongoing process of coordinating action among persons. It is to foreground the moment-to-moment interchange between and among interlocutors, and locate meaning within the patterns of interdependency.

For constructionists the social constructivist orientation remains all too tied to a dualist epistemology, and all the philosophical problems that it inherits. The epistemological riddles remain about how external and internal realities are connected. Further, in its ultimate concern with the student's cognitive enrichment the social constructivism carries with it strong vestiges of individualist ideology. These differences also make themselves manifest in the choice of domains which are elaborated by theorists and practitioners. The constructionist places the strong emphasis on the domain of the social, while simultaneously maintaining a critical reflexive posture towards his/her work. The social constructivist largely sees the social as instrumental in developing the "mind of the student". It is thus the latter world that places a prominent role in description and explanation.

Gergen has said that constructionism makes no claims to being a first philosophy, a foundation upon which a new world may be erected. There is no attempt to replace all traditions in the name of truth, ethical principle, political vision or any other universal criterion. Rather, the hope is to augment and expand on existing resources in the service of planetary well-being. All traditional practices—for good or ill and with varied efficacy—serve to construct worlds of the real and the good. In effect, all make a certain contribution to the sea of intelligibility.

Consistent with traditional views of knowledge as cumulative (exogenic) and universal (endogenic), educational institutions are built around what Freire (1985) calls a "nutritionist" model. The model is essentially hierarchical, with the ultimate authority residing in the communities of knowledge-production itself. Typically these are experts in the field, like scientists and scholars. These experts discover or reveal the truth that students will ultimately be taught—or "fed", in Freire's terms. Next within the hierarchy are educational experts such as curriculum designers, who package the knowledge into educational units. Following are administrators and bureaucrats who select among these units. Teachers enter at the end, as instruments to dispense the educational nutrients to the students. Students are expected merely to consume the knowledge.

Despite widespread criticism of this model, it continues to describe educational practice disturbingly well. Apple (1986) and others have documented the hierarchical processes through which educational content is produced and passed on to teachers. Mehan (1979) and others have shown how students remain generally passive, and expected merely to absorb the knowledge presented.

In several significant ways, social constructionists add dimension to such critique. At the outset, constructionists see all claims to knowledge as embedded within particular communities of meaning making. As a result, various bodies of knowledge will inevitably favour particular visions of the good, for example, continuous improvement in conditions (perfectibility), materialism over spiritualism, "reason" over "emotion", individualism over collectivism. In this sense a hierarchy of knowledge lends itself to totalitarianism. Or in Foucault's terms (1979, 1980), the dissemination of knowledge expands relations of power in which the user ultimately serves as pawn.

On a more subtle level, the constructionist finds the hierarchical model wanting in its tendency to suppress the contextual and pragmatic conditions that give authoritative language its significance. From the constructionist standpoint, "knowledgeable propositions" gain their meaning within particular contexts of usage, and function as means of coordinating action within these contexts. Knowledge of chemistry, for example, serves to unite a community, to define and grant value to particular projects and identities, and to help in generating outcomes of importance to this community. Yet, in the hierarchical model, the knowledgeable propositions are stripped away from this context. Educators extract bodies of discourse (and a limited number of instantiations) from the professional disciplines, and pass these extractions on to those beneath them in the hierarchy. The pragmatic function of these discourses within the communities themselves is lost. The discourses lose their significance, and students are often left with a promissory note that somehow their studies are useful and important. Further, because the authoritative discourses are treated as sacrosanct—the products of "our best minds"—they tend to travel the hierarchy in monologic fashion. That is, they do not move from communities of administrators, to teachers, to students as invitations to conversational supplementation. The recipients may clarify, order, and package, but the authoritative discourses remain, insofar as possible, intact. In the same way, students typically learn to approach the knowledgeable discourses in this way. One may enter the realm, approximate some distant approximation of its ways, and then exit. The result is that the authoritative discourses are not easily appropriated in exterior realms of life. One cannot easily employ the argots of physics, economics, experimental psychology, or algebra in cultural life more generally because their meanings are so fully tied to a specific domain of academic usage. In this sense, the professional discourses operate paramorphically, not so much altering existing forms of conduct, as co-existing in relative isolation.

In addition to problems of power and decontextualization, constructionists point to the problematics of monologic vs. dialogic practices of meaning making. The recipient of a monologue—as in the case of authoritative knowledge—is denied a voice of his/her own (Gergen). The endpoint to be achieved by monologic education is a student who has fully absorbed that which has been presented—or in effect, becomes a simulacra of the authority. Whatever talents, insights, or specialized education the individual possesses is denied entry into the conversation. And with the denial of voice comes an obliteration of identity and an invitation to lethargy. It is in this vein that Wise (1979) has described how academics and governments impose curricula and methods on schools that largely silence the teacher. Apple (1993) elaborated this analysis in discussing how the standardized curricula imposed on teachers deskill them. Because teachers are treated as technicians, and asked merely to implement prefabricated plans, they lose their capacity to reflect on the larger educational issues and to develop their own solutions (effective supplementation). Others similarly argue that the hierarchical model "deskills" the student. Jackson (1968) has described how the hierarchical relationships in schools discourage creativity and innovation among students. Wood (1988) and others have extended this analysis, arguing that students are shaped "to take their place unthinkingly in a world that operates beyond their control with no respect for their needs". Once we attend to the relational aspects of knowledge production, we can also see that deskilling does not happen equally to all social groups.

Given the inherent problems of authority based knowledge, what alternatives are suggested from a constructionist standpoint? The present analysis first calls for a de-sacralizing of professional knowledge. Rather than presuming that the traditional knowledge makers provide "the best" or "last" word, let us realize that all claims to knowledge grow from culturally and historically situated traditions. This is not at all to deny their value, but to realize that such values are also contingent. Situating knowledge in this way invites a shift from monologue to dialogue—from hierarchy to heterarchy i.e. others are invited into deliberation about the subject matter of education, its value, and relevance.

From a constructionist perspective, Gergen says that all knowledge is perspectival and value saturated. Thus, to enter a domain of knowledge is to step into a particular form of life. In this sense the present arguments lend strong support to current movements toward plurivocality in education, attempts to empower those who have traditionally been excluded from knowledge production. Beyer and Apple (1988), for instance, have argued that "meaningful curriculum reform must occur within those institutions, and by those people, most intimately connected to the lives of students: teachers, administrators, students, and community members". Instead of seeing teachers merely as technicians trained to dispense authoritative knowledge, many wish to enhance the role of "teachers as curriculum makers".

By traditional accounts, education functions to produce learned or knowledgeable individuals, who either by dint of what they know and/or their rational abilities, are equipped for effective action in whatever situations life has to offer. Inscribed on their mental slates are maps of what there is, along with the details of history, the proper modes of deduction, and so on. Education is for purposes of mastery and storage of knowledge; subsequent life provides the conditions for its use. The challenge for the educational process, then, is not that of storing facts, theories and rational heuristics in individual minds. Rather, it is to aid in generating contexts in which the value and meaning of the constituent dialogues may be most fully realized, conditions under which dialogues may be linked to the ongoing practical pursuits of persons, communities, or nations. The constructionist would favour practices in which students work together with teachers and others to decide on issues of importance, and the kinds of activities that might best allow significant engagement. For example, if students are concerned about ecology, racial tension, abortion, drugs, the rock music industry, the demands imposed by the fashion industry, forms of self-expression and so on, can projects be developed that will generate requisite skills? For the constructionist, then, educational dialogues should be wedded as closely as possible to the circumstances of application.

Traditional views of knowledge as "within individual minds" favour a distinct division between the teacher and student. The teacher "knows", and students are thrust into the position of objects to be operated on—minds to be filled with contents or rationalities. From the constructionist standpoint, the individual is not the possessor of contents or rationalities, but rather, participates in them. Knowledgeable and rational statements are not external expressions of the internal mind, but are relational achievements. What stands as reason, memory, motivation, intention and the like are the result of coordinated action and negotiation within a community (Billig, 1987; Edwards and Potter, 1992; Myerson, 1994). For the constructionist educator, the primary challenge is that of contributing to generative relationships—relationships from which the student emerges with expanded potentials for effective relating. The student's role shifts from that of object to be operated on to a subject within relationships (Gergen).

As we shift from the individual to the relationship as the center of focus, we can again appreciate the work of social constructivists on processes of teacher assisted learning, semiotic apprenticeship, and relations in the zone of proximal development are salutary (Kozulin, 1998; Wood, Cobb, and Yackel, 1995; Becker and Varelas, 1995; Larochell, Bednarz, and Garrison, 1998). All locate the site of learning within the relational matrix. However, perhaps the most visible outcome of constructionist thinking thus far is the emergence of collaborative or cooperative learning (Sharan, 1990; Bleich, 1988). As Kenneth Brufee (1993) puts it, collaborative learning is a process in which the ongoing exchange among students serves as the primary educational function. One learns through engaging, incorporating, and critically exploring with others. Ideally, through social interchange skills in articulation and responding are developed, and new possibilities of world construction are opened. Learning becomes a "shift in our language-constituted relations with others" in one inventive display of collaborative learning. Yet, collaborative inquiry may be viewed as but a beginning of exploration into the enormous potential of relationship centered education. We are thus enriched, for example, by inquiries into forms and potential of dialogue in the classroom (Barbules, 1993; Wells, 1999), and by explorations into the importance of the friendship relationship in teacher-student relations (Rawlins, 2000). Much to be welcomed is also an expansion of the concept of relationship to include more than the social relationships within the class. It is here that the pedagogical innovations fostered by the social constructivists can play a particularly important role. Inspired by Vygotsky's work, the concept of relationship is expanded to include the various tools and materials encountered in the educational process. However, there is no principled end to the perimeters of relationship.

All practices construct the world in their own way, carry values of certain sorts, and lend themselves to certain futures at the expense of others. What is being proposed is an alternative epistemology to that offered by the existing traditions, with which we might open new possibilities in education (Gergen). A social constructionist view of knowledge argues strongly for greater democracy in negotiating what counts in educational practice, the local embedding of curricula, the breaking of disciplinary boundaries, the lodgment of disciplinary discourses in societally relevant practices, educational practice in societal issues, and a shift from subject and child centered modes of education to a focus on relationships—extended so far as practicable. Many of these emphases are not new to the dialogues on education. And in this sense social constructionism does lend a strong support to certain forms of practice.

Gergen's Quotes:

"All meaningful propositions about the real and the good have their origins in relationships."

"All knowledge is perspectival and value saturated."

"The challenge for the educational process, then, is not that of storing facts, theories and rational heuristics in individual minds. Rather, it is to aid in generating contexts in which the value and meaning of the constituent dialogues may be most fully realized, conditions under which dialogues may be linked to the ongoing practical pursuits of persons, communities, or nations."

"Students should work together with teachers and others to decide on issues of importance, and the kinds of activities that might best allow significant engagement."

2.3 WHAT IS CONSTRUCTIVISM

There are multiple perspectives on constructivism. It will be unjust to present any single perspective, instead, here is an attempt to provide different perspectives on constructivism as depicted by various writers, who have contributed markedly in the development of constructivism by their lucid writings. In the education literature, constructivism is represented as a theory of learning, teaching, education, cognition, personal knowledge, scientific knowledge, and a worldview—in all a "grand theory" (Matthews, 2002). Saunders (1992) explains and agrees with Watzawick (1984): "Constructivism can be defined as that philosophical position which holds that any so-called reality is, in the most immediate and concrete sense, the mental construction of those who believe they have discovered and investigated it." Constructivism is a holistic-realistic philosophy. It is an epistemology, a learning or meaning-making theory, which offers an explanation of the nature of knowledge and how human beings learn. Tenets of this philosophy include: the need to situate learning and problem-solving in real-life contexts where the environment is very rich in information and there are no right answers (embedded knowledge); authentic tasks, cognitive apprenticeship; meaning negotiated through interactions with others; multiple perspectives on reality; nurturance of reflexivity and learning in ill-structured domains. It maintains that individuals create or construct their own new understandings of knowledge through the interaction of what they come in contact (Cannella & Reif, 1994; Richardson,

1997). One of the basic premises is that an individual learner must actively build knowledge and skills and that information exists within these built constructs rather than in the external environment. All advocates of constructivism agree that it is the individual's processing of stimuli from the environment and the resulting cognitive structures, that produce adaptive behaviour, rather than the stimuli themselves (Harnard, 1982).

Simon (1995) has summarized the constructivist perspective as deriving from a philosophical position that we as human beings have no access to an objective reality that is a reality independent of our way of knowing. Rather, we construct our knowledge of our world from our perceptions and experiences, which are themselves mediated through our previous knowledge. Experience is the central point around which learning and knowledge are generally interpreted in constructivism. It is a belief that one constructs knowledge from one's experiences, mental structures and beliefs that are used to interpret objects and events.

Jonassen (1991) talks about constructivism as follows: "Constructivism, founded on Kantian beliefs, claims that reality is constructed by the knower based upon mental activity. Humans are perceivers and interpreters who construct their own reality through engaging in those mental activities...thinking is grounded in perception of physical and social experiences, which can only be comprehended by the mind. What the mind produces are mental models that explain to the knower what he or she has perceived.... We all conceive of the external reality somewhat differently, based on our unique set of experiences with the world and our beliefs about them." Jonassen (1991) stated, "the mind is instrumental and essential in interpreting events, objects and perspectives on the base that is personal and individualized". Thus, our view of the external world differs from others because of our unique set of experiences. Senge (1995) put it this way: "We don't describe the world we see. We see the world we can describe." According to Mahoney, there are five basic themes which pervade the diversity of theories expressing constructivism.

These themes are:

1. Active agency
2. Order
3. Self
4. Social-symbolic relatedness, and
5. Lifespan development. (Mahoney, 2004)

With different language and terminological preferences, constructivists have proposed, that human experiencing involves continuous active agency. This distinguishes constructivism from forms of determinism that casts humans as passive pawns in the play of larger forces. The second contention is that much human activity is devoted to ordering processes—the organizational patterning of experience by means tacit, emotional meaning-making processes. In a third common contention, constructivists argue that the organization of personal activity is fundamentally self-referent or recursive. This makes the body a fulcrum of experiencing, and it honours a deep phenomenological sense of selfhood or personal identity. Persons exist and grow in living webs of relationships. The fourth common theme of constructivism is that individuals cannot be understood apart from their organic embeddedness in social and symbolic systems. Finally, all this active, meaningful, and socially embedded self-organization reflects an ongoing developmental flow in which dynamic dialectical tensions are essential. Order and disorder co-exist in lifelong quest for a dynamic balance that is never quite achieved. All these five themes convey a constructive views of human experience as one that emphasizes meaningful action by a developing self in complex and unfolding relationships (Mahoney, 2004).

As stated above constructivism is a philosophy of learning and knowledge founded on the premise that by reflecting on our experiences, we construct our own understanding of the world we live in. Each one of us generates our own rules and mental models, which we use to make sense our experiences. Learning, therefore, is simply the process of adjusting our mental models to accommodate new experiences.

The fundamental distinction in constructivism is that while behaviourists view knowledge as something that happens in response to external factors and cognitivists view knowledge as abstract symbolic representation inside the learner's head, constructivists view knowledge as constructed internally by each individual. Knowledge can thus not be transmitted from one person to the other; it will have to be reconstructed by each person. This means that the view of knowledge differs from the "knowledge as given and absolute" views of behaviourism. Constructivism focuses on knowledge construction, not knowledge reproduction. Conclusively it can be asserted that each individual colours and shapes the knowledge to fit within their frame of reference.

In constructivism knowledge is seen as relativistic (nothing is absolute, but varies according to time and space) and fallibilist (nothing can be taken for granted). Also, knowledge is seen as an anticipatory construction. Maturana and Varela (1997) see knowledge as a necessary component of the processes of autopsies ("self production") characterizing living organisms.

Guiding principles of constructivism:

1. Learning is a search for meaning. Therefore, learning must start with the issues around which students are actively trying to construct meaning.
2. Meaning is contextualized and rooted in experience. Meaning is internally constructed and developed on the basis of experience. Meaning requires understanding as a whole as well as parts. And parts must be understood in the context of wholes. Therefore, the learning process focuses on primary concepts, not isolated facts.
3. In order to teach well, we must understand the mental models that students use to perceive the world and the assumptions they make to support those models.
4. The purpose of learning is for an individual to construct his or her own meaning not just memorize the "right" answers and regurgitate someone else's meaning. Since education is inherently interdisciplinary, the only valuable way to measure learning is to make the assessment part

of the leaning process, ensuring it provides students with information on the quality of their learning.

5. The mind is seen as an inner representation of an outer reality.
6. Knowledge is residing in the mind, thus learning results from a personal interpretation of the world.
7. Thought is grounded in perception and bodily experience.

An important component of constructivist theory is to focus a child's education on authentic tasks. These are tasks which have "real-world relevance and utility, that integrate those tasks across the curriculum, that provide appropriate levels of difficulty or involvement" (Jonassen, 1991). According to this theory, children learn whole to part, not incrementally. The ideas and interests of children derive the learning process. The goal of the constructivism is to create learning communities that are more closely related to the collaborative practice of the real world. Students can see a problem from different perspectives, and are able to negotiate and generate meanings and solution through shared understanding.

On a slightly different note, according to Merrill (1997), the assumptions of constructivism are:

- Knowledge is constructed from experience.
- Learning is an active process in which meaning is developed on the basis of experience.
- Conceptual growth comes from the negotiation of meaning, the sharing of multiple perspectives and the changing of our internal representations through collaborative learning.
- Learning should be situated in realistic settings; testing should be integrated with the task and not a separate activity.

On a similar note as stated above, Cunningham and Duffy identified two major similarities that are the foundation of all constructivist theorists' theories. They are that "learning is an active process of constructing rather than acquiring knowledge and instruction is a process of supporting that construction rather that communicating knowledge" (Cunningham & Duffy, 1996).

On a differing note, a new trend in constructivism is enactive constructivism. The enactive constructivist position is non-foundational, meaning that it takes neither the objective world nor the subjective world as pre-given. Rather, both are mutually specified in the history of activity that is called structured coupling. This philosophy supports the idea that understanding transforms the world by transforming the self.

It is striking to mention that constructivism reminds us that the changed concepts of learning and knowledge are not only important philosophical notions but, on the contrary, they can significantly affect how we see the world and more importantly how we behave in it. Glasersfeld (1995) indicates in relation to the concept of reality: "It is made up of in our living, and on which, we believe, others rely on, too." Rather than thinking of truth in terms of a match to reality, Glasersfeld (1995) focuses instead on the notion of viability: "To the constructivist, concepts, models theories, and so on are viable if they prove adequate in the contexts in which they were created."

Constructivism implies that learners are encouraged to construct their own knowledge instead of copying it from an authority, be it a book or a teacher, in realistic situations instead of decontextualised, formal situations such as propagated in traditional textbooks and together with others instead of on their own (Kanselaar, et al., 2001). Constructivism's central idea is that human knowledge is constructed, that learners build new knowledge upon the foundation of previous learning. This view of learning sharply contrasts with one in which learning is the passive transmission of information from one individual to another, a view in which reception, not construction, is key. This new learning theory has spawned a changing view on learning and instruction since. As stated in the beginning that the constructivism is not a single concept, but can involve many aspects, the following are three important aspects:

(a) a set of epistemological beliefs [that is, beliefs about the nature of reality, whether there is an independent reality—Glasersfeld (2001)];

(b) a set of psychological beliefs about learning and cognition (e.g., that learning involves constructing one's own knowledge);

(c) a set of educational beliefs about pedagogy, the best way to support learning (e.g., that one should allow the learners to define their own learning objectives; that knowledge emerges from constructive interaction between the teacher and the student or between collaborating students) (Kanselaar et al., 2001).

Basically defined, constructivism means that as people experience something new they internalize it through past experiences or knowledge constructs that have been previously established (Crowther, 1999). Steffe (1990) explains, "constructivists view learning as the adaptations children make in their functioning schemes to neutralize perturbations that arise through interactions with the world". Resnick (1983) stated, "Meaning is constructed by the cognitive apparatus of the learner." Novak & Gowin (1986) further define constructivism as "the notion that humans construct or build meaning in their ideas and experiences as a result of an effort to understand to make sense of them. This involves at times recognition of new regularities in events or objects, inventing new concepts or extending old concepts, recognition of new relationships (propositions) between contacts, and...major restructuring of conceptual framework to see new higher order relationships." Fabricius (1983) modifies Piaget's Schema Theory interpreting it to mean, "...reality becomes the phenomena we experience through construction".

According to Spencer (2000), from the perspective of learner and learning the three principles of constructivism are: (1) knowledge is actively constructed by the learner; (2) coming to know is the process of organizing and adapting the world to the learner's experiences; and (3) the learner does not discover an independent world outside his mind (i.e. the discovery is constructed from ideas within his mind) (As quoted by Gadinidis, 1994). Bednar et al. (1991) elaborate further: "...the learner is building an internal representation of knowledge, a personal interpretation of experience. This representation is constantly open to change, its structure and linkages forming the foundation to which other knowledge structures are appended. Learning is an active process in which meaning is developed on the basis of experience.... Conceptual growth comes from the sharing of multiple perspectives and simultaneous changing of our internal representations in response to those perspectives as well as through cumulative experience." Steffe (1990) explains, "Constructivists view learning as the adaptations children make in their functioning schemes to neutralize perturbations that arise through interactions with our world."

As constructivism itself posits, knowledge is not a static phenomenon, it changes as we engage in new experiences that test what we know. These new experiences may cause us to alter or add to our understanding, sometimes in subtle ways and sometimes dramatically (Zahorik, 1997). Consistent with this view of knowledge, learning must be situated in a rich context, reflective of real world contexts, for this constructive process to occur and transfer to environments beyond the school.

Constructivists propose arranging instruction around problems that students find compelling and that require them to acquire and use skills and knowledge to formulate solutions. Constructivists call for more emphasis on engaging students in the process learning than on finding a single correct answer (Roblyer, Edwards, and Havriluk, 1996). The term refers to the idea that learners construct knowledge for themselves—each learner individually (and socially) constructs meaning—as he or she learns. Constructing meaning is learning; there is no other kind. The dramatic consequences of this view are twofold (Hein, 1991):

1. We have to focus on the learner in thinking about learning (not on the subject/lesson to be taught).

2. There is no knowledge independent of the meaning attributed to experience (constructed) by the learner, or community of learners.
3. The second point is a position which has been frequently adopted ever since people began to ponder epistemology.

Thus, constructivism acknowledges the learner's active role in the personal creation of knowledge, the importance of experience (both individual and social) in this knowledge creation process, and the realization that the knowledge created will vary in its degree of validity as an accurate representation of reality. These four fundamental tenets provide the foundation for basic principles of the teaching, learning, and knowing process as described by constructivism.

Constructivism has also been said to be post-epistemological, meaning that it is not another epistemology, or a way of knowing. It cannot replace objectivism. Rather, constructivism is a way of thinking about knowing, a referent for building models of teaching, learning and curriculum (Tobin & Tippin, 1993).

Educational theories come and go, but often the philosophical basis behind any group of theories from a similar time period is often similar. Theories and ways of thinking about education in 21st century have not simply changed, but have actually undergone a complete 'paradigm shift' in how we view education and the nature of learning and knowledge (Cooper, 1993 & Jonassen, 1991). In theory, constructivism in education means that teachers embrace a holistic way of thinking about the nature of learning, quite apart from the methodology of direct instruction, which some call instructivism. Rather than viewing learning as decontextualized, in constructivism it is assumed that learning occurs in whole experiences. Constructivism holds that knowledge does not have a separate existence from the physical nervous system; it cannot exist in some complete form outside the learner and be internalized, stored, and reproduced at some late time.

The fundamental challenge of constructivism is in its changing the locus of control over learning from the teacher to the student. Enticing the students to achieve pre-specified objectives, constructivists have said that this violates both what we know now about the nature of learning (situated, interactive) and about the nature of knowledge (perspectival, conventional, tentative, and evolutionary). They have claimed that objectives should be negotiated with students based on their own felt needs, that programmed activities should emerge from within the contexts of their lived worlds, that students should work together with peers in the social construction of personally significant meaning, and that evaluation should be personalised ongoing, shared analysis of progress (Hanckbarth, 1996).

Agreeing with this view of knowledge, learning must be placed in a rich context, reflective of real world context, for this constructive process to happen and transfer to environments beyond the school or training classroom. Learning through cognitive apprenticeship, mirroring the collaboration of real world problem-solving, and using the tools available in problem-solving situations are key. How effectual or instrumental the learner's knowledge structure is in facilitating thinking in the content field is the measure of learning (Bednar, Cunningham, Duffy, Perry, 1995).

This theory describes the process of meaning-making, in which individuals construct mental models that ground their understanding in a deeply personal and unique fashion. Constructivists believe that certain activities and environmental enrichments can enhance the meaning-making process, such as active learning using kinaesthetic, visual and auditory modalities, creating opportunities for dialogue, fostering creativity and providing a rich, safe and engaging learning environment (Brooks & Brooks, 1996).

Learning activities are characterized by active engagement, inquiry, problem-solving and collaboration with others. Rather than a dispenser of knowledge, the teacher is a guide, facilitator, and co-explorer who encourages learner to question, challenge and formulate their own ideas, opinions, and conclusions. "Correct answers" and single interpretations are de-emphasized. Cannella & Reif (1994) label the traditional model of teaching and learning as didactic, memory-oriented transmission models. Constructivists generally maintain that when information is acquired through transmission models, it is not always well integrated with prior knowledge and is often accessed and articulated only for formal academic occasions such as exams (Richardson, 1997).

Constructivist approaches, in contrast, are regarded as producing greater internalization and deeper understanding than traditional methods. Jonassen (1995) defines constructivism from the educational perspective, as learners producing and constructing their personal knowledge. The learner environment changes completely in the new paradigm to one that is more student centred. The teacher becomes facilitator, coach, motivator not demagogue or the gate-keeper of all knowledge. The term constructivism refers to a widely accepted view that individual learners construct their learning in the light of past experiences and knowledge.

Advocates of a constructivistic approach suggest that educators first consider the knowledge and experiences students bring with them to learning task. The school curriculum then be built so that students can expand and develop this knowledge and experience by connecting them to new learning. Constructivist theorists believe students improve their critical thinking and problem-solving skills when they construct new knowledge based on background experiences and multiple resources (Price, 1997).

Three primary propositions that characterize constructivism from a cognitive and social viewpoint are presented by Savery and Duffy (1995):

1. Cognition occurs as people share their understanding with each other and test the degree to which they are compatible.
2. The goal or purpose of investigation influences what is learned and what experiences the learner draws upon to construct new understanding.
3. Knowledge evolves through social negotiation, either independently or in collaborative groups. Alternative

views and additional information enable learners to test the viability or understandings and to build new propositions that are compatible with those understandings.

Definitions:

"Constructivism is a philosophy of learning founded on the premise that, by reflecting on our experiences, we construct our own understanding of the world we live in. Each of us generates our own 'rules' and 'mental models', which we use to make sense of our experiences. Learning, therefore, is simply the process of adjusting our mental models to accommodate new experiences" (Clark, 1999).

"Constructivism is a theory of how the learner constructs knowledge from experience, which is unique to each individual" (Marsh).

"Constructivism is a theory of teaching and learning that draws on a range of teaching practices including inquiry-based learning, cooperative learning, and project-based approaches."

"Constructivism involves the process of questioning, exploring and reflecting. This theory says that learners should construct their own understanding and knowledge of the world through varied experiences. By reflecting on these experiences, students assimilate useful information and create personal knowledge."

"Constructivism is fundamentally nonpositivist and as such it stands on completely new ground—often in materialism. Rather than behaviours or skills as the goal of instruction, concept development and deep understanding are the foci; rather than stages being the result of maturation, they are understood as constructivism of active learner reorganization" (Fosnot, 1996).

"Constructivism is a theory about knowledge and learning, it describes what 'knowing' is and one 'comes to know'" (Fosnot, 1996).

"Constructivism does not claim to have made earth-shaking inventions in the area of education; it merely claims to provide a solid conceptual basis for some of the things that, until now, inspired teachers had to do without theoretical foundation" (Glasersfeld, 1995).

"A definition of constructivism is based on the fundamental assumption that people create knowledge from the interaction between their existing knowledge or beliefs and the new ideas or situations they encounter" (Airasian and Walsh, 1997).

"Basically defined, constructivism means that as people experience something new they internalize it through past experiences or knowledge constructs that have been previously established" (Crowther, 1999).

2.4 TYPES OF CONSTRUCTIVISM

Constructivism is well-known for the value of multiple perspectives as the different perspectives give us a unique tool to understand the thesis as well as antithesis of the point of view to have a sound synthesis of multiple realities of the noumena (the experience itself) as well as phenomena (the happenstance of experience). With the help of multiple perspectives, it is understood that people are able to negotiate and generate meanings and solutions to various sociological, psychological and educational problems. True to its soul, today constructivism has numerous varieties with shades of meaning. Ernest (1995) points out that "there are as many varieties of constructivism as there are researchers". Burning (1999) has identified three types of constructivism: Exogenous (reconstruction of pre-existing ideas), Endogenous (new abstract knowledge developing through cognitive activity based on predictable sequences), and Dialectical (source of knowledge is based on social interactions between learners and environments). But, the perused scanning of literature related with constructivism reveals that there are following types of constructivism such as:

- Psychological Constructivism
- Cultural Constructivism
- Radical Constructivism
- Critical Constructivism

- Trivial Constructivism
- Genetic Constructivism
- Developmental Constructivism
- Epistemic Constructivism
- Epistemological Constructivism
- Metaphysical Constructivism
- Cybernetic (or Second order) Constructivism
- Transactional or Situated Constructivism
- Exogenous (or Information-processing) Constructivism
- Endogenous (or Cognitive) Constructivism
- Dialectical (or Social) Constructivism

Each of these types of constructivism should not be seen as a set of methods, or as a fixed manifesto-like set of beliefs. They are "points of view", perspectives loosely defined by a collection of writings of particular individuals in each case. Above mentioned various types of constructivism represent popular labels in constructivist literature used as shorthand to indicate these different groups of ideas. Indeed, we can also say that "constructivist literature" is defined by their use of these labels, since the ideas are related to many other philosophical labels.

The points of contact between these concepts are many, as are the connections they can make within our own life. An endeavour has been made to point out major relationships among all labels of constructivism as a referent—a perspective which can be applied to a wide variety of situations to help us make choices about our actions and to help reflect on what we do as reflective practitioner in the field of education.

Most importantly, behind all of this are values that are rarely discussed openly in constructivism literature. Why do we even want to create models of learning? Why do we feel we need to improve the quality of education? In constructivism we see a hidden value ascribed to the notions of diversity and adaptability, which in turn promote the root value: survival of our species. Learners who can adapt quickly by learning in a complex world are more likely to adapt to changing conditions and survive as an individual (Martin Dougiamas, 1998).

Psychological Constructivism: Psychological constructivism generally regards the purpose of education as educating the individual child in a fashion that supports the child's interests and needs; consequently, the child is the subject of study, and individual cognitive development is the emphasis. Learning is primarily an individualistic enterprise. This is a child-centred approach that seeks to identify, through scientific study, the natural path of cognitive development (Vadeboncocur, 1997). This approach assumes that students come to classrooms with ideas, beliefs and opinions that need to be altered or modified by a teacher who facilitates this alternation by devising tasks and question that create dilemmas for students. To a large extent, this approach assumes that development is an ingrained, natural, biological process that is pretty much the same for all individuals, regardless of gender, class, race or the social or cultural context in which learning and living take place. It is essentially a decontextualized approach to learning and teaching.

Cultural Constructivism: The view that knowledge and reality are constructed culturally. That is that two independent cultures will likely come up with different categorizations. This means that there are two completely different ways in which the world is broken down.

Radical Constructivism: Cognition serves to organize the learners' experiential world rather than to discover ontological reality (Cobb, 1996). Glasersfeld is a prominent proponent of radical constructivism, which claims that knowledge is the self-organized cognitive process of the human brain. That is, the process of constructing knowledge regulates itself and since knowledge is a construct rather than a compilation of empirical data, it is not possible to know the degree to which knowledge reflects an ontological reality.

Radical constructivism as discussed by Maturana and Varela (1987), von Foersrer (1984), and von Glasersfeld (1984), rejects the possibility of objective knowledge, since "all knowledge depends upon the structure of the knower" (Maturana and

Varela, 1987). Thus, subject and object are constructions (or operations) of the observer, and not independently existing entities: Even if there is an ontological reality, we can only know it by assessing how well our knowledge fits with it. According to Maturana and Varela (1987), living beings are autopoietic (self-creating or self-producing) systems in the sense that they are capable of maintaining their own organization, the organization which is developed and maintained" (Andrews, 1997).

Glasersfeld (1984) distinguished between trivial and radical constructivism. Radical constructivism in Glasersfeld's terms maintains that, although there probably is a reality out there, knowledge does not reflect this reality objectively, but it reflects "exclusively an ordering and organization of a world constituted by our experience" (Glasersfeld, 1984).

Mahoney (1986) distinguished radical constructivism from critical constructivism. According to him, radical constructivism denies the existence of an independent reality and is indistinguishable from idealism, while critical constructivism does not deny the existence of a real world land is basically realist.

Radical "because it breaks with convention and develops a theory of knowledge in which knowledge does not reflect an objective, ontological reality but exclusively an ordering and organization of a world constituted by our experience" (Glasersfeld, 1984).

Important features of radical constructivism:

1. Meaning exists only in the mind, hence it cannot be transmitted.
2. The only person who can make new understanding for a person is that person.
3. In the case of communication, meaning can be negotiated, but at best we can only take this negotiated meaning as shared.
4. Meaning or understanding is formulated to fit experience, and so revised when needed.

Critical Constructivism: Critical constructivism looks at constructivism within a social and cultural environment, but adds a critical dimension aimed at reforming these environments in order to improve the success of constructivism applied as a referent (Dougiamas, 1998). Taylor (1996) describes critical constructivism as a social epistemology that addresses the socio-cultural context of knowledge construction and serves as a referent for cultural reform. It confirms the relativism of radical constructivism, and also identifies the learner as being suspended in semiotic systems similar to those earlier identified in social and cultural constructivism. To these, critical constructivism adds a greater emphasis on the actions for change of a learning teacher (Dougiamas, 1998). Not only truth and reality, but also evidence, document, experience, fact, proof and other central categories of empirical research reveal their contingent character as a social and ideological construction. Thus, a realist or relativist interpretation is subject to criticism.

While recognizing the constructedness of reality, many representatives of this critical paradigm deny to philosophy the task of the creative construction of reality. They eagerly criticize realistic judgments, but they do not move beyond analytic procedures based on subtle tautologies. They thus remain in the critical paradigm and consider it to be a standard of scientific philosophy *per se*.

Trivial Constructivism: Trivial constructivism, according to Glasersfeld (1984) maintains merely that new ideas are founded on prior ones. It is also known as personal constructivism.

Genetic Constructivism: Genetic here has the proper sense of genesis of cognitive forms, but not of heredity. Thus, the schemes and cognitive structures proper of the subject-of-knowledge (community of scientists and/or community of laymen) are permanently questioned in the process of knowing. This process, essentially constructive, is similar to the Kantian position, but diverges from it in a central aspect: the cognitive construction does not refer exclusively to logical-mathematical beings: it also refers to the process of assimilation of the obstacles, aced by the subjects of knowledge.

Genetic constructivism asserts that the cognitive function is the same in any human being and is characterized by the cognitive activities of assimilation and accommodation which make the cognitive adaptation of the objects (cognitive obstacles). This adaptation is made through schemes and/or structures constructed by the subject of knowledge when confronted by social and historical needs. In this sense, there is no functional difference between common sense and scientific sense, but only a structural differentiation (Piaget, 1967).

For genetic constructivism the relation between theory, or models and reality is one of approximation. Its validity can be demonstrated in several ways among which those of argumentative strength and efficiency (efficiency and effectiveness). Nevertheless, for that theory there is no reason for claims neither of absolute truth nor of impossibility of significant knowledge. It rejects both psyrrhonism and idealism.

Developmental Constructivism: Developmental constructivism as originally discussed by Piaget (Piaget & Inhelder, 1969) and further elaborated by researchers of post-formal development (e.g. Commons, 1989) also views knowledge as a proactive construction of the knowing organism. According to developmental constructivism, knowledge is an active construction of the knowing subject, triggered by the quest for equilibrium i.e., by the cognitive system's need for order and stability. Ibanez (1992) has noted that knowledge cannot logically be viewed as a representation or a copy of reality, since in order to know whether something is a good copy of something else we need to independently access both versions so as to compare them.

Developmental constructivism also deports from the objectivist conception of truth as correspondence between mental representations and reality. According to most organismic perspectives, knowledge systems develop by means of recurrent qualitative shifts in the direction of increased complicity (Werner, 1957). Thus, knowledge can never be considered an accurate depiction of reality; since each new refinement will require justification at a newer and higher level. Developmental constructivism equates knowledge with dialectically, adaptive actions; i.e., the ability to adopt one's knowledge structures to the environment and to adapt the environment and to adapt the environment to one's knowledge structures.

Epistemological Constructivism: Epistemological constructivism is about the study of theory of knowing and not theory of knowledge as such in terms of methods. Here the main emphasis is on how a subject arrives at the process of knowing. The importance of constructivism is best understood by comparing it with the opposite, more traditional, approach in epistemology, which sees knowledge as a passive reflection of the external objective reality. This type of constructivism emphasizes more specifically on methodological aspect of knowing.

Epistemic Constructivism: Epistemic constructivism talks about nature of knowing. It emphasises less on methodological issues regarding nature of knowing.

Metaphysical Constructivism: Each type of constructivism accepts reality as constructed one. This types of constructivism too accepts reality as constructed which are not only physical or concrete but also which are abstract or beyond physical i.e. metaphysical.

Cybernetic (or Second order) Constructivism: Cybernetic (or Second order) constructivism or cybernetics of self-organization presents another kind of constructivism, which is based on the concept of *autopoiesis* (self-formation) which was formulated by the Chilean cell-biologists Humberto Maturana and Francisco Varela (1980, 1987): An autopoietic system is "organized (defined as a unity) as a network of processes of production (transformation and destruction) of components that produces the components which: (i) through their interactions and transformations continuously regenerate and realize the network of processes (relations) that produced them; and (ii) constitute it...as a concrete unity in space which they (the components) exist by specifying the topological domain of its realization as such a network" (Maturana & Varela, 1980).

In other words, autopoietic systems are self-contained and self-referential unities, which are qualified as such whenever the following six criteria are satisfied:

(i) The system is identifiable through its border.
(ii) It is analyzable through its components.
(iii) The interaction of the components obeys the general physical laws (i.e., it is a natural system).
(iv) The boundary is self-maintained by preferential neighbourhood relations (i.e., the system can stabilize its own boundary).
(v) The system is contained within and producing the boundary.
(vi) It is a self-productive system using only its own components or transformed imported material. (Mingers, 1995)

Although autopoiesis has originally developed to describe biological cells, subsequently it has been applied to a variety of disciplines covering physical, cognitive, and psychic systems (Maturana & Varela, 1987; Mingers, 1995). Particularly interesting is Luhmann's application of autopoiesis in social, communication, and legal systems (Luhmann, 1989, 1990, 1995).

The constructivist character of autopoiesis is manifested at the level of the closure of the nervous system implying that action and cognition depend on each other without any outside system of reference. According to von Foerster, "my nervous system does not, indeed, cannot, tell me what is 'out there', not because of mechanical but because of logico-semantic reasons. My nervous system cannot tell me anything because it is 'me': I am the activity of my nervous system, all my nervous system talks about is its own state of sensory-motor activity" (von Foerster, 1993). In fact, von Foerster (1984) argues that all sensory receptors (i.e., visual, auditory, tactual, etc.) send physically indistinguishable 'responses' to the cortex and that, therefore, the 'sensory modalities' can be distinguished only by keeping track of the part of the body from which the responses come, and not on the basis of 'environmental features'. From this observation von Glasersfeld concludes that "contemporary neurophysiological models may be compatible with a constructivist theory of knowing but can in no way be integrated with the notion of transduction of 'information' from the environment that any realist epistemology demands" (von Glasersfeld, 1989).

Transactional or Situated Constructivism: Knowledge about a topic acquired by participation in activities that have real world meaning to the topic. By using the topic in its context, students gain a deeper meaning. Situated cognition considers that knowledge is mostly context-dependent and symbolic descriptions elicited prior to direct experience are less important that functional units developed via direct experience with a current problem. Learners become involved in a "community of practice" which embodies certain beliefs and behaviours to be acquired. As the beginner or newcomer moves from the periphery of this community to its center, they become more active and engaged within the culture and hence assume the role of expert or old timer. Furthermore, situated learning is usually unintentional rather than deliberate. These ideas are what Lave & Wenger (1991) call the process of "legitimate peripheral participation".

Exogenous (or Information-processing) Constructivism: In exogenous constructivism, as with the philosophy of realism, there is an external reality that is reconstructed as knowledge is formed. Thus, one's mental structures develop to reflect the organization of the world. The information processing conceptualizations of cognitive psychology emphasize the representation view of constructivism, calling attention to how we construct and elaborate schema and networks of information based on the external realities of the environments we experience.

Endogenous (or Cognitive) Constructivism: Endogenous (or Cognitive) constructivism (Cobb, 1994 & Moshman, 1982) focuses on internal, individual constructions of knowledge. This perspective, which is derived from Piagetian theory, emphasizes individual knowledge construction stimulated by internal cognitive conflict as learners strive to resolve mental disequilibrium. Essentially, children as well as older learners must negotiate the meaning of experiences and phenomena that are discrepant from their existing schema. Students may be said to author their knowledge, advancing their cognitive structures by revising and creating new understandings out of existing ones.

This is accomplished through individual or socially mediated discovery oriented learning.

Cognitive oriented constructivism is based on the work of Jean Piaget. His theory has two major parts: an ages and stages component that predicts what children can and cannot understand at different ages and a theory of development that theory of cognitive development proposes that humans cannot be given information, which they immediately understand and use. Instead, humans must construct their own knowledge through experience. Experiences enable them to create schemas—mental models in their heads. These schemas are changed, enlarged and make more sophisticated through two complimentary processes: assimilation and accommodation.

Dialectical (or Social) Constructivism: Dialectical (or Social) constructivism (Brown, Collins & Duguid, 1989 & Rogoff, 1990) views the origin of knowledge construction as being the social intersection of people, interactions that involve sharing, comparing and debating among learners and mentors. Through a highly interactive process, the social milieu of learning is accorded center stage and learners both refine their own meanings and help others find meaning. In this way knowledge is mutually built. This view is a direct reflection of Vygotsky's socio-cultural theory of learning, which accentuates the supportive guidance of mentors as they enable the apprentice learner to achieve successively more complex skill, understanding and ultimately independent competence.

The fundamental nature of dialectical constructivism is collaborative social interaction in contrast to. individual investigation of cognitive constructivism. Though the cognitive give and take of social interactions, one constructs personal knowledge. In addition, the context in which learning occurs is inseparable from emergent thought. This latter view known as contextualism in psychology becomes a central tenet of constructivism when expressed as situated cognition. Social constructivism captures the most general extent perspective on constructivism with its emphasis on the importance of social exchanges for cognitive and the impact of culture and historical context on learning.

It contends that categories of knowledge and reality are actively created by social relationships and interactions. These interactions also alter the way in which scientific categories are created and scientific objects are perceived.

Another account of it asserts that social activity presupposes human beings inhabiting shared forms of life and in the case of social construction, utilizing semiotic resources (meaning making and meaning signifying) with reference to social structures/ institutions. Human knowledge structures are essentially socially constructed. Knowledge is not simply constructed, it is co-constructed.

Social constructivism emphasizes the importance of culture and context in understanding what occurs in society and constructing knowledge based on this understanding (Derry, 1999 & McMahon, 1997). This perspective is closely associated with many contemporary theories, most notably the developmental theories of Vygotsky and Bruner, and Bandura's social cognitive theory (Shunk, 2000).

Intersubjectivity is another important concept advocated by dialectical constructivism. It is a shared understanding among individuals whose interaction is based on common interests and assumptions that form the ground for their communication (Rogoff, 1990). Any personal meanings shaped through these experiences are affected by the intersubjectivity of the community to which the people belong. Intersubjectivity not only provides the grounds for communication but also supports people to extend their understanding of new information and activities among the group members (Rogoff, 1990). The construction of knowledge is also influenced by the intersubjectivity formed by cultural and historical factors of the community (Gradler, 1997; Prewat & Floden, 1994). When the members of the community are aware for their intersubjective meanings, it is easier for them to understand new information and activities that arise in the community. Variants of dialectical constructivism include situated constructivism, social re-constructivism, socio-cultural constructivism, socio-historical constructivism and emancipatory constructivism. This dialectic is examined in more detail in a strong paper by Salomon and Perkins (1998), who suggest ways that these 'acquisition' and 'participation' metaphors of learning interrelate and interact in synergetic ways. They model the social entity as a learner, compare it with the learning of an individual in a social setting, and identify three main types of relations:

1. Individual learning can be less or more socially-mediated learning.
2. Individuals can participate in the learning of a collective, sometimes with what is learned distributed throughout the collective more than in the mind of any one individual.
3. Individuals and social aspects of learning in both of these senses can interact over time to strengthen one another in a reciprocal spiral relationship.

Dialectical constructivism emphasizes education for social transformation and reflects a theory of human development that situates the individual within a socio-cultural context. Schools are the socio-cultural settings where teaching and learning take place and where cultural tools such as reading, writing, mathematics, and certain modes of discourse are utilized (Richardson, 1997). This approach assumes that theory and practice do not develop in a vacuum; they are shaped by dominant cultural assumptions (Martin, 1994). Both formal knowledge, the subject of instruction and the manner of its presentation are influenced by the historical and cultural environment that generated them. To accomplish the goals of social transformation and reconstruction, the context of education must be deconstructed and the cultural assumptions, power relationships and historical influences that undergrid it must be exposed, critiqued and when necessary, altered (Myers, 1996). Emphasis is growing on the teacher's use of multiple epistemologies, to maintain dialectic tension between teacher guidance and student-initiated exploration, as well as between social learning and individual learning. Vygotsky (1978) advocates the concept that learning occurs in the "zone of proximal development", which is defined as "the distance between the actual development level as determined by independent problem-solving and the level of potential development as determined through problem-solving under adult guidance or in collaboration with more capable peers". Thus, it is advocated that students should learn and master concepts through interaction with people who are more knowledgeable, such as teachers or peers.

2.5 IMPLICATIONS OF CONSTRUCTIVISM

Paul Ernst (1995) in his descriptions of the many schools of thought of constructivism suggests the following implications of constructivism which derive from both the radical and social perspectives:

- Sensitivity towards and alternativeness to the learner's previous constructions.
- Diagnostic teaching attempting to remedy learner's errors and misconceptions.
- Attention to metacognition and strategic self-regulation by learners.
- The use of multiple representations of mathematical concepts.
- Awareness of the importance of goals for the learner and the dichotomy between learner and teacher goals.
- Awareness of the importance of social contexts, such as the difference between folk or street mathematics and school mathematics (and an attempt to exploit the former for the later).

Wilson & Cole (1991) provide following implications which can isolate some concepts central to constructivist design, teaching and learning:

- Embed learning in a rich authentic problem-solving environment;
- Provide for authentic versus academic contexts for learning;
- Provide for learner control;
- Use errors as a mechanism to provide feedback on learners' understandings.

Jonassen (1991) has noted that many educators and cognitive psychologists have applied constructivism to the development of learning environments. From these applications, he has isolated a number of design principles:

- Create real-world environments that employ the context in which learning is relevant;
- Focus on realistic approach to solving real-world problems;
- The instructor is a coach and analyzer of the strategies used to solve these problems;
- Stress conceptual interrelatedness, providing multiple representations or perspectives on the context;
- Instructional goals and objectives should be negotiated and not imposed;
- Evaluation should serve as a self-analysis tool;
- Provide tools and environments that help learners interpret the multiple perspectives of the world;
- Learning should be internally controlled and mediated by the learner.

Jonassen (1994) summarizes what he refers to as "the implications of constructivism for instructional design". The following principles illustrate how knowledge construction can be facilitated:

- Provide multiple representations of reality;
- Represent the natural complexity of the real world;
- Focus on knowledge construction, not reproduction;
- Present authentic tasks (contextualizing rather than abstracting instruction);
- Provide real-world, case-based learning environments, rather than predetermined instructional sequences;
- Foster reflexive practice;
- Enable context and content dependent knowledge construction;

- Support collaborative construction of knowledge through social negotiation.

Apart from above mentioned facts recorded by reputed thinkers, constructivist theorists believe students improve their critical thinking and problem-solving skills when they construct new knowledge based upon background experiences and multiple resources. Students construct knowledge as individuals or as part of a social unit, but knowledge are not a separate entity unto itself, and knowledge cannot be independent of the knower. The philosophical, psychological and epistemological underpinnings of constructivist learning theories are disparate, but the common thread throughout constructivism is learner-centred teaching. Students link critically when they combine background knowledge, independent research and classroom presentations to build on their existing schema, thus expanding their foundations of knowledge. Constructivist theory lends itself well to classroom application; however, there are questions about transforming learning theory into practice. Constructivism or constructivist theory puts the students, their interests and past experiences and knowledge a paramount parts of understanding in designing curriculum (Stofflett, 1998).

Teaching strategies using social constructivism as a referent include teaching in contexts that might be personally meaningful to students, negotiating taken-as-shared meanings with students, class discussion small-group collaboration, and valuing meaningful activity over correct answers (Wood, 1995). Many critics and researches lament the fact that students who can answer complex questions and solve problems are unable to explain the underlying reasons or methods they use to reach their conclusion (Staver, 1989; Swamy, 1987). For teachers, to improve thinking implies through understanding of internal mental development, external forces and the constantly changing relationship between internal and external states. Constructivist approach is able to provide all these.

Constructivism is a more overarching theory, one that can incorporate a number of teaching practices, such as cooperative, collaborative, and inquiry-based learning. In the classroom, the constructivist view of learning can point towards a number of different teaching practices. In the most general sense, it usually means encouraging students to use active techniques (experiments, real-world problem-solving) to create more knowledge and then to reflect on and talk about what they are doing and how their understanding is changing. The teacher makes sure she understands the students' pre-existing conceptions, and guides the activity to address them and then build on them (Seigel, 2004).

Constructivism is also often misconstrued as a learning theory that compels students to "reinvent the wheel". In fact, constructivism taps into and triggers the students' innate curiosity about the world and how things work. Students do not reinvent the wheel but, rather, attempt to understand how it turns, how it functions. They become engaged by applying their existing knowledge and real-world experience, learning to hypothesize, testing their theories, and ultimately drawing conclusions from their findings (Seigel, 2004).

In the constructivist classroom, the focus tends to shift from the teacher to the students. The classroom is no longer a place where the teacher ("expert") pours knowledge into passive students, who wait like empty vessels to be filled. In the constructivist model, the students are urged to be actively involved in their own process of learning. The teacher functions more as a facilitator who coaches, mediates, prompts, and helps students develop and assess their understanding, and thereby their learning. One of the teacher's biggest jobs becomes *asking good questions* (Seigel, 2004).

In short, constructivism has important implications for teaching:

- Teaching cannot be viewed as the transmission of knowledge from enlightened to unenlightened; constructivist teachers do not take the role of the "sage on the stage". Rather, teachers act as "guides on the side" who provide students with opportunities to test the adequacy of their current understandings.

- If learning is based on prior knowledge, then teachers must note that knowledge provide learning environments that exploit inconsistencies between learners' current understandings and the new experiences before them. This challenges teachers, for they cannot assume that all children understand something in the same way. Further, children may need different experiences to advance to different levels of understanding.
- If students must apply their current understandings in new situations in order to build new knowledge, then teachers must engage students in learning, bringing students' current understandings to the forefront. Teachers can ensure that learning experiences incorporate problems that are important to students, not those that are primarily important to teachers and the educational system. Teachers can also encourage group interaction, where the interplay among participants helps individual students become explicit about their own understanding by comparing it to that of their peers.
- If new knowledge is actively built, then time is needed to build it. Ample time facilitates student reflection about new experiences, how those experiences line up against current understandings, and how a different understanding might provide students with an improved (not "correct") view of the world.
- If learning is a constructive process, and instruction must be designed to provide opportunities for such construction, then what professional development practices can bring teachers to teach in student-centred ways?

There is a need to recognize that construction in learning is not just the domain of children but of learners, all learners. Constructivist professional development give teachers time to make explicit their understandings of learning (e.g., is it a constructive process?), of teaching (e.g., is a teacher an orator or a facilitator?, and what is the teacher's understanding of content?), and of professional development (e.g., is a teacher's own learning best approached through a constructivist orientation?). Furthermore, such professional development provides opportunities for teachers to test their understandings and build new ones. Training that affects student-centred teaching cannot come in one-day workshops. Systematic, long-term development that allows practice—and reflection on that practice—is required.

It is also useful to remember the educator's maxim. Teachers teach as they are taught, not as they are told to teach. Thus, trainers in constructivist professional development sessions model learning activities that teachers can apply in their own classrooms. It is not enough for trainers to describe new ways of teaching and expect teachers to translate from talk to action; it is more effective to engage teachers in activities that will lead to new actions in classrooms.

Some other implications:

- Children learn more, and enjoy learning more when they are actively involved, rather than passive listening. When they enjoy learning, there are more likely to retain learning.
- Students learn how to think and understand. Also, they have ownership of their own learning.
- Education works best when it concentrates on thinking and understanding, rather than on rote memorization. Constructivism concentrates on leaning how to think and understand.
- Constructivist learning is transferable. In constructivist classrooms, students create organizing principles that they can take with them to other learning settings.
- Constructivism applies natural curiosity to real world situations. It promotes social and communication skill within a group setting.
- Constructivism gives students ownership of what they learn, since learning is based on students' questions and explorations, and often the students have a hand in designing the assessment engages the students' questions

and explorations, and often the students have a hand in designing the assessments as well. Constructivist assessment engages the students' initiatives and personal investments in their journals, research reports, physical models and artistic representations. Engaging the creative instincts develops students' abilities to express knowledge through a variety of ways. The students are also more likely to retain and transfer the new knowledge to real life.

- By grounding learning activities in an authentic, real-world context, constructivism stimulates and engages students. Students in constructivist classrooms learn to question things and to apply their natural curiosity to the world.
- Constructivism promotes social and communication skills by creating a classroom environment that emphasizes collaboration and exchange of ideas.
- Students must learn how to articulate their ideas clearly as well as to collaborate on tasks effectively by sharing in group projects. Students must, therefore, exchange with others and to evaluate their contributions in a socially acceptable manner. This is essential to success in the real world, since they will always be exposed to a variety of experiences in which they will have to cooperate and navigate among the ideas of other.

Principles of learning from an information processing perspective such as recognizing the limits of short-term memory, providing many opportunities for students to connect prior knowledge to current learning, and recognizing the need for spaced practice can also be implemented within a constructivistic approach. Again, the major distinction is in where to start: with a pre-designed curriculum or with the students' experiences and knowledge base. What is the correct approach? If we start with the students' knowledge base before we have established desired goals, there is a tendency to have the students simply 'make progress', "thereby limiting students who are not adequately prepared". These students may develop adequate thinking skills but can have large gaps in their knowledge and skills. On the other hand, if we focus only on desired end goals, especially knowledge goals, without consideration of the student's acquired knowledge and background, we run the risk of developing knowledge and skills that have no meaning to the learner and are therefore easily forgotten.

Teaching strategies using social-constructivism as a referent include teaching in contexts that might be personally meaningful to students, negotiating taken-as-shared meanings with students, class discussion, small-group collaboration, and valuing meaningful activity over correct answers (Wood, 1995). Cobb (1944) contrasts the approach of delivering mathematics as "content" against the technique of fostering the emergence of mathematical ideas from the collective practices of the classroom community. Emphasis is growing on the teacher's use of multiple epistemologies, to maintain dialectic tension between teacher guidance and student-initiated exploration, as well as between social learning and individual learning. Constructivism-related strategies such as these are starting to be used more often in science and mathematics classrooms, but perhaps not surprisingly, have been common for a longer time in humanities subjects like social studies and communication (Dougiamas, 1998).

In the classroom, the constructivist view of learning can point towards a number of different teaching practices. In the most general sense, it usually means encouraging students to use active techniques (experiments, real-world problem-solving) to create more knowledge and then to reflect on and talk about what they are doing and how their understanding changing. The teacher makes sure he or she understands the students' pre-existing conceptions, and guides the activity to address them and then build on them.

Book reports and literature analysis is one of the areas as advocated by constructivism could be useful in promoting higher level thinking. Once a student digests a book, the student has to take what he has read and somehow relate his understanding of the world with the new knowledge, concepts, or themes that he identified in the book. Critical thinking here is key, because different students are going to read the book with a different worldview or idea as to what is important in the world. Because of this, we can't just instruct or drill into a student what the underlying message or themes of work of literature are. To properly interpret literature, it is probably useful to be involved in some group discussion and to learn by trial and error. Unfortunately, analyzing literature is one of those skills that doesn't lend itself to standardized multiple choice testing. A certain amount of comprehension is going to be testable, but higher level critical thinking is probably best judged on a subjective scale...i.e., book reports, essay questions.

There are several other uses that we can see constructivism being useful, such as science application through science experiments and identifying themes in history. Constructivism provides one theoretical approach to the use of computer-based systems, and, as such, deserves careful consideration. Duffy and Jonassen (1992) argue that instruction should not focus on transmitting plans to the learner but rather on developing the skills of the learner to construct (and reconstruct) plans in response to situational demands and opportunities. Thus, instruction should provide contexts and assistance that will aid the individual in making sense of the environment as it is encountered. Plans must be constructed, tested, and revised as a function of the particular encounters in the environment. Learning environments based on the objectivist view of learning are problematic because: Computer models of mind rely on a formalization of knowledge. Experiences must be represented in some propositional form. However, any propositionalization is simply one representation of that prior experience. The individual, but not the computer or the computer model of mind, can reconceptualize, reconstruct, and repropositionalize that experience in many different ways. It is the storage of experiences (unformalized background) that the computer systems and models cannot achieve....

Conclusively, constructivism represents one of the big ideas in education. Its implications for how teachers teach and learn to teach are enormous. If our efforts in reforming education for all students are to succeed, then we must focus on students. To date, a focus on student-centred learning may well be the most important contribution of constructivism.

3

Constructivist Epistemology

It is said that a question is the beginning of a quest which has to be more important than even the conquest, similarly an epistemological question is the beginning of epistemological quest. Epistemological quest is a journey and its destination is not achievable until and unless epistemic quest is satisfied as in the domain of any epistemology, the two routes are followed such as Epistemic and Epistemological. Epistemic enquiry provides us nature of knowledge and epistemological enquiry provides us methodology of knowledge. In the case of constructivist epistemology too, first there is a need to find the nature of knowing and secondly methodology of knowing as constructivism is not a study of knowledge but a study of knowing which have been time and again has been reaffirmed by many constructivist epistemologists.

3.1 EPISTEMIC ASPECT OF CONSTRUCTIVISM

This physical world is found always in a constant flux and that is why it is not exaggerated to say that the change is only permanent thing. The dynamicity of change has always affected every aspect of human life and knowledge. This change is explicitly evident in epistemology too where the trend has been to move from a static, passive view of knowledge towards a more adaptive and active view (Heylighen, 1993). Each theory emphasized knowledge as being awareness of objects that exist independent of any subject. According to this objectivist view, objects have intrinsic meaning and knowledge is a reflection of a correspondence to reality. In this tradition, knowledge should represent a real world that is thought of as existing, separate and independent of the knower, and this knowledge should be considered true only if it correctly reflects that independent world. In contrast, the constructivists argue that knowledge and reality do not have an objective or absolute value or at the least, that we have no way of knowing this reality. Von Glasersfeld (1995) indicates in relation to the concept of reality: "It is made up of the network of things and relationships that we rely on in our living, and on which, we believe, others rely on, too." The knower interprets and constructs a reality based on his experiences and interactions with his environment. Rather than thinking of truth in terms of a match to reality, von Glasersfeld focuses instead on the notion of viability: "To the constructivist, concepts, models, theories, and so on are viable if they prove adequate in the contexts in which they were created."

Constructivism is an epistemology, a philosophical explanation about the nature of knowledge. Constructivist epistemology is a view that reality, or at least our knowledge of it, is a value-laden subjective construction rather than a passive acquisition of objective features. Basically, constructivism views that knowledge is not 'about' the world, but rather 'constitutive' of the world (Scherman, 1995). To social constructivists knowledge is a human product and is socially and culturally constructed (Ernest, 1999, Gardner, 1997, & Prat & Floden, 1994). Individuals create meaning through their interactions with each other and with the environment they live in.

Constructivist epistemology in general has provided a remarkable description of people's spontaneous epistemology and of the structures that organize their knowledge. It has sketched out a general architecture of knowledge in terms of a given epistemic subject's structures. Piaget has used the term "epistemic subject" and defined it as the nucleus common to every individual's knowledge at a given developmental level.

Constructivism views all of our knowledge as "constructed", because it does not reflect any external "transcendent realities; it is contingent on convention, human perception, and social experience. It is believed by constructivists that presentations of physical and biological reality, including race, sexuality and gender are socially constructed. Constructivism prefers constructed reality instead ontological reality. The interpretation of reality derives from the child's natural epistemology. That epistemology engenders "worldview" focused either on understanding the world or on understanding oneself as a thinking subject. Thus, we can say that knowledge is nothing but human constructs.

The constructivist perspectives affirm that the mind constructs its own reality. Constructivism emphasizes the importance of the knowledge, beliefs, and skills an individual brings to the experience of learning. It recognizes the construction of new understanding as a combination of prior learning, new information, and readiness to learn.

The epistemic of constructivism was made explicit by Vico who wrote a treatise on the construction of knowledge and said "the human mind can only know what the human mind has made". This statement differentiates between knowledge of the real world and knowledge of the world as a mental image that we create from our experiences. Vico has insisted that we in some ways construct our own worlds through our actions, beliefs and thoughts and then we live in the worlds we have constructed. More subtly, he maintained that human can understand only what they have themselves constructed.

In constructivism, knowledge is seen as Relativistic (nothing is absolute, but varies according to time and space) and Falliblist (nothing can be taken for granted). In the view of constructivists, knowledge development is an active process in which meaning is accomplished on the basis of experiences. This view of knowledge does not necessarily reject the existence of the real world and agrees that reality places constraints on the concepts that are but contends that all we know of the world are human interpretations of our experience of the world. Constructivism emphasizes the importance of the world knowledge, beliefs and skills an individual brings to bear on learning. Viewing the construction of new knowledge as a combination of prior learning matched against new information, and readiness to learn, this theory opens up new perspectives, leading individuals to informed choices about what to accept and how to fit it into their existing schemata, as well as what to reject.

Constructivism rejects the traditional philosophical position of realism and adopts a relativist position. The traditional view of realism sees knowledge as a representation of an absolute reality—a world "out there" prior to having been experienced. The constructivists see knowledge as "something that is presently constructed by individuals, in an active way, as they try to give meaning to socially accepted and shared notions". As von Glasersfeld himself says, "Knowledge is the result of an individual subject's constructive activity, not a commodity that somehow resides outside the knower and can be conveyed or distilled by diligent perception or linguistic communication."

Epistemic of constructivism is also a learning or meaning-making theory that offers an explanation of the nature of knowledge. Constructivists see knowledge as an interconnection among ideas. Some epistemic aspect of constructivism as stated by different writers:

- Constructivist approaches view knowledge as personally and socially constructed, rather than 'objective' and revealed; theories as provisional, not absolute (R. Miller and R. Driver, 1987).
- Knowledge is an intellectual construct, and what are referred to as the laws of nature are merely the result of this human activity (R. Nadeau and J. Destautels, 1984).
- The fact that scientific knowledge enables us to cope does not justify the belief that scientific knowledge provides a picture of the world that corresponds to an absolute reality (Glasersfeld, 1989).
- Although we may assume the existence of an external world we do not have direct access to it; science as public knowledge is not so much a discovery as a carefully checked construction (R. Driver and Oldham, 1986; quoted by Mathews, 1992).
- Put into simple terms, constructivism can be described as essentially a theory about the limits of human

> knowledge, a belief that all knowledge is necessary a product of our own cognitive acts. We can have no direct or unmediated knowledge of any external or objective reality. We construct our understanding through our experiences, and the character of our experience is influenced profoundly by our cognitive lens (J. Confrey; quoted by Mathews, 1992).

For most constructivists our knowledge does not tell us about the world at all, it tells us about our experiences and how they are best organized.

In the view of constructivists, knowledge development is an active process in which meaning is accomplished on the basis of experiences. This view of knowledge does not necessarily reject the existence of the real world and agrees that reality places constraints on the concepts that are but contends that all we know of the world are human interpretations of our experience of the world. Constructivism emphasizes the importance of the world knowledge, beliefs and skills an individual brings to bear on learning. Viewing the construction of new knowledge as a combination of prior learning matched against new information, and readiness to learn, this theory opens up new perspectives, leading individuals to informed choices about what to accept and how to fit it into their existing schemata, as well as what to reject.

Constructivism rejects the traditional philosophical position of realism and adopts a relativist position. The traditional view of realism sees knowledge as a representation of an absolute reality—a world "out there" prior to having been experienced. The constructivists see knowledge as "something that is presently constructed by individuals, in an active way, as they try to give meaning to socially accepted and shared notions". As von Glasersfeld himself says, "knowledge is the result of an individual subject's constructive activity, not a commodity that somehow resides outside the knower and can be conveyed or distilled by diligent perception or linguistic communication" (http:// www. math.upatras.gr/~m bounder//articles/constr.html).

Jonassen (1991) provides a summary of objectivism: "Knowledge is stable because the essential properties of objects are knowable and relatively unchanging. The important metaphysical assumption of objectivism is that the world is real, it is structured and that structure can be modelled for the learner. The epistemic of objectivism holds that the purpose of the mind is to 'mirror' that reality and its structure through thought processes that are analyzable and decomposable. The meaning that is produced by these thought processes are external to the understander, and it is determined by the structure of the real world."

In contrast, the epistemic of constructivist view argues that knowledge and reality do not have an objective or absolute value or, at the least, that we have no way of knowing this reality. Glasersfeld (1995) indicates in relation to the concept of reality: "It is made up of the network of things and relationships that we rely on in our living, and on which, we believe, others rely on, too." The knower interprets and constructs a reality based on his environment. Rather than thinking of truth is terms of a match to reality, Glasersfeld focuses instead on the notion of viability: "to the constructivist, concepts, models, theories and so on are viable if they prove adequate in the contexts in which they were created".

Heylighen (1993) explains that social constructivism "sees consensus between different subjects as the ultimate criterion to judge knowledge. 'Truth' or 'reality' will be accorded only to those constructions on which most people of a social group agree."

Epistemic of constructivism views all of our knowledge as "constructed", under the assumption that it does not necessarily reflect any external "transcendent" realities; it is contingent on convention, human perception, and social experience. Last but not the least, epistemic aspect of constructivism describes what is knowledge and "knowing".

The premises of epistemic of constructivism are:

- Knowledge is constructed, not transmitted.
- Prior knowledge impacts the learning process.

- Initial understanding is local, not global.
- Building useful knowledge structures requires effortful and purposeful activity.

Following are epistemic theses of constructivism based on von Glasersfeld's philosophy:

- Knowledge is not about an observer-independent world.
- Knowledge does not represent such a world; correspondence theories of knowledge are mistaken.
- Knowledge is created by individuals in a historical and cultural setting.
- Knowledge refers to individual experience rather than to the world.
- Knowledge is constituted by individual conceptual structures.
- Conceptual structures constitute knowledge when individuals regard them as viable in relationship to their experience; constructivism is a form of pragmatism.
- There is no preferred epistemic conceptual structure; constructivism is a relativist doctrine.
- Knowledge is the appropriate ordering of an experiential reality.
- There is no rationally accessible, extra-experiential reality.

3.2 EPISTEMOLOGICAL ASPECT OF CONSTRUCTIVISM

Constructivism is an epistemological view of knowledge acquisition emphasizing knowledge construction rather than knowledge transmission and the recording of information conveyed by others. The role of the knowledge constructor is conceived as one of building and transforming knowledge. But, what does it mean to construct knowledge? Within constructivism there are different notions of the nature of knowledge and the knowledge construction process or in other words, there are different versions of methodologies of knowledge construction.

Individual know-how involves a variety of cognitive schemas are more heuristic than general structures are.

Glasersfeld has stated, "to claim that one's theory of knowing is true, in the traditional sense of representing a state or feature of an experiencer-independent world, would be perjury for a radical constructivist". One of the central points of theory is precisely that this kind of "truth", can never be claimed for the knowledge (or any piece of it) that human reason produces. To mark this radical departure, it is appropriate to call a theory of knowing rather than a "theory of knowledge". Noddings is right in saying that radical constructivism should be "offered as a post-epistemological perspective". One of the consequences of such an appraisal, however, must be that one does not persist in arguing against it as though it were or purported to be a traditional theory of knowledge. Another consequence is that constructivism needs to be radical and must explain that one can indeed, manage without the traditional notion of Truth. That the task is possible may become more possible if the sources are traced of some of the ideas that made the enterprise seem desirable.

Quoting Xenophanes, Glasersfeld says that we may credit the insight that even if someone succeeded in describing exactly how the world really is, he or she would have no way of knowing that it was the "true" description. This is the major argument the sceptics have repeated. It is based on the assumption that whatever ideas or knowledge we have must have been derived in some way from our experience, which includes sensing, acting and thinking. If this is the case, we have no way of checking the truth of our knowledge with the world presumed to be lying beyond our experiential interface, because to do this, we would need or access to such a world that does not involve our experiencing it.

He says that throughout the occidental history of ideas and right down to our own days, two requisites have been considered fundamental in any epistemological discussion of knowledge. The first of these requisites demands that whatever we would like to call "true knowledge" has to be independent of the knowing subject. The second requisite is that knowledge is to be taken seriously only if it claims to represent a world of "things-in-themselves" in a more or less veridical fashion. In other worlds, it is tacitly taken for granted that a fully structured and knowable world "exists" and that it is the business of the cognizing human subject to discover what that structure is. He has asserted, "What the sceptics failed to stress was that, though no truths about a 'real' world could be derived from experience, experience nevertheless supplied a great deal of useful knowledge."

Vico (1858) has very clearly said that the human mind can know only what the human mind has made. In other words, knowledge is a human constructs. Pursuing the way of thinking one is led to have reconstruction of the concept of knowledge (Glasersfeld, 1985). Some reconstruction is needed because, on the one hand, one can no longer maintain that the cognizing activity should or could produce a true representation of an objective world, and on the other, one does not want to end up with a solipsistic form of idealism. He further says that the only way out, then, would seem to be a drastic modification of the relation between the cognitive structures we build up and that "real" world which we are inclined to assume as "existing" beyond our perceptual interface. Instead of the illusory relation of "representation", one has to find a way of relating knowledge to reality that does not imply anything like match or correspondence. To propose a conceptual alternative, the credit goes to Darwin's theory of evolution in general and the concept of "fit" in particular. Hans Vaihinger (1913), who is famous for his work ("Philosophy of As If") reintroduced the idea of conceptual construction. After him, Piaget is the one who is credited the most as a pioneer of the constructivist theory of knowing. New concept of knowledge (based on Piaget's thinking) proposes the following principles based on constructivism:

(a) Knowledge is not passively received either through the senses or by way of communication.
(b) Knowing is actively built up by the cognizing object.
(c) The function of cognition is adaptive, in the biological sense of the term, tending towards fit or viability.

(d) Cognition serves the subject's organization of the experiential world, not the discovery of an objective ontological reality.

Lerman (1989), following Kilpatrick, suggests that the core epistemological theses of constructivism are:

> Knowledge is actively constructed by the cognizing subject, not passively received from the environment.
>
> Coming to know is an adaptive process that organizes one's experiential world; it does not discover an independent, pre-existing world outside the mind of the knower.

Glasersfeld says that if taken seriously, they are incompatible with the traditional notions of knowledge, truth and objectivity and they require a radical reconstruction of one's concept of reality. Instead of an inaccessible realm beyond perception and cognition, it now becomes the experiential world we actually live in. This world is not an unchanging independent structure, but the result of distinctions that generate a physical and a social environment to which, in turn, we adapt as best we can. Consequently, one cannot adopt the constructivist principles as an absolute truth, but only as a working hypothesis that may or may not turn out to be viable. That is the main reason why the constructivist orientation is unequivocally post-epistemological.

Now the question arises how does it come about that the reality we construct is in many ways remarkably stable? And, one might also ask why, if we ourselves construct our experiential reality, can we not construct any reality we might like? The first question is answered in a categorical way by George Kelly: "to the living creature, then, the universe is real, but it is not inexorable unless he chooses to construe it that way" (1995). Each living organism thrives by abstracting regularities and rules from experience that enable it to avoid disagreeable situations and, to some extent, to generate agreeable ones. This "abstracting of regularities" is always the result of assimilation. No experience is ever the same as another in the absolute sense. Repetition and consequently regularity can be obtained only by disregarding certain differences. No schemes could be developed if the organism could not isolate situations in which a certain action leads to a desirable result. It is the focus on the result that distinguishes a scheme from a reflex and makes possible the form of learning that Piaget called accommodation. It takes place when a scheme does not lead to the expected result. This produces a perturbation, and the perturbation may lead either to modification of the pattern that was abstracted as the "triggering situation" or to a modification of the action. All this concerns the experiential world of the acting organism, not any "external reality". And the patterns a cognizing organism can and does abstract from experience depend on the operations of distinction and coordination the organism can and does carry out.

The second question—why we cannot construct any reality we like—can be raised only if the concept of viability is misunderstood or ignored. The absurdity of solipsism stems from the denial of any relation between knowledge and an experiencer-independent world.

If the view is adopted that "knowledge" is the conceptual means to make sense of experience, rather than a "representation" of something that is supposed to lie beyond it this shift of perspective brings with it an important corollary: the concepts and relations in terms of which we perceive and conceive the experiential world we live in are necessarily generated by ourselves. Radical constructivism does not suggest that we can construct anything we like but it does claim that within the constraints that limit our construction there is room for infinity of alternatives. It, therefore, does not seem ultimately to suggest a theory of knowing that draws attention to the knower's responsibility for what the knower constructs.

Constructivist epistemology has reemphasized that every knowledge is constructed knowledge. Let us see how different constructivist writers have viewed the construction of knowledge. By definition, knowledge construction is an active, rather than a passive process. The process of constructing one's knowledge can involve cognition (Cunningham, 1988, 1993) and physical constructions (Harel and Papert, 1991) of meaning, through the development of mental models or schemas (Johnson-Laird, 1980), as well as physical or virtual representations of knowledge (McClellan, 1996; Winn, Hoffman and Osberg, 1995; Mones-Hattel and Mandes, 1996). Construction of knowledge is a process of self-regulation that surpasses simple memory explanations (Palmer and Goetz, 1988; Schmeck, 1988; Weinstein, Goetz and Alaxander, 1988).

According to constructivists, there is nothing systematic about how we learn or construct knowledge. Rather, constructivists believe that knowledge is constructed socially using language (Vygotsky, 1962) and everyone has different social experiences resulting in multiple realities (Jonassen, 1996). Constructing knowledge, then, is a socio-linguistic process where there is gradual advancement of understandings built upon previous knowledge resulting in multiple dimensions of the truth (Spiro & Jehng, 1990; Spiro, Feltovich, Jacobson, & Coulson, 1991).

As far as content and process is concerned, it has been pointed out (Noddings, 1990) that constructivism raises serious questions from an epistemological position. What does it mean, for example, to talk of individual construction as 'knowledge'? The attempt to separate content and process, or to make one subservient to the other, belies a faulty epistemology. James (1974) tells us that knowledge involves both question (process) and answer (product or content). Thus, the epistemic and epistemological aspects of constructivism should not be viewed as distinct or absolute exclusive; rather, both are inseparable and mutually inclusive.

Time and again, majority of constructivists have re-emphasized that constructivism is a theory of knowledge construction, not a theory of pedagogy. Constructivism posits that knowledge construction occurs amid four assumptions:

- Knowledge involves active cognizing by the individual.
- Knowledge is adaptive, facilitating individual and social efficacy.
- Knowledge is subjective and self-organized, not objective.

- Knowledge acquisition involves both socio-cultural and individual processes.

Knowledge is a function of how the individual creates meaning from his or her own personal experiences; it is not a function of what someone else says is true. Each of us conceives of external reality somewhat differently, based upon our unique set of experiential mappings with the world and our beliefs about them. "What biology shows us is that the uniqueness of being human lies exclusively in a social structural coupling that occurs through languaging, generating (a) the regularities proper to the human social dynamics, for example, individual identity and self-consciousness, and (b) the recursive social human dynamics that entails a reflection enabling us to see that as human beings we have only the world which we create with others—whether we like them or not" (Maturana & Varela, 1987).

Epistemological aspect of constructivism is also a learning or meaning-making theory that offers an explanation of how human beings learn. It maintains that individuals create or construct their own new understandings or knowledge through the interaction of what they come in contact (Cannella and Reiff, 1994; Richardson, 1997). Knowledge is acquired through involvement with content instead of imitation or repetition (Kroll and La Boskey, 1996).

3.3 CONSTRUCTIVIST LEARNING: A NEW APPROACH TO LEARNING

For so many years, education has been dominated by approaches to teaching and learning that reflect the following assumptions (Feden, 1994):

- Learning is the process of accumulating bits of information and isolated skills.
- The teacher's primarily responsibility is to transfer knowledge directly to students.
- The process of learning and teaching focuses primarily on the interactions between the teacher and individual students.

In this tradition, the teacher transmits information that the learner receives. Teaching practices focus on lecture as a means of conveying information and on the traditional paper/pencil, multiple choice types of assessment (Allenspach, 1996). Learning emphasis is on propositional knowledge—knowledge "that" (facts, assertion, concepts and propositions). The objectivist philosophy, described by Jonassen (1991), reflects these assumptions for knowledge transfer. Objectivists believe that there is reliable knowledge about the world that teachers must transmit and that learners must replicate this knowledge in their thinking (Murphy, 1997).

In the view of constructivist, learning is a constructivist process in which the learner is building an internal illustration of knowledge, a personal interpretation of experience. This representation is continually open to modification, its structure and linkages forming the ground to which meaning is accomplished does not necessarily reject the existence of the real world, and agrees that reality places constraints on the concepts that are, but contents that all we know of world are human interpretations of our experience of the world. Conceptual growth comes from the sharing of various perspectives and the simulations changing of our internal representations in response to those perspectives as well as through cumulative experience (Bednar et al., 1995). Learning is a process through which human beings adapt to the experiential world.

Constructivist model of learning emphasizes meaning-making through active participation in socially, culturally, historically and politically situated contexts. A crucial element of active participation is dialogue in shared experiences, through which situated collaborative activities, such as modelling, discourse and decision-making, are necessary to support the negotiation and creation of meaning and understanding. Also, contemporary constructivist theory of learning acknowledges that individuals are active agents, they engage in their own knowledge construction by integrating new information into their schema, and by associating and representing it into a meaningful way.

Constructivism theorists ask the following questions (Hofer and Pintrch, 1997; Jonassen, 1996):

- What does it mean to know something?
- How do we come to know it?
- How does this knowledge influence our thinking processes?

A basic assumption is that "children learn when they are in control of their learning and know that they are in control" (Green & Gardner, 2002). Wheatley (1991) suggests two principles of learning embodied in the constructivist theory: "Principle one states that knowledge is not passively received, but is actively built up by the cognizing subject. Principle two states that the function of cognition is adaptive and serves the organization of the experiential world, not the ontological reality."

Learning is essentially a social and learners are particularly motivated by rewards provided by the community. However, because knowledge is actively constructed by learner, learning also depends to a significant extent on the motivational drive to understand and promote the learning process. Central to constructivism is its conception of learning. Von Glasersfeld (1995) argues: "From the constructivist perspective, learning is not a stimulus-response phenomenon. It requires self-regulation and the building of conceptual structures through reflection and abstraction." In this paradigm, learning emphasizes the process and not the product. How one arrives at a particular answer, and not the retrieval of an 'objectively true solution', is what is important. Learning is a process of constructing meaningful representations, of making sense of one's experiential world. In this process, students' errors are seen in a positive light and as a means of gaining insight into how they are organizing their personal experiential world.

Jonassen (1991) notes that many educators and cognitive psychologists have applied constructivism to the development of learning environments. From these applications, he has isolated a number of design principles:

- Create real-world environments that employ the context in which learning is relevant;

- Focus on realistic approaches to solving real-world problems;
- The instructor should be a coach and analyser of the strategies used to solve these problems;
- Stress conceptual inter-relatedness, providing multiple representations or perspectives on the content;
- Instructional goals and objectives should be negotiated and not imposed;
- Evaluation should serve as a self-analysis tool;
- Provide tools and environments that help learners interpret the multiple perspectives of the world;
- Learning should be internally controlled and mediated by the learner.

Jonassen (1994) has also summarised what he refers to as the implications of constructivism for instructional design. The following principles illustrate how knowledge construction can be facilitated:

- Provide multiple representations of reality;
- Represent the natural complexity of the real world;
- Focus on knowledge construction, not reproduction;
- Present authentic tasks (contextualizing rather than abstracting instruction);
- Provide real-world, case-based learning environments, rather than predetermined instructional sequences;
- Foster reflective practice;
- Enable context and content dependent knowledge construction;
- Support collaborative construction of knowledge through social negotiation.

Wilson and Cole (1991) provide a description of cognitive teaching models which "embody" constructivist concepts. From these descriptions, we can isolate some principles central to constructivist design, teaching and learning:

- Embed learning in a rich authentic problem-solving environment;
- Provide for authentic versus academic contexts for learning;
- Provide for learner control;
- Use errors as a mechanism to provide feedback on learners' understanding.

In the view of constructivists, learning is a constructivist process in which the learner is building an internal interpretation of experiences that he/she has accumulated in his/her life journey. This representation is continually open to modification, its structures and linkages forming the ground to which other knowledge structures are attached. Learning is an active process in which meaning is accomplished on the basis of experience. This view of knowledge is not necessarily reject the existence of the real world, and agrees that reality places constraints on the concepts that are, but contends that all we know of the world are human interpretations of our experience of the world. John Dewey (1910) has rightly said, "Only by wrestling with the conditions of the problem at hand, seeking and finding his own solution (not in isolation but in correspondence with the teacher and other pupils) does one learn."

Within the constructivist paradigm, the accent is on the learner rather than the teacher. It is the learner who interacts with his or her environment and thus gains an understanding of its features and characteristics. The learner constructs his or her own conceptualizations and finds his or her own solutions to problems, mastering autonomy and independence. Thus, learning is the result of individual mental construction, whereby the learner learns by dint of matching new against given information and establishing meaningful connections, rather than by internalising mere factoids to be regurgitated later on. In constructivist thinking, learning is inseparably affected by the context and the beliefs and attitudes of the learner. Here, learners are given more latitude in becoming effective problems, as well as deciphering to these problems. "If a student is able to perform in a problem-solving situation, a meaningful learning should then occur because he or she has constructed an interpretation of how things work using pre-existing structures. This is the theory behind constructivism. By creating a personal interpretation of external ideas and experiences, constructivism allows students the ability to understand how ideas can elate to each other and pre-existing knowledge" (Drapikowski).

The constructivist learning presents the learner with opportunities for autopoietic learning with a view to prior knowledge and understand how to construct new knowledge from authentic experience—creating a view in keeping with Rogers' experiential learning (Rogers, 1969, 1994). Rogers, one of the exponents of experiential learning—the tenets of which are inextricably related to, and congruent with, those of constructivism—made the distinction between cognitive learning, which he deemed meretricious, and experiential learning, which he considered significant (Drapikowski). For him, the qualities of experiential learning include:

- Personal involvement;
- Learner intention;
- Evaluation by learner; and
- Previous effects on learner.

It could be argued that constructivism emphasizes the importance of the world knowledge, beliefs and skills an individual brings to learn on learning. Viewing the construction of new knowledge as a combination of prior learning matched against new information, and readiness to learn, this theory opens up new perspectives, leading individuals to informed choices about what to accept and how to fit it into their existing schema, as well as what to reject. We can say that constructivism emphasizes learning, encourages learner autonomy and personal involvement in learning, looks to learners as agents exercising will and purpose, fosters learners' natural curiosity, and also takes account of learners' affect, in terms of their beliefs, attitudes and motivation. In addition, within constructivist theory, context is accorded significance, as it renders situations and events meaningful and relevant, and provides learners with the opportunity to construct new knowledge from authentic experience. After all, "Learning is contextual: we do not learn isolated facts and theories in some abstract ethereal land of the mind separate from the rest of our lives: we learn in relationship to what else we know, what we believe, our prejudices and our fears. On reflection, it becomes clear that this point is actually a corollary of the idea that learning is active and social. We cannot divorce our learning from our lives" (Hein, 1991). What is more, by providing opportunities for independent thinking, constructivism allows students to take responsibility for their own learning, by framing questions and then analyzing them. Reaching beyond simple factual information, learners are induced to establish connections between ideas and thus to predict, justify and defend their ideas (Brooks & Brooks, 1993).

This way we find that time and again, constructivists have reiterated that constructivism is a philosophy of learning founded on the premise that by reflecting on our experiences, we construct our own understanding of the world we live in. Each of us generates our own rules and mental models, which we use to make sense of our experiences. Learning, therefore, is simply the process of adjusting our mental models to accommodate new experiences. Here are some explanations which may be helpful to all who are engaged in teaching, learning and curriculum construction process:

- **How does learning occur?** The learner creates meaning from experience. The mind reflects input from the external world to create its own singular version of reality.
- **What factors influence learning?** Learning is a search for meaning. Therefore, learning must start with the issues around students are actively trying to construct meaning. Meaning requires understanding wholes as well as parts. And parts must be understood in the context of wholes. Therefore, the learning process focuses on primary concepts, not isolated facts, and the interaction between the learner and the environment.
- **What is the role of memory in learning?** Memory is just the method by which learners accumulate experiences,

generate concepts, and evolve information with each new situation. Constructivist view memory as the repository not for intact knowledge, but for flexible threads of information that can be recognized in an unending variety of ways.

- **How does transfer of knowledge occur?** Transfer of knowledge can occur by involving learners in completion of authentic tasks which are anchored within a context meaningful to them.
- **What types of learning are best explained by constructivist theory?** This type of learning structure may not be best for introductory knowledge acquisition which may require rote memorization of rules and facts, or building knowledge in a linear manner. However, for advanced knowledge acquisition, this learning theory works quite well. There are no preconceived limitations or barriers to knowledge. The student is free to create his or her own construct.
- **How should learning be evaluated?** The purpose of learning is for an individual to construct his or her own meaning, not just memorize the right answers and regurgitate someone else's meaning. Since education is inherently interdisciplinary, the only valuable way to measure learning is to make the assessment part of the learning process, ensuring it provides students with information on the quality of their learning. Constructivism calls for the elimination of grades and standardized testing. Instead, assessment becomes part of the learning process so that students play a larger role in judging their own progress.

Authenticity of task plays a crucial role in constructivist settings of learning as constructivist theory of learning is rooted in the learners' ability to build upon existing knowledge by completing meaningful, authentic tasks. Knowledge is assembled through the assimilation of new information which is compared to pre-existing notions and modified to from a new understanding based on the input of new data. According to Chen, "The goal of constructivist learning environment is to engage learners in active (manipulative), constructive, intentional, complex authentic cooperative (collaborative and conversational) and reflective learning activities." In other words, students learn by doing and they will learn more when the tasks that they are completing are exciting and have meaning to them i.e., it must be authentic one.

Constructivist learning is student-centred and involves the building of knowledge through cognitive and physical constructions, mental modelling and virtual representations of knowledge (Osberg, 1997). The building of knowledge also involves dialogue and collaboration with others who share common interests and learning goals. Reflective thought and critical enquiry through "mental representation, visualization and the process of developing, testing and discarding hypotheses are also indicative actions of an individual activity engaged in the knowledge construction process.

Reinsmith (1996), has suggested following ten truths about constructivist learning:

- Learning first takes place through osmosis. He claims, making an analogy between the initial learning of babies who live immersed in an environment and any learner, who perhaps should be immersed in an active learning atmosphere.
- Authentic learning comes through trial and error. That is, learning occurs when people try out ideas and see if their guesswork applications work or not.
- One of the tragic defects of mass education is the waste of not following or building students' interests.
- Besides determining readiness and interest for course topics and tasks, teachers have to get students to affirm that they can learn.
- Learning occurs in a context.
- Use it or lose it. Why can't students who passed a class use all the information and skills from it? They have to try out ideas in various situations and keep

using them; of course, it's impossible to use all of the information from a course, so students' experiences yet the information and skills to preserve only the most useful.

- A learner moves from imitation to intrinsic ownership, from external modelling to internalization and competence. How? Teachers can be catalysts in this process (perhaps by including modelling a progressive series of discoveries toward course concepts).
- Learning can be joyful, fun.
- Real learning often follows tangents.
- Tasks are a very poor indicator of whether an individual has really learned something. Nevertheless tests could be used to diagnose how students think if teachers can uncover why students think if teachers can uncover why students answer in a particular way.

Two valued tenets of the constructivist practice are the process of collaborative learning and deep personal introspection into one's own learning process (Brooks & Brooks, 1993, 1996). Through dialogue, we form a network of understanding, a community of others with whom we can learn and share through discourse. Dialogue, however, is not the only active means of knowledge construction at our disposal. Mental manipulation, visualization, and the process of developing, testing and discarding hypotheses (Shank, 1992; Shank, 1994) are also indicative actions of an individual activity engaged in the knowledge construction process. According to Marton et al. (1987, 1992) a traditional way of learning means that the individual learns facts and reproduces these facts correctly, a kind of quantitative nature. An alternative way of learning, a phenomenographic view, is according to Marton (1987) that man in his relation to the world around him, in order to be able to handle it, tries to form meaning and understanding. This means that there already is a conception about what is to be learnt within the learning man. Learning means that a change has taken place from one conception to another, where the latter is qualitatively different from the first (Dahlgren, 1997). Compared to the traditional quantitative view, learning is looked upon as a qualitative change of the learner's view of something in the surrounding world, not as a quantitative growth of the amounts of facts. Accordingly, learning should be seen as a qualitative change in a person's view of seeing, experiencing, understanding, to conceptualize something, rather than as a quantitative change in the amount of knowledge someone possesses.

Theories about constructivism involve the belief that better learning occurs when knowledge is the result of a situated construction of knowledge (Wilson, 1996). Learning means a personal process of knowledge construction that takes place in an encounter between what is in the learner's power of imagination and what is brought about. Knowledge building and higher order learning occurs when learners explore issues, examine arguments, and question positions from new or different perspectives. The collaborative and interactive nature of non-linear learning is supported by new constructivist learning paradigms.

Crotty (1994) defined the type of environment a constructivist will try to create, where learners "are required to examine thinking and learning processes; collect, record, and analyze data; formulate and test hypotheses; reflect on previous understandings; and construct their own meaning". Jonassen (1992) researched constructivism as the philosophical foundation for situated learning. Later, Jonassen (1994) further defined constructivist learning environments as those that are best designed for "advanced learners"..."constructivistic environments stress situated problem-solving tasks, because those are the nature of tasks that are called on and rewarded in the real world".

3.3.1 Constructivist Learning Principles

For the learners to construct meaning, he or she must actively strive to make sense of new experiences and in so doing must relate it to what is already known or believed about a topic. Learners must build their own understanding and in this process how information is resented and how learners are supported in the process of constructing knowledge are of major significances. The pre-existing knowledge that learners bring to each learning task is emphasized too. Students' current understandings provide the immediate context for interpreting any new learning. Regardless of the nature of sophistication of a learner's existing schema, each person's existing knowledge structure will have a powerful influence on what is learnt and whether and how conceptual change occurs. Knowledge is conceived as being embedded in and connected to the situation where the learning occurs. As a consequence, thinking and knowledge that is constructed are inextricably tied to the immediate social and physical context of the learning experience.

Constructivism is not only about knowledge and knowing but about learning also. The fundamental assumption about the learners is that they construct knowledge for themselves. Each learner individually constructs meaning as he or she learns. There are nine general principles of learning that are derived from constructivism. These nine principles are (Epslein, 2002): (1) Learning is an active process in which the learner uses sensory input and constructs meaning out of it. (2) People learn to learn as they learn. Learning consists both of constructing meaning and constructing systems of meaning. (3) Physical actions and hands on experience may be necessary for learning, especially for children, but is not sufficient; we need to provide activities which engage the mind as well as the hand. Dewey called this reflective activity. (4) Learning involves language: the language that we use influences our learning. Lev Vygotsky, a psychologist that helped in the theory of constructivism, argued that language and learning are inextricably intertwined. (5) Learning is a social activity: our learning is intimately associated with our connection with other human beings, our teacher, our peers, our family, as well as casual acquaintances. Dewey pointed out that most of traditional learning is directed toward isolating the learner from social interaction, and towards seeing education as a one-on-one relationship between the learner and the objective material being learned. (6) Learning is contextual: we learn in relationship to what else we know, what we believe, our prejudices and our fears. (7) One needs knowledge to learn: it is not possible to absorb new knowledge without having some structure developed from previous knowledge to build on. The more we know, the more we learn. (8) Learning is not instantaneous: it takes time to learn. For significant learning we need to revisit ideas, ponder them, try them out, play with them, and use them. (9) The key component to learning is motivation.

Bruner (Kearsley, 1999) provides the following principles of constructivistic learning:

1. Instruction must be concerned with the experiences and contexts that make the student willing and able to learn (readiness).
2. Instruction must be structured that it can be easily grasped by the student (spiral organization).
3. Instruction should be designed to facilitate extrapolation and/or fill in the gaps (going beyond the information given).

We all know that at least there are fifteen forms of constructivism such as contextual, dialectical, empirical, humanistic, information-processing, methodological, moderate, Piagetian, post-epistemological, pragmatic, radical, rational, realist, social, and socio-historical and many of these terms relate to overlapping concepts and assumptions there are striking differences too. Despite the differences among all types of constructivism, there is important congruence among most constructivists with regard to central learning principles:

1. learners construct their own learning;
2. the dependence of new learning on students' existing understanding;
3. the critical role of social interaction; and
4. the necessity of authentic learning tasks for meaningful learning (Bruning, Royce & Dennison, 1995; Pressley, Harris & Marks, 1992).

On a similar line of central principles there are four epistemological assumptions at the heart of the constructivist learning process.

- Learners who are involved in active learning physically construct knowledge.

- Learners who are making their own representations of action symbolically construct knowledge.
- Learners who convey their meaning to others socially construct knowledge.
- Learners who try to explain things they don't completely understand theoretically construct knowledge.

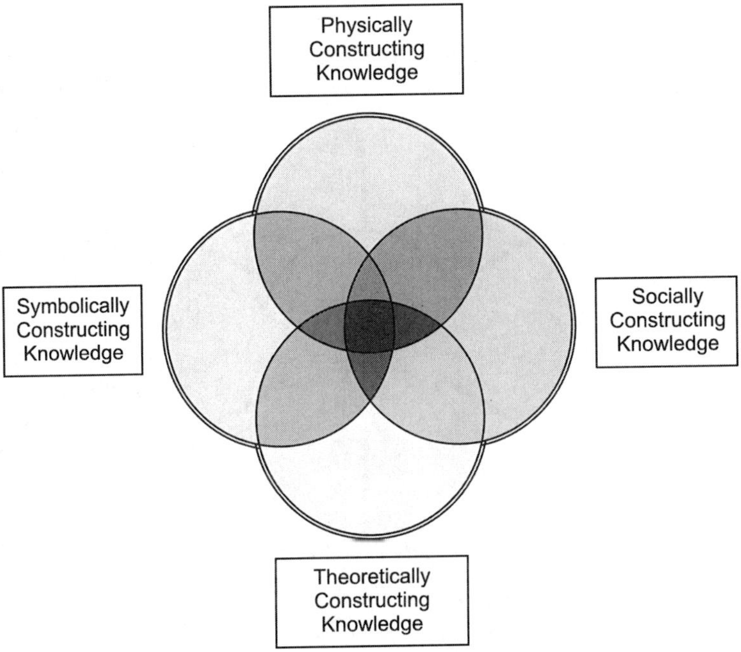

Figure 1

Apart from the above stated principles of learning along with its epistemological assumptions, designing a constructivist view of learning has six important elements: situation, groupings, bridging, questions, exhibit and reflection. These six elements combine together to give the student a constructivist experience of learning.

Situation: What situation are we as the teacher going to arrange for the student to explain? Give this situation a title and instruct the student that they are to explain the situation by describing a process of solving a problem, answering questions, creating a metaphor, making a decision, drawing conclusions, or setting goals. This situation should include what we expect the student to do and how the student will make their own meaning out of this experience.

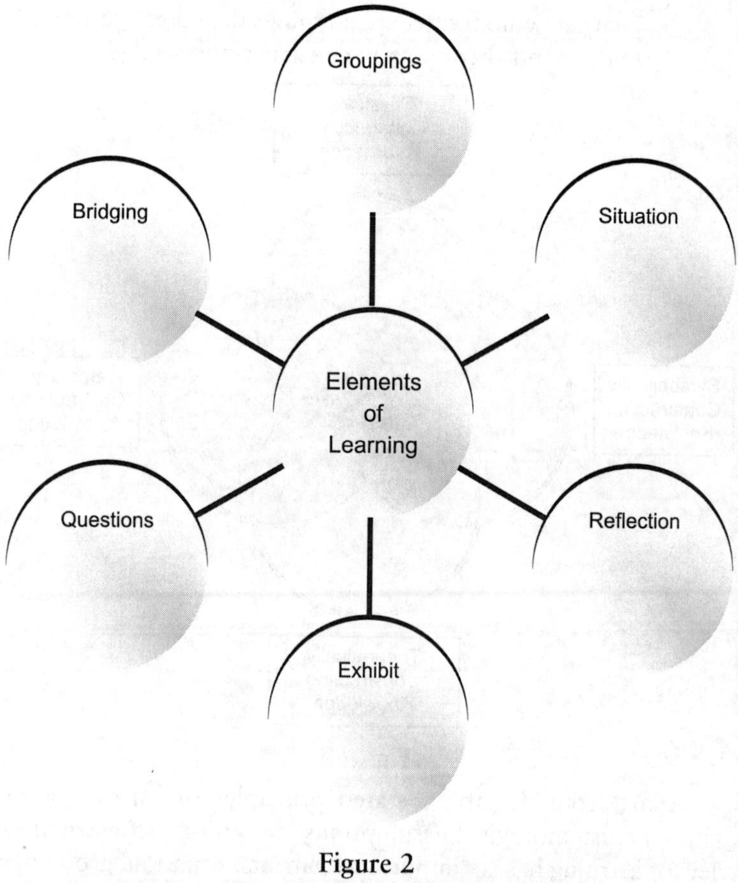

Figure 2

Grouping: There are two types of grouping in the constructivist view of learning. First, how is the teacher going to group the students in the class so each student can maximize their learning experience? Second, how is the teacher going to group the materials, resources and information the student will use to explain the situation as it has been assigned by the teacher. Keep in mind, the explanation may take the form of problem-solving, physical modelling, graphically representing, numerically describing, or the student individually writing about his collective experience.

Bridging: This initial activity is intended to determine what the student already knows and bridging that information with what they might learn by exploring the situation. This activity can involve such activities as giving the student a simple problem to solve, having a whole class discussion, playing a game, or making a list.

Questions: Questions should be an active part of every phase of the learning process. Well-constructed questions by the teacher or the student can help the student become aware of what they are learning and how this learning experience is connected to their prior knowledge.

Exhibit: The exhibit element of this process is designed to give the student a metacognitive awareness of their learning experience. In the exhibit phase the student is to record their thinking as he or she is explaining the situation. This activity can include writing a description on cards, giving a verbal presentation, creating a cognitive map, acting out or role playing their impressions, constructing a physical representation with models, making a video or audio presentation.

Reflection: In the final stage of the constructivist view of learning the student reflects on what they have just learned. Though this is one of the most important elements of a learning experience it is the one that is most overlooked by educators. Reflection is the phase of the learning process where integration between what the student has just learned is incorporated into what the student already knows. Reflection is the heart and soul of the constructivist view of learning.

What is importance of constructivist learning principles for the teachers? Driscoll (2000) has categorized constructivist learning conditions into five recommendations for teachers:

- Embed learning in complex, realistic and relevant environments.
- Provide for social negotiation as an integral part of learning.

- Support multiple perspectives and the use of multiple modes of representation.
- Encourage ownership in learning.
- Nurture self-awareness of the knowledge construction process.

Thus we as teacher educators or as teachers must keep in mind following things:

1. Learner should be encouraged to raise questions, generate hypotheses and test their validity.
2. Learners should be challenged by ideas and experiences that generate inner cognitive conflict or disequilibrium. Students' error should be viewed positively as opportunities for learners and teachers to explore conceptual understanding.
3. Students should be given time to engage in reflection through journal writing, drawing, modelling and discussion. Learning occurs through reflective abstraction.
4. The learning environment should provide ample opportunities for dialogue and the classroom should be seen as a "community of discourse engaged in activity, reflection and conversation" (Fosnot, 1989).
5. In a community of learners, it is the students themselves who must communicate their ideas to others, defend and justify them.

Students should work with big ideas central organizing principles that have the power to generalize across experiences and disciplines.

3.3.2 Constructivist Learning Theory

We can identify three fundamentally different approaches regarding the nature of knowledge and the nature of learning. These three basic approaches are referred to behaviourism, cognitivism and constructivism. Behaviourism is based on behavioural changes. It focuses on a new behavioural pattern being repeated until it becomes an automatic. Cognitivism is based on the thought process behind the behaviour. Changes in behaviour are observed, but only as an indicator to what are going on in the learner's mind. Constructivism is based on the premise that we all construct our own perspective of the world, based on individual experiences and schema. Each of us generate our own 'rules' and 'mental models', which we use to make sense of our experiences. Learning, therefore, is simply the process of adjusting our mental models to accommodate new experiences. Cognitivists view knowledge as abstract symbolic representations inside the learner's mind, constructivists view knowledge as constructed internally by each individual. That is, no knowledge can be transferred intact from one individual to another. Each individual colours and shapes the knowledge to fit within their frame of reference. Byrnes (1996) and Arseneau & Rodenburg (1998) contrast objectivist and constructivist approaches to learning:

Objectivist view	Constructivist view
1. Knowledge exists outside of individuals and can be transferred from teachers to students.	1. Knowledge has personal meaning. It is created by individual students.
2. Students learn what they hear and what they read. If a teacher explains abstract concepts well, students will learn those concepts.	2. Learners construct their own knowledge by looking for meaning and order; they interpret what they hear, read and see based on their previous learning and habits. Students who do not have appropriate backgrounds will be unable to accurately hear or see what is before them.
3. Learning is successful when students can repeat what was taught.	3. Learning is successful when students can demonstrate conceptual understanding.

In view of constructivist, learning is a constructive process in which the learner is building an internal illustration of knowledge, a personal interpretation of experience. This representation is continually open to modification, its structure and linkages forming the ground to which other knowledge structures are attached. Learning is an active process in which meaning is accomplished on the basis of experience. This view of knowledge does not necessarily reject the existence of the real world, and agrees that reality places constraints on the concepts that are, but contends that all we know of the world are human interpretations of our experience of the world. Conceptual growth comes from the sharing of various perspectives and the simultaneous changing of our internal representations in response to those perspectives as well as through cumulative experience (Bender et al., 1995).

What each person sees (or observation) depends more on what is already stored in that person's mind than on light being emitted (or not) from the image (Beneze, 2005). This suggests that learning from our environment (through our senses) is an active rather than a passive process. In a way, we seem to project onto phenomena what we already know about them. In other words, we each construct a unique mental image by combining information in our heads with the information we receive from our sense organs. In many ways, this is self-assuring. Each of us is an individual, viewing the world in ways like no other person on earth.

While many theorists emphasize each person's right and tendency to construct unique meanings, many people also believe that these are not completely unique. Simply put, because we share common language and conduct much of our thought through language and other communal symbols, is thinking. In a sense, an individual's thought is never his or her own.

Constructivist learning theory suggests a number of points about teaching and learning:

Learners have ideas: Educational research advises that students begin their study of topics with pre-conceived notions about concepts teachers want them to learn. Learner's ideas often contradict those of teachers! Students' current ideas (also called 'prior', 'alternative' or children's conceptions) often contradict the prevalent concepts. Students cannot, therefore, be treated like their brains are blank slates to be written upon or empty vessels to be filled up. Learners are not in other words, passive. Rather, they often are quite active in learning.

Learners need first-hand experiences: Sharing ideas, skills, etc. with learners by telling or showing often is insufficient for them to learn. Learners need to use and test ideas, skills, etc. through relevant activities. Often, this involves concrete experiences that combine with abstract ideas that have been presented to learners.

Students' and scientists' inquiries are self-fulfilling: Students' current ideas can affect all procedures associated with science and technology, including observing, classifying, measuring, hypothesizing, predicting, choosing variables to change or monitor, controlling variables, analyzing tests, and drawing data-based conclusions. All of these scientific skills are therefore, theory-based; i.e., how a person conducts the skill depends on what ideas he/she already holds. How a person classifies, for instance, depends on what categories he/she already has in mind.

Learners need other people: Students can't change their thinking on their own, even if they want to; they lack the understanding of what laws, theories, and inventions are available to them. For students to learn, therefore, experiences alone are not sufficient. They need other experienced people to guide and help them.

Learners like their ideas: Interestingly, just like scientists, students are very reluctant to give up their favoured ideas! Once a person sees a thing in one way, it is difficult to see it any other way. Indeed, students often are emotionally attached to their ideas; they don't even want to hear that someone may have a better explanation. That might threaten their self-worth. As a consequence, they may not even want to deal with what other recommend!

Learners see what they want to see: It has been said that observing something tells you more about the observer than what is being observed. To a great extent, people project what they already have in their hands onto phenomena to be observed. They see what they want to see.

Learner often is not aware of what they know: Students are frequently not consciously aware of reasons (e.g., laws and theories) for their actions; they just innately know why they do things a certain way. Teaching and learning should begin by encouraging learners to express and clarify their pre-instructional conceptions.

Learners may not discover experts' conclusions: Because students will 'see what they want to see' it seems inappropriate for teachers to simply provide students with experiences and then expect them to discover planned conclusions, especially since it took scientists years to do so. Consequently, familiar 'inquiry', 'discovery' (and certain constructivist) practical activities (laps) are inappropriate. Students, invariably, 'discover' what is apparent to them; not necessarily, what would be apparent to a professional scientist or engineer. Accordingly, it is important for educators to carefully present ideas, skills, attitudes, etc. to students to which they want them to have access. Teachers must, therefore, take purposeful steps to get to see things in new ways. Moreover, learners deserve access to knowledge of different communities as knowledge is communally based. Learning should not be so conservative as to ignore knowledge and ways of knowing of different races, cultures and societies. In other words learning must be pluralist—rather than conformist.

Students need to know how to learn: Students may not know even if they have access to ideas and an urge to change, how to change their thinking. They may lack skills necessary to re-consider their ideas. They may not know how to think about their own ideas, how to learn new ones or how to decide what they believe. Therefore, as with conceptual change, students need others (often teachers) to introduce them to new skills; e.g., how to develop concept maps to exhibit ideas.

Students deserve the right to determine their beliefs: Scientists are never, because of the development, absolutely certain that their explanations are correct. There always is a possibility for change. Consequently, we could ask whether or not society (through teachers) has the right (or, even ability!) to change a student's beliefs. While getting students to understand new ideas may be (is) society's right and responsibility, forcing them to accept certain beliefs may be problematic. Should education be about convincing others or about enlightening others? Perhaps students deserve the right to determine their own beliefs in school settings and beyond. That may occur if students have opportunities to conduct scientific investigations and inventions project under their control.

Park (2001) has given following principles of Constructivist Learning Theory which may be very helpful for the teachers who want to situate their teaching and learning in constructivist settings:

- Knowledge and beliefs are constructed within the learner. Learners both *create* and *own* their knowledge. The kind of *ownership* discussed here relates to *pride of ownership*; the learner's ability to learn is reinforced with each discovery.
- Knowledge formation involves constructing meaning. Learning must be self-regulating; the learner must take control of the process and progress at his/her own level of competence. The problem space must not be over-prescribed; the learner must have the opportunity for discovery.
- Knowledge formation involves integration with prior knowledge. The integration process, itself, is rich in opportunity for new discoveries.
- Learning is a social process, greatly enhanced by shared experiences and shared memory.
- Learning involves reflection and metacognition. In order to form meanings, learners must reflect on their own methods of learning. Learners must also participate in the assessment of their own learning. Assessment must take into account alternative views and contexts.

- Learning outcomes are varied and often unpredictable. Individuals are likely to form meanings from experiences that are unique to and guided by their overall experience.

3.4 CONSTRUCTING KNOWLEDGE OF CONSTRUCTIVISM

Any structural or systemic change is unique in the sense that it brings with it a lot of challenges along with wonderful prospects provided people are ready to accept and implement it with right attitude and perspective. This is true with the recent changes that are taking place in the light of NCF-2005 which establishes the need to recognize the child as a natural learner, and knowledge as the outcome of the child's own activity. Very clearly it (the NCF-2005) asserts that there is an urgent need to have a fundamental change in how we think of learners and the process of learning. In other words, there is need to engage in detail with the underpinnings and implications of 'child-centred' education. More precisely, there is need to have 'child-centred' pedagogy means giving primacy to children's experiences, their voices, and their active participation. The learning plans therefore must respond to physical, cultural and social preferences within the wide diversity of characteristics and needs. Our school pedagogic practices, learning tasks, and the texts we create for learners, tend to focus on the socialization of children and on the 'receptive' features of children's learning. Instead, we need to nurture and build on their active and creative capabilities—their inherent interest in making meaning, in relating to the world in 'real' ways through acting on it and creating, and in relating to other humans. Learning is active and social in its character. The draft has highlighted that children's voices and experiences do not find expression in the classroom—often the only voice heard is that of the teacher when children speak, they are usually only answering the teacher's questions or repeating the teacher's words. They rarely do things, nor do they have opportunities to take initiative. The curriculum must enable children to find their voices, nurture their curiosity—to do things, to ask questions and to pursue investigations, sharing and integrating their experiences with school knowledge—rather than their ability to reproduce textual knowledge. Reorienting the curriculum to this end must be among our highest priorities, informing the preparation of teachers, the annual plans of schools, the design of textbooks, learning materials and teaching plans, and evaluation and examination patterns. It has again and again asserted that the teaching should be for the construction of knowledge. Conclusively we can say that it urges the teachers and the teacher educators to situate teaching and learning in a Constructivist Paradigm which is possible if we know how to construct knowledge of constructivism.

Now the question arises how to construct knowledge of constructivism? We are well acquainted with the fact that as educators, our practice is informed by the beliefs and personal theories that we hold about teaching, learning and knowledge. Beliefs about how we come to know, what it means to be a teacher or how students learn constitute our own 'philosophies' which are reflected in and guide our practice (Murphy). These beliefs may not be explicit in that we may never have actually articulated them. Nonetheless, if we stop to reflect on our practice, or especially if we try to explain our actions and behaviours, our beliefs surface and we become more aware of them. In becoming aware, we bring them to a more conscious level so that we can actually question, challenge, compare and communicate them or even replace them by new beliefs that we might consciously decide to embrace.

In short, thus, epistemological beliefs or beliefs about what constitutes knowledge and how we come to know are fundamental because they influence or provide a basis for our beliefs about teaching, learning and construction of knowledge and teaching. As Ernest (1998) argues, all practice and theories of learning and teaching rest on an epistemology, whether articulated or not. Thus, we as teachers and teacher educators need to bring change in our epistemological belief system if we really want to bring change in educational system for better prospects at all costs. Another important point is how to bring change in our role as educator. The role of the teacher is to engender learning by supporting the student in this construction process. A linear model might look like this:

Steps in the construction of knowledge	Supporting activity of the teacher
(a) Exposure to alternative perspectives.	Ensure alternative perspectives are accessible readily to students.
(b) Empathetic experience of entering into those perspectives for understanding.	Establish a conducive environment and encourage the student to empathetically enter the alternative perspectives.
(c) Understanding of the body of theory relating to the subject.	Provide access to the "conversation of the knowledge community".
(d) Evaluation of the alternatives through reflection and critical thinking.	Enable the social environment in which cognitive interactions and dialogic processes can evaluate the alternatives.
(e) Construction of a personal perspective, the matter that is learned.	Provide incentives to encourage learners to complete the knowledge construction process.

We all need to ask ourselves following questions if we are genuinely interested to construct knowledge of constructivism:

- How to acquaint with constructivist paradigm of teaching and learning as it will require a lot of learning and de-learning as well?
- Is there any formal agency to orient them if the Teacher-Educators are ready to adopt constructivist approach of teaching and learning?
- Supposing that there are such agencies then how to approach them for the necessary knowledge and education advocated by constructivism?
- How to procure variety of literature related with constructivism?

- How to be sure enough that the understanding one has developed on the basis of self-reading or self-learning is sufficient enough to be implemented in the actual classroom teaching and learning situation?
- How to convince the receiver i.e., students and their guardians that this paradigm of learning and teaching is better than the present paradigm i.e., behaviouristic paradigm of teaching and learning?
- How far will it be feasible to implement constructivist paradigm of teaching and learning in the actual classroom situation?
- What kind of assessment policy and practices will have to be adopted if there is complete adoption of constructivist paradigm of teaching and learning?
- How to integrate children's knowledge and the community's knowledge to which they belong to?
- How to integrate school knowledge and local knowledge?
- What strategies will they have to adopt in case of multiple interpretations?
- How to promote critical pedagogy (critical pedagogy provides an opportunity to reflect critically on issues in terms of their political, social, economic and moral aspects) inside and the outside classroom situation?
- What perspective change is required to view learning as a search for meaning out of personal experience, and knowledge generation as a continuously evolving process of reflective learning?
- What kind of attitudinal change is required to view knowledge not as an external reality embedded in textbooks, but as constructed in the shared context of teaching-learning and personal experience?

Challenges are many in kinds and types. Good thing about human potentiality is that the humans are capable to develop a strategy to overcome any challenge. International experiences indicate that there are strategies which are very successful if we educators situate ourselves in constructivist paradigm of teaching and learning. First and foremost need is to bring attitudinal change in ourselves only then the question of feasibility arises. Are we ready to construct knowledge of constructivism?

4

Constructivist Pedagogy

4.1 CONSTRUCTIVIST TEACHING—NATURE AND PROCESSES

In the traditional classroom the child is not permitted to use whole experiences or learn dynamically but is usually limited to narrow "active" processes: concentrating to pay attention and posing self-questions or creating mnemonics. Viewing traditional teaching from the child's point of view, classroom learning is mysterious, confusing and arbitrary. As Pechman (1992) notes, schools try to teach children to use the formal tools of academic disciplines—vocabulary, mathematical formulae, scientific procedures—lent many children find few opportunities outside of school to practice what they are taught. "The resulting inauthenticity of classroom activity makes it difficult for children to see how school learning applies to their lives."

In short, constructivists would not hesitate to pose the following as the state of much education today: The traditional classroom is dominated by teacher talk (Goodlad, 1984).

- Most teachers rely heavily on textbooks (Ben-Pertz, 1990).
- Most classrooms ask students to work individually, not cooperatively, and on relatively low-level skills.
- Students' thinking is devalued in most classrooms, except for finding the "right" answer.
- Most schooling is built on the premise that there is a fixed world that students must come to know. Mastery is valued over construction of new knowledge.

The constructivist approach to teaching is based on a combination of a subset of research within cognitive psychology and a subset of research within social psychology, just as behaviour modification techniques are based on operant conditioning theory within behavioural psychology. The basic premise that an individual learner must actively "build knowledge and skills" (Bruner, 1990) and that information exists within these built constructs rather than in the external environment. However, all advocates of constructivism agree that it is the individual's processing of stimuli from the environment and the resulting cognitive structures, which produce adaptive behaviour, rather than the stimuli themselves (Harnard, 1982).

In constructivist perspective, students are not blank slates upon which knowledge is etched. They come to learning situations with already formulated knowledge, ideas, and understandings. This previous knowledge is the raw material for the new knowledge they will create. The student is the person who creates new understanding for him/herself. The teacher coaches, moderates, suggests, but allows the students room to experiment, ask questions, and try things that don't work. Learning activities require the students' full participation (like hands-on experiments). An important part of the learning process is that students reflect on, and talk about their activities. Students also help set their own goals and means of assessment. Students control their own learning process, and they lead the way by reflecting on their experiences. This process makes them experts of their own learning. The teacher helps create situations where the students feel safe questioning and reflecting on their own processes, either privately or in group discussions. The teacher should also create activities that lead the student to reflect on his or her prior knowledge and experiences. Talking about what was learned and how it was learned is really important.

A constructivist teaching approach views learners as actively engaged in making meaning, and teaching with that approach looks for what students can analyze, investigate, collaborate, share, build and generate based on what they already know, rather than what facts, skills, and processes they can parrot. To do this effectively, a teacher needs to be a learner and a researcher, to strive for greater awareness of the environments and the participants in a given teaching situation in order to continually adjust their actions to engage students in learning, using constructivism as a referent (Dougiamas, 1998).

Some of the tenets of constructivism in pedagogical terms are following (Dougiamas, 1998):

- Students come to class with an established worldview formed by years of prior experience and learning.
- Even as it evolves, a student's worldview filters all experiences and affects their interpretation of observations.
- For students to change their worldview requires work.
- Students learn from each other as well as the teacher.
- Students learn better by doing.
- Allowing and creating opportunities for all to have a voice promotes the construction of new ideas.

As far as quality of student's education is concerned it is result of the school learning environment and the importance attached to education by the student and his/her family peers. Obviously, if students come prepared to learn, they will have a better experience, especially if most peers also value learning, but the environment must be conducive to learning through encouragement and support.

The changing environment of education can create complications, such as reconciling constructivism with such trends as outcomes based education—which is funded on the intention to define, design, deliver and document instruction and assessment in terms of intended outcomes. Outcomes can apparently be intermediate or minimal competencies (mastery) and developmental outcomes (integrated products). Thus, the emphasis is on mastery which contrasts sharply with constructivism. Outcomes-based education is employed to change schools, holds them accountable and monitor them based on expressed outcomes. Standards, even if, documented in "real-world" ways can be antagonistic to constructivism, depending upon the structure developed by the school curriculum.

In keeping with the definition of constructivism, Constructivist Teaching is teaching that allows students to "interpret" their experiences in class and try to make sense of them. There is no one single teaching methodology that is called "constructivist teaching". For example, constructivist teaching is not limited to discovery learning (where students learn through discovery) nor does it necessarily imply that lecturing cannot be part of constructivist teaching. It only implies the need to diagnose what is already in the student's mind (usually used to initiate instruction) and that the focus is on student learning rather than teacher teaching. In neither case does it does specify how.

Bruner provides the following principles of constructivist teaching:

1. Teaching (instruction) must be concerned with the experiences and contexts that make the student willing and able to learn (readiness).
2. Teaching (instruction) must be structured so that it can be easily grasped by the student (spiral organization).
3. Instruction should be designed to facilitate extrapolation and of fill in the gaps (going beyond the information given).

The constructivist view of teaching can point towards a number of different teaching practices and processes. In the most general sense, it usually means encouraging students to use active techniques (experiments, real-world problem-solving) to create more knowledge and then to reflect on and talk about what they are doing and how their understanding is changing. The teacher makes sure he/she understands the students' pre-existing conceptions, and guides the activity to address them and then build on them.

The main activity in constructivist settings is solving-problems. Students use inquiry methods to ask questions, investigate a topic, and use a variety of resources to find solutions and answers. As students explore the topic, they draw conclusions, and, as exploration continues, they revisit those conclusions. Exploration of questions leads to more questions. Constructivist learning is transferable. In constructivist perspective, students create organizing principles that they can take with them to other learning settings. Students learn to question things and to apply their natural curiosity to the world.

The constructivist teaching relies heavily on collaboration among students. There are many reasons why collaboration contributes to learning. The main reason it is used so much in constructivism is that students learn about learning not only from themselves, but also from their peers. When students review and reflect on their learning processes together, they can pick up strategies and methods from one another.

Constructivist teaching promotes social and communication skills by creating a kind of environment that emphasizes collaboration and exchange of ideas. In this mode of teaching, students get an opportunity to learn how to articulate their ideas clearly as well as to collaborate on tasks effectively by sharing in group projects. Thus, this teaching advocates that the students must therefore exchange ideas and so must learn to "negotiate" with others and to evaluate their contributions in a socially acceptable manner. This is essential to get success in the real world, since they will always be exposed to a variety of experiences in which they will have to cooperate and navigate among the ideas of others.

Constructivist teaching practice expects a classroom teacher that he/she must be in a position to: (1) Influence or create motivating conditions for students, (2) Take responsibility for creating problem situations,... (3) Foster acquisition and retrieval of prior knowledge..., and (4) Create a social environment that emphasizes that attitude of learning to learn.... The learning process not the product of learning is the primary focus of constructivism..." (Olsen, 1999). The constructivist teacher has to guide and not tell. The student has to make their own meanings and decisions. They are not to be handed to them by the teacher. To facilitate real learning, teachers need to organize their classroom and their curriculum so that students can collaborate, interact, and raise questions of both classmates and the teacher.

The whole idea of a constructivist teaching is characterized by the mutual respect between the teacher and the children. In most classrooms the respect is one way. The children have to respect the teacher. A constructivist teacher must respect the children by allowing the children rights to their feelings, ideas, and opinions. The teacher must refrain from using their power unnecessarily. A characteristic of constructivist teaching is that the responsibility for decision-making is shared by everyone in the classroom (de Vries & Zan, 1995).

As far as teaching processes are concerned, constructivist methodology: (1) emphasizes the learner's role in the education process—the more active the role, the better; (2) focuses student attention on pursuing questions or problems that occur to them rather than on answers supplied by a teacher or expert text; (3) focuses teacher attention on the creation of learning environments rich in "construction materials" rather than in creating good information delivery system; (4) emphasizes activity-based or project-based learning.

Teaching methods based on constructivist view are very useful to help students' learning. The following are practices which can help students understand, recall and apply essential information, concepts and skills. They are used to make lessons relevant, activate students' prior knowledge, help elaborate and organize information, and encourage questioning. Important concepts from this perspective are (Slavin, 1994):

1. Advanced Organizers: General statements given before instruction that relate new information to existing knowledge to help students process new information by activating background knowledge, suggesting relevance, and encouraging accommodation;
2. Analogies: Pointing out the similarities between things that are otherwise unlike, to help students learn new information by relating it to concepts they already have;
3. Elaboration: The process of thinking about new material in a way that helps to connect it with existing knowledge.

Welson & Cole (1991) have provided a description of teaching models which "embody" constructivist concepts of teaching. From these descriptions, we can isolate some concepts central to constructivist design, teaching and learning:

1. Embed learning in a rich authentic problem-solving environment;
2. Provide for authentic versus academic contexts for learning;
3. Provide for learner control;
4. Use errors as a mechanism to provide feedback on learner understanding.

Constructivism as a philosophy of teaching would cause a teacher to provide experiences where students can create their own meaning, rather than lecturing and drilling students is specific facts and skills. A prime example of constructivism is in letting students read widely of their own literature selections from a rich array. Constructivist teachers would not see the need to ask students to answer ten questions at the end of each book, because they would trust if the students are reading, they are understanding, because they are bringing meaning to their activity. Their learning is far beyond our ability to test with narrow measures. Constructivist teachers believe in the child's desire to learn a rich nurturing learning environment. Free play in a well-stocked kindergarten environment is a good example of this philosophy at work.

Constructivist teaching help students make and implement plans, and evaluate their own progress. Following six principles of learning are consistent with constructivist thought:

1. Teachers need to find content that is important to children? Kids want to know!
2. We should put skills like reading, writing and maths in a content where they are needed, rather than on drill-and-kill worksheets or for tests.
3. We need to help children connect their learning to their lives and understanding.
4. We should try to engage children in active processes of discovery, experimentation, discussion, prediction and inquiry.

5. We should allow and encourage children to represent their learning in many ways (graphically, artistically, musically, physically, etc.).
6. We need to provide a scholastic community of support, not criticism from teachers and other students (Dalton & Watson, 1997).

Time and again, majority of constructivists have re-emphasized that constructivism is a theory of knowledge acquisition, not a theory of pedagogy. Constructivism posits that knowledge acquisition occurs amid four assumptions:

1. Knowledge involves active cognizing by the individual.
2. Knowledge is adaptive, facilitating individual and social efficacy.
3. Knowledge is subjective and self-organized, not objective.
4. Knowledge acquisition involves both socio-cultural and individual processes.

These four assumptions have led, indirectly, to eight primary pedagogical recommendations:

1. Learning should take place in authentic and real-world environments.
2. Learning should involve social negotiation and mediation.
3. Content and skills should be made relevant to the learner.
4. Content and skills should be understood within the framework of the learner's prior knowledge.
5. Students should be assessed formatively, serving to inform future learning experiences.
6. Students should be encouraged to become self-regulatory, self-mediated, and self-aware.
7. Teachers serve primarily as guides and facilitators of learning, not instructors.

8. Teachers should provide for and encourage multiple perspectives and representations of content.

In the end, Driscoll (1994) also has defined five constructivist characteristics that should form the pedagogical foundation for designing learning:

1. Provide complex learning environments that incorporate authentic activity.
2. Provide for social negotiation as an integral part of learning.
3. Juxtapose instructional content and include multiple modes of representation.
4. Nurture reflexivity (reflect on learning).
5. Emphasize student-centred instruction.

In the light of above discussion, the striking point is that in constructivist teaching the most important point is matching teaching style to student learning style.

4.2 CONSTRUCTIVIST PRINCIPLES OF TEACHING

It is important to realize that the constructivist approach borrows from many other practices in the pursuit of its primary goal; helping students learn *How to Learn*. Here are some of the core ideas, partly based on the analysis of Taber (2006) that may be helpful for us to understand the constructivist principles of teaching:

1. Knowledge is actively constructed by the learner, not passively received from the outside. Learning is something done by the learner, not something that is imposed on the learner.
2. Learners come to the learning situation (in science, etc.) with existing ideas about many phenomena. Some of these ideas are *ad hoc* and unstable; others are more deeply rooted and well developed.
3. Learners have their own individual ideas about the world, but there are also many similarities and common patterns in their ideas. Some of these ideas are socially and culturally accepted and shared, and they are often

part of the language, supported by metaphors, etc. They also often function well as tools to understand many phenomena.

4. These ideas are often at odds with accepted scientific ideas, and some of them may be persistent and hard to change.
5. Knowledge is represented in the brain as conceptual structures, and it is possible to model and describe these in some detail.
6. Teaching has to take the learner's existing ideas seriously if they want to change or challenge these.
7. Although knowledge in one sense is personal and individual, the learners construct their knowledge through their interaction with the physical world, collaboratively in social settings and in a cultural and linguistic environment. (The relative stress on such factors account for the different 'versions' of constructivism earlier alluded to.)

For pedagogic purposes, the tenets of constructivist principles of teaching can be rephrased as follows:

- Students come into our classrooms with an established worldview, formed by years of prior experience and learning.
- Even as it evolves, a student's worldview filters all experiences and affects their interpretation of observations.
- Students are emotionally attached to their worldviews and will not give up their worldviews easily.
- Challenging, revising, and restructuring one's worldview requires much effort.

Duffy and Kirkley (2004) explained methods for applying constructivist teaching principles to design learner-centred online education: The primary pedagogical goals for constructivist learning environments as identified by Duffy and Kirkley are:

1. "Engage the student in inquiry that will lead to the students' useful understanding of the concepts and skills identified in the course objectives."
2. "Provide structure and support to the learners as they engage in goal-oriented inquiry and problem-solving."
3. "Facilitate interaction, collaboration, and a community-based learning environment."
4. "Design an assessment system that is performance oriented, calling for a demonstration of useful understanding."
5. "Promote transfer of knowledge to other contexts through reflective activities and diverse experiences."

In their book *A Case for Constructivist Classroom*, J.G. Brooks & M.G. Brooks state twelve principles essential to constructivist teaching:

1. Encouragement and acceptance of student autonomy and initiative.
2. Utilization of raw data and primary sources along with manipulative, interactive and physical materials.
3. When planning, teachers use cognitive terminology such as "classify", "analyze", and "create".
4. Allowance of student responses to drive lessons shift instructional strategies and alter content.
5. Inquiry concerning students' understanding of concept before sharing their own understanding of those concepts.
6. Encouragement of students to engage in dialogue, both with the teacher and with one another.
7. Encouragement of student's inquiry by asking thoughtful, open-ended questions and encouraging students to ask questions of each other.
8. Pursuit of elaboration of students' initial responses.
9. Engagement of students in experiences that might engender contradictions to their initial hypotheses and then encourage discussion.

10. Allowance for wait time after posing questions.
11. Providing time for students to construct relationships and create metaphors.
12. Nurturing students' natural curiosity through frequent use of the learning cycle model.

On the basis of above stated constructivist principles of teaching we educators can design our teaching instructions and teaching strategies as per the need.

4.3 CONSTRUCTIVIST NOTION OF A TEACHER

A constructivist teacher creates a context for learning in which students can become engaged in interesting activities that encourages and facilitates learning. The teacher does not simply stand by, however, and watch children explore and discover. Instead, the teacher may often guide students as they approach problems, may encourage them to work in groups to think about issues and questions, and support them with encouragement and advice as they tackle problems, adventures, and challenges that are rooted in real life situations that are both interesting to the students and satisfying in terms of the result of their work. Teachers thus facilitate cognitive growth and learning as do peers and other members of the child's community.

Constructivist teachers encourage students to constantly assess how the activity is helping them gain understanding. By questioning themselves and their strategies, students in the constructivist classroom ideally become "expert learners". This gives them ever-broadening tools to keep learning with a well-planned classroom environment, the students learn how to learn.

The teacher might look at it as a spiral. When they continuously reflect on their experiences, students find their ideas gaining in complexity and power, and they develop increasingly strong abilities to integrate new information. One of the teacher's main roles becomes to encourage this learning and reflection process.

For example: Groups of students in a science class are discussing a problem in physics. Though the teacher knows the "answer" to the problem, he or she focuses on helping students restate their questions in useful ways. He or she prompts each student to reflect on and examine his or her current knowledge. When one of the students comes up with the relevant concept, the teacher seizes upon it, and indicates to the group that this might be a fruitful avenue for them to explore. They design and perform relevant experiments. Afterward, the students and teacher talk about what they have learned, and how their observations and experiments helped (or did not help) them to better understand the concept.

All the constructivist thinkers have felt that the teacher was a very vital part of the theory. A constructivist teacher sets up problems and monitors student's exploration, guides the direction of student inquiry and promotes new patterns of thinking (Brooks & Brooks, 1995). It is up to the teacher to facilitate the constructivist learning process. The structure of the learning environment should promote opportunities and events that encourage and support the process of understanding.

In a classroom where the teacher asks a question to the students and hands fly up excitedly because the student feels that they know the answer. The teacher then looks around the room and chooses a student. The student answers, and the teacher says, "No". The teacher then calls on another student who answers and the teacher says, "close but not quite". The teacher then proceeds to call on a third student who answers and then teacher replies, "Yes, that is the right answer!"

The teacher conveys many lessons to the students by conducting his/her classroom in this manner. The students now know that there is one answer to the teacher's questions and they have to find that one right answer. Another thing is that the students now know that they put themselves at risk if they raise their hand, unless they are certain that they have to right answer. The teacher should respond to the student's answers by saying, "I never thought of it that way" or "That is a creative way of looking at it."

The teacher's response "no" causes the students to feel foolish. The teacher needs to encourage the student and support them. This is the idea of constructivism and what it means to be a constructivist teacher. The purpose of a constructivist teacher is to make the students think for themselves, and not to wait for the teacher to tell them what to think. In traditional classrooms the teacher seeks the correct answer to validate student learning, whereas in a constructivist classroom the teacher seeks the students' point of view (Brooks & Brooks, 1999). The students will learn to proceed with less focus and direction from the teacher. With a constructivist teacher the students can express their own ideas clearly in their own words and not have to respond restricted question.

Contrary to criticism by some educators, constructivism does not dismiss the active role of the teacher or the value of expert knowledge. Constructivism modifies the role, so that teachers help students to construct knowledge rather than to reproduce a series of facts. The constructivist teacher provides tool such as problem-solving and inquiry-based learning activities with which students formulate and test their ideas, draw conclusions and inferences, and pool and convey their knowledge in a collaborative learning environment. The teacher functions more as a facilitator who coaches, mediates, prompts and helps students develop and assess their understanding and thereby their learning. One of the teacher's biggest jobs becomes *Asking Good Questions.*

According to constructivist notion of teachers they may:

- Prompt students to formulate their own questions (inquiry).
- Allow multiple interpretations and expressions of learning (multiple intelligence).
- Encourage group work and the use of peers as resources (collaborative learning).
- Encourage and accept student autonomy and initiative.
- Allow student responses to drive lessons, shift instructional strategies and other content.

- Inquire about students' understandings of concepts before sharing their own understandings of those concepts.
- Encourage students to engage in dialogue both with the teacher and with one another.
- Encourage students' inquiry by asking throughout, open-ended questions and encouraging students to ask questions of each other.
- Seek elaborate of students' initial responses.
- Engage students in experiences that might engender contradictions to their initial hypotheses and then encourage discussion.
- Allow a waiting time after posing questions.
- Nurture students' natural curiosity through frequent use of the learning cycle model (Brooks & Brooks, 1993).

There is a growing recognition that effective teachers are people who are becoming guides on the side requires expertise with group work, performance tasks, reflective activities and a variety of teaching strategies that most of us did not observe when we were students, and most of the teachers have not been taught to teach.

It is found that teachers who are comfortable with one of the strategies required to conduct a learner centred classroom (cooperative learning, performance tasks authentic assessment, journaling, etc.), they always have the same story to tell: they have worked at least three years to achieve a comfort level with the strategy, they had someone as a collaborator (a friend, spouse, or teacher down the hall), they gradually changed their approach to teaching, it did not happen over night, and there was a great deal of trial and error.

To have success with a constructivist classroom activity, it is important for the teacher to be a good facilitator. The teacher should encourage the students to make discoveries for themselves while conducting active dialogue. For conceptual learning to occur, the teacher should seek to fuse the constructions of students and experts. By comparing and contrasting their constructions with experts' constructions, the students gain insights into both and begin to reconceptualize their constructions in the direction of those of the experts (Zahorik, 1997).

Pat Flynn, Don Mesibov, Paul Vermette and Mike Smith suggest that teachers must think of lessons as a two-step process based on "Two-Step" model which is based on three simple concepts:

1. Student engagement with information must precede teacher explanations.
2. Instruction (guidance) should come in the form of interventions as students engage with information, ideas and concepts.
3. Authentic tools create an environment for student engagement and teacher interventions.

Exploration must be followed by discovery. In the discovery phase the teacher engages students in an authentic task that enables them to demonstrate mastery of the learning objectives of the lesson. In the exploratory phase, the teacher grabs the learners' attention, activates their prior knowledge, and motivates students to engage in the authentic task that will be the focus of the discovery phase.

4.4 DESIGNING THE CLASSROOM IN A CONSTRUCTIVIST SETTING

Let us begin with a comparison between the traditional classroom and constructivist classroom:

Traditional Classroom	Constructivist Classroom
1. Curriculum begins with the parts of the whole. Emphasizes basic skills.	1. Curriculum emphasizes by concepts, beginning with the whole and expanding to include the parts.
2. Strict adherence to fixed curriculum is highly valued.	2. Pursuit of students' questions and interests is valued.
3. Materials are primarily text-books and workbooks.	3. Materials include primary source of material and manipulative materials.

(Contd.)

4. Learning is based on repetition.	4. Learning is interactive, building on what the student already knows.
5. Teachers disseminate information to students; students are recipients of knowledge.	5. Teachers have a dialogue with students, helping students construct their own knowledge.
6. Teacher's role is directive, rooted in authority.	6. Teacher's role is interactive, rooted in negotiation.
7. Assessment is through testing, correct answers.	7. Assessment includes student works, observations and points of view, as well as tests. Process is as important as product.
8. Knowledge is seen as inert.	8. Knowledge is seen as dynamic, ever changing with our experiences.
9. Students work primarily alone.	9. Students work primarily in groups.

From the above table it is clear that in the constructivist classroom, the focus tends to shift from the teacher to the students. The classroom is no longer a place where the teacher ("experts") pours knowledge into passive students, who wait like empty vessels to be filed. In the constructivist model, the students are urged to be actively involved in their own process of learning. The teacher functions more as a facilitator who coaches, mediates, prompts and helps students develop and assess their understanding, and thereby their learning. One of the teacher's biggest jobs becomes *Asking Good Questions*.

And, in the constructivist classroom, both teacher and students think of knowledge not as inert factoids to be memorized, but as a dynamic, ever-changing view of the world we live in and the ability to successfully stretch and explore that view.

The constructivist classroom relies heavily on collaboration among students. There are many reasons why collaboration contributes to learning. The main reason it is used so much in constructivism is that students learn about learning not only from themselves, but also from their peers. When students review and reflect on their learning processes together, they can pick up strategies and methods from one another.

The main activity in a constructivist classroom is solving-problems. Students use inquiry methods to ask questions, investigate a topic, and use a variety of resources to find solutions and answers. As students explore the topic, they draw conclusions, and, as exploration continues, they revisit those conclusions. Exploration of questions leads to more questions.

Students control their own learning process, and they lead the way by reflecting on their experiences. This process makes them experts of their own learning. The teacher helps create situations where the students feel safe questioning and reflecting on their own processes, either privately or in group discussions. The teacher should also create activities that lead the student to reflect on his or her prior knowledge and experiences. Talking about what was learned and how it was learned is really important. Now, let us turn to the four critical components of a constructivist classroom:

a. It's about constructing knowledge not receiving it; each of us constructs our own learning based on our past experiences;
b. It's about thinking and analysing, not accumulating and memorizing information; they use the content not memorize it;
c. It's about understanding and applying, not repeating back;
d. It's about being active, not passive.

All classrooms in which instructional strategies compatible with constructivist approach are used don't necessarily look alike. The activities and the format can vary considerably. The students can construct new knowledge and relate new knowledge to prior knowledge through interacting with others. In general, four principles are applied in any constructivist classroom (Chen, 1997):

1. Learning and development is a social, collaborative activity.
2. The Zone of Proximal Development can serve as a guide for curricular and lesson planning.
3. School learning should occur in a meaningful context and not be separated from learning and knowledge children develop in the "real world".

4. Out-of-school experiences should be related to the child's school experience.

One of the basic tenets of constructivism is that students learn by doing rather than observing. Students bring prior knowledge into a learning situation in which they must critique and re-evaluate their understanding of it. This process of interpretation, articulation and re-evaluation is repeated until they can demonstrate their comprehension of the subject. Constructivism often utilizes collaboration and peer criticism as a way of provoking students to reach a new level of understanding. Active practice is the key of constructivist lesson.

The constructivist teacher sets up problems and monitors student exploration, guides the direction of student inquiry and promotes new patterns of thinking. Classes can take unexpected turns as students are given the autonomy to direct their own explorations. Constructivist teachers refer to new data, primary sources and interactive materials to provide experiences for their students rather than relying solely on another's set of data. For teachers who have used only one printed text, a shift to other sources may take some adjustment. For example, rather than read about the census, students examine and interpret census data. Or better yet, they plan a mini-census, gather their own data, and interpret the results.

Students represent a rich array of different backgrounds and ways of thinking. Myths, taboos, and things we learn from our families, friends and teachers—all are part of cultural influence. Context is embedded in culture and it is difficult to separate the two. When presented with information in the classroom that contradicts existing ideas, a student may try to accommodate both interpretations, rather than change deeply held beliefs. Unless the teacher realizes what views the students hold, classroom teaching can actively help students constructs faculty ideas.

If the classroom can provide a natural zone where students exchange their personal views and test them against the ideas of others, each student can continue to build understanding based on empirical evidence. Hands-on activities and observations of the natural world provide shared experiences for those constructions. For example, to study the phases of the moon, the class could keep an observational log of the moon and its shape in the sky for several weeks. Small groups discuss the various observations and speculate about their meanings. If models, text references, or illustrations are available as resources students could know that these are the results of others' observations and speculations. Such references are actually the construction by others of the current understanding of the world around us.

Just as students do not easily let go off their ideas, neither do school boards, principles, parents or for that matter, teachers. Ideas like student autonomy and learner-driven inquiry are not easily accepted. Required course content and externally applied assessments are realities that teachers must accommodate. A teacher inspired to change to constructivist instruction must incorporate those realities into his/her approach. He or she might begin gradually, turning on one or two constructivist explorations in the regular curriculum. Listening to students as they discuss ideas together is a good way to start shifting the balance of responsibility to the learners. Another step is using primary sources and raw data as the basis of inquiry, rather than relying solely on the text.

If students begin thinking about accumulated knowledge as an evolving explanation of natural phenomena, their questions can take on an exciting dimension. In the coming decades, research will change the way most of the accepted facts of today are perceived. Our challenge is to foster students' abilities so they can continue to learn and build their understanding based on the changing world around them.

Brooks and Brooks have suggested the following measures to design the classroom in constructivist setting (Brooks & Brooks, 1993):

1. Student autonomy and initiative are accepted and encouraged or students are encouraged to take initiative and take ownership for their own learning, thereby developing their own intellectual identity: By respecting students' ideas and encouraging independent thinking,

teachers help students attain their own intellectual identity. Students who frame questions and issues and then go about analyzing and answering them take responsibility for their own learning and become problem-solvers.

a. Students' ideas are respected.

b. Independent thinking is encouraged.

c. Students develop questions and identify issues, then gather and analyze information to create their own answers.

2. The teacher asks open-ended questions and allows wait time for responses: Reflective thought takes time and is often built on others' ideas and comments, the ways teachers ask questions and success of student inquiry.

   a. What time is allowed—it takes time to reflect and build on the ideas of others.

   b. Higher level thinking is encouraged.

3. Higher level thinking is encouraged or students are challenged to reach beyond factual answers: The constructivist teacher challenges students to reach beyond the simple factual response. He encourages students to connect and summarize concepts by analyzing, predicting, justifying and defending their ideas.

   a. Students are encouraged to connect and summarize concepts by analyzing, predicting, justifying and defending their ideas.

4. Students are engaged in dialogue with the teacher and with each other: Social discourse helps students change or reinforce their ideas. If they have the chance to represent what they think and hear others' ideas, students can build a personal knowledge base that they understand. Only when they feel comfortable enough to express their ideas will meaningful classroom dialogue occur.

a. Discussion helps students reflect on their ideas and either change or reinforce them.
b. Sharing their own ideas and listening to the ideas of others helps students construct their own knowledge.
c. The classroom environment must be comfortable and non-threatening to allow meaningful dialogue.

5. Students are engaged in experience that challenge hypotheses and encourage discussion or opportunities are provided for students to test hypotheses: When allowed to make predictions, students often generate varying hypotheses about natural phenomena. The constructivist teacher provides ample opportunities for students to test their hypotheses, especially through group discussion of concrete experiences.
   a. Discussion of concrete experience is encouraged.
   b. Students are engaged in experiences that challenge hypotheses and encourage discussion.
6. The class uses raw data, primary sources, manipulations, physical and interactive materials or students are involved in real-world situations from which they can generate abstract concepts: The constructivist approach involves students in real-world possibilities, and then helps them generate the abstractions that bind phenomena together.
   a. Students use raw data and primary sources.
   b. Students have access to manipulative and interactive materials.

Let us discusses some of the key points (KP) of constructivist classroom one by one with suitable examples:

(KP-1): In a constructivist classroom, learning is constructed. Students are not blank sheets upon which knowledge is etched. They come to learning situations with already formulated knowledge, ideas and understandings. This previous knowledge is the raw material for the new knowledge they will create.

Example: An elementary school teacher may present a class problem to measure the length of a Maize Plant. Rather than starting the problem by introducing the ruler, the teacher should allow students to reflect and to construct their own methods of measurement. One student may offer the knowledge that his mother said he is four feet tall. Another may say she knows things are measured by hands too. The students may discuss these and other methods they have heard about, and decide on one to apply to the problem.

(KP-2): The student is the person who creates new understanding for him or herself. The teacher coaches, moderates and suggests. But allows the students' room to experiment, ask questions, tries things that don't work. Learning activities require the students' full participation (hands-on experiments). An important part of the learning process is that students reflect on and talk about, their activities. Students help set their own goals and means of assessment.

Examples: A language teacher may set aside time each week for a writing exercise. The emphasis should be on content and getting ideas down rather than memorizing grammatical rules, though one of the teacher's concerns may be the ability of his or her students to express themselves well through written language. The teacher may provide opportunities for students to examine the finished and earlier drafts of various authors. He or she may allow the students to select and create projects within the general requirements of building a portfolio. Students serve as peer editors who value originally and uniqueness rather than the best way to fulfil an assignment.

(KP-3): Constructivism believes that the students control their own learning process, and they lead the way by reflecting on their experiences. This process makes them experts of their own learning. The teacher helps create situations where the students feel safe questioning and reflecting on their own processes, either privately or in group discussions. The teacher should also create activities that lead the student to reflect on his or her prior knowledge and experiences. Talking about what was learnt and how it was learnt is really important. Thus, the teacher should ask the student to maintain a class-diary where they should be asked to record how they felt about the class projects, the reactions of others to the projects and how they felt their own writing had changed. Periodically the teacher should read the class-diary and hold a meeting with the students where the two assess: (1) what new knowledge the student has created; (2) how the student learns best; and (3) the learning environment and the teacher's role in it.

(KP-4): The constructivist classroom relies heavily on collaboration among students. There are many reasons why collaboration contributes to learning. The main reason it is used so much in constructivism is that students learn about learning not only from themselves, but also from their peers. When students review and reflect on their learning process together, they can pick up strategies and methods from one another.

Example: In the course of studying ancient civilizations, students may be asked to undertake an archaeological dig. As the students find different objects, the teacher introduces classifying techniques. The students should be encouraged to (1) set up a group by developing criteria and choosing which objects should belong and (2) collaborate with other students who worked in different quadrants of the dig. Each group may then be asked to develop theories about the civilizations that inhabited the area.

(KP-5): The main activity in a constructivist classroom is solving problems. Students use inquiry methods to ask questions, investigate a topic, and use a variety of resources to find solutions and answers, they resist those conclusions. Exploration of questions leads to more questions.

Example: Students may be asked to figure out how to purify water. The investigation solutions may range from filter paper, to a stove-top distillation apparatus, to piles of charcoal, to an abstract mathematical solution based on the size of a water molecule. Depending upon students' responses, the teacher should encourage abstract as well as practical, creations of new knowledge.

(KP-6): Students have ideas that they may later see that they were invalid, incorrect or insufficient to explain new experiences.

These ideas are temporary steps in the integration of knowledge. For instance, a child may believe that all trees lose their leaves in the fall, until he or she visits an evergreen forest. Constructivist teaching takes into account students' current conceptions and builds from there.

(KP-7): What happens when a student gets a new piece of information? The constructivist model says that the student compares the information to the knowledge and understanding he or she already has, and one of three things can occur:

- The new information matches up with his previous knowledge pretty well (it's consonant with the previous knowledge), so the student adds it to his understanding. It may take some work, but it's just a matter of finding the right fit, as with a puzzle piece.
- The information doesn't match previous knowledge (it's dissonant). The student has to change his or her previous understanding to find a fit for the information. This can be harder work.
- The information doesn't match previous knowledge, and it is ignored. Rejected bits of information may just not be absorbed by the student. Or they may float around; waiting for the day when the student understanding has developed and permits a fit.

Wiske (1994) describes how teaching for deep understanding changes the rules in the classroom, especially how the intellectual property of the classroom can be best utilized. She says: "Understanding is not a private possession to be protected from theft, but rather a capacity to be developed through the free exchange of ideas."

Using the Teaching for Understanding framework, Wiske (1994) makes note of shifting roles and responsibilities in a classroom dedicated to emphasizing understanding. First and foremost, the lines between the teacher and the learner become blurred, and at times the roles are reversed. This provides an opportunity for students to demonstrate their skills to a wider audience, and the teacher to acknowledge individual's scholastic capabilities in a different light than might normally occur. Role reversal opportunity should be provided at the schools. This can be done by asking students to become teachers and discharge the duty of teachers. Also, the teacher must be willing to share what Wiske (1994) refers to as intellectual authority. Instead of the objective knowledge base and commensurate power residing strictly with the teacher, intellectual authority is shared under this framework, leading to respect, consideration, and empowerment for both teachers and students.

In Wiske's (1994) words: "Certainly teachers must not abandon their authority, which derives legitimately from the knowledge of subject matter and their responsibility for guiding students. But they must encourage students to develop their own ways of exercising authority. In short, teachers must be in authority, without being authoritarian."

Wiske (1994) uses the metaphor of the key of knowledge being granted to every student by simply "leaving the door (to knowledge) unlocked". In this fashion, we can create an open atmosphere for learning that provides for guidance and assistance, yet celebrates students' intrinsic value and autonomy (Brooks & Brooks, 1996).

"Creating a constructivist classroom requires that the classroom teacher must be in a position to: (1) Influence or create motivating conditions for students, (2) Take responsibility for creating problem situations, (3) Foster acquisition and retrieval of prior knowledge, and (4) Create a social environment that emphasizes that attitude of learning to learn. The learning process not the product of learning is the primary focus of constructivism" (Olsen, 1999). The constructivist teacher has to guide and not tell. The student has to make their own meanings and decisions. They are not to be handed to them by the teacher. To facilitate real learning, teachers need to organize their classroom and their curriculum so that students can collaborate, interact and raise questions of both classmates and the teacher.

The whole idea of a constructivist classroom is characterized by the mutual respect between the teacher and the children. In most classrooms the respect is one way. The children have to respect the teacher. A constructivist teacher respects the children by allowing the children rights to their feelings, ideas and opinions. The teacher refrains from using their power unnecessarily. A characteristic of constructivist education is that the responsibility for decision-making is shared by everyone in the classroom (de Vries & Zan, 1995).

In the classroom, the constructivist view of learning can point towards a number of different teaching practices. In the most general sense, it usually means encouraging students to use active techniques (experiments, real-world problem-solving) to create more knowledge and then to reflect on and talked about what they are doing and how their understanding is changing. The teacher makes sure he/she understands the students' pre-existing conceptions, and guides the activity to address them and then build on them.

With regard to classroom practices, constructivism also owes a substantial debt to the new social studies recommendations. Emphasizing open-ended questions, student-centred inquiry, and primary source materials, these reforms foreshadowed many of the ideas and techniques of the constructivist movement.

In a constructivist classroom, the focus is on how individual students accommodate information into their existing mental schemata. They are challenged to reorganize their cognitive world to account for new experiences. They embrace problems as their own, use prior knowledge as a starting point, accommodate new information and construct tentative solutions by integrating old and new knowledge together. Learning is anchored around "big ideas" that can be generalized across experiences. Instead of focusing on discrete pieces of data and collections of facts, students conceptualize in a more global sense. Facts and information are not merely memorized and reproduced, rather they are used as tools to form generalizations and understandings with greater meaning. Students pursue open-ended investigations and generate several possible solutions or explanations to a problem, which may be expressed as concepts or generalizations. They actively question and interpret materials to develop conceptual understandings. In such a setting, student "learning is deeper, more comprehensive and longer lasting". In such an environment the classroom teacher is both a facilitator of inquiry and a facilitator of knowledge. As Steffe and Gale have pointed out, "From a didactic perspective, a teacher is a presenter of knowledge. From a discovery perspective, he or she is simply a provider of experiences." In a constructivist approach, both these functions are combined.

Twenty Indicators of Constructivist Practice which include:

1. Students often work individually answering questions.
2. Students often do hand-on/laboratory activities.
3. Students often work on projects that take a week or more.
4. Students often write a journal/diary in which they record their learning experiences.
5. Students often suggest or help plan classroom activities.
6. Students often work in small groups to come up with a solution.
7. Students work on problems for which there is no solution.
8. Students often write an essay explaining their thoughts.
9. Students often hold a debate and argue for a point of view.
10. Students often have to design their own problems to solve.
11. Students often decide on their own procedures for solving problems.
12. Students often assess their own work on an assignment.
13. Students often have to represent the same relationship in more than one way.
14. Students often make a product that will be used by someone else.

15. Students often demonstrate their work to an audience.
16. Students often have tasks for which there is no correct answer.
17. Teacher does not often lead a whole-class discussion.
18. Students often lead a discussion or give a presentation.
19. Students do not often work on their own on assignments at their desks.
20. Students often work together in small groups to complete assignments.

Although most constructivist classrooms feature active, social and creative learning, different kinds of knowledge invite different constructivist responses, not one standard constructivist approach (David Spencer, 2000). How can a teacher create appropriate targeted constructivist responses to learners' difficulties? One approach to the challenge recognizes that different kinds of knowledge—inert, ritual, conceptually difficult, and foreign —are likely to prove troublesome for learners in different ways (Perkins, 1999). Inert knowledge is that knowledge that is hidden and not easily applied to everyday experiences. Ritual knowledge is that which is applied without forethought and concern for context. Conceptually difficult knowledge is that which is distant from most experience and therefore difficult to place in context. Foreign knowledge is difficult to accept in time or place such as history or culture. Each type of knowledge is best acquired by different approaches to construction.

In 1991 Wheatley proposed a model of constructivist teaching using the problem centred learning approach. Wheatley (1991) quotes Kozmetsky (1980) stating that "each student must be encouraged to build his/her own conceptual constructs that will permit the ordering of knowledge into useful problem-solving schema". Then Wheatley proposed that the teacher's role is to "provide stimulating and motivational experiences through negotiation and act as a guide in the building of personalized schema".

Wheatley's (1991) problem centred learning approach has three components: tasks, groups, and sharing. The model is a simple one to follow. Wheatley (1991) suggests that "in preparation for a class a teacher selects tasks which have a high probability of being problematical for students—tasks which may cause students to find a problem. Secondly, the students work on these tasks in small groups. During the time the teacher attempts to convey collaborative work as a goal. Finally, the class is convened as a whole for a time of sharing." Wheatley (1991) then goes in further detail of the selection of tasks being based upon student beliefs and that the tasks should contain the following ten attributes:

1. Be accessible to everyone at the start.
2. Invite students to make decisions.
3. Encourage "what if" questions.
4. Encourage students to use their own methods.
5. Promote discussion and communication.
6. Be replete with patterns.
7. Lead somewhere.
8. Have an element of surprise.
9. Be enjoyable.
10. Be extendable.

While the students are working together on the problem, the elements of cooperative learning as outlined by Johnson and Johnson (1987) should be taken into consideration including Positive interdependence, Face to face interaction, Individual accountability, and the Appropriate use of interpersonal and small group skills. After the children have had an opportunity to explore the problem for about 25 minutes, Wheatley (1991) suggests that the teacher lead the class in a discussion in which each of the groups present their solution methods, inventions, and insights. It is important for the teacher to maintain a neutral stance during this session and to not correct any "wrong" answers, but allowing the students to discuss them. The sharing both models and promotes higher level thinking and reasoning skills and often leads the students to further "conversations" and thinking in their own heads.

Wheatley's (1991) problem centred approach to learning is a simple and open-ended approach to learning which many teachers already use or could adapt current curriculum to fit within. The bonuses of Wheatley's model are the metacognitive skills in understanding how one solves problems as compared with others in the classroom. Wheatley's model is also open to any subject or content desired by the practitioner.

Another approach to pedagogy, but more specifically related to science education is Saunders' (1992) four step approach. Saunders (1992) states that in being a constructivist in science education does have implications and that the implications lead to a certain approach to teaching science. His first step is to organize hands-on investigative labs. These are problem centred and differ from the traditional "recipe" labs in that there are no prescribed methods or procedures to solving the problem or exploring the phenomena. Saunders (1992) states that in using the inquiry approach, that the students must utilize their own schema to formulate expectations about what is likely to be observed.

The second implication is that there is active cognitive involvement. This is in contrast to the passive learning that takes place in many teacher "centred" oriented classrooms. Saunders (1992) explains that learning is made meaningful through activities like "thinking out loud, developing alternative explanations, interpreting data, participating in cognitive conflict (constructive arguing about phenomena under study), development of alternative hypothesis, the design of further experiments to test alternative hypothesis, and the selection of plausible hypotheses from among completing explanations".

The third component to Saunders' (1992) model is that students work in small groups. Saunders (1992) explains that "small-group work tends to stimulate a higher level of cognitive activity among larger numbers of students than does listening to lectures and thus provides expanded opportunities for cognitive restructuring.

The last implication of Saunders' (1992) model is higher level assessment. Although vague to what is really meant for this implication, the literature on alternative assessment is vast. Saunders (1992) explicitly states that by incorporating the above three strategies without assessing the way that was taught that student cognitive activity will remain at a low level. I also agree that the tool should fit the task and reflect the way that learning took place in the classroom. This has real implications for the traditional fill in the blank and multiple choice tests. Saunders (1992) has some great advice and relevance to the person who claims to be a constructivist. Although the strategies fit well within the science classroom, they may be easily adapted to fit any subject area and accommodate many different learning styles.

Finally, constructivism is not a methodology. There is no prescription for "how to teach like a constructivist". The best one can do is to give students opportunities to construct knowledge. When it is said as to "construct knowledge", it means that one should philosophically not to believe that one can open up a kid's brain and pour information into it. The student has to work and take responsibility for learning. Since one cannot magically transfer knowledge from his/her brain to the brains of students, it simply means to try to create the moments and activities in which learning can occur. It simply means relinquishing some control in the classroom and allowing students to explore their interests. It means providing opportunities for different types and ways of learning, and of evaluating learning.

4.5 BECOMING A CONSTRUCTIVIST TEACHER

Brooks and Brooks (1993) clearly state that "in order for learning to take place in schools, teachers must become constructivist teachers, that is, in the classroom, they must provide a learning environment where students search for meaning, appreciate uncertainty, and inquire responsibly". Constructivist teachers encourage students to constantly assess how the activity is helping them gain understanding (Seigel, 2004). Contrary to criticisms by some (conservative/traditional) educators, constructivism does not dismiss the active role of the teacher or the value of expert knowledge. Constructivism modifies that role, so that teachers help students to construct knowledge rather than to reproduce a series of facts. The constructivist teacher provides tools such as problem-solving and inquiry-based learning activities with which students formulate and test their ideas, draw conclusions and inferences, and pool and convey their knowledge in a collaborative learning environment. Constructivist teacher transforms the student from a passive recipient of information to an active participant in the learning process. Guided by the teacher, students construct their knowledge actively rather than just mechanically ingesting knowledge from the teacher or the textbook.

Constructivist teachers pose questions and problems, and then guide students to help them find their own answers. They use many techniques in the teaching process. For example, they may:

- Prompt students to formulate their own questions (inquiry).
- Allow multiple interpretations and expressions of learning (multiple intelligences).
- Encourage group work and the use of peers as resources (collaborative learning).

The book "The First Days of School" says that if you dare to teach, then you must dare to learn. Teachers must continually make efforts to bring new ideas into the classroom, try them, and learn from them. Learning to become a teacher does not stop after a particular course (degree in general or degree in education); it is a long-term journey and commitment to our students, our colleagues and ourselves. Teachers should be leaders. Leaders think, make decisions, and solve problems; they do not wait for someone to do it for them. However, leaders are always willing to learn from someone else.

If we really want to become a constructivist teacher then it is important to have a sound understanding of what constructivism means to evaluate its promise and use it knowledgeably and effectively (Applefield, Huber & Moasllem, 2001). We all know very well that, Teachers' personal theories of learning have long been viewed as having considerable influence on virtually all aspects of teachers' decisions about instruction whether behaviouristic or constructivistic. Thus, first of all, the teachers will have to bring change in their personal theories of learning say, for example, from behaviouristic to constructivistic.

To refer to constructivism, today we have so many terms such as generative learning (Wittrock, 1985); situated learning and authentic instruction (Brown, Collins & Duguid, 1989), post-modern curricula (Hlynka, 1991) and educational semiotic (Cunningham, 1992). Even though constructivists cannot be adequately represented by a single voice or an entirely universal point of view, there is a conception of learner and learning that is unmistakable in its central tenets. Thus, a constructivist teacher must acquaint himself or herself with the fundamental principles of constructivist learning and in its divergence from an objectivist tradition of learning theory based on either behaviourism.

To become a Constructivist Teacher, there is a need to take into consideration of eighteen indicators of Constructivist Philosophy:

1. Students are ready for meaningful learning before acquiring basic skills.
2. Students should decide what activities are to be done.
3. Instruction should not be on problems with clear answers.
4. How much students learn does not depend on their background knowledge.
5. Teachers should act as facilitators versus explainers.
6. Student thinking is more important than content of the curriculum.
7. Interest in academic work is more important than content of the curriculum.
8. A variety of activities is better than the same assignment for all.
9. Short-answer and multiple-choice tests are not useful.
10. Open-ended problems are useful.
11. Individual and group projects are useful.

12. Student presentations/performances are useful.
13. Teachers don't know more than students and should not explain answers.
14. A quiet classroom is not needed for effective learning.
15. Teacher feels comfortable facilitator versus explainer.
16. Students gain more knowledge from teacher as facilitator versus explainer.
17. Students gain more useful skills from teacher as facilitator versus explainer.
18. Students prefer discussions with teacher as a facilitator versus explainer.

Based on the above constructivist philosophy, a constructivist teacher must use methods such as Mental Models, Facilitation, etc. if he or she is really willing to become a constructivist teacher. Some researchers link constructivism with a novice-to-expert model of learning where step-like progressions via experiences are accelerated by connecting to the conceptual understanding, or mental models, of experts. A model of the target system, roughly what the teacher expects as outcomes, must connect to a mental model in order to be internalized. The conceptual model of the target is the teacher's representation of the knowledge to be transferred. But constructivists recognize this is a place where novices can be exposed to the kind of concepts, which an expert gains through years of experience. In developing a conceptual model a teacher should take into account the kinds of things an expert considers, such as what problems and errors are likely to be encountered in a given situation. What are the most important concepts? How can they feed into a broader conceptualization? How will they attach to the user's mental models? "...when experiences are carefully facilitated which support the conceptual model of the target, learners are able to adapt and reshape internal mental models and construct knowledge for themselves" (Brandt, 1997).

The teacher as facilitator initiates the class discussion by presenting the experts' mental model to the students and then steps out of the discussion to let mental models develop in the learners through interaction. The discussion can include all members of the class and is nearly unlimited in time. Learners unsure of the 'correctness' of their own current mental model can read others' models and prefer their own for inspection by the class. Is Teacher a Facilitator or Collaborator? This question can be categorized into two basic views, cognitive and social. If, as Piaget suggested, knowledge is acquired when cognitive stability is directly challenged, then the primary role of the teacher as facilitator is to pose problems that stretch learners to a point of intellectual disequilibrium (perturbation). If, as Vygotsky suggested, cognitive development is "the transformation of socially shared activities into internalized thought processes", then the primary role of the teacher as collaborator is to monitor classroom learning and participate actively with students in its evolution (Scheurman, 1998).

Facilitation is a balance of pull and push interaction with the students (Airasian and Walsh, 1997). How often should the teacher comment and should those comments be questions or suggestions? Since the asynchronous media allow the teacher to analyze the discussion, the interjection can be a course correction rather than a lecture. The important concept is not whether students construct understandings of concepts but how good are their constructions. The teacher's role is to facilitate a learning environment that helps students create good schemas of understanding. By facilitating students working with others, the teacher creates a 'community of scholars'. Students communicate ideas and make sense of others' ideas.

In using constructivist methods teachers may err on the side of students' constructs or on the side of scholars. That is, by either not correcting the students' constructions to bring students to consider scholarly constructs or allowing too little exploration of the students' constructs before presenting the 'right' answer. "What is essential for bringing the two types of constructions together, however, is teacher-student dialogue" (Zahorik, 1997). Teachers must join the discussion to challenge both students and scholarly constructions. The objective of the teacher-facilitator is to continue the discussion so that students continue to view their constructions in terms of the experts.

An important aspect of constructivism has to do with conflict. Within a context of growth and cooperation, conflict is the source of developmental progress. It is not the teacher's intent to avoid conflict. It is the facilitator/teacher's job to help students negotiate the frictions that inevitably surface and provoke them to challenge ideas (Brooks, 1990). The facilitator models higher-order thinking by asking questions that probe students' knowledge deeply. Interactions remain at the meta-cognitive level. The facilitator's role is to challenge the learner's thinking. The facilitator and students will constantly ask questions such as: What does this mean? What are the implications of that? The students gradually will take over the role in collaboration (Duffy and Cunningham, 1996). A constructivist teacher is a facilitator and a guide who works and learns alongside his/her students. Such a teacher is involved in processing learning with students as they experiment, cooperate, invent, and communicate. He/she is a scribe when needed but he/she may also be a code-breaker—unlocking children's thinking patterns and developing relationships for purposes of understanding students, celebrating discoveries, or inventing theories. A constructivist teacher tries to question strategically so that children can examine their assumptions without questioning their self-worth as thinkers. A constructivist teacher is open to the children's ideas, she trusts children as sense-makers and helps them develop reasoning skills by allowing them to reason, even though that reasoning may not be logical in the adult sense. Although the constructivist teacher values children's language, representations, and relationships, she also expects them to learn and develop. She is a collaborator in the process we call learning rather than a source of the way to learn.

For constructivist teachers, curriculum is fluid and flexible. Teachers must be ready to incorporate children's interests through discussions, class meetings, interviews, and observations of children's actions. Teachers must be able to offer materials and situations that have the potential to be experimented with by children's evolving thinking and growing knowledge. Teachers must build a socio-moral environment with children in which they discover lifelong dispositions toward learning, and in which they learn by cooperating with adults and peers. Constructivist curriculum is not easy to pin down and define. It cannot be prescribed. It must be invented by a teacher and the children, for whom the curriculum is a living, developing experience of people, places, events, and things. Constructivist teachers use processes to help children curriculum relationships. The curriculum evolves and is not a finite entity.

Constructivist teachers are process-oriented. They are interested in children's thinking, in the relationships their students can explain, and in developing dispositions toward learning. A constructivist teacher takes his/her teaching clues from children's interests, not from curriculum outlines. He/she accepts that children are unique and tries to find out where they are on the thinking continuum. A constructivist teacher values invention, experimentation, cooperation, and caring relationships. He/she believes that children are already learners when he/she meets them and tries to help them develop an awareness of thinking processes and develop confidence in their own sense-making mission. Constructivist teachers value parents as important partners and build relationships with them that will lead to knowledge of their children as thinkers and problem-solvers. Constructivist teachers understand that thinking from experiential contexts, as well as social contexts, can help children develop relationships and response processes that build on these contexts equally. It's not what the teacher knows, but what the child knows that is important. A teacher that thinks about his/her student's thinking and understanding, and look for ways to help children express and document these processes, and he/she provides opportunities for children to build relationships, experiment, and cooperate... he/she is probably a constructivist teacher. He/she observes his/her students and reflects on his/her observations. He/she includes students in class meetings and discussions about topics, experiences, events, etc. that interest them. He/she works to create contexts for learning. He/she thinks about what materials can be used to create interest. What relationships are children developing that will be strengthened or challenged? How can the social context for learning be strengthened so children can learn from each other? He/she must understand that knowledge has three sources: objects, relationships between objects, and social conventions. He/she involves students in thinking about what they already know and what they want to learn more about. He/she involves students in explaining or demonstrating what has been learned so that he/she can tell what thinking or skills are developing and which ones may be stagnant or immature.

A constructivist teacher promotes an atmosphere of mutual trust and respect. Getting to know children for who they are as thinkers and doers is also essential. Inviting children to express ideas in many forms like art, construction, drama, dance, music, cooking, aiming, board and card games, group games, as well as with conventional oral and written language options also help to develop literacy. Sharing with children the many ways people use to express themselves encourages children to represent their ideas.

Representing ideas is the heart of language and literacy. Language and literacy are also promoted by valuing children's language. A constructivist teacher would write, record, videotape, and listen to children. She would read and share her love for reading processes such as rhyming, alliteration, onomatopoeia, vocabulary development, context, syntax, and grammar. By accepting children and the language they bring to the classroom, a constructivist teacher creates a context where the language she brings is of interest to children causing them to acquire increasing use of receptive and expressive language processes. A constructivist classroom is a natural environment for promoting language and literacy development since it integrates the children's interests into learning contexts. The children are responsible for their learning so they have a need to read and write and so they try very hard.

A constructivist teacher evaluates children's progress through processes such as observations, questioning, reflecting, and listening to children's reasoning, theories, and accounts of events. A constructivist teacher looks for development along a continuum of knowledge and relationship building. Each child is compared to him or herself rather than against each other. A constructivist teacher looks for developing dispositions toward learning like taking initiative, being confident, curious, and creative as well as conventional forms of knowledge acquisition and is equally concerned with social relationship building as with mathematics and scientific relationship building, knowing that one reinforces the other. A constructivist teacher looks for learning processes such as classification, serration, enumeration, spatial and temporal awareness, comparing and contrasting, as evidence of progress, rather than right answer to particular questions. The teacher considers process over the product and is tuned into the children's demonstrations and explanations of their own learning.

To become a constructivist teacher is to be in the process of becoming more thoughtful, insightful, observant, caring...a flexible, questioning, human being. Teachers try to make sense of student's thinking just as students try to make sense of the world. A teacher can become more or less of a teacher depending upon how he/she incorporates or makes sense of his/her teacher preparation as he/she involves herself in the life and work of being a teacher. Exposure to as many ideas as possible during teacher preparation leaves those who truly seek to become teachers with building blocks to make sense out of the experience. It is the sense making that is important. Those who use their teacher preparation to help them make sense of teaching will become more constructivists only if constructivism adds meaning and understanding to their work with children. The quest for making sense will lead some to become effective teachers whether they are constructivist or not.

One of the best ways for the teacher to really become a constructivist teacher in his/her classroom is by seeing with others about it, and trying in himself or herself. He/she can become a constructivist teacher by following measures:

- Constructivist teachers pose questions and problems, and then guide students to help them find their own answers. They use many techniques such as inquiry, multiple intelligence, collaborative learning, etc. in the teaching process.

- Constructivist teachers encourage students to constantly assess how the activity is helping them gain understanding.
- A constructivist teacher sets up problems and monitors students' exploration, guides the direction of student inquiry and promotes new patterns of thinking (Brooks & Brooks, 1995). It is up to the teacher to facilitate the constructivist learning process. The structure of the learning environment should promote opportunities and events that encourage and support the process of understanding.

Last but not the least, a constructivist teacher must resist himself or herself giving the impression that there is always the right answer. In fact, the impression should be to have a possibility of having always an answer particularly in social studies. The teacher should respond to the students' answers by saying (in a situation when students give inexact answer), "I never thought of it that way" or "That is another creative way of looking at it."

4.6 CONSTRUCTIVIST TEACHING STRATEGIES

A teacher must have positive expectations. This means believing in each student and believing that the student can learn and be successful. Students only learn as much as the teacher expects; teachers who set high expectations for their students will receive higher achievement from their students. It is amazing to see what students can accomplish when they know and sense that someone believes in them. The main aspiration as a teacher should be to help students meet their fullest potential by establishing an environment where their students feel safe, are comfortable taking risks with new learning and presents them with opportunities to share their thoughts and ideas.

The teacher should try and encourage students to discover principles by themselves. The teacher should give them the opportunity to have dialogue among their peers and with the teacher. The main task as a teacher should be to present information to be learned that matches or closely matches the student's current level of learning. The curriculum should be organized in a spiral manner, so that students continually build upon what they have already learned. The teacher should also try to modify his/her teaching strategies to student responses and encourage the students to analyze, interpret and predict information in the course of their learning.

In a constructivist framework, following teaching strategies may be adopted:

1. Planning: What do I want my students to do?
   a. Objectives (in own words form curriculum)
   b. Organization and Materials
   c. Groupings
2. Pre-Assessment:
   a. What do my students already know?
   b. What assessment and instructional tools I will use?
3. Connections:
   a. How will my students focus, be engaged and make connections with prior knowledge in order to learn new knowledge?
4. Exhibits:
   a. How will my students show that they know?
5. Evaluation:
   a. How will I assess what the students have learnt?
6. Reflections:
   a. Teacher:
      (1) What worked well?
      (2) What would I do differently?
      (3) What will I do if the students have not learnt the material?
   b. Student:
      (1) What did I learn?
      (2) What helped me to learn the material?
      (3) How do I learn best?

Many active teaching and learning techniques reflect the constructivist approach. These include problem-based learning, real-world simulations, case study approaches and scientific experiments. Metacognition or thinking about thinking is an important activity in the constructivist classroom. Students are encouraged to constantly raise questions and explore ideas.

Problem-Based Learning/Anchored Instruction: Problem-Based Learning (PBL)/anchored instruction, is a student-centred, contextualized approach to schooling. In this approach, learning begins with a problem to be solved rather than content to be mastered. This is consistent with new models of teaching and learning that suggest the emphasis of instruction needs to shift from teaching as knowledge transmission to less teacher-dependent learning. The concept of anchored instruction was stimulated by the "inert knowledge problem" which states that the knowledge can be recallable only when individual is questioned explicitly in the context in which it was learned. The issue of learning transfer, situated cognition and collaborative learning are primarily concerns in anchored instruction. It emphasizes the importance of creating an anchor or focus that generates interest and enables students to identify and define problems and to pay attention on their own perceptions and comprehension of these problems (Bransford, 1990).

The goals of PBL include: (1) developing scientific understanding through real-world cases, (2) developing reasoning strategies, and (3) developing self-directed learning strategies. As students articulate and reflect upon their knowledge in PBL, they develop more coherent understandings of the problem space (Hmelo, 1995). The active learning used in PBL should promote the self-directed learning strategies and attitudes needed for lifelong learning (Bereiter and Scardmalia, 1989). Self-directed learning objectives of PBL are particularly important because PBL may facilitate development of lifelong learning strategies necessary to stay current in the face of rapid technological advances.

Distributed Cognition: The concept of distributed cognition emphasizes the interaction among individuals, environment and cultural artifacts. It claims that development and growth of cognitions of individuals should not be isolated events rather the changes should be a reciprocal process. It starts from the minds of individuals, through the reciprocal teaching and guide each others or acquainting themselves with the tools. It leads to the changes of the subsequent joint performances and products, the improved competencies then can distribute among and reside in individuals. As who plays the leading role in influencing distributed cognitions is really situated bounded. For example, in a well-balanced group competencies may play a dominate role, in the presence of powerful tools, the tools may help to guide individual, and in absence above two sources, individual's competence will dominate. Sshima, Bereiter and Scardamalia (1995) based on distributed cognition, examines students in knowledge construction and transforming in CSILE network environments. The results indicated that students, who benefited the most from the activities, engaged more in knowledge-transformation. This system allows students to distribute information and interact with information resources in a joint space, can prompt conceptual progress (knowledge assimilation and knowledge construction). Dede (1996) predicted a distributed learning and knowledge building community will be the new paradigm of 21st century education.

Three sources emerge from the theory of distributed cognition: First, the increasingly important role that technology plays to handle intellectual tasks to ease individual cognitive load. Second, the reemphasis on Vygotsky's socio-cultural theory, a theory that describes how the character of social interactions and externally mediated action makes explicit certain processes that come to be internalized in the private thought of the individual. Third, dissatisfied with cognition is only in one's mind, shifting attention on cognitions that are situated dependent and distributed in nature (Salomaon, 1994).

Cognitive Flexibility Theory: Spiro (1998) suggested that people acquire knowledge in ill structured domains by constructing multiple representations and linkages among knowledge units. This can be achieved by designing hypermedia documents that present multiple cases where similar concepts are linked across cases (Spiro & Jehang, 1990). Learners visit and more importantly revisit the same case or concept information in a variety of contexts.

Spiro's Cognitive flexibility theory and criss-crossed landscape theory approaches address important issue in transfer, how general knowledge is transferred in ill-structured domains. They suggest a mixture of well and ill-structuredness in the early stages, to familiar learners with grounded knowledge yet avoid establishing rigid presentation. Intermediate course of cases were selected to seek a balance between continuity and discontinuity; a partial overlapping across cases rather than from any single perspective that running through many cases. Spiro (1995) has illustrated in detail how to apply cognitive flexibility and constructivism theories into designing instruction in ill-structured domains that promote advanced knowledge acquisition.

Cognitive Apprenticeship: Cognitive apprenticeship is a term for the instructional process that teachers provide and support students with scaffolds as the students develop cognitive strategies. Wilson and Cole (1994) describe the core characteristics of cognitive apprenticeships model: heuristic content, situated learning, modelling caching, articulation, reflection, exploration, and order in increasing complexity. Cognitive apprenticeship is a culture that permits peers to learn through their interactions, to build stories about common experiences and to share the knowledge building experiences with the group. Collaborative discussion occurring in CSCL is important for student learning because it activates prior knowledge which facilitates the processing of new information. CSCL is designed to help students at acquiring cognitive and meta-cognitive knowledge by means of observation and guided practice (Collins, 1984).

Situated Cognition: It is not possible to separate cognitive tasks from social tasks, because all cognitive tasks have a social component (Perret-Clermont, 1993). Constructivists view cognition as situated-bound and distributed rather than decontextualized tools and product of mind (Leve, 1998; Pea, 1994). Thinking is both physically and socially situated that problem tasks can be significantly shaped and changed by the tools make available and the social interactions that take place during problem-solving. Situational cognition, a new paradigm of learning, emphasizes apprenticeship, coaching, collaboration, multiple practices, and articulation of learning skills, stories and technology (Brown, Collins & Duguid, 1989). "Community of Practice", a concept emerging from situated cognition, emphasizes sharing and doing, construct meaning in a social unit (Roschelle, 1995). Situated learning occurs when students work on authentic tasks that take place in real-world setting (Winn, 1993). However, the very difference between metacognition approach of learning and situated belief of learning is that situated learning is usually unintentional rather than purposeful. These ideas are what Lave & Wenger (1991) call the process of "legitimate peripheral participation".

As Lave (1991) states that learning is a function of the activity, context and culture in which it occurs, which contrasts with most classroom learning which is abstract and out of context. Education can apply the two basic principles of situated cognition into classroom practice: (1) Present in an authentic context, (2) Encourage social interaction and collaboration. It is believed that rich contexts can reflect students' interpretation of the real world and improve their knowledge being transferred in different situation. Collaboration can lead to articulation of strategies that can then be discussed, which, in turn, can enhance generalizing grounded in students' situated understanding.

Self-Regulated Learning/Metacognition: Flanell (1976) first invented the term metacognition. He defined metacognition as one's knowledge regarding one's own cognition as well as control and monitor one's own cognition. The term self-regulated learning and metacognition are interchangeable.

A self-regulated learner is aware when he or she knows a fact or has a skill and when he or she does not. He or she views acquisition as a systematic and controllable process, and she accepts greater responsibility for him or her achievement. In other words, he or she is the initiator of the learning process. Self-regulated learning has played a part in constructivist theory. In behavioural theory, regulation is equivalent to metacognition, knowing about and regulating cognition. Social cognition theory views self-regulation as combining self-observation, self-judgment and self-reaction.

Self-regulation plays a crucial role in all phases of learning and cross domains. Schoenfeld (1987) states that self-regulation has the potential to increase the meaningfulness of students' classroom learning, and the creation of a "mathematics culture in the classroom best fosters metacognition. Schoenfeld (1983) showed that many problem-solving errors are due to metacognitive failure rather than lack of basic mathematics knowledge. He further insists that all metacognitive strategies are illustrated in action, should be developed by students, and not declared by the teachers. Study metacognitive strategies are important as well, in reading to learn and can be applied to enhance text processing (Grow, 1996). To teach students to become active, motivated, self-regulated learners is a continuing issue in education. Authentic and meaningful classroom activities that are relevant to real-life situations are likely to engender students' cognitive activity and conceptual change (transfer). Scaffolding, dual instructions (verbal persuasion and modelling), and teaching appropriate cognitive strategies are believed to have positive impact on increasing students' efficacy.

Teachers or instructors can help students set achievable goals and provide feedback highlighting progress toward goals (Rerald, Grow's SSDL Model, 1996). Linking students' success and failure with cause, is a highly persuasive source of efficacy. Ensure appropriate learner control in the task that requires students to become self-directed learners. It is assured that students can be taught to become more self-directed learners. It is assumed that students can be taught to become more self-regulated learners by acquiring effective strategies and by enhancing perceptions of self-efficacy. Poor learners can benefit from reciprocal teaching that through process of modelling, guiding and collaborative learning. The major responsibility of teachers is not to dispense knowledge, and no single teacher can teach students everything they need to know in their entire lifetime. Equipping students with self-regulated strategies will provide them with necessary techniques for becoming independent thinkers and lifelong learners. Dede and Palumbo (1991) indicate that develop constructive instructional systems should be grounded in the psychology of learning and transfer rather than in the human factors and technological design issues. They further claim that the development of constructive systems should support metacognition and problem-solving skills development.

Scaffolding: Scaffolding in construction is a means to an end; as soon as it's no longer needed, it disappears. Instructional scaffolding is similarly transient (Lawson, 2002). Scaffolding in an educational context is a process by which a teacher provides students with a temporary framework for learning. Done correctly, such structuring encourages a student to develop his or her own initiative, motivation and resourcefulness. Once students build knowledge and develop skills on their own, elements of the framework are dismantled. Eventually, the initial scaffolding is removed altogether; students no longer need it.

According to McKenzie (1999), the defining features of successful scaffolding include clear direction, purpose, and expectation. Results include on-task activity; better student direction; reduced uncertainty, surprise, and disappointment; increased efficiency; and palpable momentum. "...Scaffolding requires continuous sorting and sifting as part of a 'puzzling' process—the combining of new information with previous understandings to construct new ones. Students are adding on, extending, refining and elaborating. It is almost as if they are building a bridge from their preconceptions to a deeper, wiser, more astute view of whatever truth matters for the question or issue at hand", McKenzie says.

There are different ways to scaffold instruction for students. According to Bransford, Brown and Cocking (2000), some educators favour an apprenticeship model whereby an expert models an activity, provides the learner with advice and examples, guides the student in practice and then tapers off support until the student can do the task alone; others prefer methods that encourage ongoing use of tools and consultation with other people, arguing that in real life few people ever work exclusively on their own. Most agree that scaffolding is particularly effective in areas in which students need to be more self-reliant, such as technology-based learning (Banaszynski, 2000).

An example of scaffolding through apprenticeship is the writing workshop model used by Dorn and Soffos (2001), who explain that the nurturing activities of an expert are critical to fostering children through different stages of writing ability, from emergence (writing letters and single words; understanding that we write and read English from left to right) to early writer status (recognizing such patterns as paragraphs and pages) to transitional writer status (mastering the ability to edit and revise an original work).

"Writing is by nature a social process.... Children learn how to become writers through meaningful interactions with more knowledgeable people", Dorn and Soffos write (2001). Moreover, "Writing is a learned skill that is shaped through practice and constructive feedback. It requires motivation, strategies, skills and knowledge."

Dorn and Soffos, who work primarily with elementary school children, suggest that in order to successfully write, a student must master three interrelated skills: comprehension of ideas, expressive language and facility with mechanics. "The ultimate goal of teaching", they say, "is to promote an orchestration process. It is important to note that orchestration occurs at the point where old knowledge meets new knowledge: if the child has too many new things to learn, this can interfere with the orchestration process" (Dorn & Soffos, 2001).

What, specifically, does a teacher do to orchestrate, or scaffold, student learning in the area of writing? Dorn and Soffos (2001) suggest that teachers ask four simple questions before they begin: *What is easy for the writer to do? What is hard for the writer to do? What does the teacher expect the writer to do? What does the teacher expect to do for the writer?* Constantly re-evaluating allows a teacher to plan activities that will encourage developing writers to attempt new skills; once mastery is underway, new goals can be set and new support systems devised.

Based on theory and research, and reiterating the hallmarks of successful scaffolding (McKenzie, 1999) a teacher can expect the following outcomes when using scaffolding as an instructional method:

- Students should be able to appreciate (if not articulate) directions and expectations after those elements have been introduced by the teacher. Provided that the purpose of the lesson has been made clear, this reflecting back on the part of the student should not be regurgitation of information—recitation by rote—but a sincere report of what he/she understands to be the scope of the work at hand and the evaluation strategy of the teacher.
- As long as the lesson has been planned with students' zones of proximal development in mind, progress should be made with a minimum of non-constructive frustration. In other words, students should be challenged but share enough of an expectation of success to keep working on-task. Levels of uncertainty and disappointment stand to be lower than those experienced by students with no confident sense of mastery.
- Teachers and students should both recognize increased efficiency and momentum because the two parties will be working symbiotically—teachers introducing, demonstrating, guiding and pulling back; and students exploring, attempting, internalizing self-motivation and then understanding (and perhaps initiating the next cycle of scaffolded activity).

Co-operative Learning: Co-operative Learning is an increasingly popular instructional strategy. Johnson and Johnson's (1993) model identifies five basic elements which should be built into activities for effective co-operation:

- Positive interdependence;
- Individual and group accountability;
- Explicit teaching of social skills;
- Face to face primitive interaction;
- Group processing of learning.

Alongside this development is the Critical Skills Programme (CSP) promoted by Network Educational Press in Scotland, and gaining increasing numbers of practitioners (Weatherley, 2000). The training manual for CSP states this approach to co-operative learning as:

> "a practical response from teachers working in real classrooms to the theoretical arguments supporting constructivist, collaborative, experiential, authentic and democratic learning environments. CSP can provide a real life "how-to" model to address the worthy ideals espoused throughout recent literature."
>
> (Network Educational Press, 1997)

Co-operative learning provides an approach to teaching which is conducive to the development of the skills required for a changing world and its benefits are well documented. There is extensive research into the effectiveness of co-operative learning as a particular method of structuring this social interaction, which increases pupil attainment. There are three major benefits to co-operative learning: higher achievement and greater productivity, more positive relationships and greater psychological health, social competence and self-esteem. There is a possibility that there may be no other teaching strategy that simultaneously may achieve so many different outcomes.

Again, co-operative learning is an approach to learning and teaching which delivers the key components of formative assessment by offering the opportunity for regular and rigorously designed group work, where children are very clear about the learning intentions and success criteria and are encouraged to work collaboratively while still encouraging individual accountability.

Broud and Miller (1996) argue five key propositions about learning from experience:

- Experience is the foundation of, and stimulus for, learning. It is a central consideration and cannot be bypassed.
- Learners actively construct their own experience, influenced by their unique past, as well as current context.

- Learning is holistic and the connectedness of knowledge must be highlighted.
- Learning is socially and culturally constructed and it is challenging to move beyond the influence of context and culture.
- Learning is influenced by the socio-emotional context in which it occurs—"Denial of feelings is denial of learning." (Broud & Miller, 1996)

Students are actively involved in making meaning, processing and relating information to their own experience through dialogue and collaboration. There is an emphasis on understanding and the learner's increasing responsibility for his or her own learning. This reflects a holistic view of learners, which takes account of the emotional aspects of learning.

The following procedures for teachers are suggested by Yager (1991):

1. Seek out and use student questions and ideas to guide lessons and whole instructional units.
2. Accept and encourage student initiation of ideas.
3. Promote student leadership, collaboration, location of information and taking actions as a result of the learning process.
4. Use student thinking, experiences and interests to drive lessons.
5. Encourage the use of alternative sources for information both from written materials and experts.
6. Encourage students to suggest causes for event and situations and encourage them to predict consequences.
7. Seek out student ideas before presenting teacher ideas or before studying ideas from textbooks or other sources.
8. Encourage students to challenge each other's conceptualizations and ideas.

9. Encourage adequate time for reflection and analysis; respect and use all ideas that students generate.
10. Encourage self-analysis, collection of real evidence to support ideas and reformulation of ideas in light of new knowledge.
11. Use student identification of problems with local interest and impact as organizers for the course.
12. Use local resources (human and material) as original sources of information that can be used in problem resolution.
13. Involve students in seeking information that can be applied in solving real-life problems.
14. Extend learning beyond the class period, classroom and the school.
15. Focus on the impact of science on each individual student.
16. Refrain from viewing science content as something that merely exists for students to master on tests.
17. Emphasize career awareness—especially as related to science and technology.

Yager (1991) has suggested following strategies for implementing a constructivist lesson:

1. Starting the lesson:	Observe surroundings for points to question. Ask questions. Consider possible responses to questions Note unexpected phenomena. Identify situations where student perceptions vary.
2. Continuing the lesson:	Engage in focused play. Brainstorm possible alternatives. Look for information. Experiment with materials.

	Observe a specific phenomenon.
	Design a model.
	Collect and organize data.
	Employ problem-solving strategies.
	Select appropriate resources.
	Students discuss solutions with others.
	Students design and conduct experiments.
	Students evaluate and debate choices.
	Students identify risks and consequences.
	Define parameters of an investigation.
3. Proposing explanations and Solutions:	Communicate information and ideas.
	Construct and explain a model.
	Construct a new explanation.
	Review and critique solutions.
	Utilize peer evaluation.
	Assemble appropriate closure.
	Integrate a solution with existing.
	Knowledge and experiences.
4. Taking action:	Make decisions.
	Apply knowledge and skills.
	Transfer knowledge and skills.
	Share information and ideas.
	Ask new questions.
	Develop products and promote ideas.
	Use models and ideas to illicit discussions and acceptance by others.

Finally, the introduction of constructivist ideas into a classroom does not eliminate lecturing as an instructional tool. It is still worthwhile to spend significant class time behind the podium. While lecturing may continue to provide an efficient means of covering information, in a constructivist framework, it serves a more complex function. Not just a device for imparting facts, lecturing establishes a context in which to place class discussions of critical issues. Lectures serve as a foundation upon which students can build further understandings. They provide a structure of major events that allow students to construct a larger mosaic of conceptual awareness. Even in the constructivist classroom, lecturing may remain an important pedagogical tool. It is an effective means to build an intellectual scaffolding upon which to build new information configurations. Nor does the introduction of constructivism into a class preclude other traditional teaching methods. A teacher may still provide direct instruction. The question is really how much intervention and how much direct instruction is appropriate. As one supporter of constructivism said "it is difficult to imagine any learning encounters without a certain amount of transmission [of knowledge] on the part of teachers. Primary sources play a fundamental role in the constructivist setting. In fact, these materials are the conduit by which constructivist theories and methods enter survey courses. Documents, as the raw materials of history, are the vehicle that students use to practice historical skills as they construct new understandings. Working with them, students decode data, debate their meaning, and establish new interpretations. Overall, they move away from "the pre-digested summarization of history served up" in many history classes and build upon previous knowledge to construct new meaning and understanding. The use of documents in the construction of new knowledge fuels genuine excitement as the human element of a historic movement emerges. Dealing with documents in a classroom also provides students with another important skill—putting questions to data. One cannot construct new knowledge without making reasoned judgments and one cannot make reasoned judgments without asking good questions. In class, students are often so preoccupied with getting the "right" answer that they ignore the need to ask the "right" questions. Thomas Holt has stated that being able to pose questions "is part of the process of learning about history. It is about the questions as well as answers." The skill of asking questions is not innate to students, they need directions in how to pose good questions just as they need guidance in developing other critical thinking skills. Further, when students interact and question sources, they will confront conflicting ideas and positions. As they weigh evidence, they will question their classmates, their teacher and themselves. Often the questions raised will generate new issues that cannot be clearly answered by the available evidence. The combination of lecturing and analyzing documents in a constructivist-oriented setting allows the instructor to give students an enriched academic programme. The skills of analysis and synthesis, which are fundamental to the constructivist paradigm, can be promoted by a series of in-depth, sustained concentrations on a limited number of topics or questions. The class sequence may be designed to move students back and forth from assimilation (perceived current reality) to accommodation (challenging students to reorganize their cognitive view). Students may be asked to deal with new information as they read various primary sources and to revise their views and understandings of the topics.

Apart from above mentioned strategies, following are three examples of instructional methods (Debate, Case Method and Brainstorming) that facilitate constructivist learning principles and translate well to face to face classroom teaching and technology-mediated learning environments, too.

Debate: The debate is an instructional method that facilitates articulation of thoughts and argumentation through the use of language. Instructors can use debates to enhance their learners' confidence and ability to express viewpoints as well as help them to develop coherent organization and precise expression of ideas structured in a manner that matches the speaker's (or writer's) purpose and intended audience. To maximize the effectiveness of debates, instructors should establish a few ground rules before beginning. Debates can range from highly structured, formal interactions, to quite casual exchanges of viewpoints. There is, however, a tendency for technology-mediated debates to be more successful when they are structured and formal. Whether or not the debate is formal, there needs to be a moderator and judge. The moderator's role is to enforce the rules of the debate and the judge's role is to determine the winning team. To help contribute to a successful debate, instructors should adhere to a structure similar to the following:

- The class size should not consist of more than 25-30 participants and not be less than 10-15.
- There should be two teams with an equal number of team members on each side.
- There should also be a moderator and a judge, who is usually (but not always), the instructor.
- When there are an odd number of class participants, one learner may be chosen to be the debate moderator.
- The topic should be an issue related to the course content and one where there are polarized views on the issue presented.
- Content on the topic and the related issues should be presented to the learners, but they should not be told which team they will be assigned to in the debate until the onset of the debate.
- The instructor should make every effort to get to know where each class participant stands on the issues presented and have them argue on the side that they do *not* agree with.
- Members of the team have a predetermined time limit to present their position on the issues.
- If using synchronous technologies (such as audio or video conferencing), the time limit should be two to three minutes to present for individual team members.
- If the technology is asynchronous (such as a listserv or computer mediated conferencing software), the time limit might be 24 to 48 hours with an opportunity for each team member to post one message no longer than one screen of information.
- After each team has presented their most important points, the opposing teams may take turns to counter any points raised by their opposing team members.
- The debate should be concluded with an opportunity for each team to present concluding remarks.

The desired learning outcome of a debate is to force learners to confront situations that that result in contradictions that challenge the learner to acquire better understandings. To make the debate effective at facilitating constructivism principles, the instructor will need to ensure learners take a stand that is contrary to their current belief system. This will help the learners to actively challenge their understandings by searching out new information and experiences of which they have little working knowledge.

Case Method: Much of the literature on constructivism learning principles stresses the importance of experiential learning. Case studies provide one such opportunity to enhance learning through the examination of real life situations tailored to raise those issues that are important for learners to consider (Boyd, 1980; Dixon, 1991). A case study provides information about a simulated (or sometimes real) situation; learners respond to predetermined questions or develop an action plan (Marsick, 1990). If cases are developed so as to bring about a questioning of learner assumptions and if learners are also provided with the opportunity to examine those assumptions in interactions with others, critical self-reflection will be fostered (Hudspeth, 1991; Stolovich & Keeps, 1991). Writing case studies includes the following (Graf, 1991; Lacey & Merseth, 1993):

- Selecting *objectives*. These will depend on the subject and quite often involve such interpersonal skills as revolving conflict, leadership or management techniques.
- Providing *background* in the form of a clear description of the actual problem. Only one major problem should be presented and focused on. Information on the nature of the environment, the players in the case, the resources available, and any time frames that apply need to be included.
- The inclusion of *relevant information* of major influences on people in terms of specific events, facts, and circumstances which relate directly to the incident or problem. These may be social contexts, previous experiences, or cultural backgrounds. These should also be made as authentic as possible.

- Formulation of discussion questions need to be developed to guide the activities of the learners and facilitate the exploration of the issues contained in the problem situation. The questions should lead the learners to recognize alternative solutions, consider contributing influences, and anticipate probable consequences.

Other elements to include when writing case studies are as follows:

- Select facts and incidents that will be easily recognizable.
- Identify characters and keep to four at the most; one or two is best. Describe clear pictures so readers do not get confused.
- Include brief dialogues that give a sense of the characters involved.
- Introduce key characters early and link them clearly to the problem.
- Include social/organizational content.
- The concluding sentence should point out a need for somc form of action.

When using case studies in technology-mediated learning environments, the web would be an appropriate medium to present the case study and following discussion questions. If the web is not being used, the case should be presented in paper based format. To make the case study as effective as possible at facilitating constructivism principles, consideration should be given to having the class participants develop the cases, rather than the instructor. Irrespective of whether the learners or the instructor develops the case study, it should be presented to the class prior to the discussion and read individually. Once the class has read the case, the instructor should use heterogeneous discussion groups to discuss particular points of view. Groups that include a mix of gender, culture, socio-economic status, and age will provide multiple perspectives to the problem presented in the case. If the instructor is using synchronous technologies, the learners should be provided with approximately 30-45 minutes for discussion on the questions followed by a presentation of their findings, opinions, or beliefs to the entire class. If the instructor is using asynchronous technologies, the instructor should have access to an online learning environment capable of dividing the class into small groups. The small groups should have approximately one week for discussion. The discussion should then be followed with a summary developed by each group of their findings, opinions or beliefs and presented to the entire class. Opportunities for all class participants to respond to the group summaries should also be provided in both asynchronous and synchronous environments.

Case studies can be made more effective at facilitating constructivism learning principles in asynchronous environments through the use of role play. According to Renner (1997), role playing is experiential learning at its best and can be used to "insert a slice of life into the classroom, connect theory with everyday practice, practice unfamiliar skills in a safe setting, and learn to appreciate contradictory viewpoints". Role play can be made even more interesting with asynchronous software that allows for users to have an *alias*. The alias option is where a user can be assigned an alternate user name on the conferencing software. Using the alias, the instructor can assign roles from the case study to class participants where they are a different gender, socio-economic status, ethnic origin, or age. In this way, the learners must not only *act* from an alternative perspective, but also *respond* to their fellow class mates who will not know the 'true' identity of each class member. This kind of learning activity helps learners to understand that much of what we know to be true (our objective and external realities) is often contextually and culturally situated.

Brainstorming: Brainstorming is an instructional method that works well when used in combination with the nominal group technique (group problem-solving) (Korhonen, 1990). Brainstorming is most often used to channel a group's collective thoughts through structured group input over a short period of time in ways that invite uninhibited participation (Renner, 1997). This process can result in fresh solutions to old problems.

Brainstorming works well with group sizes that are not larger than eight (Renner, 1997). When using synchronous technologies, such as video or audio conferencing, one participant should be assigned recorder of the ideas generated while the rest of the group spontaneously contribute their ideas. The time required should range from five to fifteen minutes with an equal amount of time for evaluation and discussion. When using asynchronous technologies, such as computer mediated conferencing software, group sizes should also be limited to eight. Limiting group size with computer-mediated conferencing software is important in that it will as ensure that all class participants have an opportunity to generate their ideas, yet will not result in an overwhelmingly large number of messages to read—as can often happen when group sizes are too large. One to three days is the time frame suggested for brainstorming with asynchronous technologies; longer periods of time can often result in the degeneration of fresh ideas. Rather than a final discussion on evaluation, as is suggested with synchronous technologies, the group should work together through a negotiation process and produce a summary of the most worthwhile ideas generated.

The desired outcomes of brainstorming include, according to Renner (1994), the development of new solutions to existing problems, inspire collective creativity, and effect group synergy. Brainstorming supports constructivism learning principles through the facilitation of a collaborative group process where shared understandings are negotiated through a socio-linguistic process.

4.7 ASSESSMENT FROM A CONSTRUCTIVIST PERSPECTIVE

Assessment and evaluation of constructivist learning is also different than that of traditional methods. Traditional methods generally focus on the reproduction of the context and mastery of the symbol system that is associated with a particular discipline. Assessment in a constructivist environment should focus on the students' ability to "organize, structure, and use information in context to solve complex problems" (Osberg, 1997). Bednar (1991) suggests that there are two ways in which constructivist learning can be evaluated. The first assesses how well a student functions within a particular learning domain and if they used the tools and their understanding of the domain to solve problems. The second focuses on the reflective thought process and the documentation of this process that was used to solve a problem. In such a case, the product is of lesser importance than the process used to develop that product. The use of technology can enhance both the learning and assessment process in a constructivist learning environment.

Alternative Assessment: Part of rhetoric surrounding the reform movement is specifically tied to the desire for accurate representation of what a student knows (Rose, 1995; Jonassen, 1992) and how that knowledge can be transferred to domains outside the school room (Sweet & Zimmerman, 1992). The focus is on providing non-traditional means that allow students to show their understanding of a concept for process. It is also a much more complex; holistic approach to assessment.

Alternative assessment techniques, such as criterion-referenced, performance based assessment, relate strongly to real-world experiences (Rose, 1995; Resnik, 1989). Performance assessments replicate the actions required to actually do the tasks, rather than referencing the tasks obliquely. However, it is not easy to develop or administer performance-based on other alternative assessment procedures (Herman, Aschabacher & Winters, 1992). It requires more time, more willingness to engage on a personal level with students and more analysis. It also requires that the student be prepared to perform in a different manner than might have previously been expected (Perkins, 1993).

However, it is perceived that the benefits of performance-based assessment to the student can be extensive (Rief, 1990; Newman, Griffin & Cole, 1989; Bruner, 1990). There is often a heightened sense of personal accomplishment, more initial motivation to engage in the task and the perception of a stronger relationship between in a school and out-of-school activities (Herman, Aschabacher & Winters, 1992).

The process of developing performance based assessment rubrics is similar in some ways to the design of traditional assessment. The designer must still tie the assessment to the instruction, determine the purpose of the assessment, select the tasks, develop criteria and ensure reliable scoring of the performance itself. The largest difference lies in the nature of the tasks that the student must undertake (Herman, Aschabacher & Winters, 1992), and the manner in which the data is interpreted. As stated by Winn (1993), "...instructional designers are wrong to assume that they can base instructional strategies on the analysis of an objective, standard on the analysis of an objective, standard world. Evaluation of learning can only tell us what students appear, or pretend to know, not what they really know."

Constructive learning is an active process and alternative assessment celebrates this active process. Instead of testing for the presence or absence of instead provides a means to understand whether "students organize, structure and use information in context to solve complex problems" (Herman, Aschabacher & Winters, 1992). This relates to the manner in which the semiotic model of sign can be used as an alternative assessment tool. By analyzing the relationship between signs and symbols instead of evaluating the discrete signs themselves, a holistic picture of the students' understanding emerges. The process by which these relationships come into being is an emergent phenomenon (Shank, 1992); which is iterative, personal and ongoing.

Simmons too (1994) states the case for iterative, ongoing and embedded assessment, which can be both self and instructor administered. She states: "Assessment is not something that we tack onto learning: it is an essential ongoing component of instruction that guides the process of learning. Ongoing assessment uses exhibitions, student explanations of concepts, the writing of a poem or a song or any number of other thought demanding performances to evaluate and reflect on students work."

Assessment can be used to build understanding through reflective and iteration. There is great promise for deeper understanding and appreciation of the creative, generative process we call learning when a student is aware of scholastic expectations and understands how to effectively review and critique his or her own work. Simmons (1994) outlines this process in three steps:

1. The teacher must help students understand from the outset the standards by which their work will be judged.
2. Students must document their work process for the duration of the project or unit.
3. Through performance and feedback, students come to understand the complex nature of judging and improving upon one's work.

This last point is especially crucial, as "taking the time and energy to reflect on and improve one's work is essential to the understanding process itself". Instead of the traditional black-and-white, single score assessments usually meted out by traditional instructors, students learn instead that there are indeed many shades of grey, that it is difficult to judge and to be judged.

Rief (1990) also supports self-assessment, especially in middle-school aged children. In her utilization of self-assessment techniques of student writing over the course of a year, Rief came to understand that it was the student's personal dialogue that was most valuable. In establishing criterion for portfolio work, she found that it was best if she imposed external criteria by which the portfolio would be judged, and allowed the students themselves determine the internal criteria: "I discovered that the students knew themselves as learners better than anyone else. They set goals for themselves and judged how well they had reached those goals. They thoughtfully and honestly evaluated their own learning with far more detail and introspection than I thought possible. Ultimately, they showed me who they were as readers, writers, thinkers and human beings" (Rief, 1990).

In essence what Rief (1990) discovered was the intrinsic motivation so necessary for developing deep understanding and personal meaning. As one of her students states: "Now I know that in order to write something well, you have to care about it. The first important thing is that you like a piece of writing, and then you worry if anyone else likes it." At the core of the learning process is to acknowledge the intrinsic value of learning to ourselves. At the end of the year, in describing the above students' work, Rief (1990) states, "she has a message for his reader, because the message is always for her, first".

In practice, both traditional and alternative assessment of students' performance should require an understanding of how a particular student came into the learning process, including their cultural background, personal learning style and what they accomplished in relative terms while engaged in the learning process. It becomes a very delicate, finely tuned relationship between assessors and assessed. This balance is easier to maintain when working with alternative practices (Simmons, 1994).

Brooks & Brooks (1993) describe what assessment in a constructivist classroom looks like! Rather than saying "NO" when a student does not give the exact answer being sought, the constructivist teacher attempts to understand that student's current thinking about the topic. Through non-judgmental questioning, the teacher leads the student to construct new understanding and acquire new skills. Constructivists believe that assessment should be used as a tool to enhance both the student's learning and the teacher's understanding of the student's current understanding. It should not be used as an accountability tool that makes some students feel good about themselves and causes others to give up.

According to Grant Wiggins (1989), authentic assessments have four qualities: (1) They require that the student engage in creating a product that relates directly and authentically to the skill being taught. For example, students' writing is assessed through evaluation of real writing tasks, rather than through spelling tests, grammar exercises, or other decontextualized measures. (2) The standards for excellent performance are articulated clearly and specifically to students throughout the entire process. (3) Self-assessment is a critical component of the assessment process, as students reflect on their own performance as compared to the stated standards and modify their efforts in order to improve their performance. (4) Students present their work publicly and are expected to justify their decisions in front of other people.

Authentic assessment is thought to provide a broader window into the minds of students and create greater opportunity for students to participate in their own evaluative and learning processes. If truly actualized, authentic assessment is deeply embedded in teaching and learning: "...It is designed to provide the student with a genuine rather than a contrived learning experience that provides both the teacher and student with opportunities to learn what the student can do. The demonstration of learning occurs in a situation that requires the application and production of knowledge rather than the mere recognition or reproduction of correct answers" (Darling-Hammond, Ancess, & Falk, 1995). These types of assessments require that students actually perform certain learning tasks, thereby demonstrating their skill and understanding and their ability to apply what they have learned (McTighe, 1997). Performance assessments are those "which model real tasks, i.e., require the pupil to perform in the assessment what we wish them to learn in the classroom; usually they focus on higher levels of cognitive complexity" (Gipps, 1995).

Authentic assessment is also thought to enhance the learning process, because the evaluation tools used fall naturally from daily classroom activities, rather than being separate, summative measures at the end of a learning unit. "This kind of assessment does not drive the curriculum; it grows out of the curriculum and is part and parcel of the curriculum.... Thumbing through a portfolio with a student or watching a student perform a task...adds a degree of intimacy that can be refreshing in an age of depersonalized appraisal" (Maeroff, 1991). In other words, students learn as they create the assessment data, and authentic assessment allows the teacher to witness this learning as it happens.

Finally, forms of assessments that are authentic influence students affectively in positive ways. When students perceive activities as having personal and real-world relevance, they are more likely to feel positive about those activities and put effort into them. "What we assess sends a strong signal to students about what is important for them to learn. When authentic performance tasks play a key role in teaching and assessing, students will know that we expect them to apply knowledge in ways valued in the world beyond the classroom" (McTighe, 1997).

As a constructivist teacher, one may find authentic assessment appealing because of its student-centredness. Its implementation, however, is far from easy, particularly if one's evaluative experiences as a student or teacher were traditional: pencil and paper objective and/or essay tests, five-paragraph expository papers, and so on. To evaluate authentically meant taking risks and constantly experimenting.

In essence, much of what a teacher has experienced and what he or she may witness others experience is autocratic in nature. Teachers and professors at all levels take primary responsibility for the events, outcomes, and evaluations in the classroom. Henry Giroux (1988) defines this teacher-as-authoritarian role as reflective of a conservative tradition of male-dominated Western culture, one that focuses only on the performance of the intellect as determined and evaluated by the teacher. Others, in an attempt to redefine and reshape "authority", have advocated feminist pedagogical principles, because patriarchal pedagogical structures deny women and others "the authority of their experiences, perspectives, emotions, and minds" (Friedman, 1985). This "feminist pedagogy" has a variety of qualities, most consistently the following: student-centred instruction, decision-making, and evaluation; nonhierarchical classroom structures; empowerment of the individual; celebration of differences; collaboration between students; and full participation and engagement of all students (Brown, 1992).

Maxine Greene (1978) asserts, "A new pedagogy is obviously required, one that will free persons to understand the ways in which each of them reaches out from his or her location to constitute a common continent, a common world. It might well be called a democratic pedagogy, since, in several respects, the object is to empower persons to enact democracy. To act upon democratic values, I believe, is to be responsive to consciously incarnated principles of freedom, justice, and regard for others." Here again, the focus is placed upon the student as an individual, and equity rather than authority is central.

The roots of authentic assessment are grounded in these theoretical principles. Greene (1978) suggests that education of teachers must bring them "in touch with their own landscape". If the focus of teacher education is mastery of techniques or demonstration of "competencies", rather than critical, reflective thinking, teachers become, in Greene's words, "mere transmission belts" or "clerks". Teachers must have opportunities to learn how to explore the world critically and find their place in it before they can challenge children to do so. The emphasis of authentic assessment on process and product and the value that authentic assessment places upon the individual create the ideal scenario in which to help teachers find their own landscapes. Lucy M. Calkins (1995) articulates this "practice what we preach" philosophy effectively in Writing Between the Lines: "Minds-on teaching is something that happens deep within the self. If we teachers want to reform our methods of assessment..., it's important to realize that the place to begin is within ourselves.... 'Authentic assessment' cannot exist unless we, as teachers, inhabit and claim the process as our own."

Rief and Atwell both emphasize the need for effective reading and writing teachers to continue to evolve as readers and writers themselves. We find, however, that our busy schedules and priority lists allow little time for this type of growth. During the next week, your task is to rediscover yourself as a reader and writer, by immersing yourself in the following experiences (Benner, 2000):

1. Read something that you have been meaning to read for a long time and have never had the chance to. This could be a book of poems, an adult work of fiction, a young adult novel, a collection of picture books by a particular author, a biography, a professional book, etc. The choice is yours. Concentrate on becoming a reflective reader...what elements of the writer's style appeal to you? turn you of? How do you relate your personal life experiences to this piece of writing? What do your eyes and mind do as you read? Why do they do these things? What parts of the book touch you emotionally? Why?

2. Experiment with writing in a genre with which you are unfamiliar or uncomfortable. Perhaps take a stab at poetry, a short piece of fiction, a persuasive essay, an autobiography, a picture book for children. Again, the choice is yours. Try to engage in all stages of the writing process as you do so, and reflect upon how you do this—linearly, cyclically, spirally? What succeeded in your writing? What frustrated you?
3. As you read and write, keep a reader's/writer's log with your reflections. Try to form connections between the two processes as you reflect. Then, at the end of your log, provide a self-evaluation of your reading and writing ability. What are your strengths and weaknesses as a reader and a writer? How would you grade yourself on your reader's/writer's log? Why?

When the teacher presents the exam to the students, they seem generally positive. A few may have questions, perhaps testing the teacher to see if their choice of reading material could truly be their choice. When the teacher decides to read the midterms without pen or pencil in hand, to form general impressions, and then make comments and assign marks/grades later. What the teacher may discover is that the students may handover to him/her images and glimpses of who they were as human beings, imprints of their hearts so compelling, etc.

Much of the student writing may be in narrative form, particularly the journal writing, and the teacher may began to see the true potential of using this form of writing to engage students in deeper reflection about literature, the writing process, and teaching. Suzanne Rice (1993) emphasizes the value of learning through story and dialogue, a pedagogical technique suggestive of a feminist epistemology. She cites the work of Carol Witherell and Nel Noddings (1991), who claim that "stories give special voice to the feminine side of human experience—to the power of emotion, intuition, and relationships in human lives". They assert that "narrative capacity is the way each of us reorganizes, reassesses, realigns our life experience so that it is continually integrated into our present personal schema.... The power of narrative is that it allows the individual to continually locate and relocate his or her own voice within a social and cultural context." Indeed, the teacher may witness this type of personal transformation occurring, as the students may find ways to connect what they were reading and writing to their own life experiences and conflicts.

One of the most difficult aspects of this process for the teacher is the dilemma of assigning grades to the projects. As a classroom teacher, when a teacher uses the workshop approach with children, it may be challenging to quantify each child's effort and writing progress and settle upon a grade. Some pertinent questions may naturally recur such as: Do I evaluate each person based on simple completion of the tasks outlined? How do I assess the amount of effort and "heart" each person put into his/her work? What about students' past experiences with taking risks as readers and writers and their current levels of expertise? Pat Belanoff (1991) elaborates on the "messiness" of evaluating writing: She asserts that writing teachers have difficulty agreeing on what constitutes good writing and whether individual pieces of writing meet those criteria. She points out that even the same evaluator reading the same piece of writing in two different sittings frequently evaluates it differently each time. And then, even if the evaluator could come to terms with grading or rating the piece, that piece is but one representation of a student's ability: "To what degree does a particular piece of writing represent a student's total ability? Are we assessing the student's ability or the quality of the piece of writing? In fact the only thing it's really possible to find out is if the particular piece of writing before us does or does not accomplish some particular purpose. Could the student duplicate the piece, do something else like it just as well again? And even if so, can writing tasks be so much alike that we can be sure that if a student does one he/she can do the other?"

In evaluating this assignment, teacher has to decide whether what he/she was evaluating was actually the quality of the writing the students did or the quality and depth of the thought put into their experimentation with print. One of the goals for the students may be that they would play with words and dabble with types of writing that were unfamiliar and perhaps even threatening. As Belanoff (1991) states, "We want them to take risks, to try harder things which may make their writing look as though it's deteriorating depending on when we decide to look at it. We don't want them to write what they already know how to write; we want them to write something that pulls and stretches their skills—and that pulling and stretching can result in some pretty messy stuff."

All of these issues may complicate the "authentic" assessment process for the teacher and may make objectivity an unrealistic (and perhaps even undesirable) goal. Ultimately, the teacher may place the quality of students' writing in the context of their quality of thought and effort and establish a sort of "gestalt" impression in his/her mind of what that quality of thought would represent. With this impression providing the framework for teacher's thoughts, he/she began to respond to the students' efforts.

Linda Darling-Hammond, Jacqueline Ancess, and Beverly Falk (1995) state, "It is the action around assessment—the discussions, meetings, revisions, arguments, and opportunities to continually create new directions for teaching, learning, curriculum, and assessment—that ultimately have consequence. The 'things' of assessment are essentially useful as dynamic supports for reflection and action, rather than as static products with value in and of themselves." The reading and writing workshop experience may launch a teacher to higher levels of self-discovery and understanding of the world around him/her. The teacher may find his/her own landscape. Experiencing truly authentic assessment may strengthen his/her resolve and feel empowered with the knowledge and confidence to implement it in his/her classroom. Finally, the teacher must provide experiences and assessments that inspire and nurture lifelong learning and enable the students to discover their own landscapes.

Fortunately, classroom landscapes are changing, some for the better, some for the worse. Test score accountability, in particular, is compelling many teachers in public schools to take backward steps from democratic pedagogy into autocratic modes of information transmission. The "powers that be" are demanding that administrators, teachers, and students "prove" that learning has occurred in ways that can be measured quantitatively. Unfortunately, quantitative accountability tends to reduce student learning to acquisition and transmission of isolated bits of knowledge. Teacher educators and future teachers have the opportunity (and the responsibility) to change this landscape. We have the potential to impact the landscape of education in profound ways through practice of authentic teaching, learning, and assessing. The roots of reform germinate within our own belief systems and ways of knowing and learning. Greene (1978) eloquently proposes that, in order to foster democratic values and authentic learning in our classroom landscapes, "self-reflectiveness be encouraged, that teacher educators and their students be stimulated to think about their own thinking and reflect upon their own reflecting. This seems to be inherently liberating and likely to invigorate their teaching and their advocacy."

How is self-reflectiveness encouraged? We believe that all students need to be engaged in activities rooted in authenticity that help them become writers, mathematicians, scientists, or teachers (Benner, 2000). According to Linda Darling-Hammond (1996), teacher education reformers are beginning to recognize that prospective teachers, like their students, learn by doing: "As teacher educators, beginning teachers, and experienced teachers work together on real problems of practice in learner-centred settings, they can begin to develop a collective knowledge base and a common set of understandings about practice." This is what happened to us as a result of this immersion in the workshop experience. Students learned readers' and writers' workshop by reading about it, discussing it, and actually doing it. In this process, we identified and grappled with the many challenges involved in implementing authentic experiences and assessments. The most central challenge, for both professor and students, involved deepening our response to our own writing, others' writing, and ultimately, ourselves.

Darling-Hammond (1996) asserts that teachers must "understand learners and their learning as deeply as they comprehend their subjects". This is the essence of authentic assessment. Teachers need to develop a capacity to analyze and respond to what is happening in their classrooms and in the lives of their students. In order to do this, teachers need to develop productive relationships with their students. Skilful teachers in settings where they know their students well make the greatest difference in what children learn. Robert J. Tierney (1998) states, "To be both accountable and empowered, readers and writers need to be both reflective and pragmatic. To do so, readers and writers need to be inquirers—researching their own selves, considering the consequences of their efforts, and evaluating the implications, worth, and ongoing usefulness of what they are doing or have done. Teachers can facilitate such reflection by encouraging students to keep traces of what they do, by suggesting they pursue ways to depict their journey... and by setting aside time to contemplate their progress and efforts. These reflections can serve as conversation starters—conversations about what they are doing and planning to do and what they did and have learned."

Indeed, learning is a journey, for students of all ages. Teacher education must help each teacher to first find his/her own landscape, and then develop the confidence to bring others into this landscape. The most powerful teachers are those for whom learning is an exciting and continuous opportunity, for both themselves and the children they inspire. These teachers are not just receptacles and transmitters of information; they can act upon this knowledge in ways firmly grounded in personal belief and conviction. The most powerful assessment, therefore, is that which empowers, encourages, and strengthens learners, particularly those who will be tomorrow's teachers. It is through our example as teacher educators that our students will learn to someday empower, encourage, and strengthen the children in their care (Benner, 2000).

Sign Theory as an Assessment Tool: Sign theory can be used as an assessment tool to evaluate the meaning inherent in a representation. However, a balance must be maintained between the value of interpretation and the value of consensual undertaking. For example, to understand the value of a virtual learning environment, one must ask both creators and experienced what they derived from their design or experiential encounter with the environment. It is not just a question of whether students remember discrete aspects of the environment. It is more a question of what they derived from it in a holistic fashion.

Formative Assessment from a Constructivist Perspective: Formative assessment is assessment that informs—it informs teachers about what students think; it informs students what their classmates think; it informs individuals what they themselves think. It promotes awareness and communication in the classroom. The emphasis is on finding out what isn't known, and it tells teachers and students early enough in the course that something can be done about it. If done well, it is extremely low-stakes. If done often, both students and teachers can modify their approaches based on the outcome. In this way, formative assessment can be a valuable learning experience for students and teachers. Summative assessment is different. It is used to evaluate—in the sense of assigning a value label. It is high-stakes. The emphasis is on finding out what is known. Both students and teachers tend to focus on the score rather than the details. It is done at the end of a topic, and thus, it cannot generally be used as a learning experience.

QUESTION CYCLE

- Present an item.
- Let students work individually or in groups.
- Collect answers.
- Show histogram.
- Discuss as a class.
- Wrap-up.

The question cycle: One way in which formative assessment can be used is called the question cycle. The typical class period can be broken down into two or three cycles of six phases, as listed to the right. Although this cycle does not need to be followed strictly at all times, it is a good starting point, especially for teachers who are new to conducting an interactive classroom. The cycle makes relatively efficient use of class time by always asking a question first. Discussion and wrap-up can then be shortened or lengthened to take into account students' answers.

Presenting an item: Although the act of "presenting" an item is straightforward, the relevance of this phase is that it is first. There is no lecturing needed beforehand; students merely answer the questions based on their current knowledge and understanding, and preferably, without worrying about whether their answers are right or wrong. However, the choice of question, problem, or task is critical. There should be a variety of types of items, and they should vary in their subtlety, abstractness, and level. It is often a good idea to let students read and interpret the item themselves, without any immediate intervention from teachers. All questions contain some level of ambiguity, and it is often the case that the ambiguity leads to a range of defensible responses. By leaving the ambiguity there, teachers can help discourage students from focusing on the "right" answer and can help them develop interpretational and communication skills.

Let students work individually or in groups: Whether individually or in groups, students should be given sufficient time to reason toward an answer. When done individually, students should still be allowed time to share and defend their answers with a neighbour or small group of classmates. This will happen more naturally when students work in small groups, so in both cases, students are given opportunities to articulate their thinking, to become more aware of the thinking of their classmates, to prepare for the class-wise discussion, and to develop better listening skills. One variation is to have students work individually and to submit their answers. The histogram is not displayed yet. Then they work in groups as described above and submit their answers again. This mode permits comparison of the distribution of answers before and after group work, and in some cases can help motivate students who do not appreciate the value of group work. Part of the class-wide discussion can focus on why the distribution of answers changed as a result of working in groups. The amount of time needed for this phase depends on the item, and sometimes it can be hard to predict how much time a particular class will need for a certain item. Often, the noise level can be a good indicator of where the students are in the process of working on the item. Just after the item is sent, the noise level is often very low, as students are reading and interpreting the item. Then the noise level begins to rise as groups begin to discuss the item. When the noise level has peaked and begins to fall, it is soon time to collect answers.

Collect answers: Collecting answers is a good way to get students out of group work smoothly with minimal disruption. It also forces students to commit to an answer—something they will avoid if teachers let them. By committing to an answer, students will be more actively engaged during the other phases of the question cycle, and they will get more out of the experience. When possible, teachers can monitor the answers as they come in, and begin to think about the upcoming class-wise discussion.

Show histogram: One of students' favourite parts of the question cycle is the histogram display, in which they get to see how the class is distributed. The immediacy of the feedback helps students see how they fit in to the rest of the class, and serves as an excellent focus for the class-wide discussion. Showing the histogram also returns control of the class to the teacher, and it is done without all the confusion, frustration, and loss of time usually associated with bouncing back and forth between group work and teacher-facilitated activities.

Discuss as a class: During this phase, teachers typically ask for volunteers to defend or otherwise explain their choices. Because students have had the opportunity to explain their reasoning in the small group format, they are often more likely to share their reasoning in the whole-class setting. Because they can see from the histogram that there are classmates who gave the same answer, they are often more comfortable participating, even if they are in the minority. If students are unwilling to share their reasoning, teachers can ask for volunteers who will explain why someone might choose a certain answer, even if it isn't the one they chose. If the item sent is to predict what will happen during a demonstration, then it is best to do the demonstration after the choices have been discussed. After the demonstration, the discussion should center on any mismatches between predictions and observations. It is critical to keep the discussion student-directed, even if it is moderated by the teacher. The teacher's role should be to draw out student reasoning and help clarify it. To do this, it is helpful for the teacher to remember that there are no wrong answers and that silence and patience are most likely to instil confidence and willingness to participate. Some paraphrasing can be done, but it is valuable to make sure that the student agrees with the paraphrase and that it is not done so much that students fail to develop appropriate communication skills.

Wrap-up: If necessary, and only if necessary, teachers can give a short lecture in order to summarize the discussion, clarify any lingering confusion, introduce useful concepts or principles, emphasize the major points of discussion, indicate connections to earlier questions and discussion, or otherwise address the state of knowledge exhibited by students during the discussion. Another way of wrapping up is to ask students "what if" questions, such as special and limiting cases. An entire question cycle is not needed for these—just a few, short, follow-up questions should suffice. Still another technique is to present the same item again, collect answers, and show a new histogram. The discussion would center on changes in the distribution of answers, and possibly there would be no need of a formal wrap-up. In some cases, rather than any wrap-up, it is more instructive for students to immediately consider another item, preferably an item that is related to the one just completed. The discussion and wrap-up can then focus on a pair or even a group of items, rather than only on a single item.

Choosing and sequencing items: Before any items can be sent, teachers must select which items they are going to present and decide the order in which they will be presented. Items should vary in style, difficulty, and purpose. It is usually best if most of the questions yield a range of responses. In other words, it is not necessary—and perhaps even undesirable—that questions have only one right answer. Teachers should look for questions that will stimulate a lively debate during the class-wide discussion. Both the habits of mind and the cognitive goals are useful for guiding teachers through this step. Thus, it is recommended that teachers first decide which cognitive goal to target within any particular topic or subtopic. Then, to help maintain interest and motivation, teachers should vary the targeted habit of mind. However, particular habits of mind are more suitable for certain cognitive goals than others. For instance, "seeking alternative representations" is good for honing concepts, and "comparing and contrasting" is good for clustering concepts. Also, a particular habit of mind can advance more than one cognitive goal. Teachers should remember, however, that they do not need to wait until all the early stages of cognitive development are addressed before moving on to the later stages. All the cognitive skills should be targeted from the very beginning of the course. In addition, students do not need to understand every concept, subtopic, or topic completely before moving on to the next. This means that sometimes students will have to reach and stretch a little. Teachers should keep in mind that student confusion does not mean that they are lacking information. A little confusion can be beneficial for providing the internal need that spawns the motivation to learn.

Preparing for the class-wide discussion: Another important step that should be completed before an item is sent is to get ready for the class-wide discussion. It is common for teachers to be caught off-guard by their students' responses, so some preparation both in the anticipated distribution of answers and in the possible range of explanations will side-step much awkwardness and help maintain a friendly, non-threatening classroom environment. Teachers must convince students that items are formative not summative. In other words, the items "inform" rather than "represent a value judgment". This can be difficult, because students often have years of prior experience trying to determine the "right" answer, and they have lots of emotional "baggage" associated with getting questions right or wrong. Teachers therefore must disarm students' quest for the right answer, which sometimes happens at the very end of the question cycle, when students want the teacher to summarize the discussion and tell them what the "right" answer was. This tendency should be avoided, and when students insist on knowing the right answer, teachers should shift the focus of the discussion by meta-communicating about why students are so interested in the right answer and why they should be interested instead in the assumptions and thought processes leading up to the answers they chose. Teachers also must learn to use the information they get back from students. We expect students to deal with information in real time, so why not teachers as well? Therefore, teachers need to learn how to listen and respond to students' answers and explanations.

5

Constructivism and Teacher Education

Teacher education programmes play an important role in our society because they serve the public interest. One of the primary responsibilities of teacher education programmes is to produce effective classroom teachers. Pedagogical research has demonstrated that constructivism can help teachers become successful in the classroom (Emmer & Gerwels, 2002; Vaughan, 2002; Deeds & Allen, 2000; Carlin & Ciaccio, 1997). Therefore, it is in the best interest of pre-service teachers that they become familiar with a constructivist philosophy of teaching and learning.

Present Teacher Education is found weak on at least two major accounts:

- Epistemological (assumptions of knowledge and knower), and
- Pedagogical.

Thus to make the foundations of teacher education programme stronger, it is apt to bank upon constructivism. Constructivism is an approach to teaching and learning that acknowledges that information can be conveyed but understanding is dependent upon the learner. In recent years, constructivism has received considerable attention in education scholarship, practitioner preparation, and policy formation (MacKinnon & Scarff-Seatter, 1997; Richardson, 1997; Teets & Starnes, 1996). It has been heralded as a more natural, relevant, productive, and empowering framework for instructing both school students and teacher education students (Cannella & Reiff, 1994).

As an approach to teaching, constructivism may be examined as much for what it is NOT as for what it is. It challenges what Oldfather, Bonds, and Bray (1994) characterize as the default mode in education—an empiricist/reductionist approach to teaching and learning. They cite Freire who considers this approach to be a "banking" model—the teacher fills students with deposits of information considered by the teacher to be true knowledge, and the students store these deposits, intact, until needed. Cannella & Reiff (1994) label these traditional models didactic, memory-oriented transmission models. Constructivists generally maintain that when information is acquired through transmission models, it is not always well integrated with prior knowledge and is often accessed and articulated only for formal academic occasions such as exams (Richardson, 1997). Constructivist approaches, in contrast, are regarded as producing greater internalization and deeper understanding than traditional methods.

5.1 FOUNDATIONS OF TEACHER EDUCATION

Epistemologically and pedagogically both, present teacher education is found to be based on behaviouristic paradigm which considers knowledge as objective and fixed and teacher's role is to impart or transmit it to the students ignoring importance of students' own experiences. On the contrary, the demand of the time is to situate entire paradigm of teacher education programme on constructivist paradigm as it believes in multiple realities and considers knowledge largely as subjective and thus it emphasizes teacher's role as a facilitator who helps the students to construct his/her knowledge on the basis of his/her own experience and understanding.

Translation of any theory into practice is an arduous task. Similar practical problem is found with constructivism too. Constructivist theory while it may inform and influence practice, constructivism is a theory of learning, not a theory of teaching (Wolffe & McMullen, 1996), and translating theory to practice is both difficult and imprecise (MacKinnon & Scarf-Seatter, 1997). However, education literature documents several large- and small-scale efforts to do so (DeJong & Grooms, 1996; Kaufman,

1996; Richardson, 1997). Constructivist teacher education generally reflects two major traditions—the developmental and social reconstructionist traditions (Cannella & Reiff, 1994). Programmes influenced by the developmental tradition attempt to teach students how to teach in a constructivist, generally Piagetian, manner. They are typically characterized by substantial direct instruction in theory and practice, often without complementary opportunities for inquiry, discovery, or self-examination. This approach can easily become overly prescriptive. If this occurs, the teacher educator models an approach to teaching that is essentially antithetical to the approach students are intended to employ in their future classrooms (Oldfather, Bonds, & Bray, 1994).

Programmes influenced by social reconstructionist tradition attempt to help teacher education students deconstruct their own prior knowledge and attitudes, comprehend how these understandings evolved, explore the effects they have on actions and behaviour, and consider alternate conceptions and premises that may be more serviceable in teaching. Critical analysis and structured reflection on formal course knowledge and everyday practical experience are incorporated.

Richardson (1997) identifies two factors that appear to affect the approach teachers and teacher educators take in forming constructivist settings—the extent to which the social is acknowledged as a critical factor in learning and individual cognitive development and the specific content, subject matter, or discipline. Some subjects, such as mathematics, are more "bounded" than others by rules, formulae, and procedures. They are more likely to be regarded by teachers as producing problems and tasks to which there are "correct" answers. Individual interpretations and construction of ideas and concepts are less likely to be encouraged by teachers than in subjects such as literature and writing.

The overarching challenge constructivism presents to teachers and teacher educators is the formidable task of translating a learning theory into a theory of teaching (MacKinnon & Scarff-Seatter, 1997), which in turn raises questions about what teachers need to know and be able to do. For teacher educators, among other tasks, this involves balancing the need to acknowledge the different discipline-specific requirements of teaching with the need to model constructivist methods in teacher education courses and practicums. Richardson (1997) also notes the limits of a perspective on teaching that values students' understandings at the expense of "right" answers. Student knowledge becomes idiosyncratic; 30 different students may arrive at 30 different understandings or interpretations of a concept, all of which are not equally appropriate. Inappropriately applied, constructivist approaches may lead to the "abandonment" style of teaching (MacKinnon & Scarff-Seatter, 1997). Several authors cite the importance of teacher educators' modelling constructivist approaches that engage students in interdisciplinary exploration, collaborative activity, and field-based opportunities for experiential learning, reflection, and self-examination (Kaufman, 1996; Kroll & LaBosky, 1996) if future teachers are to be able to employ these strategies in schools.

To derive culturally relevant and socially just pedagogy and practice from constructivist epistemologies, Martin (1994) and Vadeboncoeur (1997) urge teacher educators to deconstruct and scrutinize cultural assumptions that underlie various interpretations of constructivism to expose how social beliefs have influenced the development of theory and practices. Without such scrutiny, societal inequities and historical forms of oppression may be perpetuated in supposedly constructivist classrooms, and the very constraints on individual development constructivists seek to remove or ameliorate will be reinforced.

A final challenge faced by educators is the pitfall of regarding constructivism as the only viable theoretical framework for teaching and learning. It is one way of thinking about how knowledge and understanding are formed, but it is not the only way. Nor are various interpretations of constructivism necessarily incompatible with one another (MacKinnon & Scarff-Seatter, 1997; Oldfather, Bonds, & Bray, 1994). Prospective teachers should be exposed to varying perspectives and given opportunities to develop the discretion needed to choose most appropriately and the skills to implement their choices.

Thus, the Foundations of Teacher Education programme must be based upon the constructivist principles of: (a) integrated curriculum; (b) organized yet flexible learning environment and schedule; (c) developmentally appropriate curriculum; (d) continuous assessment and progress, and (f) teaching for understanding.

The faculty's conception of what is important to the preparation of educators, and the relationships between the key elements are crucial aspects. According to this conception, a safe, caring, and diverse community of learners in which each is respected allows people to collaborate in the socially mediated process of constructing knowledge. This leads to a sense of individual and collective empowerment allowing one the confidence, courage, and desire to reflect critically on one's aims and practices, as well as the context in which these occur. This process of critical reflection is essential if one is to improve the quality and appropriateness of one's future actions or the context in which those actions will occur. Educators serve the needs of a pluralistic society by working to meet the needs of all students; they serve the needs of a just society by challenging the inequities of the status quo.

This conceptual framework must not only define what is expected of the college's students, but also what is expected of the faculty. This is reflected in the statement of philosophy for the college. The statement reads, "The College of Education is a community of learners—faculty, staff, and students—committed to encouraging dialogue and cooperation, to facilitating a process by which learners actively construct meaning, and to continuing improvement through critical reflection and action." Conclusively the emphatic point is that we must strive all the possible ways to base our Teacher Education Programme on constructivist principle of teaching, learning and assessment.

Meaningful teacher education, then, involves not just mastering content and pedagogical strategies (although these are necessary and important aspects of expert teaching), but understanding the nature and purpose of both, so that teachers are better able to recognize, reflect on, and solve the problems encountered in practice. In keeping with a constructivist, reflective practitioner model of professional development, pupil-teachers are viewed as researchers of their own practice as well as critical analysts of the theory and research of others. Our aim is to provide an environment in which the reflective practitioner contemplates prior experiences, weighs successes and difficulties associated with these experiences, and considers strategies for extending successes and reducing difficulties.

This model presumes a collaborative relationship between graduate students and university/college of education faculty in determining and addressing the professional development needs of individual candidates. This is a labour intensive process, requiring sustained time and effort by all involved, so that pupil-teachers work is guided by a shared commitment to continuous improvement based on reflection, evaluation, and ongoing research (Swanson, 1995). In this sense, then, the areas of *research, reflection, learning,* and *leading* may be woven together in all core course work within the programme.

The characteristics of reflective decision-making and continuous professional development included in programmes in the Department/Colleges of Education should be derived from concepts of reflective practice and cognitive apprenticeship. The intent should be to encourage individual open mindedness, that is, the ability to actively challenge personal beliefs by continually seeking and evaluating new information. Open-mindedness goes hand-in-hand with whole-heartedness and intellectual responsibility. Whole-heartedness is an absorbing enthusiasm for and dedication to one's work. Intellectual responsibility includes caring enough about the consequences of one's professional duties and actions to seek necessary information on which to base intelligent decisions. These characteristics inform and direct the actions which constitute reflection.

The programme's conceptual framework should be consistent with the unit's conceptual framework but it must focus more specifically on understanding the dynamics of teaching and learning in specific content areas or disciplines as well as in particular socio-cultural contexts.

An aim of professional preparation should be the development of an ability to reflect on and learn from practical experiences (Tynjala, 1999). The integration of theoretical and practical knowledge and the eventual ability to be a reflective practitioner are logical aims for teacher education programmes. However, Mandl, Gruber, and Renkl (1996) observed that in traditional university/college of education settings, pre-service teachers normally make use of the knowledge acquired in the instructional setting but cannot generalize this to professional contexts. If abstract theoretical content studied in the university/college of education setting does not transfer to practical knowledge or future teaching practice, then theory is not influencing professional preparation. Nothing more than rote knowledge can be expected when methods of assessment tend to encourage students to memorize and discourage students from achieving deep understanding (e.g., Entwistle, 1995). A challenge in teacher education is to develop instructional practices that integrate theories of learning (based on constructivism) and instruction with practical pedagogical skills.

Dewey (1965) has argued that if learning is to be meaningful, it must begin with what is already relevant. Dewey would support the use of qualitative evaluations such as essays that can represent students' current understanding and show individual growth. Essays should be used in the current study as they engage students in discussing theory and practice, largely in light of personal experience, at various levels of complexity. In order to implement this type of assessment, one must ask about the kinds of outcomes that are indicative of the quality of students' growth. Evaluations promoting recognition-based items inhibit enthusiastic engagement with ideas and are a barrier to the acculturation of students into reflective practitioners.

As universities are learning communities, members accepted into these communities have the privileges and responsibilities afforded to membership. Pre-service teachers and professors must acknowledge their mutual obligations for learning in order to achieve the university's ultimate goal of student growth and learning. Professors are responsible for providing opportunities for student interaction and for establishing a climate conducive to student participation. In turn, students are responsible for actively engaging in such environments. All members of the university must have a shared purpose and sense of responsibility in order to collectively engage in the learning process. Students' sense of responsibility for learning is not independent from their academic setting; institutions must therefore create learning communities that nurture student responsibility (Pace, 1984). Pace proposed that academic achievement is dependent on responsible student behaviour and that university environments serve to either encourage or discourage these responsible student behaviours.

Several authors cite the importance of teacher educators' modelling constructivist approaches that engage students in interdisciplinary exploration, collaborative activity, and field-based opportunities for experiential learning, reflection, and self-examination (Kaufman, 1996; Kroll & LaBosky, 1996) if future teachers are to be able to employ these strategies in schools. To derive culturally relevant and socially just pedagogy and practice from constructivist epistemologies, Martin (1994) and Vadeboncoeur (1997) urge teacher educators to deconstruct and scrutinize cultural assumptions that underlie various interpretations of constructivism to expose how social beliefs have influenced the development of theory and practices. Without such scrutiny, societal inequities and historical forms of oppression may be perpetuated in supposedly constructivist classrooms, and the very constraints on individual development constructivists seek to remove or ameliorate will be reinforced.

A final challenge faced by educators is the pitfall of regarding constructivism as the only viable theoretical framework for teaching and learning. It is one way of thinking about how knowledge and understanding are formed, but it is not the only way. Nor are various interpretations of constructivism necessarily incompatible with one another (MacKinnon & Scarff-Seatter, 1997; Oldfather, Bonds, & Bray, 1994). Prospective teachers should be exposed to varying perspectives and given opportunities to develop the discretion needed to choose most appropriately and the skills to implement their choices.

5.2 A NEW APPROACH TO TEACHER EDUCATION

Elliot Eisner (1994) reminds us that would-be teachers have been trained in the profession from the age of five, some even younger. They learned from their own teachers just as we did. They had models of what to say and do and how to act. Teaching them about a different way of doing things usually has little effect: Students often enter a college/department/institute of education with a set of conservative expectations and predispositions. They want to become teachers like those they have known, and they expect to teach students just like the ones who were their friends. Accordingly, their acculturation into the profession requires little break with their past and their childhood values. In short, teacher education students tend to avoid alternative ways of seeing; they often show little interest in finding new lenses through which to conceptualize knowledge and pedagogy. Instead they walk into their classes searching for information delivery recipes and classroom discipline approaches. Question of purpose, context and power are alien and irrelevant. What, they ask does such information have to do with teaching (Kincheloe, 2000)?

We can tell our students in our classroom management class that the more engaged their students are, and the more empowered they feel, and the more control that the teacher is willing to give up, the better the classes will be. The students in these classes will tend to value learning that they help to create. Their needs have a greater chance of being met. We can tell our students all of this. However, telling the students simply won't work. They must participate in it. They must feel it. They must appreciate it from the inside, as an affective impact. This is what makes it stick. This is what allows them to trust that the community will actually work. This is what allows them to trust enough to give up control. Not only do they begin to trust in the idea, they begin to know the power of trusting their own students to create meaningful learning environments for themselves because they have done it as students. They begin to understand not only that their students want to learn but how they want to learn. In a positive, equal, respectful environment most students will flourish as they participate in their own creation of knowledge.

Even university professors who believe strongly in the ideas of student-centred learning, communities of inquiry, constructivism, and philosophical dialogue and the power of these ideas to affect genuine, positive change also have difficulty as they attempt to create courses which exemplify these ideas. As was stated earlier, students demand to learn the methods for which they believe they will be accountable. If they have never had a chance to see what it's like outside of the box, then they would not even be able to recognize an opportunity when it presented itself. Awareness of possibility allows for freedom and choice. At the very least, we must give our students that. Patiently and caringly, we need to awaken our students. Of course, shaking them up, breaking open the box will lead to frustration. But that disillusion may lead to change. Blind compliance certainly won't.

Richard Morehouse and Melinda Williams studied student use of argument skills over a period of three years and found that their ability to construct a written argument was enhanced:

Principle 1: Learning about teaching involves continuously conflicting and competing demands.

Principle 2: Learning about teaching requires a view of knowledge as a subject to be created rather than as a created subject.

Principle 3: Learning about teaching requires a shift in focus from the curriculum to the learner.

Principle 4: Learning about teaching is enhanced through (student) teacher research.

Principle 5: Learning about teaching requires an emphasis on those learning to teach working closely with their peers.

Principle 6: Learning about teaching requires meaningful relationships between schools, universities and student teachers.

Principle 7: Learning about teaching is enhanced when the teaching and learning approaches advocated in the programme are modelled by the teacher educators in their own practice.

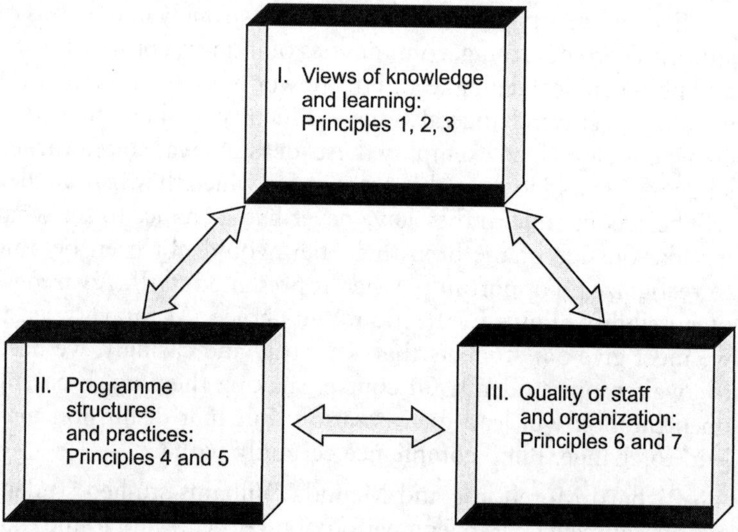

Clustering of the seven principles into components of programmes and programme change.

Above mentioned principles reflect constructivist principles based on constructivist epistemology and pedagogy. Thus our teacher education preparation requires a new approach and this new approach must be constructivist approach. Professional development in a constructivist paradigm, it seems, promotes the predisposition toward inquiry into and interpretation of educational situations. This orientation stands in opposition to the traditional deficit orientation, which marginalizes the quest for understanding.

Lieberman and Miller (1990) very nicely describe the notion of professional development that searches for understanding as "continuous inquiry into practice". In this construction of professional development we see the teacher as a "reflective practitioner", someone who has a tacit knowledge base and who then builds on that knowledge base through ongoing inquiry and analysis, continually rethinking and re-evaluating values and practices. Teacher development is not only the renewal of teaching, but it is also the renewal of schools—in effect, culture building.

Professional development as inquiry into practice involves learning from teaching as opposed to learning to teach (Zumwalt, 1988). This approach privileges teachers as "the primary knowledge generators of the profession" (Lambert, 1988); professional development and teacher research are closely woven in this "systematic and intentional inquiry carried out by teachers" (Cochran-Smith, 1990).

The new paradigm of professional development for teachers recognizes that the interests of others are being served when teachers are the targets of "applied approaches". Rather than engaging in rational processes of resolving problems by choosing from available "received" knowledge, teachers are raising questions about the relevance of such "applied" approaches, and whose interests are being served by it anyway. Practitioner-generated knowledge that is embedded in and emerges out of action, is coming to be seen increasingly as the basis for a new and emerging paradigm in teaching (Smyth, 1991).

This view of professional development has at its center, the purpose of increasing to some extent "choice, authority, and responsibility" in exercising teaching duties (Lambert, 1988). Learning from teaching is the antithesis of popular forms of staff development that have "colluded with the forces that would continue the colonization of teachers". In the process of inquiring into their practice, teachers determine the focus of reflection and action.

A teacher educator's epistemology is crucial in that the "conception of knowledge can promote a view of the teacher as either technician or intellectual, and the extent to which values are rendered explicit can either inhibit or encourage a more critical pedagogy" (Britzman, 1986). A logistical view of theory and practice (Butt, Townsend, Bc Raymond, 1990) permeates courses in teacher education presenting theory as truth and denying both the social construction of reality and the subjectivity of the students. Theory is perceived as separate from and superior to experience. This perpetuates a traditional view of knowledge as objective, static, and derived from authorities, ensuring the maintenance of present structures and interests in schools. This technological view of knowledge treats prepositional knowledge as privileged and nonproblematic, usually in the form of "putting into practice of research findings" (Grimmett et al., 1990).

Prescriptive theoretical knowledge about teaching frames a particular discourse that negates problematic aspects of teaching. Learners consume knowledge rather than critically identifying and examining the privileged discourse. Pedagogy becomes dichotomized focusing on knowledge transmission and not on the learner's understanding. Consequently, getting through the text takes precedence over the construction of knowledge. In the process, authorship of learning is lost. Another mode of knowing, termed deliberate (Grimmert et al., 1990), understands the relationship between theory and practice to be dialectical, treating "theory and practice as different but equal aspects of the same phenomena, each being capable of informing the other" (Butt et al., 1990). Competing views of teaching are considered by the practitioner in light of the context of practice, knowledge is authority-oriented informing rather than directing practice. Finally, a problematic view of knowledge "holds the practical problem in a specific context as the focus for deriving both situation-specific theory and practical action". Since knowledge is subjectively constructed and personal, a compatible pedagogy aims at making tentative knowledge explicit and useful to the learner. As knowledge is reconstructed, the learner functions as a generator of knowledge. Smyth (1989) sees the distinction between receiving knowledge and creating knowledge as Friere's "distinction between the pedagogy of the question and the pedagogy of the answer". The form of knowledge generated is personal in nature and therefore useful in transforming practice. This latter view of knowledge, increasingly prevalent in the literature in teacher education, is often referred to as "personal practical knowledge" (Connelly & Clandinin, 1988), or "craft knowledge" (Grimmett K. MacKinnon, 1992), which is "time bound and situation specific, personally compelling and oriented toward action" (Feiman-Nemser Ec Floden, 1986). Because of its complexity, some researchers view it as organized nonlinearly according to rules of practice, practical principles, and images

(Elbaz, 1991). It is an "embodied" integrated knowledge which is "simultaneously emotional, evaluative, and cognitive", permeated with personal meaning. Personal practical knowledge is contextual and therefore useful to the teacher's practice, interactive in that it is developed in the teacher's practice, and speculative in that it is subject to change (Clark & Lampert, 1986).

This emerging view of knowledge in teacher education requires that theory as presented in the preservice programme be treated as problematic, and that the cultural, social, political, and economic forces shaping various discourses be examining theory, rather than construed as imposed, superior, and separated from practice, gives way to knowledge as constructed by those who practice. The practice of theorizing teaching is returned to the lived world of the teacher.

A number of knowledge bases have been proposed as necessary for the practicing teacher. Goodlad (1990) identifies "knowledge of a nation's government and its expectations for citizens", "intellectual tools to participate broadly in the human conversation", "pedagogical knowledge and skills necessary to arrange optimal conditions for educating the young", knowledge of "the commonplaces of schooling" such as pupils, goals, organization, evaluation, curriculum, instruction, and "promising alternatives". Shulman (1987) identifies a similar set of knowledge bases. However, these are not readily translated into classroom action. For example Calderhead (1988) notes that the "translation of subject matter knowledge into practice requires interaction between this knowledge and other knowledge such as that concerning children or teaching strategies. And it seems likely these transactions are highly complex".

The knowledge bases as outlined by Goodlad, Shulman and others should not become prescriptive decontextualized content in preservice programmes. Teacher educators need to allow for the interaction of students' personal practical knowledge and the knowledge bases in the real world of teacher practice. This rather wide sweeping review of the teacher education literature portrays movement from a normative prescriptive and conventional paradigm entrenched in a training orientation, toward a constructivist paradigm in which teachers "become simultaneously students of schooling and architects of their own professional development" (Bullough, Knowles, & Crow, 1992). The new paradigm recognizes that meaning develops in context and that teachers need to "recognize themselves as centers of meaning-making, as producers of legitimate knowledge that is worthy of being shared and deserving to be acted upon". An inquiry orientation to teaching subscribes to the notions that the teacher is a center of meaning-making, and that meaning is constructed within context. Inquiry into the teacher's biography as well as the teaching context is essential to the development of deeper understandings of teaching.

Inquiry-oriented teacher education has been defined by Tabachnich and Zeichner (1991) as follows: "This general approach to preparing teachers emphasizes the development of knowledge, skills and dispositions by prospective teachers and teachers that enable them to be reflective about their teaching and the social contexts in which their teaching takes place (e.g., the classroom, the school, the local community, the society)." Situated in the dialogical paradigm, inquiry-oriented teacher education is more of a sense-making of practice recognizing than any teaching situation is open to multiple interpretations because of varying perspectives. It encompasses a wide array of "kinds of conversation and thinking" (Sykes and Bird, 1992) which compose "knowledge in themselves". The "pragmatic mode" involves exploration of problems of practice with recourse to abstract knowledge as it is useful. The "narrative mode" envisages inquiry as the sharing of stories of practice in order to excavate meaning. The "casuistical mode" relies on the comparison of traditional cases and the case at hand. These three modes, according to Sykes and Bird, have been marginalized by the "foundational mode".

According to Gadamer (1988), interpretation is the most basic way of being in the world and cannot be reduced to anything simpler. Learning to teach is an ongoing process of interpretation of practice. This appears to be normative for pupil-teachers, and the faculty. The contingency of practice demands that educational situations be continually interpreted for new meaning. Learning to teach requires immersion in the "real world" of practice, not just for "experience" but for the development of interpretive experience in the "teaching world". However, this teaching world, in which pupil-teachers dwell, is riddled with tensions. In dialogue, and only in dialogue according to Gadamer, do we use language to "go to the essence of the matters themselves". Dialogue is interpretation. In dialogue we are really interpreting. Speaking then is interpreting itself. It is the function of the dialogue that in saying or stating something a challenging relation with the other evolves, a response is provoked, and the response provides the interpretation of the other's interpretation. Learning to teach requires an extended dialogue among the participants in order to share interpretations of pedagogical situations by "building a common language, so that of the end of the dialogue we will have some ground". The central task in constructing the internship in a teacher education programme is to provide structures that privilege dialogue. The extended dialogue is an interpretive activity which seemed to naturally gravitate toward the lived experiences of teaching—the personal struggles in making sense of pedagogy.

The Need for a New Approach

Possibilities and opportunities for refinement continue to emerge as experiences open new avenues, offering choices and a path to true freedom: the freedom to be the best one can be. If education is growth as suggested by Dewey, the kind of educative process necessary to this growth requires that our schools and universities provide experiences which nurture the whole of us—bringing us to wonder, which sustains our search for meaningful knowledge; cultivating critical thought, enhancing the quality not only of that knowledge but also our beliefs; fostering dispositions of care and compassion which informs our choices, our judgments; and freeing our creative expression, leading us to new metaphors and possibilities and back again to wonder. This transformative approach to learning and knowledge requires that teachers be willing to relinquish attitudes and beliefs that inhibit the child's growth towards personhood, and forgo those restrictions which narrow the educative process. When knowledge is imposed, as in a mimetic approach, students are denied opportunities for questioning and reflecting. Knowledge is given, received, and regurgitated. For many students, little learning occurs. For Freire (1970) the imposition of knowledge is oppressive; and further, the oppressed are depersonalized-dehumanized. Further, Maxine Greene (1986) sees freedom as the power to act and choose and to overcome obstacles which keep us from defining ourselves and being the best we know how to be. Knowing or recognizing the barriers in our personal paths is impossible in an environment which makes our choices for us and tells us what we should know and how we should act. Lacking autonomy we haven't the opportunity for cognitive praxis which would open avenues of possibility for each of us. If we are unaware of the obstacles which keep us from being the best we can be, we can never really be free for we cannot overcome something which is out of our awareness. In an oppressive, imposed school environment how can a person fulfil his or her potential? Students either blindly comply or they simply cease caring. Lacking empowerment in the form of autonomy to make choices or take action, many of our students grow up without realizing their potentials. Often they don't even have a clue as to what their possibilities might have been since they were denied opportunities to see and know. There are some who continue to follow their intuitive and knowing hearts and minds, creating learning environments that do promote growth and autonomy. Others have wonderfully enlightened moments which sustain them and their students with brief glimmers of the way it could be. Unfortunately, the pressures and mandates which teachers face daily work at wearing them down and at forcing them to comply with models they don't believe in. In their disempowered state, most give in, sometimes even forgetting why they became teachers in the first place. Thus there is a need to have a new approach to teacher education.

In our experience, it is often the case that the teacher does not have the thinking skills that he/she is trying to teach to her students. If he/she cannot reach deep knowledge and understand a concept himself/herself, it follows that he/she won't know how to go about teaching it. These comments are wake up calls which bring us back to work in community. It is believed that this depth of knowledge and understanding can be realized through philosophical dialogue that takes place in a community of inquiry. Teachers must have opportunities to practice their thinking skills, too. We have an obligation to provide those opportunities for constructing knowledge together with our students at the university/college level, even if it means that we don't cover all that we think is important. The student-centred classroom, as a classroom community could be called, requires that the teacher assume certain things about his or her students. At the very core of this model is the belief that given an opportunity for meaningful engagement, the student will actually want to learn. This seems obvious at first glance. However, if we examine the practices of traditional education and classroom management, we see that the basic assumption about students is that they would not learn on their own unless we somehow coerced them. In the constructivist model, teachers are expected to encourage students to engage in dialogue, both with the teacher and with one another. Also, thoughtful, open-ended questions are encouraged and utilized among teacher, students, and peers (Brooks and Brooks, 1999). However, it doesn't just happen. Both teachers and students need practice. Gordon Wells (1999) states, inquiry does not refer to a method (as in discovery learning), still less to a generic set of procedures for carrying out activities. Rather, it indicates a stance toward experiences and ideas—a willingness to wonder, to ask questions, and to seek to understand by collaborating with others in the attempt to make answers to them. At the same time, the aim of inquiry is not knowledge for its own sake but the disposition and ability to use the understandings so gained to act informedly and responsibly in the situations that may be encountered both now and in the future.

Intellectual development is essentially a process of making meaning with others. Students of all ages can engage in meaning-making and a community of philosophical inquiry provides fertile ground for this practice. Students are empowered by their roles as co-enquirers, and construct knowledge as a means of making sense of their world. The meaning this holds for each involved is incentive for willing participation. Knowledge is a social construction deeply rooted in a nexus of power relations. It is heavily dependent upon culture, context, custom and historical specificity (McLaren, 1994).

Culturally responsive teaching is also central to any vision of developing a diverse community of learners. Gibson and Ogbu (1991) alluded to this concept when they wrote that teachers and administrators "need to show themselves receptive to learning from the diverse cultures in their midst and they need also to teach majority-group students the value of interethnic reciprocal learning". Gay (2000) identifies five key characteristics of culturally responsive teaching:

- It acknowledges the legitimacy of the cultural heritages of different ethnic groups, both as legacies that affect students' dispositions, attitudes, and approaches to learning and as worthy content to be taught in the formal curriculum.
- It builds bridges of meaningfulness between home and school experiences as well as between academic abstractions and lived socio-cultural realities.
- It uses a wide variety of instructional strategies that are connected to different learning styles.
- It teaches students to know and praise their own and each others' cultural heritages.
- It incorporates multicultural information, resources, and materials in all the subjects and skills routinely taught in schools.

Villegas and Lucas (2002) identify the importance of culturally responsive teaching in the preparation of educators. The new approach to teacher education must incorporate elements like collaborative learning, empowerment, importance of reflection and self-assessment, action, service learning, etc.

Collaborative learning (sometimes called cooperative learning) (Baloche, 1998; Bruffee, 1993; Cohen, 1994; Johnson, Johnson, & Holubec, 1994; Slavin, 1995) supports the process of constructing meaning as multiple experiences and perspectives provide opportunities for individuals to question and adapt their private knowledge and interpretations. Bruffee (1993) proposed that knowledge is "constructed through negotiation with others in a community of peers". This highlights the critical relationship between a community of learners and the constructivist view of learning. The new approach to teacher education must facilitate a Constructivist Approach to Teaching, Learning and Leading. The constructivist view of learning is based on the work of Jean Piaget, Lev Vygotsky, Jerome Bruner, and Howard Gardner among others (Brooks & Brooks, 1993; Fosnot, 1996).

Lambert, et al. (2002) and Lambert (2003) have developed a constructivist theory of leading which extends theories of adult learning to the work of school administrators. Lambert defines a constructivist view of leading as "The reciprocal processes that enable participants in an educational community to construct meanings that lead toward a shared purpose of schooling" (Lambert et al., 2002). This view is echoed in the work of House and Sears (2002) as they put forward a new view of the role of the school counsellor. House and Sears (2002) state, "It is critical that school counsellors move beyond their current roles as helper-responders in order to become proactive leaders and advocates for the success of all students." In order for school counsellors to take on this role, counsellor preparation programmes must help preservice counsellors "by emphasizing the value of experience, promoting active learning, engaging in reflective practice, and inviting dialogue among students and faculty" (House & Sears, 2002).

Empowerment: Bergsma (2004) defines empowerment as "a process by which people gain control of their lives, democratic participation in the life of their community, and a critical understanding of their environment". Freire (1970) stresses the importance of people identifying their own problems, analyzing the roots of those problems, and then joining with others to take action and overcome challenges. This vision of individual and social transformation calls for including issues of knowledge, power and social change in the curriculum. Banks (1993) and Vavrus (2002) make clear the importance of transformative academic knowledge for teaching and for teacher education, while Anderson and Saavedra (1995) provide related insights for educational administration and Marri's (2005) research highlights a role for educational technology in developing such knowledge. Critical to this conception is the intentional inclusion of multiple perspectives, as well as "concepts, paradigms, themes, and explanations that challenge mainstream academic knowledge and that expand the historical and literary canon" (Banks, 1993).

Educators do not bestow empowerment upon others; individuals discover empowerment through learning of new possibilities and potentialities, and through effecting change in their environment when applying their learning. Empowerment helps provide a desire to question and to reflect critically, as well as the courage to work toward change.

Reflection: The body of literature demonstrating the importance of reflection and self-assessment in learning to teach, lead, and counsel grows daily (Gipe & Richards, 1991; Moallem, 1997; Rovegno, 1992; Zeichner, 1987). Reflective teaching implies a willingness on the part of the educator to critically examine her or his own assumptions, aims, and practices (Schon, 1983, 1987; Zeichner, 1987). It is particularly important in creating culturally relevant and responsive practices (Howard, 2003). Reflection takes place before, during, and after teaching (e.g., Schon, 1987) and is focused and stimulated by analysis of critical incidents (Griffin, 2003). According to Mezirow (1990), transformative reflection leads to emancipatory learning.

Action: As valuable a practice as reflection is, it is without legitimate purpose if it does not lead to action. Professionals must be willing and prepared to make changes in their own practice as well as in those elements of the larger context that may frustrate learners' efforts (Zeichner, 1987). This process of working as a reflective professional to resolve context-bound problems requires an educator to reflect "in action", as well as "on action" (Schon, 1987), and to be always aware of the impact of their choices on students of different social, economic, and cultural communities.

Service Learning: Since 1970, there has been a growing body of research supporting the effectiveness of service learning for students and preservice teachers (Conrad & Hedin, 1991; Root, 1997). Rooted conceptually in the work of John Dewey (1998), and closely related to experiential learning, service learning blends service activities with academic curriculum in order to meet real community needs. Root and Batchelder (1994) concluded that preservice teachers who completed a service learning project made significant gains in the complexity of their thinking about social problems and critical incidents in their teaching. Wade (1995) found that preservice teachers who participated in service learning developed more positive attitudes toward parent and community involvement in their classrooms and schools. Vadeboncoeur, Rahm, Aguilera, and LeCompte (1996) found that preservice teachers engaged in service learning showed an increased commitment to social justice and a reduction in teacher biases. Cochran-Smith (2004) argues for making social justice a key outcome of teacher education programmes, but attention to social justice is not limited to teacher education. Vera and Speight (2003) make a case for counsellors to ground their views of multicultural competence in "a commitment to social justice".

5.3 THE ISSUE OF PRESERVICE TEACHER EDUCATION

In the light of constructivism, there are several issues which need to be addressed if we are really at all serious about adopting constructivism in the process of teaching and learning at various levels of education at wider level. All the teachers who are engaged in teaching at various levels of education are generally from preservices teacher education programmes. Preservice teachers join the course having very high expectations believing this that after the completion of this course; they will be in a position to establish themselves as ideal teachers from all perspective.

Preservice teachers possess constructed knowledge, attitudes, assumptions, beliefs, and values about teaching and learning (Pankratius and Young, 1995). These preexisting ideas include: (a) well-established teacher role identities (Crow, 1987); (b) unrealistically optimistic expectations about their future teaching performance (Weinstein, 1989); (c) strong convictions about teaching and how to teach (Clark, 1988); and (d) an extensive inventory of "personal practical knowledge composed of such experiential matters as images, rituals, habits, cycles, routines, and rhythms" (Connelley & Clandinin, 1985). Such perspectives frame preservice teachers' beliefs about effective teaching (Perry & Rog, 1990) and serve as preexisting knowledge structures on teaching (Stoddart & Roehler, 1990).

Knowledge—especially knowledge about teaching—is constructed by preservice teachers in order to make sense of their world. With hours of classroom experience from which to draw, varying and disparate repertoires of beliefs and values about teaching and learning shape the preservice teachers' views (Pankratius and Young, 1995). These prospective teachers tend to construct primitive, underdeveloped knowledge bases that influence their teaching styles and affect their responses to teacher education programmes (Powell, 1991). Book, Byers and Freeman (1986) argue that this prior knowledge is a key reason "many candidates come to formal teacher preparation believing that they have little to learn".

There are numerous issues which need to be discussed such as:

- How to lay the groundwork at preservice teacher education?
- How to get started at preservice teacher education programme?
- How to reaching inside?
- How to explore and enhance understanding?
- How to design Lesson planning?

The main issue is how to lay the groundwork at preservice teacher education. Thousands of students annually enter our secondary education preservice programme. Now the question is how to design the entry-level course for the pupil-teachers who join the preservice course? With the belief that constructivism undergirds our preservice teachers' thinking, two of the four faculty may be assigned to design the entry-level course decided by them to introduce a constructivist "theme" in their sections of the initial preservice secondary course. Grounded in constructivist learning principles, the assigned teachers may develop an entry-level preservice secondary education course to unearth and address teacher candidates' preconceptions about teaching.

Undergirding the curriculum is our belief that the principles and consequences of constructivism significantly influence the teaching and learning process. Learners construct views and perceptions that they relate to preexisting knowledge structures. They actively construct the structures (or schemata) that help them do this. In turn, those cognitive structures are refined and restructured. It is upon this framework that preservice teachers build their rationale for teaching as well as bolster their personal practical knowledge about teaching.

In designing this course, the assigned teachers may develop activities and strategies to "promote the development of more powerful and effective constructions" (Confrey, 1990). This influence might lead the teachers to provide opportunities for the pupil-teachers to "critically evaluate the various philosophies and methods [they] encounter in terms of [their] own goals, values, and principles" (Henderson, 1992). An effective and convincing example of this type of activity is early concept mapping of our teacher candidates' knowledge bases about teaching.

Constructivist learning principles must provide the course framework; students should be encouraged to examine and evaluate their beliefs, attitudes, and knowledge about teaching. Active student involvement is of paramount significance as we examine the social setting, group processes, and personal growth through reflection. Saunders's (1992) constructivist instructional strategies identified as hands-on investigations, active cognitive development, group work, and higher-level assessment may support the curriculum. These strategies help learners build personal meanings, encourage them to reflect on their own knowledge, and clarify understanding.

In providing a process-centred, developmental course, broad goals may be implemented in place of specific outcomes. Glodin (1990) states: "Often, the exclusively behavioural characterization of desirable learning outcome leads educators to rely on the teaching of discrete, disconnected skills...rather than developing meaningful patterns, principles and insights." Our intent should be to provide techniques that enable our students to prove implicit knowledge that underlies their emergent professional judgment in classroom decision-making (Pankratius and Young, 1995). In assisting in examining our students' belief systems, knowledge structures, and individual's goals, we must facilitate in identifying and reconstructing their knowledge. With these principles in mind we should develop the learner goals for our introductory course: (a) develop the process of self-reflection based on an examination of personal practical knowledge; (b) display an awareness of the role of self-analysis in constructing a view of teaching; (c) examine preservice teachers' belief systems, knowledge structures, and individual goals as they relate to the concept of the emerging teacher; (d) investigate personal and theoretical views of effective secondary school teaching and effective secondary schools; (e) analyze the goals, issues, and problems of the secondary school; (f) explore the impact of technology and societal changes on schools as a basis for understanding the emergent teacher; (g) prove preservice teachers' implicit theories that underlie their emergent professional judgment in classroom decision-making; (h) evolve a sense of professional ethics through self-examination in relation to the expectations of the professional dimensions of teaching; and, (i) begin to unfold a personal and professional rationale for teaching (Pankratius and Young, 1995). These goals, along with the principles of constructivism, may give us a course that demanded the active participation of the teacher candidates in building on or reconstructing their preconceptions about teaching.

Student-centred activities provide the learners and instructors with vital information about their personal models of teaching. Some of these are, on the basis of Hunt's (1987) notion of outside in (external activities and factors that shape and influence the individual) and inside out (internal predispositions and attitudes; these often serve as the filters or monitor for examining external influences) as metaphors to describe the teaching central to our emerging constructivist programme. In this context, students' conceptions are challenged as they apply their assumptions, values, and beliefs to unique situations throughout the course.

How to get started at preservice teacher education programme?: During the first week of the class, a suitable measure/inventory may be used to help teacher educators and student-teachers to gain insights into the ways in which students' temperaments may influence the teaching act. This is an important measure because it provides an outside-in look at students, allowing both the teacher educators and student-teachers to gain a greater understanding of how the students see their world. Compatibility with and contrast between the teacher educators and student-teachers serves as a starting point in discussing how the individual's temperament influences the art of teaching. While teaching and learning styles are related to constructivist ideas of teacher education, the measure/inventory may act as a catalyst in helping students to construct ideas about styles and temperament in the classroom. Student-teachers may be grouped based on particular styles, allowing for initial experiences based on interaction with individuals who tend to share the same perspectives. The student-teachers may realize and think of how different they are and how this difference effects how they learn and behave. It may also make them realize that they all don't learn the same. They all take information and process it differently.

An informal outside-in questionnaire may be designed to examine students' views about teaching. The questionnaire may contain questions designed to probe the students' awareness of critical personal issues in teaching which may bring their assumptions, values, and beliefs about teaching to the surface. Questions may include: "Why do you want to become a teacher?", "What comes to mind when you use the phrase 'a really good teacher'?" "What are your strengths and weaknesses that you think will affect how well you do as a student-teacher and during your first year of teaching?" The questionnaire may also include questions related to how students think knowledge is best produced, what they believe will distinguish them from other teachers in their subject area, and a question about their fears and apprehensions about teaching. Following this assessment, student-teachers may be interviewed to discuss the questionnaire. The purpose of the interview is to: (a) discern the student's teaching style; (b) determine influences on that teaching style; and (c) create a bond between instructor and students (Pankratius and Young, 1995). Family influences, personal experiences, educational background, career paths, and experiences with children and youth are examined at this time.

How to reaching inside?: Student-teachers may be asked to begin reflecting on their past experiences in education. They may be asked to write a three to five pages paper reflecting on their relationships, hardships and successes with teachers from their past experiences with school. They may be asked to describe teachers as vividly as possible, to "show" that teacher and why this particular teacher is memorable. Students may be encouraged to report on their strongest as well as their weakest teachers. Then we should discuss the qualities these students identify as significant in the teaching-learning setting. Past teachers are the models who influence expectations about teaching. Students quickly do not realize that there is no one best type of teacher, nor is there complete agreement on the qualities that good teachers should demonstrate.

Another example of an inside-out assignment is the "Heroes and Villains" paper in which students are asked to select both a hero and a villain in the students' learning life (Brookfield, 1990). Teachers, fellow students, principals, and even parents may be the focus of this exercise. The crucial objective of this assignment is to help students probe their assumptions about education that underlie their selections. A third example is the "Educational Autobiography" which serves as a chronicle of students' experiences as learners in both formal and informal settings (Pankratius and Young, 1995).

In keeping with the reflective nature of the assignments, students may also be asked to report critical incidents, based on specific events in which they remember a learning high, when they felt affirmed as a learner, and the most important insights students realized about themselves as learners. Additionally, students are asked to relate critical incidents in which they recall being most distressed or disappointed, a learning low, or the times of despair or frustration about learning activities. These reflections help students understand what they have internalized about teaching and learning. In sharing their responses with one another in a social setting, they gain understanding in how differently teaching and learning are understood.

How to explore and enhance understanding?: Learning logs or learning journals are assigned as a process-based activity in which students develop ongoing records of their immediate learning experiences. Reactions and reflections on class readings, articles related to educational issues collected from newspapers and magazines, in-class activities, i.e., film reviews, speaker presentations, student presentations, and homework assignments may be included. Students may be encouraged to jot down responses to class activities at the close of each class. The responses are based on questions designed to determine, for example, what gave them the most intense learning high or low (Brookfield, 1990)? What was the most important insight they realized about their own emotional responses to the learning process? Students may be encouraged to review their journals prior to class and to reflect on their journals over the weekend, between classes. They may be encouraged to look for patterns, rhythms, and regularities. An important part of the log of journal is its interactive quality. It may provide opportunities to dialogue about the events in class and to capture the students' immediate experiences that influence their development.

The learning journals also provide students with a longitudinal look at their learning. It is rewarding and meaningful to observe their growth in their learning journals (Pankratius and Young, 1995). The exercises and scenarios are designed to challenge the students to restructure their knowledge bases. Another important facet of the constructivist approach is in the bonding that takes place among the students. Concept mapping is another activity that may stimulate and bring pre-existing conceptions about teaching to the surface (Pankratius, 1991; Powell, 1991). In providing micro-teaching early in the semester, students examine teaching styles and content knowledge. A probing interview induces the students to elaborate on their awareness about teaching as expressed in their micro-teaching and concepts maps. An additional concept map exercise at the conclusion of the course reveals the growth in their beliefs and attitudes about teaching. Panel presentations based on issues or field papers also reflect direct experiences in which teacher candidates are encouraged to reflect, construct, and restructure their knowledge base about learning, teaching, and teacher education. Portfolios serve as ways for students to account for the various assignments and using portfolios also serves as a process that allows students to construct their path, using multiple sources of evidence, to becoming a teacher (Geiger & Sugarman, 1988). Portfolios, as an additional assessment, are invaluable to both student and faculty as an important construction of student growth.

In examining the potential of a beginning constructivist teacher education course we, as teacher educators, must look at the implications of constructivism for preservice teachers, the faculty, the programme, and teaching expectations. We also must explore the obstacles to the implementation of a constructivist teacher education programme; in so doing we arrive at several unanswered questions that may stimulate further research (Pankratius and Young, 1995).

As constructivist educators, we expect changes and challenges in the classroom. If we accept the likelihood of multiple perspectives then teaching is not the mere transmission of knowledge; it becomes a quest in which the role of the teacher educator is to probe, acknowledge, encourage, and challenge. It is a more active role that shifts with the class make-up from a session to a session. The constructivist educator places his or her attitudes, beliefs, values, and assumptions on the table alongside those of the learners. Teaching becomes a vibrant practice of mutual exploration and enlightenment. We also need to understand the development of the constructivist educator and we need to define the qualities that enhance the transition to constructivism.

As students exit this constructivist-based course, questions arise about their future preservice experiences. How will these students respond to methods that tend to be didactic in nature? What long-term effect does constructivist teaching have on their knowledge bases about teaching, learning, and about knowledge itself? In what ways will field experiences with non-constructivist teachers influence preservice teachers' constructivist philosophies? When these preservice teachers enter the "real world" as classroom teachers, will the school climate be one that will nurture or destroy their constructivist perspectives? How will these students react to more behaviouristic teaching methods and styles? (Pankratius and Young, 1995).

"The great strength in constructivism is that it leads us to think critically and imaginatively about the teaching-learning process" (Noddings, 1990). When we teach in a constructivist manner, we learn and grow with our learners. When preservice teachers learn in a constructivist manner, they learn first-hand the principles of active learning and the power of pre-existing conceptions. They also sense the empowerment that comes with learning how to learn. In following constructivist learning principles, even the teacher-educators may feel liberated.

If, as Combs (1972) claimed, "the production of an effective teacher is a highly personal matter, dependent primarily upon the development of an appropriate system of beliefs"; then a constructivist, reflective, and introspective approach that encourages the exploration, illumination, evaluation, and restructuring of that system of beliefs enhances the process of teacher education. An environment may be created in which teacher candidates may build their knowledge base at the same time they may examine models, constructs, and behaviours of teaching. In the true sense of the constructivist spirit, students may be engaged actively in molding their perceptions and constructing knowledge. This introductory course may provide the right environment for a constructivist preach because the students bring extensive knowledge and beliefs about teaching to the course. Ultimate consequences of a constructivist teacher education programme is the knowledge and understanding gained about students. We, as teacher-educators, must know our students well enough to build models of their understanding of teaching and teacher education. "The results will be that a teacher creates a 'case study' of each student" (Confrey, 1990). With that understanding of our teacher candidates we can guide their exploration and study to best meet their needs. We can also assist students in their modes of inquiry and provide opportunities for them to strengthen their existing knowledge base. "Ultimately", Confrey (1990) realized, "the student must decide on the adequacy of his or her construction". The growth, stability, and organization of our students' knowledge bases are their responsibility. We need to give them the opportunity to build and reflect, and the chance to change (Pankratius and Young, 1995).

Our experience in developing and implementing an alternative teacher education programme will be very challenging as we redefine our roles, beliefs, and commitments about teaching. Some of the major challenges we will have to face may include (a) reorganization of programme offerings and content; (b) use of alternative forms of student assessment and grading; (c) teacher education innovation embedded in a bureaucratic university system; (d) placement of interns with mentoring teachers who demonstrate best practices in classroom instruction; and (e) state licensure requirements restricting the unification of teacher education programmes (Pankratius and Young, 1995). Working as an integrated, interdisciplinary team will be essential for meeting these challenges. The team will have to share a fundamental assumption that course content should not be separate, offering splintered skills, but rather integrated, teaching themes that cross disciplines. The reorganization of programme offerings and course content into an integrated block of courses should have a specific meaning in the context. Sometimes, this constructivist approach may not be captured in traditional university guidelines for curriculum. The solution lies in creating a new structure that retains the names of old courses. The argument is that change need not be universal and comprehensive to be effective.

The shifting of student learning styles from information processing to constructivist analysis and synthesis is possible within the structure of this programme. However, participating faculty must acknowledge that in the initial weeks students can be expected to experience dissonance and frustration as they face the challenge of altering their usual approaches to learning.

Issue of Lesson Planning: Lebow (1993) has proposed the following five principles toward a new mindset, to influence the design of constructivist lesson plans:

- Maintain a buffer between the learner and the potentially damaging effects of instructional practices.
- Provide a context for learning that supports both autonomy and relatedness.
- Incorporate the reasons for learning into the learning activity.
- Support self-regulated leaning by promoting attitudes that enable the learner to assume responsibility for learning.
- Strengthen the tendencies of the learner to engage in learning processes, by encouraging exploration of mistakes.

On the basis of above mentioned principles of lesson planning, the teacher-educators must devise a suitable strategy to help their student-teachers to design their lesson plans so that it may meet the needs of constructivist learning environment as suggested by Honbein (1996) who describes seven goals for the design of constructivist learning environment:

- Provide experience with the knowledge construction process.
- Provide experience in and appreciation for multiple perspectives.
- Enable learning in realistic and relevant contexts.
- Encourage ownership and voice in the learning process.
- Embed learning in social experience.
- Encourage the use of multiple modes of representation.
- Encourage self-awareness in the knowledge construction process.

There are some more important educational issues that need to be raised with respect to the structure and duration of learning tasks and the nature and efficiency of learning challenges posed to learners.

ISSUE 1: Very often new teachers preparing to enter the profession or in-service teachers engaged in school change efforts ask the same question about their ability to transform constructivist learning theory into classroom practice. They ask: how could I possibly maintain a structural learning environment if students spend so much time designing their own investigations and I spend so much time mediating those various investigations? How could I keep everyone focused, on-task and learning with so little structure.

The structure in the constructivist classroom may look different than what some teachers organizing envision when they think of the term, but it is there nonetheless. Structure in the constructivist classroom is negotiated with the child and can include norms, procedures and policies that could easily go unnoticed by the novice eye. In one setting, students might move about the classroom freely to get supplies, meet study group members, confer with the teacher or return to work started at an earlier point. And students have the opportunity to be self-directive or not as they desire.

The constructivist teacher incorporates lessons of all types into classroom life depending upon his/her analysis of the needs of his/her learners. One day a visitor might find this teacher encouraging students to share their interpretations of characters in the book they are each reading. Or, they might find this teacher leading a session in which he/she is sharing the conventional forms of a business letter to a group of student with rough drafts. In these cases, the structure (small group meetings with the teacher) may look similar, but the teachers instructional objectives and students' opportunities to change their current perspectives are different.

In another constructivist classroom, the students may be seated in rows facing the chalkboard, working on an arithmetic problem. Let's examine a particular problem and the teacher's role in guiding students to solving it. The teacher has presented an ill-defined problem involving how to configure the tables for that evening's parent open house with the constructivist that the tables seat a maximum of 6 and there are 87 parents attending that evening. The students are trying to determine how many tables they need to set up for the open house. The teacher encourages multiple pathway solutions. Of particular interest to the teacher is how the students deal with the remainder, since six is not a factor of 87. The students' differential responses will help him/her determine which students' understandings of the part/whole relationship will make instruction with more sophisticated division problems appropriate and which students can benefit more from further problems with the part/whole/ remainder relationships.

The above classroom illustrations serve to describe the variability of classroom structure compatible with constructivist pedagogy. Constructivist learning theory is not prescriptive, neither dictating classroom structure nor teaching technique. It does explicitly state that conceptual change is the key to cognitive growth and development, and thus conceptual change becomes an essential quest for the teacher's professional action. The precise nature of that endeavour is derived from the teacher's negotiations with the learners.

ISSUE 2: Efficiency of Learning: because teachers have limited instructional time, the manner in which time is used in the classroom will always be a concern for teachers. Teachers feel considerable pressure to complete the requirements of their assigned curriculum. Thus, it is predictable that teachers and educators in general will raise questions about how to accomplish the most with the time that is allocated. However, answers to questions of efficiency are not easily answered. There is neither universal agreement concerning precisely what the outcomes of schooling should be, not agreement about what methods yield efficient and lasting learning. And if one's goal is to enhance the transfer of learning, the answers become even more varied.

Constructivists value asking big questions, giving students time to think, and providing opportunities to explore to find answers. While this way of teaching requires more time, by ensuring sufficient time, students gain a better grasp of complex ideas. Moreover, deliberate investigation by students tends to foster the disposition to pursue issues and phenomena more completely, even those that are more difficult. Many lament the fact that school curricula contain so much material that it is almost impossible to cover it all. But where is the learning in "coverage"? When the emphasis in school is placed too heavily on information and its recall, the invariable result will be prodigious amounts of forgetting. Thus, the position of constructivist educators is not to worship efficiency, but instead to value the quality of the learning. They substitute to the principle that "more is less". On the surface it may appear that efficiency is satisfied, but the more important outcome for learners of all ages, it is argued, involves learning with depth.

This is certainly not to say that teachers should be unconcerned about how they manage their instructional time, for nothing could be further from the truth. One may badly squander precious learning time through the poor application of any instructional methodology.

Therefore, it is of utmost importance for effective constructivist teaching that the conditions for learning be carefully structured, and that student's learning activities and learning be carefully monitored. Competent constructivist teaching demands not only full engagement by students, but also meaningful engagement and accountability by teachers. Where tension arises over efficiency of instruction, constructivists will accentuate the goal of achieving depth of learning rather than breath of learning (Brooks & Brooks, 1993). In the final analysis, what is of enduring significance is that learners acquire deeper levels of understanding, see their learning in a meaningful context, become increasingly competent (and yes efficient) learners and have the awareness and ability to apply their learning in non-school contexts.

ISSUE 3: Efficiency of Learner "Struggle" in the Process of Learning: Constructivists believe that meaningful learning or "purposeful knowledge" may be promoted by a learning environment that has three main features. First, one should use authentic problems that are tasks having the contextual feel of the real world. Secondly, the learning environment should represent the natural complexity of the real world and avoid oversimplification of the task and instruction. And thirdly, a constructivist learning environment should support collaborative knowledge construction through social negotiation (Jonassen, 1991). It is believed that such learning environments invite learners through interaction with others to engage in problem finding, problem-solving and inquiry learning. Through the combination of complex, real-world problems and meaningful social interaction among learners and teacher, constructivists assert that learners are encouraged to discover or invent new rules or revise old rules and in the process come to a deeper understanding of underlying concepts and principles. The discovery process embedded in a constructivist learning environment also allows learners to re-evaluate what they know, and to change their understanding based on what they have directly learned from their environment. Constructivists agree that the open-ended, problem-based, inquiry learning characteristics of constructivist learning environments require learners to struggle with the ill-structured, real-world problems in order to solve them.

One of the fundamental underlying principles of constructivism is the concept of "socio-cognitive conflict". This mechanism for learning, derived from the work of Piaget and his followers, proposes that cognitive conflicts lead to higher levels of reasoning and learning (Weble & Palinscar, 1996). Cognitive conflicts arises through the dynamics of social exchange when the learner realizes that there is a contradiction between his/her existing understanding and what he/she is experiencing.

Constructivists claim that it is reasonable to believe that the best environment for creating such conflict is an environment in which problems are posed, questions are raised and alternative perspectives are presented. Problem-based environments also promote peer collaboration and exchange of ideas, which are the major sources of cognitive conflict (Piaget, 1976). Evidence shows that giving up one's current understanding in order to reach a new perspective will be best attained by an exchange of ideas (Damon, 1984; Radziszewska & Rogoff, 1991).

From a motivational perspective, evidence shows that since problem-based, inquiry learning environments simulate real world situations, students' natural curiosity is stimulated and learners find their learning experiences to be more interesting, more engaging and more relevant. Furthermore, problem-based environments make higher cognitive, meta-cognitive, affective, and resource management demands upon the learner. These high level demands encourage learners to develop expertise in how to learn as well as in learning to construct useful knowledge (Perkins, 1991). A problem-based learning environment is much more likely to engage learners in the learning process through identification, formulation and restructuring of goals; planning; development and execution of plans; self-monitoring and appropriate use of resource management strategies.

Finally, the purposes of preservice teacher education have, for the most part, been treated as distinct. Preservice has traditionally existed to maintain professional standards by presumably fully preparing teachers for licensing, and for the "rigorous application of standards of practice" (Bernier L. McClelland, 1989). It does this by providing them with the knowledge and the status to teach. The expansion of the knowledge base, increased demand on education by society, the need for school change, and increased research on staff development, all serve to increase the necessity for continuous professional development in the future. Because "all fields are moving towards a continuous professional development model" in a rapidly changing world, preservice teacher education needs to be reconceptualized in the light of constructivism. Credentialism as the focus of preservice will be forced to give way to professional development as a process of learning from practice. The ability to adapt to changing societal conditions increasingly demands a professional who continues to learn and change.

5.4 TEACHER-EDUCATOR PARADIGM REVISITED

Teacher-educators are considered as the backbone of any teacher education programme. If teacher-educators themselves are not comfortable with constructivism how can we expect to base our teacher-education programme on constructivism? Majority of teacher-educators are found hesitant to come out of the shell of behaviourism in which they have been educated and which they have been practicing. They find themselves happy with their comfort zone. However, there are some who want to come out of their comfort zone (zone of Behaviourism) then there is a lot of resistance. This resistance is due to fear of ignorance about the constructivism. Those who have embraced constructivism view their profession (teaching) much satisfying and fulfilling. When teacher-educators situate their teaching on constructivism, they have been found using various constructivist strategies consciously or unconsciously like:

- Prompting students to formulate their own questions (inquiry).
- Allowing multiple interpretations and expressions of learning (multiple intelligence).
- Encouraging group work and the use of peers as resources (collaborative learning).
- Encouraging and accepting student autonomy and initiative.
- Allowing student responses to drive lessons, shift instructional strategies and other content.
- Inquiring about students' understandings of concepts before sharing their own understandings of those concepts.
- Encouraging students to engage in dialogue both with the teacher and with one another.
- Encouraging students inquiry by asking throughout, open-ended questions and encouraging students to ask questions of each other.
- Seeking elaborate of students' initial responses.
- Engaging students in experiences that might engender contradictions to their initial hypotheses and then encourage discussion.
- Allowing a waiting time after posing questions.
- Nurturing students' natural curiosity through frequent use of the learning cycle model (Brooks & Brooks, 1993).

Thus what we need is to redefine and revisit Teacher-educator paradigm of teaching, learning and research based on constructivism. Some researches have shown that the Teacher educators have reported that their notion of classroom have got changed as they started practicing constructivism in their classrooms. They have realized that a classroom is a place for constructing knowledge not receiving it; each of us constructs our own learning based on our past experiences. Classroom teaching is about thinking and analyzing, not accumulating and memorizing information. Students must use the content not to memorize it. Learning is about understanding and applying, not repeating back.

Teacher-educators must realize that the students are the individuals who create new understanding for themselves. The teacher merely coaches, moderates and suggests. Also, he/she must allow the students' room to experiment, ask questions, tries things that don't work. Learning activities require the students' full participation by providing hands-on experiments. A vital part of the learning process is that students reflect on and talk about their activities. If teacher-educators start believing in constructivism then they will start believing also that the students are capable of controlling their own learning process, and they can lead the way by reflecting on their experiences. This process also enables them experts of their own learning strategies. Here the teacher-educators' job is to educate the pupil-teachers to help create situations where the students feel safe questioning and reflecting on their own processes, either privately or in group discussions. The teacher-educators' should also create activities that lead the students to reflect on their prior knowledge and experiences. Talking about what was learnt and how it was learnt is really important. Thus, the teacher-educators must ask the pupil-teachers that they should ask the student to maintain a class-diary where they should be asked to record how they felt about the class projects, the reactions of others to the projects and how they felt their own writing had changed. Periodically the teacher should read the class-diary and hold a meeting with the students where the three assess: (1) what new knowledge the student has created; (2) how the student learns best and (3) the learning environment and the teacher's role in it.

Effective approaches to teacher development mirror what we know about learning; they are continuous, build on learners' current knowledge and skills, and include sufficient intensity and practice that new learnings can become part of teachers' ongoing practice.

What we know: An analysis of research and experience in staff development (Loucks-Horsley et al., 1987) suggests that programmes that effectively support teacher growth have the following characteristics:

- Content that is either based on research or has demonstrated its effectiveness in schools and classrooms.
- Opportunities for teachers to work together as they learn, plan to use, and implement their new knowledge and practices.
- Opportunities for teachers to participate in decisions about what they will learn, how they will learn, and how they will use what they learn.
- Norms that support experimentation and risk taking.
- Time for teachers to participate fully in the learning experience, to practice, to master new behaviours, and to incorporate new practices into their teaching routines.
- Integration of staff development into other initiatives of the school or district, with a connection between individual, school, and district goals.
- Leadership that provides direction and clear expectations, coupled with ongoing support for teachers to learn and to use what they learn.
- Appropriate and sufficient incentives and rewards; and
- Designs based on knowledge about learning and the process of change.

All of these characteristics are critical to the success of teacher-educators' development. Yet the last is of particular interest here, since it is closely connected to our perspective of learning. Although the implications of current cognitive research for adult learning strategies are not entirely clear, the constructivist perspective suggests some ways in which teacher learning mirrors the learning of students. It follows, then, that teacher-educators' development should have much in common with what described earlier as good teaching. Among the characteristics they share are:

- Active leading techniques.
- Attention to what teachers already know (i.e., their current conceptions of teaching, and of learning).
- Sufficient time to consider new ideas and 'try them on' for fit; and multiple opportunities to observe and then apply new knowledge in practice.
- Thus, effective teacher-educators development can be an excellent model for good teaching.

Taking action on what we know: A constructivist-driven teacher development model suggests a certain course of action that is unlike traditional (primarily one-shot, workshop-oriented) teacher-educators development approaches.

Attention should be paid to prior teacher knowledge: Teachers at all levels of preparation come to teaching with their own experiences and observations of what works with student, what should be taught, and what instructional strategies work best. Preservice teachers, for example, may assume that engaging students with a good dose of creativity and enthusiasm is in and of itself enough fuel to ignite the learning fire. Experienced teachers may accept that engagement is essential to good learning but might also believe that reading about science/mathematics qualifies as a stand-in for the exploration stage of the learning model. How can we begin to help teachers actively reconstruct their views about teaching and learning science/mathematics if we don't attempt to pinpoint the prior knowledge teachers bring with them?

Concepts should be developed and introduced over sufficient periods of time: Just reading or hearing about new concepts is rarely enough to advance authentic learning. Teachers need to participate in multiple, interactive, collaborative experiences. For example, rather than learn about the topic of pond life via a one-time, facts-to-be-learned presentation, teachers can work in small groups to share what they know and then, visiting an actual pond, work together to reconstruct their views. This type of learning will allow them to develop their understanding of such concepts as diversity and systems over time.

Theory should be tied to experience by using learning activities that make abstract concepts personal: Such experiences are the catalysts that help teachers learn. Follow this with activities that give teachers time to reflect on their experiences. Then introduce new information that prompts teachers to focus on the formation of abstract concepts and generations. To continue with our pond life example, teachers can design aquariums for their classrooms so they (and their students) can observe and answer questions that relate to pond life. They can also divide readings, relate the readings to what they observe, and share their findings with each other. Concept development continues in this phase as teachers digest new information. The instructor slowly adds fuel as discussions turn to formal theories such as food webs, interdependency of pond organisms, ecosystem factors that enable pond life, and so on. Learners can personally experience concepts when the methods of experiential engagement and exploration, along with theory conceptualization and the pedagogical techniques of small working groups, are employed. Here theory ties closely to experience.

In the final step, teachers should have opportunities to try out developing concepts by making multiple applications in their classrooms: Teachers need the chance to experiment with new concepts and techniques with their students. At meetings held after their trials, teachers can compare successes and strategies about back-to-the-drawing-board activities.

As a follow-up, a long-term plan should be instituted for supporting novices: Give teachers a voice in how this process win work. They may elect to form support or check-in groups, designate those who are most expert as mentors, or continue to refine applications with their original work group. This model suggests that we view the teacher development process, from beginning coursework through inservice opportunities, from a constructivist perspective that encourages teachers to explore, experience, and incorporate new strategies. Teachers need to decide when, how, and under what conditions these new strategies should be used. This approach prepares teachers to deal with increasing classroom diversity and a multitude of daily decisions. It also allows them to construct an evolving instructional theory in the classroom, regardless of which curriculum they use.

Learning more about subject knowledge: Most of today's schoolteachers have limited knowledge of the subject they teach. They are not required to take much of the subject knowledge as undergraduates, and the courses they take are not taught in a way that allow them to develop concepts they would need to teach. Thus, the course, institute, or university department would:

Be taught in a way that reflects constructivist learning. This means learners would do the subject (for example, science or mathematics or any subject) by pursuing real questions about the natural world and mixing investigative methods with knowledge about the important facts and concepts of science or mathematics as a discipline. Depth of content rather than breadth of coverage would lead to desirable concept formation instead of rote memorization of science or mathematics trivia.

Use an interdisciplinary approach: So that a geology course, for example, would incorporate biology, chemistry, mathematics, and physics. Teachers will then see the interrelationships that occur naturally in the real world and are not separated into disciplines.

Include historical and philosophical assumptions and contexts: Some early philosophical theories can help us understand present-day laws and ideologies, including a few of the misconceptions students (and teachers) bring to class. For instance, Aristotle believed that forced motion is maintained by force. Buriden's impetus theory developed from Aristotle's notion and maintains that the impetus is an Intel source of force that maintains the motion. These views contrast with Newton's laws, which suggest that an object in motion tends to stay in motion unless a force acts upon it.

Help teachers relate science/mathematics content to technological and societal issues: Thereby connecting science/mathematics to the real world and how we live in it. A unit on waste pollution, for example, might consider an alternative to the present use of Styrofoam materials.

Use instructional strategies: Like cooperative learning, wait time, discussion techniques, inquiry, problem-solving, and assessment, so that teachers' witness for themselves how these methods serve as important vehicles for science/mathematics learning.

Induce problem-solving: As an active means for learning the important facts and concepts of science/mathematics.

Require collaboration among faculty from several disciplines or fields: Whatever course is being taught would benefit from a number of perspectives, especially when instructors make it a point to connect content of different disciplines. This can be done using a science or mathematics team or a science and mathematics pedagogy team.

Conclusively, the Teacher-Educator paradigm may be revisited by following constructivist measures:

Learning More About Learning

What teacher development approach would foster a rich understanding of how student learn?

Extend over a long period of time, encouraging developing teachers to incorporate into their knowledge bases an expanding picture of how student develop and learn. They are continually involved in constructing a more elaborate understanding of student, how they most effectively learn science/mathematics, and, subsequently, what instructional strategies are most appropriate to use and how and when they could be used best.

Provide teachers with knowledge about the complete range of theories and research on student's learning, including developmental findings from research on social learning, cognitive learning and constructivist theory of learning. Constructivism has had and will continue to have an important impact on school science or mathematics and how it is taught. Teachers need to understand the theory behind constructivism and see the implications it has for curriculum, instruction, and assessment.

Be simultaneously rich in theory and research and experientially based. Coursework in how student learn must allow preservice teachers to work directly with student during science/mathematics learning to see how to apply the theoretical principles they are learning. Constructivism provides a model of how such a course might be framed. Early in the course, for example, participants might visit classrooms to observe how student learn science/mathematics. They share observations and discuss in teams which of the instructional strategies and techniques worked and which did not, as well as why and how they worked. At this point teachers are ready to learn some new information, perhaps something about developmental learning theory, that will enhance their developing concept of how student learn.

Not confine learning about learning to courses devoted solely to theories of learning. For instance, in some buildings teachers may form collegial teams to share their insights into how student learn science/mathematics and to invite expert guests to share with them aspects of how student learn. Teachers could examine curriculum materials and see how the instructional format reflects one or more learning theories. The format for the Elementary science/mathematics study units is quite different from the materials for science/mathematics: A Process Approach. A major determinate of those differences lies in the different theories of learning that the curriculum developers used to structure activities.

Schools and districts can choose among several approaches for teacher development that can incorporate these characteristics (see Sparks and Loucks-Horsley, 1989 for detailed discussion):

Training with coaching. Most frequently equated with staff development, this approach can result in demonstrable changes in teacher behaviour and, subsequently, in the behaviours of student. The model includes development of the theory and rationale behind the new behaviours to be learned, demonstration or modelling, practice in training settings, and guided practice or peer coaching in the classroom with supportive feedback from a colleague. The process of peer coaching is particularly important in helping teachers change their teaching practices, in providing them with opportunities to discuss their changing ideas about teaching, and in giving them the psychological support they need to persist in learning (Joyce and Showers, 1988).

Observation and assessment. This approach involves careful observation of teaching with attention to certain behaviours and an open discussion of the results. The model is labelled in various ways, primarily as forms of supervision and coaching. Teachers agree on a focus for the observations, with the observer recording behaviours as they occur. A conference follows, in which the observations are discussed, strengths and weaknesses assessed, and goals set for the future. Both the observed teacher and the observer can gain insight into effective pedagogy and how to incorporate it into daily teaching practice.

Inquiry. This approach incorporates such practices as action research and reflective inquiry. Teachers, alone or collaboratively, decide what problem or situation they are interested in examining, gather and analyze data, and interpret the results in light of changes they might make in their classrooms or in school practice.

Individually guided teacher development. In this approach, teachers, individually or in collegial teams, identify their interests and concerns; establish a goal; and seek input by way of coursework, workshops, library research, field trips, and other forms of self-study to reach the goal.

These approaches to staff development can complement, and in some cases replace, the traditional inservice workshop. When well designed, they can help teachers increase their knowledge of science/mathematics (or any subject), learning, and teaching in ways that they can apply directly to classroom teaching.

5.5 BRINGING CHANGE IN TEACHERS' THINKING

Knowing that we all construct our own understanding, there will undoubtedly be other perspectives on what is meant by particular principles and how those principles may be implemented in daily interactions with students. There is a need to have continuous dialogue among the teacher-educators to bring change in our thinking (Rodgers & Chaille, 1997). Teacher-Educators face the challenge of preparing teachers to participate in the increasingly complex profession of educating young children. Beginning teachers must be able to address curriculum guidelines for their particular grade level, make decisions regarding the selection of curriculum materials, meet the needs and provide appropriate challenge for individual students, increase parent involvement in the classroom prepare students to take standardized tests, and promote multicultural education; along with countless other responsibilities. As additional mandates are passed down from decision-making bodies regarding the preparation of future teachers, teacher-educators must determine the best course of action in programme development. How can we get students "ready" for this ever-changing culture of education? One approach might be to address each task as it comes along so that we make sure that students "know" what they need to know. Yet, each of the external forces that are influential in determining requirements for certifying new teachers may have its own idea of what beginning teachers should know when they enter the profession. How can we possibly satisfy all of those different sets of expectations? More importantly, how can we make sure that our students know the material? Our constructivist perspective is consistent with Harrington's (1994), in that the challenge for teacher-educators lies in encouraging our students to struggle with the notion of what it means to "know" and what knowledge is of most worth. "Teaching education is not about knowledge but, rather, about knowing" (Harrington, 1990). It is about the active construction of knowledge; specifically, it is about building personal theories about teaching and learning. Chaile and Britain (1997) describe children as theory builders and compare their actions to those of scientists. As children gain information about their world through interactions with objects and other people, they make inferences as they interpret their new information. They use those inferences to predict subsequent trials; they make inferences as they interpret their new information. They use those inferences to predict subsequent trials, in a sense, testing hypotheses. The theory building is not exclusive to young children, but is continued throughout our lives. With that in mind, let's examine what experiences our university students have had and what theories they may have constructed over the course of their lives about the nature of learning. Most of our students have had years of experience in educational settings that reinforce the notion that learning means knowing the right answer. Their classroom experiences could be characterized by the use of worksheets and other product-oriented forms of assessment, an emphasis on external forms of motivation such as grades, and other strategies used to control their behaviour. Through these experiences, many students have constructed personal theories about teaching and learning that are inconsistent with constructivist theory (Rodgers & Dunn, 1997). Most have not experienced classrooms where they were encouraged to solve their own problems, develop their own questions and search for answers, or use critical analysis and reflection to develop their own ideas about issues. Participation in such experiences might have encouraged them to build theories about the learning process as a search for meaning rather than a search for the right answer. Understanding the personal theories, our students have constructed throughout their lives is vital to our roles as constructivist teacher-educators. We need that information to build our theories about how we can help them make sense of constructivist theory. We all use the theory building process as we look with our students. We also learn about our students' theories as we interact during class and this increased understanding drives our further interactions with students. There is not one right way to be a constructivist teacher. Consistent with constructivist theory, we must all make sense of what learning is all about, what that means for teaching practice. The moot point is there is an urgent need to bring change in our thinking about teaching, learning, assessment and knowledge itself all from constructivist perspective. Without bringing change in

Teachers' thinking nothing is going to change. For the suitable change our teacher-educators must be exposed to the concepts like Portfolios, grading rubrics, developmental checklists, holistic writing evaluations, performance assessments, etc. which are based on constructivist principles. The author believes that unless our concept and mode of assessment is changed it is not possible to bring change in our thinking about teaching and learning. A suitable change in our thinking about assessment will certainly bring change in our thinking regarding teaching and learning too. Teacher-educators and curriculum planners must expose themselves to the alternative (constructivist) paradigms of teaching and learning.

There are several challenges behind bringing change in Teachers' thinking. The overarching challenge constructivism presents to teachers and teacher-educators is the formidable task of translating a learning theory into a theory of teaching (MacKinnon & Scarff-Seatter, 1997), which in turn raises questions about what teachers need to know and be able to do. For teacher-educators, among other tasks, this involves balancing the need to acknowledge the different discipline-specific requirements of teaching with the need to model constructivist methods in teacher education courses and practicums. Richardson (1997) also notes the limits of a perspective on teaching that values students' understandings at the expense of "right" answers. Student knowledge becomes idiosyncratic; 30 different students may arrive at 30 different understandings or interpretations of a concept, all of which are not equally appropriate. Inappropriately applied, constructivist approaches may lead to the "abandonment" style of teaching (MacKinnon & Scarff-Seatter, 1997).

Several authors cite the importance of teacher-educators' modelling constructivist approaches that engage students in interdisciplinary exploration, collaborative activity, and field-based opportunities for experiential learning, reflection, and self-examination (Kaufman, 1996; Kroll & LaBosky, 1996) if future teachers are to be able to employ these strategies in schools.

To derive culturally relevant and socially just pedagogy and practice from constructivist epistemologies, Martin (1994) and Vadeboncoeur (1997) urge teacher-educators to deconstruct and scrutinize cultural assumptions that underlie various interpretations of constructivism to expose how social beliefs have influenced the development of theory and practices. Without such scrutiny, societal inequities and historical forms of oppression may be perpetuated in supposedly constructivist classrooms, and the very constraints on individual development constructivists seek to remove or ameliorate will be reinforced.

A final challenge faced by educators is the pitfall of regarding constructivism as the only viable theoretical framework for teaching and learning. It is one way of thinking about how knowledge and understanding are formed, but it is not the only way. Nor are various interpretations of constructivism necessarily incompatible with one another (MacKinnon & Scarff-Seatter, 1997; Oldfather, Bonds, & Bray, 1994). Prospective teachers should be exposed to varying perspectives and given opportunities to develop the discretion needed to choose most appropriately and the skills to implement their choices.

However, constructivist educators agree that the teachers' thinking change requires learning opportunities supporting in-depth examination of educational theories and practices in light of teachers' beliefs and experiences if they are to help pupils develop conceptual understandings of subject matters and a critical view of education (Maria Teresa Tatto, 1998). Several conditions are necessary for the development of learning opportunities allowing teachers freedom to develop new understandings of teaching and learning. A necessary point of departure is the development of a theoretical view of learning to guide teacher education in which knowledge, curriculum, and learning are socially constructed; the curriculum and instruction are discipline based; the focus is on teachers' and children's sense making; and authority is socially accorded (Cochran et al., 1993; Condon et al., 1993; Schon, 1987; Zeichner & Gore, 1990).

Constructivist teachers require learning opportunities that encourage reflection, dialogue, critical thinking, knowledge ownership, and understanding in context and within learning communities (Black & Ammon, 1992; Cochran et al., 1993; Condon et al., 1993; Mosenthal & Ball, 1992; O'Loughlin, 1992; Zeichner & Gore, 1990). This reconceptualization of teacher education requires the creation of norms of discourse, which provide cohesiveness of purpose and facilitate constructive dialogue about teaching and learning within and across learning communities. Constructivist-oriented approaches often require teacher education students and teacher-educators to engage in dialogue, reflection, and inquiry and are more likely to influence teacher change in desired directions.

It is very important to have changing teachers' beliefs to bring change in teachers' thinking. Purposes of education may shape teachers' beliefs about what is appropriate in teaching and teachers' conceptions about their professional role. Conceptions of their role may, in turn, shape their teaching practice (Buchmann, 1986). Reflecting and attempting to understand how their beliefs influence their teaching are critical to teachers' development and change in role conceptions and teaching practices.

How to bring change in one's thinking:

- We should be sincere about our personal theory about the process. A personal theory about the process includes the premise that students will be more likely to understand how children learn by simultaneously examining and reflecting on their own investment in the learning process. This premise is supported by the research (Anderson & Roth, 1989) indicating that regardless of how well the ideas are presented, they will not be understood unless students make personal use of them to understand their world.
- As we search for meaning in our discussions about issues embedded in the complex field of teacher education, we can address our own questions about how to best approach the issues in light of constructivist theory.
- There is a need to think about how does our understanding of the learning process, and of our student's personal theories, inform our practices with preservice and in-service teachers?

- How can we help our students develop an appreciation for curiosity to the point that they pursue their own need to know?
- How can we support the autonomy of our students while we simultaneously expect them to strive for high standards?
- Above all, how can a focus on the goal of autonomy help our students to become more capable of addressing the complexity inherent in education?

5.6 REDESIGNING TEACHER PREPARATION PROGRAMME

Today, the operant issue is teacher education—not teacher training. Unfortunately, some programmes are still based on the principles of normal schools rather than research-based constructivist principles. Clearly, we need to produce beginning teachers who are critical thinkers and reflective practitioners and to help practicing teachers to develop the critical stance and strategies necessary to become reflective practitioners. This involves more than just mimicry, mechanical use, and classroom management of inquiry based teaching.

The development of critical thinking in which preservice teachers and in-service teachers are challenged by pedagogical issues and required to deliberate about the alternative solutions, to reflect and to justify their instructional decisions should be a fundamental part of every teacher education or professional development programme. Major adjustments to some dimensions are necessary to ensure a more accurate match with the worldview, ontological, epistemic, psychological, pedagogical, and linguistic assumptions of our desired image of teaching and learning.

Thus, seeing the prevalent scenario, there is a need for developing more powerful teacher-education, with more emphasis on pupil-centred learning and with dissemination of research evidences on effective constructivist teaching, to help teachers develop a more sophisticated understanding of how pupils learn and extend their understanding to teaching practices that support pupil's active learning. And most importantly, to address the influences of textbooks and worksheets on constructivist teaching to prepare teachers to a more proper use of textbook in their teaching.

The design for Teacher Preparation Programme would include following main features such as: (a) non-gradedness; (b) multi-age grouping; (c) developmentally appropriate practice; (d) child-centred learning; (e) integrated thematic instruction; (f) team teaching; (g) community involvement; and (h) parent involvement, with an emphasis on creating a sense of community within the classroom (Pamela Evanshen, 2005).

Non-gradedness: As referred to by Gaustad (1992), "non-graded education is the practice of teaching children of different ages and ability levels together, without dividing them into group labelled by grade designations". Children make continuous progress at their own rates of speed, remaining with the same teacher for more than one year. Individuals are different and should not be treated as items on an assembly line. A non-graded organizational structure allows students to complete the curriculum at an individual rate rather than requiring them to proceed in lock-step with their peers (Gaustad, 1994). Anderson & Pavan's (1993) eleven elements of non-gradedness may be chosen when redesigning the teacher education programme:

1. Individual differences in the pupil population are accepted and respected, and there is ample variability in instructional approaches to respond to varying needs.
2. Learning, which is the "work" of the child, is intended to be not only challenging but also pleasurable and rewarding.
3. Students are viewed as a whole; development in cognitive, physical, aesthetic, social, and emotional spheres is nurtured.
4. The administrative and organizational framework, for example, with respect to pupil grouping practices, is flexible and provides opportunities for each child to interact with children and adults of varying personalities, backgrounds, abilities, interests, and ages.
5. Students are enabled through flexible arrangements to progress at their own best pace and in appropriately

varied ways. Instruction, learning opportunities, and movement within the curriculum are individualized to correspond with individual needs, interests, and abilities.

6. Curricular areas are both integrated and separate. Instructional, programmatic, and organizational patterns are flexible, with outcomes rather than mere coverage of content as the primary focus.
7. The expected standards of performance (in terms of outcomes) in the core areas of the curriculum are clearly defined, so that the points to be reached by the end of a designated (e.g., a three- or four-year) period are well known. However, the time taken to reach that end, and the path followed to that end, is allowed to vary for students with different histories and potentialities.
8. Within the curriculum and related assessment practices, specific content learning is generally subordinate to the understanding of major concepts and methods of inquiry, and the development of the skills of learning: inquiry, evaluation, interpretation, and application.
9. Student assessment is holistic, to correspond with the holistic view of learning.
10. Evaluation of the learner is continuous, comprehensive, and diagnostic. Except for reference purposes as necessary to parental and staff understanding, chronological age and grade norms play a much smaller role in evaluation and reporting activities than does the child's own growth history and potential.
11. While there are some core components of the curriculum that are especially valued (as reflected in performance standards in the major content areas), the system is largely teacher-managed and controlled. Thus, it empowers teachers to create learning opportunities and to use instructional strategies at their own discretion, based on the perceived needs of the students they are serving. Assessment procedures are similarly flexible, individualized, and teacher managed. These elements of

non-gradedness coupled with a constructivist framework served as a guide for planning the programme and designing the building. According to Brooks and Brooks (1993), "a constructivist framework challenges teachers to create environments in which they and their students are encouraged to think and explore". Wilson (1996) defines a constructivist learning environment as "a place where learners may work together and support each other as they use a variety of tools and information resources in the guided pursuit of learning goals and problem-solving activities".

Multi-age grouping: This type of a grouping encourages collaboration between and among teachers and children. Vygotsky's (1962) theory emphasizes that social interaction plays a fundamental role in the development of cognition. The range of skill that can be developed with adult guidance or peer collaboration exceeds what can be done alone (Vygotsky, 1978). By combining multi-age grouping, team teaching and the philosophy and practices of non-gradedness, a truly child-centred environment can be created (Anderson, 1993).

Developmentally appropriate practices: Developmentally appropriate practices are at the heart of multi-age classrooms. A developmentally appropriate approach is very child-centred and allows teachers to focus on individual student needs. Bredekamp and Copple (1997) define developmentally appropriate practices as the result from the process of professionals making decisions about the well-being and education of children based on at least three important kinds of information or knowledge:

1. What is known about child development and learning-knowledge of age-related human characteristics that permits general predictions within an age range about what activities, materials, interactions or experiences will be safe, healthy, interesting, achievable, and also challenging to children.
2. What is known about the strengths, interests, and needs of each individual child in the group—to be able to adapt for and be responsive to inevitable individual variation.

3. Knowledge of the social and cultural contexts—in which children live to ensure that learning experiences are meaningful, relevant, and respectful for the participating children and their families.

The teachers must teach the whole child, supporting intellectual, social, emotional, and moral growth. They strongly recommend curriculum integration, which actively involves the child both physically and cognitively (Bredekamp & Copple, 1997). According to Lolli (1998), "Curriculum in the multi-age classroom is based upon a constructivist view of learning." Information is more easily learned and remembered when it is taught in a meaningful context, when it is relevant to the learner, and when the learner takes an active role in learning (Gaustad, 1992). Children create meaning from the experiences and modelling that occurs around them. Developing deeper bonds with peers, as a result of multi-age grouping over a three-year period, extends and expands a variety of scaffolding opportunities between all learners.

Team teaching: Teaming requires sharing of materials, skills, territory, equipment and recognition for successes and student achievement (Gaustad, 1994). It also involves brainstorming, documenting, discussing, interpreting and analyzing teaching and learning. Team teaching is a requirement for the programme. Each member of the team needs to be comfortable with the other's style of teaching and learning. The goal is to develop and maintain trust in an effort to assist all students in their learning process. Learning community teams (learning centre team, administrators, and related-arts specialists) are responsible for the development and implementation of the integrated thematic units of instruction.

Thematic instruction: Moving from a teacher-directed method of instruction to more of a child-centred or constructivist approach is a challenge in a public school system. Kovalik's (1994) "Integrated Thematic Instruction" model may be selected as the guide for the integration of the curriculum. Thematic units may be created to address curriculum standards. A framework may be created by teams of teachers utilizing standards as a guide. Teachers and students may begin each study accessing prior knowledge and planning learning experiences. This integrated approach may be employed based on constructivist principles such as student-initiated questions, student-to-student interactions, textbooks as only one of the sources of information, cooperative learning opportunities, valuing student expression of thoughts, and construction of new knowledge in constructivist programmes. Reading and writing experiences may be integrated into the thematic study as well. Reading and writing, and mathematics may also be studied outside of the designated theme time using a hands-on interactive approach.

Parent involvement: Parents are welcomed and encouraged to participate in the learning process. Parents may be asked to volunteer in the classrooms. Beyond the typical scenarios of adults reading with individual children, parents may be engaged in inquiry-based learning experiences at learning centers. They may guide children through active exploration of concepts, problem-solving and reflection. This hands-on, active-learning approach allows parents to assist with teaching and learning, and witness evidence of student success.

Sense of community within the classroom: The quality and nature of the relationship between the teacher and his/her students is the key to building a sense of community (Kovalik, 1994). Building a culture where students feel respected, cared about, and bonded to classmates, teachers, and the school makes a "caring community" (Goleman, 1994). The students may become familiar with the life-skill terms: (a) integrity, (b) initiative, (c) flexibility, (d) perseverance, (e) organization, (f) sense of humour, (g) effort, (h) common sense, (i) problem-solving, (j) responsibility, (k) patience, (l) friendship, (m) curiosity, (n) cooperation, and (o) caring. They learn the importance of such skills as they use them regularly. All children are "members" of the classroom. Children with special needs are included and easily become contributing members of the classroom community. Children, teachers, and parents become "school families" in the years to come as they spend growing and learning with one another.

The implementation of constructivist teaching must (1) allow enough time to address prior conceptions and facilitate students' incorporation of new ideas, (2) limit the breadth of content taught, (3) explicitly introduce students unfamiliar with scientific inquiry to methods they will use to learn the content, and (4) take steps to avoid the common pitfalls of group work (Diggs & Kimbrough, 2002).

For the successful implementation of constructivist practices, we have identified three essential factors that must be present: First, when employing a constructivist teaching style, the time spent on individual topical exercises must expand at the expense of content breadth. This is an old truth, and it remains difficult to accomplish in introductory classes, where breadth is favoured over depth. However, a constructivist approach is helpful for creating a meaningful understanding of the material and models good teaching practices that preservice teachers will later use in their own classrooms, provided this teaching approach is implemented correctly. An inquiry-based approach is easiest to implement in specialized survey classes, because these classes stand alone and are not generally part of a majors' sequence that depends on a prescribed amount of content coverage in each course. Especially in courses designed to reach the broadest population of students and future citizens, we should take steps to include the best possible teaching techniques in classes accessible to all.

Secondly, most preservice teachers are not familiar with constructivist learning or methodology, even if they have been exposed to the general theory before in education courses, so the time for each topic must increase as the students are learning not only new content but are also learning how to conduct scientific inquiry.

Finally, while lecture classes and examinations are based on individual understanding, much constructivist learning involves group work, allowing a few students to build understanding for a group, leaving weaker students at a disadvantage on examinations. It is clear that more homework reinforcement of in-class exercises is desired by students to overcome this difficulty, and to help those students whose learning styles are not amenable to group work.

Linking ontology and pedagogy: The radical constructivist may well respond that whether or not radical constructivism could give birth and nurture to a young science is irrelevant since science is in fact established. They may also cite the increasing attention that philosophers of science have given to subjectivist views of knowledge. These views range from the moderate position taken by Kuhn in The Structure of Scientific Revolutions to the extremism of Feyerabend's Against Method. More to the point of the above question, however, radical constructivists argue that their position promotes better teaching and thus better learning. To bolster this assertion the radical constructivists point to research such as Clement (1987) and Briscoe et al. (1990).

Pedagogical constructivism rejects the idea that an identity exists between knowledge within and knowledge without. For example, we may agree that at the end of a lesson a student has successfully gained knowledge about plants, but is there an identity between the student's knowledge (knowledge within) and the knowledge the teacher presented in the instructional process (knowledge without)? Pedagogical constructivism says no. Learning is not the relatively simple process of transplanting knowledge from the teacher or textbook to the student. Rather, learning is an interpretive process. Learning occurs when a person under the influence of experience (in this example teaching) constructs personal knowledge that makes the experience meaningful. In the tradition of pragmatism, this learning is subsequently validated or invalidated by further experience. This view of learning suggests the use of instructional procedures that foster higher order cognitive thinking as exemplified in Clement (1987).

The unique position of radical constructivists is that ontology and pedagogy are vitally linked. Radical constructivists maintain that constructivist teaching will increase with teacher acceptance of radical constructivist ontology. The four spheres of the radical pedagogical constructivist linkage represent ontology, epistemology, psychology, and pedagogy. The radical constructivists discount the first sphere as unknowable. They collapse or link the second and third spheres with the equation, knowledge-knowing; and they assert that this equation logically leads to a particular view of pedagogy. The linkage argument is: If I understand that reality is inherently unknowable, then I also will understand that what I know is a construction and the only meaningful reality. It is only logical that methods of instruction should facilitate the personal construction of meaning and stress higher order cognition. Radical constructivists also maintain that the alternative to this view is naive realism: If I understand that the world is real and knowable, then I also will understand that knowledge corresponds to reality. It is only logical then that instruction be the transplanting of knowledge to the learner, i.e., rote learning.

Based on this argument, radical constructivists maintain that teacher education should work at persuading teachers to adopt radical constructivist ontology (von Glasersfeld, 1989). The realist teacher who asks students to memorize facts because the facts are objective, once converted to radical constructivism will more readily adopt pedagogical constructivist teaching strategies (Briscoe et al., 1990).

The Teacher-Educator during the preservice teacher education programme can develop a format based on constructivism for the observations of pupil-teachers when they go to school for teaching practices.

Ratings:

1. Strongly Agree............................ = 3 Points
2. Agree... = 2 Points
3. Slightly Agree............................ = 1 Points
4. Not Agreed................................. = 0 Points

(1) Use pupils' existing knowledge to guide teaching.

1.1 Teacher's awareness of pupil's existing ideas.

1.2 Elicit pupil's ideas before presenting teachers' own ideas or before studying ideas from textbook or other sources.

1.3 Challenge pupils' initial ideas.

1.4 Make new ideas accessible to pupils.

(2) Guide pupils to generate explanations and alternative interpretations.

2.1 Pupils observe phenomenon.

2.2 Pupils describe phenomenon.

2.3 Pupils generate explanations and interpretations.

2.4 Probe pupils' responses for clarification and justification.

2.5 Pupils explain contradictions and misconception.

(3) Devise incisive questions.

3.1 A question rich learning environment.

3.2 Questions based on pupils' responses.

3.3 Pupils expand on their questions and justify their responses.

3.4 Accept and value pupil's answers and suggestions.

(4) Choose materials and activities for test ideas.

4.1 Pupils work with materials and activities.

4.2 Pupils engage in scientific inquiry.

4.3 Pupils work independently with minimal help from the teacher.

4.4 Pupils put their ideas to test (disprove or prove what they think).

4.5 Pupil's suggestion about the direction of the activity/experiment.

(5) Provide a classroom atmosphere conducive to discussion.

5.1 Pupils put forward and discuss ideas with the teacher.

5.2 Pupils put forward and discuss ideas with peers.

(6) Provide opportunities for pupils to utilise new ideas.

6.1 Relate current teaching points to previous knowledge.

6.2 Pupils apply knowledge to new situations or real-life problems.

Teacher's teaching performance in their observed lessons may be rated according to the above mentioned 22 features that describe constructivist teaching with a 4-point rating ranging from strongly agree (3); agree (2); slightly agree (1) to not observed (0).

The teaching of each student teacher may be rated towards the end of lesson observation to the extent to which it reflected constructivist teaching. For example, a teacher who started the lesson by involving pupils in talking about the knowledge/content/concept learned in previous lesson/year was considered as exhibiting awareness of pupils existing ideas. However, the rating of this practice of teaching with either "strongly agree" or "agree" and "slightly agree" will depend on the breadth and depth of treatment. Another example may be on the rating of the category "pupils explain phenomenon". Some times teachers may not be found to involve pupils in explaining phenomenon throughout the whole lesson, the rating would then be "0"—"not observed". If this practice of teaching is rarely found the rating would then be 1—"slightly agree", so on and so forth. The ratings of the teaching may be clarified and confused by studying the video-recordings of lessons and cross-checking with the observational field notes. This is to ensure the ratings are really describing teachers' performance with each particular item.

6

Constructivism and Distance Education

Today, the major issues in Instructional Design in Distance Education are not the contents and methodologies (in narrower sense) but the epistemological and pedagogical in nature (in broader sense). Here is an attempt to outline some thoughts relevant to the new educational milieu providing insights into constructivist instructional design (traditional such as correspondence learning, etc. and modern such as web-based learning, etc.) for distance education.

6.1. ISSUES IN INSTRUCTIONAL DESIGN IN DISTANCE EDUCATION

Distance education is growing to meet the needs of traditional and non-traditional students. With broadband Internet technologies reaching urban areas as well rural areas, a diverse course offering can be provided to students throughout the country. Equitable access to courses can benefit the learning experiences of students. The quality and diversity of education will increase as the number of online courses and access develops. However, the instructors of web-based distance education courses are critical to the success of the learner. Through utilizing the virtual learning scaffolding model, teachers can incorporate multiple instructional routes to include all learners, fostering active and social learning. Through the facilitation of various student-learning styles, the student may become engaged with the material and take on the responsibility of learning.

The complexity of the online learning environment must be based on a conceptual framework utilizing constructivist elements

(Jeff Boulton, 2002). Situated learning as a model of instruction for web-based courses can foster apprenticeship-style learning that engages the learner with authentic context. Moore stated that the basic principle in setting up a constructivist learning environment is to establish the minimum structure that allows the maximum degree of dialogue between the students. What this right balance of structure and dialogue is depends on the educational sophistication of the students and the subject to be learned. He further states that to achieve constructivist learning, we want to create learning communities. The learning community is one in which students build knowledge together; they also support each other emotionally and in practical ways (Moore, 2004). The learning community is the vehicle through which learning occurs online. Members depend on each other to achieve the learning outcomes for the course. Without the support and participation of a learning community, there is no online course (Smith, 2005). Another area that affects the change of the role of the instructor in distance education is the Transactional Distance Gap. Moore's Theory of Transactional Distance defines the role of faculty in distance education. This concept of "transactional distance" defines the relationship of instructor and learner (Moore and Anderson, 2003). According to Moore, transactional distance is the gap of understanding and communication between the teachers and learners caused by geographic distance. It is filling this 'gap' of understanding and communication between the teacher and learner that defines the role of the instructor. The instructor must be the one to bridge that gap through special teaching techniques, distinctive procedures in instructional design and the facilitation of interaction (Moore and Kearsley, 2005).

Reconceptualization of distance education courses involves the study of virtual learning communities. Understanding student epistemology and ontology is essential for the design, support, and growth of the virtual learning community (Jeff Boulton, 2002). Legitimate peripheral participation helps us understand the virtual community of learners and the progressive involvement and encouragement required for the student to be part of the community (Goldberg, 2005). Much of the emphasis in the literature is focused on the technicalities of the course creation and, unfortunately, the outcome measurements are questionable because of the methodologies employed.

Before we discuss the issues, let us have a look at the concept of Distance Education. The California Distance Learning Project defines distance learning as follows: "Distance Learning is an instructional delivery system that connects learners with educational resources. Distance Learning provides educational access to learners not enrolled in educational institutions and can augment the learning opportunities of current students. The implementation of Distance Learning is a process that uses available resources and will evolve to incorporate emerging technologies." The terms "distance education" or "distance learning" have been applied interchangeably by many different researchers to a great variety of programmes, providers, audiences, and media. Its hallmarks are the separation of teacher and learner in space and/or time (Perraton, 1988), the volitional control of learning by the student rather than the distant instructor (Jonassen, 1992), and noncontiguous communication between student and teacher, mediated by print or some form of technology (Keegan, 1986; Garrison and Shale, 1987).

Several key features define distance learning. The importance of the teacher-learner communications cannot be overstated.

- the separation of teacher and learner during at least a majority of each instructional process
- separation of teacher and learner in space and/or time
- the use of educational media to unite teacher and learner and carry course content
- the provision of two-way communication between teacher, tutor, or educational agency and learner, and
- control of the learning pace by the student rather than the distance instructor.

These definitions apply equally to high tech and low tech approaches to distance learning. There are two distance education delivery system categories—synchronous and asynchronous. Synchronous instruction requires the simultaneous participation of all students and instructors. The advantage of synchronous instruction is that interaction is done in "real time" and has an immediacy. Examples include interactive tele-courses, teleconferencing and web conferencing, and Internet chats.

Asynchronous instruction does not require the simultaneous participation of all students and instructors. Students do not need to be gathered together in the same location at the same time. Rather, students may choose their own instructional time frame and interact with the learning materials and instructor according to their schedules. Asynchronous instruction is more flexible than synchronous instruction, but experience shows that time limits are necessary to maintain focus and participation. The self-paced format accommodates multiple learning levels and schedules. Examples of asynchronous delivery include e-mail, listservs, audiocassette courses, videotaped courses, correspondence courses, and WWW-based courses.

Three elements are of paramount importance to any successful distance education programme:

- Instructional design
- Technology
- Support

Support is often undervalued in design and implementation. Technology implementation studies show that teacher preparation and ongoing support are undervalued.

Why Distance Learning? Distance education increases access to learning opportunities. Well organized distance learning accommodates multiple learning styles. Distance learning serves learners who are not likely to attend traditional classroom instruction (*effectiveness*). In some cases it can serve as many or more learners per rupee spent (*efficiency*). Adult life for many is complex and demanding. Many adults are unable to or unwilling to attend traditional adult education schools and classrooms for many reasons including:

- Having work and family obligations that make attending a regular class time difficult, learning more effectively from video, audio, and web-based media when moving at their own pace.

- Experiencing the dearth of public transportation systems in many parts of the state, needing more practice of skills to achieve mastery.
- Living in locations without convenient access to traditional classes, and/or
- Lacking the full confidence to participate in a large classroom setting in front of other students.

People who can't attend traditional classes because of these and many other realities need alternatives. These adults are prime targets for distance learning. They are motivated to continue their education, but limited by circumstances as to how they participate in adult basic education. Flexible learning approaches that are not classroom centred appeal to these potential learners. One challenge for adult educators is to transition to interactive Internet based instruction that offers a much richer palate of learning materials, communications, and testing possibilities.

The following set of common assumptions was developed for the California Distance Learning Project by a resource team. It was developed to help guide collective thinking and discussions about distance learning policies and priorities.

- Anytime, any place, any pace instruction is one goal for California adult education.
- Faced with an increasingly competitive global market, California, a state of immigrants, will look to adult education to play a key role in developing and maintaining a world class workforce.
- The potential demand for adult basic education services in California far outstrips the supply. New methods must be found to effectively and efficiently reach out and serve more adult learners.
- Distance learning provides access for learners not presently served in traditional settings and enhances learning opportunities for those not being served in traditional programmes.
- Distance learning should be used as a strategic tool to support individual institutional missions. However, there

are institutional structures and cultures that do not foster an environment where distance learning can be easily utilized.

- Distance learning offers unique opportunities for adult schools to provide access to persons not otherwise served; and thus has the potential to continue to expand adult education in new ways.
- Distance learning often requires resource sharing and collaboration among providers. It can be enhanced by many kinds of partnerships.
- Distance learning, incorporating emerging information technologies, provides both an opportunity and a challenge to adult schools in expanding their missions and services.
- Distance learning is most effective when staff, along with learners, acquire new knowledge and skills. Thus, on-going staff development must be an essential part of the distance learning development process.

Core values: These principles assume that the practice of distance learning contributes to the larger social mission of education and training in a democratic society. With that in mind, the principles reflect the following tenets and values:

- Learning is a lifelong process, important to successful participation in the social, cultural, civic, and economic life of a democratic society.
- Lifelong learning involves the development of a range of learning skills and behaviours that should be explicit outcomes of learning activities.
- The diversity of learners, learning needs, learning contexts, and modes of learning must be recognized if the learning activities are to achieve their goals.
- All members of society have the right to access learning opportunities that provide the means for effective participation in society.

- Participation in a learning society involves both rights and responsibilities for learners, providers, and those charged with the oversight of learning.
- Because learning is social and sensitive to context, learning experiences should support interaction and the development of learning communities, whether social, public, or professional.
- The development of a learning society may require significant changes in the roles, responsibilities, and activities of providers, organizations and personnel as well as of the learners themselves.

Schlosser and Anderson (1993) identify the new skills which teachers must learn as they assume the role of distance educators:

- Understanding the nature and philosophy of distance education.
- Identifying learner characteristics at distant sites.
- Designing and developing interactive courseware to suit each new technology.
- Adapting teaching strategies to deliver instruction at a distance.
- Organizing instructional resources in a format suitable for independent study.
- Training and practice in the use of telecommunications systems.
- Becoming involved in organization, collaborative planning, and decision-making.
- Evaluating student achievement, attitudes, and perceptions at distant sites.
- Dealing with copyright issues.

Issues in distance learning: Distance education technologies are expanding at an extremely rapid rate. Too often, instructional designers and curriculum developers have become enamoured of the latest technologies without dealing with the underlying issues of learner characteristics and needs, the influence of media upon the instructional process, equity of access to interactive delivery systems, and the new roles of teacher, site facilitator, and student in the distance learning process. The issues include redefining the roles of key participants, technology selection and adoption, design issues, strategies to increase interactivity and active learning, learner characteristics, learner support, operational issues, policy and management issues, equity and accessibility, and cost/benefit trade-offs.

The theoretical basis on which instructional models is based affects not only the way in which information is communicated to the student, but also the way in which the student makes sense and constructs new knowledge from the information which is presented. Currently, there are two opposing views which impact instructional design: symbol-processing and situated cognition. Until recently, the dominant view has been the traditional, information processing approach, based on the concept of a computer performing formal operations on symbols (Seamans, 1990). The key concept is that the teacher can transmit a fixed body of information to students via an external representation. He/she represents an abstract idea as a concrete image and then presents the image to the learner via a medium. The learner, in turn, perceives, decodes, and stores it. Horton (1994) modifies this approach by adding two additional factors: the student's context (environment, current situation, and other sensory input) and mind (memories, associations, emotions, inference and reasoning, curiosity and interest) to the representation. The learner then develops his own image and uses it to construct new knowledge, in context, based on his own prior knowledge and abilities.

The alternative approach is based on constructivist principles, in which a learner actively constructs an internal representation of knowledge by interacting with the material to be learned. This is the basis for both situated cognition (Streibel, 1991) and problem-based learning (Savery & Duffy, 1995). According to this viewpoint, both social and physical interaction enters into both the definition of a problem and the construction of its solution. Neither the information to be learned, nor its symbolic description, is specified outside the process of inquiry and the conclusions that emerge from that process. Prawat and Floden (1994) state that, to implement constructivism in a lesson, one must shift ones focus away from the traditional transmission model to one which is much more complex, interactive, and evolving.

Distance education systems now must involve a high degree of interactivity between teacher and student, even in rural and isolated communities separated by perhaps thousands of miles. Moreover, virtual learning communities can be formed, in which students and researchers throughout the world who are part of the same class or study group can contact one another at any time of the day or night to share observations, information, and expertise with one another (VanderVen, 1994; Wolfe, 1994).

Although technology is an integral part of distance education, any successful programme must focus on the instructional needs of the students, rather than on the technology itself. It is essential to consider their ages, cultural and socio-economic backgrounds, interests and experiences, educational levels, and familiarity with distance education methods and delivery systems (Schamber, 1988). The most important factor for successful distance learning is a caring, concerned teacher who is confident, experienced, at ease with the equipment, uses the media creatively, and maintains a high level of interactivity with the students.

Many important issues stem from the characteristics of distance learners, whose aims and goals may be quite different from those of traditional students. Adult learners have a wide variety of reasons for pursuing learning at a distance: constraints of time, distance, and finances, the opportunity to take courses or hear outside speakers who would otherwise be unavailable, and the ability to come in contact with other students from different social, cultural, economic, and experiential backgrounds (Willis, 1993). As a result, they gain not only new knowledge but also new social skills, including the ability to communicate and collaborate with widely dispersed colleagues and peers whom they may never have seen.

Another important variable in learning effectiveness is the preference of the student for a particular mode of learning, i.e., cooperative, competitive, or individualized (Johnson & Johnson, 1974). Thus the issue is how the current distance education projects incorporate cooperative learning, collaborative projects, and interactivity within groups of students as well as between sites?

Effective learning, however, requires both knowledge of learner styles and advance preparation on the part of the teacher or site facilitator. Teachers and site facilitators are better able to make curriculum decisions to suit the preferences of their students, such as grouping certain students productively for project work, or assigning particular students to individual research projects, if they can determine the prevalent learning modes within their own classrooms. Site facilitators have the advantage of eye-to-eye contact and personal contact with students in their classrooms, whereas studio teachers must often rely on televised images, telephone conversations, or electronic messaging for feedback on student preferences.

If a teacher recognizes the existence of these alternate learning styles, and if he/she attempts to make a match between these modes and the content to be learned, then he/she can develop a local instructional theory. As with most distance learning situations, a localized theory has a greater prospect of success than a general instructional theory intended to function satisfactorily in variety of settings, with a variety of practitioners (Owens & Straton, 1980). Porter (1994) found that teacher mediation increases the completion rate for distance education courses. Students need support and direction to enable them to make the transition from traditional classroom environments to self-directed learning particularly tools to help them monitor their progress and obtain timely feedback on their activities.

The next area to be considered is the instructional aspect of creating the web-enhanced course. Some of these concerns involve technical operations, such as appropriate file formats. However, the initial focus is best directed to the instructional concerns of student access, "demands on the reader", and utilization of the web site used to enhance a face to face course (Wolfe, 2001). A constructivist approach for the instructional use of web sites is evident in some of the literature using the technology to help students adapt a pro-active attitude in learning. For example, Berge, Collins, and Dougherty (2000) indicate that "students in web-based courses can become problem-solvers involved in real-world problems as they take responsibility for their own learning". Certainly, the open-ended learning environments rely on technology to provide resources and tools to assist students with projects (Hannafin, Land, & Oliver, 1999).

Another area of concern to be addressed is the evaluation of the course design when presented to students. This area is somewhat difficult because students cannot take the same course twice with the same instructor in a different format to determine which had better measurements of success. Anastasiades and Retalis (2001) advocate that simply evaluating the success of the marriage of technology and instruction is insufficient "to reverse the linear traditional model. The creation of an open learning environment requires the evolvement of the teacher's and the student's roles, as well as the optimum use of the training tools in the direction of changing the learning approaches and training methods" (Anastasiades & Retalis, 2001). The general theme of the literature leans towards constructivism and indicates that success in adding technology requires changes not only the delivery of certain aspects of the course, but also in the class environment.

Educators need to be cautioned that a poorly designed course cannot be saved by technological enhancements. Nicoll and Laudato (1999) advise to "keep the emphasis in training on the functionality and instructional purpose of the technology, using the technology as a tool and not as an end". Instructional design is a system of procedures for developing education and training programmes in a consistent and reliable fashion (Gustafson & Branch, 2002). Instructional design is a complex process whose origins could be followed back to the writings of Silvern (1965), which applies a systems approach to solve problems efficiently. System refers to an integrated set of elements that interact with each other (Banathy, 1987). Systems are:

- Interdependent (i.e., no elements can be separated from the system).
- Synergistic (i.e., all the elements can achieve more than the individual elements alone).
- Dynamic (i.e., systems can adjust to changing conditions in environments), and
- Cybernetic (i.e. elements communicate among them efficiently) (Gustafson & Branch, 2002).

It can be claimed that instructional systems design techniques became common after the 1970s first in military, and then in other industrial and commercial training applications. Silvern's (1965) writings followed the principles of behaviourism while further studies, particularly that of Gagné, Briggs, and Wager (1992) followed a more cognitive approach focusing on information processing (Gustafson & Branch, 2002). All these studies have made contributions to the theory of instructional design. Similarly there is a need to have some sound instructional designs based on constructivist principles as following an instructional design procedure in a systematic way is believed to make instruction more effective and relevant (Gustafson & Branch, 2002). Some pertinent issues are:

- How can instructional materials be designed to help learners use higher order thinking skills?
- Should evaluation competencies be developed independently of design and development competencies (i.e., is evaluation separate or integral in the process of instructional design and development)?
- To what extent are existing research findings and case study results applicable in new settings?
- How can computer-assisted instruction be integrated into the curriculum?
- Can interactive video be justified as a cost-effective teaching tool?
- Which face-to-face instructional functions can effectively be replaced by distance education materials?

- What changes are necessary in the programmes to prepare professionals for service in the field of educational technology in light of the many technological changes that have occurred recently?
- How can learners of all ages be taught critical viewing and listening skills? (Preston, 1989)

The web-based learning environment requires a constructivist learning setting for a healthy learning environment to exist. Traditionally distance education courses of the 'industrial era' were based on an objectivist learning setting. In this setting teachers delivered content through satellite technologies to the passive student. Few opportunities for student-initiated questions, independent thought, or interaction between students occur in this environment. Still today this method of delivery is used and unfortunately has been transferred to some web-based courses. The online environment encourages individual cognitive growth through independent learning as well as through social interaction or inter-subjectivity. The environment is monitored by the teacher who is there as a mentor and as a guide for the learner. It is in the locus of the inter-subjectivity in which Vygotsky and Piaget differ in perspective (Rogoff, 1990); "In Vygotsky's perspective, joint problem-solving occurs between partners, whereas in Piaget's view, individuals work with independence and equality on each other's ideas." Piaget's theories describe the independent learning of the individual, and Vygotsky's theories describe the learning that takes place from social interaction. The combination of these theories provides a theoretical framework for the virtual learning community. Constructivism is grounded in the work of Piaget and Vygotsky. Leve and Wenger as well as Barbara Rogoff extend our understanding of the learning environments of Piaget and Vygotsky. The understanding of these theories helps develop the 'big picture' of the cognitive processes of learners, which can be extended and applied to virtual learning. This theoretical framework for learning in a web-based environment is essential in the first step of the design of the online community of learners. There is a need to have a shift away from objectivist environment to a learner-centred collaborative environment utilizing constructivist learning theory. For this we can keep in mind Katy Campbell's (1999) three main principles of constructivism from a design point of view, which are:

1. Instruction be concerned with the experiences, convictions and constructs that learners already possess.
2. Instruction be structured so that it can be easily understood and modified by the learner.
3. Instruction be designed to facilitate exploration, extrapolation, and elaboration.

6.2 CONSTRUCTIVISM IN INSTRUCTIONAL DESIGN IN DISTANCE EDUCATION

Duffy and Jonassen (1992) argue that instruction should not focus on transmitting plans to the learner but rather on developing the skills of the learner to construct and reconstruct plans in response to situational demands and opportunities. Thus, instruction should provide contexts and assistance that will aid the individual in making sense of the environment as it is encountered. Plans must be constructed, tested, and revised as a function of the particular encounters in the environment.

Any comprehension must involve the construction of meaning. The information contained in the text must be combined with information outside of the text—including the prior knowledge of the learner—to form a complete representation of the text's meaning. Secondly, emphasis must be shifted from the retrieval of intact knowledge structures to support the construction of new understandings. Learners should be able to bring together from various knowledge sources an appropriate ensemble of information suited to the particular problem-solving needs of the situation at hand—instead of retrieving from memory a previously packaged prescription for how to think and act. This kind of constructivism is doubly constructive: (a) understandings are constructed by using prior knowledge to go beyond the information given; and (b) the prior knowledge that is brought to bear on is itself constructed, rather than retrieved intact from memory, on a case-by-case basis.

In current times, continual re-skilling is a fact of life (Bonk and Wisher, 2000), especially for teachers who must keep up with new teaching strategies, the latest professional standards, and constantly changing technologies. Coincidentally, new technologies promise to facilitate access to learning at times and places chosen by the learner (Albion and Gibson, 1998). These web-based environments have the potential to transform teacher professional development through the use of new models of teaching and learning. Online environments also have the potential to facilitate a sustained culture of sharing, collaboration, mentoring, and support for teachers.

Jonassen (1991) argues that "the most effective learning contexts are those which are problem or case based and activity oriented, that immerse the learner in the situation requiring him or her to acquire skills or knowledge in order to solve the problem or manipulate the solution". Problem-based learning is a curriculum development and instructional system that simultaneously develops both problem-solving strategies and disciplinary knowledge bases and skills by placing students in the active role of problem-solvers confronted with an ill-structured problem that mirrors real-world problems (Finkle and Torp, 1995). Traditionally, problem-based learning is used in face-to-face environments, with a facilitator guiding collaborative teams of students in solving a problem. Problem-based learning environments are often reported to increase student motivation, to help develop critical thinking skills, to increase use of outside learning resources, and to increase understanding of content knowledge in context of its use (Albanese and Mitchell, 1993; Torp and Sage, 1997).

The constructivist approaches argue that learning should be durable, transferable and self-regulated (Di Vesta and Rieber, 1987 cited by Hannafin & Rieber, 1989). Mechanisms need to be in place to promote the deeper internal processing required for such learning to occur. Most Social Constructivist models, such as that proposed by Jonassen (1994), however, also stress the need for collaboration among learners, in direct contradiction to traditional competitive approaches. One Vygotskian notion, that has significant implications for peer collaboration, is that of the 'Zone of Proximal Development'. Defined as "the distance between the actual developmental level as determined by independent problem-solving and the level of potential development as determined through problem-solving under adult guidance or in collaboration with more capable peers" (Vygotsky, 1978), it differs from the fixed biological nature of Piaget's stages of development. Through a process of 'scaffolding' a learner can be extended beyond the limitations of physical maturation to the extent that "the development process lags behind the learning process" (Vygotsky, 1978).

This has significant implications for Instructional Design as a communications medium. While it may not be highly interactive in a physical sense, the web has strong potential for social interactivity. The goal of this type of approach is the achievement of 'virtual communities' of learners on the Internet working in small collaborative groups to achieve a common goal (Dillenbourg & Schneider, 1995). While it would appear that care is necessary in the formation of such groups, it has been proposed that heterogeneous grouping can assist in the creation of zones of proximal development (Walker & Lambert, 1996).

In constructivist learning environments, we think of Web-based Problem-based learning Instructional Model. According to Problem-based learning model, which is very similar to traditional Problem-based learning models (Barrows and Myers, 1993), the learner goes through the series of phases in order to finally generate a problem solution. The problem scenario begins with identification of key concepts from the content domain and a typical context in which the following concepts might be used:

This *Presentation Phase* is intended to situate the learner in the problem context and to begin the process of activating relevant prior knowledge. Additionally, it is in this phase that learners have the option of beginning to customize their interpretation of the problem to make the context as specific as possible.

The *Exploration Phase* provides opportunity for recall and reconfiguration of prior knowledge relevant to the specific problem and exploration of additional, content specific knowledge and 'experience' gained during problem solution. Learners have access to a collection of resources relevant to the concepts encapsulated in the problem. We want them to identify possible solutions and resources needed for understanding the problem.

The *Integration Phase* emphasizes relevant knowledge transfer, analysis, integration, synthesis and evaluation of selected, content specific knowledge and problem based 'experience'. The problem in each module is divided into a series of tasks/sub-problems to facilitate scaffolding by considering the types of artifacts, typically documents of various kinds, which might be produced by the learner in association with a stepwise solution to the problem situation. Because problem-based learning is intended to increase the capacity of learners to solve real problems and because identifying critical elements may be counter-productive, the learners are required judgment in selection from what is provided and initiative in employing material from alternative sources in order to be able to solve the problem. But we need to note that resource collection and analysis to some extent is embedded into each phase of the process.

Capability to zoom in and out to different levels of detail or content. In addition, students select the "labels" on their authored notes and graphics ensuring that these items can be recalled in multiple contexts.

Cognitive Flexibility Theory employs a number of instructional prescriptions to address advanced knowledge acquisition and transfer. These include: the use of multiple knowledge representations (e.g., multiple themes, analogies, case examples, lines of argument); explicitly linking and tailoring concepts to practice and case examples (i.e., situating conceptual knowledge in contexts that are similar to those required for the application of the knowledge); incrementally introducing complexity in small, cognitively manageable units; stressing the interrelatedness and web-like nature of knowledge (instead of isolated and compartmentalized knowledge); and encouraging the assembly of appropriate knowledge from various conceptual and case resources (rather than the intact retrieval of previously memorized information) (Jacobson & Spiro, 1991).

The above instructional features are realized in a Cognitive Flexibility Hypertext, which is a hypermedia learning environment that allows "multiple juxtapositions of instructional content" through a large and complex conceptual structure (Spiro et al., 1987).

In summary, to incorporate constructivist principles, a learning objects system must generally be able to:

- Support learner-generated artifacts by incorporating learner contributions.
- Consist of multiple levels of granularity to afford reusability, flexibility, accessibility and adaptability of learning objects capitalizing on Wiley's (1998) concept of Fundamental Information Object (FIO) or taxonomy of learning object types (Wiley, 2000).
- Contain frameworks as learning objects that provide structure for instructional experiences and incorporate a linking system to facilitate their content population.

In the incorporation of generative learning activities learning object systems need to: afford discovery, reuse, and manipulation of existing and learner-created objects allow for learner designed and created artifacts that could become learning objects if posted to the system, and permit multiple versions of objects to be incorporated into the system incorporate an archival engine to clear the database of unwanted and outdated contributions allow for learner produced artifacts to be generated or according to levels in the taxonomy of learning object types (Wiley, 2000) and tagged according to standards to allow further discovery, retrieval and manipulation. Following factors could be quite handy in designing any instructional design on the basis of constructivist principles.

Cognitive and Metacognitive Factors

1. *Nature of the learning process.* The learning of complex subject matter is most effective when it is an intentional process of constructing meaning from information and experience.

2. *Goals of the learning process.* The successful learner, over time and with support and instructional guidance, can create meaningful, coherent representations of knowledge.

3. *Construction of knowledge.* The successful learner can link new information with existing knowledge in meaningful ways.

4. *Strategic thinking.* The successful learner can create and use a repertoire of thinking and reasoning strategies to achieve complex learning goals.

5. *Thinking about thinking.* Higher order strategies for selecting and monitoring mental operations facilitate creative and critical thinking.

6. *Context of learning.* Learning is influenced by environmental factors, including culture, technology, and instructional practices.

Motivational and Affective Factors

7. *Motivational and emotional influences on learning.* What and how much is learned is influenced by the learner's motivation. Motivation to learn, in turn, is influenced by the individual's emotional states.

8. *Intrinsic motivation to learn.* The learner's creativity, higher order thinking, and natural curiosity all contribute to motivation to learn. Intrinsic motivation is stimulated by tasks of optimal novelty and difficulty, relevant to personal interests, and providing for personal choice and control.

9. *Effects of motivation on effort.* Acquisition of complex knowledge and skills requires extended learner effort and guided practice. Without the learner's motivation to learn, the willingness to exert this effort is unlikely without coercion.

Developmental and Social Factors

10. *Developmental influences on learning.* As individuals develop, there are different opportunities and constraints for learning. Learning is most effective when differential development within and across physical, intellectual, emotional, and social domains is taken into account.

11. *Social influences on learning.* Learning is influenced by social interactions, interpersonal relations, and communication with others.

12. *Individual differences in learning.* Learners have different strategies, approaches, and capabilities for learning that are a function of prior experience and heredity.

13. *Learning and diversity.* Learning is most effective when differences in learners' linguistic, cultural, and social backgrounds are taken into account.

14. *Standards and assessment.* Setting appropriately high and challenging standards and assessing the learner as well as learning progress—including diagnostic, process, and outcome assessment—are integral parts of the learning process.

> *Some constructivists theories may be quite helpful in instructional design in distance education.*

Cognitive Apprenticeship: In asserting that learning is most effective when it approximates real-world situations or problem scenarios, socio-cultural research on collaborative technology also draws on insights from cognitive apprenticeship theory (Collins, 1990; Collins, J.S. Brown, & Newman, 1989; Pea, 1993). Situating students as "legitimate peripheral participants" within an authentic community, apprentices or guides their learning until they can assume a more engaged and central role in that activity (Lave & Wenger, 1991). As mentors negotiate and support novice learners through experiences suitable to their ZPDs, they, in turn, gradually cede control of the task to the student (J.S. Brown et al., 1989). When the learning participants gradually assume greater task responsibility, they begin to internalize standard cultural practices (Rogoff, 1995). Such apprenticing situations and activities do not always imply vertical "teacher-to-student" relationships, however. Teachers may, in fact, assume co-learner or co-participant role in some of these learning situations, whereas their role in others may center on performance feedback and review. Collins et al. (1989) provided a rationale for at least six teaching methods of these cognitive apprenticeships: (a) modelling, (b) coaching, (c) scaffolding and fading, (d) articulation, (e) reflection, and (f) explorations.

Assisted Learning. Not only is the environment transformed when adopting socio-cultural practices, but so, too, is the pedagogical role of the teacher. Clearly, the focus here is on assisting learning, not directing it (Tharp & Gallimore, 1988). According to Tharp (1993), adept socio-cultural teaching is responsive in nature; instead of assigning tasks, relying on text readings, and fostering standard practices (e.g., teacher *i*nitiation of a question or comment followed by pupil *r*esponse and teacher *e*valuation; known as the I-R-E recitation script), socio-cultural teacher's value assisting or supporting the performance of their students. Tharp further argued that there are seven basic ways for teachers to "assist" in the learning process: (a) modelling, (b) feedback, (c) contingency management, (d) instructing, (e) cognitive structuring, (f) questioning, and (g) task structuring. Bonk and Kim (1998) pointed out that merging these seven forms of learning assistance with Collins et al.'s six cognitive apprenticeship techniques, mentioned above, renders the following socio-culturally based teaching techniques: (a) *modelling* to illustrate performance standards and verbalize invisible processes, (b) *coaching* to observe and supervise students, thereby guiding them toward expert performance, (c) *scaffolding* and *fading* to support what learners cannot yet do and gradually removing that support as competence is displayed, (d) *questioning* to request a verbal response from learners while supporting them with mental functions they cannot produce alone, (e) encouraging student *articulation* of their reasoning and problem-solving processes, (f) pushing student *exploration* and application of their problem-solving skills, (g) fostering student *reflection* and self-awareness (e.g., through performance replays), (h) providing *cognitive task structuring* by explaining and organizing the task within students' ZPDs, (i) *managing instruction* with performance feedback and positive reinforcement, and (j) using *direct instruction* to provide clarity, needed content, or missing information. When these means of assistance are woven together, the teaching-learning situation evolves into a rich "instructional conversation" (Gallimore & Tharp, 1990, p. 196; Tharp & Gallimore, 1988, p. 111). By using this instructional framework to imagine rich, interactive conversations among students and teachers and beyond, we are optimistic that CSCL technologies can provide effective learning assistance within learner ZPDs.

Tele-apprenticeship: In merging the aforementioned strategies with global networking technologies for "tele-apprenticeship" (Teles, 1993), many universities and public schools are exploring CSCL tool features that provide unprecedented student-student social interaction opportunities and momentous cross-cultural activities and events (Harasim, 1990; Levin, Kim, & Riel, 1990; Riel, 1993). Now, online apprenticeships can involve experts and peers demonstrating ideas, posing questions, offering insights, and providing relevant information when needed. Recent breakthroughs in video conferencing tools showcase such authentic avenues for student and instructor social interaction and dialogue (Fetterman, 1996b). Such tools and strategies collectively function to electronically apprentice and assist in student learning. Another celebrated example of a cognitive apprenticeship is to involve students in genuine scientific data collection and reporting about the weather.

Scaffolded Instruction: Such cognitive apprenticeships are, of course, inherently reliant on a mentor or guide who effectively uses "scaffolded instruction". In selecting scaffolded instruction, a mentor or guide provides the learner with the support or assistance necessary to complete a task that would not have been completed without the help. Examples of this support might include prompts, hints, comments, explanations, questions, counterexamples, and suggestions. A learning scaffold may be embedded in an explicit request to include additional information or a more general question or comment intended to spur new idea linkages or course connections. Of course, these learning aids are faded and removed as the learner assumes control over the activity. Through such assistance, the learner (or a team of learners) solves a problem, generates solutions, and gains insights that would ordinarily rest beyond his or her independent abilities. In terms of such scaffolded learning activities, collaborative technologies can offer opportunities for both peer and mentor electronic guidance and feedback that stimulate student discussion and internal reflection. On the other hand, experts might also provide electronic demonstrations and task assistance. Such electronic tool support and scaffolded assistance is especially important for young children because the support structure aiding the acquisition of oral communication, which has developed over many thousands of years, is not available for young readers and writers.

Intersubjectivity: According to the socio-cultural perspective, scaffolded instruction is bound to be more effective when the players of the learning situation experience intersubjectivity. Intersubjectivity refers to a temporary shared collective understanding or common framework among learning participants. As learners find common ground (Rogoff, 1990) or shared thoughts (Levine & Moreland, 1991), they can more easily exchange their ideas, build new knowledge, and negotiate meanings. In addition to the many apprenticeship possibilities, therefore, electronic conferencing tools open up new avenues for students to take the perspective of peers and better understand their expectations and potential reactions (Bonk, Appelman, & Hay, 1996).

Distributed Intelligence in a Learning Community: Whereas an activity system includes subjects, rules, communities, objects, and divisions of labour (Cole & Engestrom, 1993), it is the tools that mediate the activity and connect humans to objects and other people (Wells, 1996). There are a myriad of CSCL tools to create new forms of activity settings for both human-human and human-computer interaction and collaboration. The current generation of collaborative educational learning tools present unique opportunities for supporting and organizing human conversations and creating new communities of learning (Blumenfeld et al., 1996). Because human mental functioning is rooted in social relations and intellectual performance is distributed among members of a learning community, it is critical to begin to understand how electronic tools might enhance the collective intelligence of such a community. What types of electronic tools foster the negotiation of meaning and sophisticated conversations among community participants? How can they be married with other learning resources—experts, mentors, teachers, text resources, and the local community—to foster learning? When socio-cultural theory is finally merged with electronic tool development and use, the answers to these questions may arise in rich, instructional conversations (Tharp

& Gallimore, 1988) among learning participants wherein new meanings and insights are co-constructed and debated. Certainly that should be the benchmark for this field.

Some socio-cultural "Ifs": Although the research on collaborative technologies is in a prime position to test and extend socio-cultural theory, many questions and issues remain. For instance, if the mind is distributed in society, then the tools for collaboration should offer a unique way to illustrate this in action. But have they? Second, if cultural artifacts and institutions underpin human development, then we need to grasp unique opportunities for human development as new collaborative educational learning tools spring forth and intersect. Instead of simply purchasing the latest CSCL tools and systems, therefore, one must first grasp their utility as scaffolded learning devices. Even the social context of extremely popular instructional techniques, such as using a word processor for collaborative writing, for instance, are only beginning to be documented and better understood (Daiute & Dalton, 1988; Kumpulainen, 1996). In terms of activity settings, collaborative tools should also offer interesting windows on the negotiation of meaning and learner interaction. If the interaction with experts and more capable peers on a social plane leads to student intellectual growth and new competencies, then we need to create and test electronic situations wherein students represent and share knowledge (Pea, 1994; Vosniadou, 1996). In order to test whether development moves from the external to the internal plane, the activities appearing within collaboration tools must be later seen in students' independent problem-solving acts. And, if speech is a bridge for movement from the external plane to new strategic behaviours, then the dialogue patterns of electronic social interaction as well as any ensuing journal writings and private reflections must be captured and inspected. Still other socio-cultural questions face collaborative learning tool advocates. For instance, if scaffolded instruction is important in moving students from novice to more expertlike behaviour, then we need to create situations wherein the cognitive apprenticeship and dialogue possibilities of collaborative tools can be fostered and examined. Pedagogically intriguing electronic apprenticeship tools should allow for various types of learning assistance and social interaction.

The constructivist path that we could and can take as designers, teachers, and administrators will lead us far beyond this traditional view of instructional design. The question is do we want to go there? And if we do, what do we have to do to get us to there from here? What supports, structures and goals need be in place in order to facilitate this transition? Various technological applications that promote the social interaction necessary to help students construct knowledge can be applied such as computer-mediated communication, computer-supported collaborative work, case-based learning environments, and computer-based cognitive tools. Using synchronous and asynchronous communication, hypertext based programmes to promote debate, "real life" problems, and computer programmes like databases and artificial intelligence, distance education learners can work together to solve problems and provide the social interaction necessary to translate educational material into meaningful experiences which constructivism advocates.

7

Constructivism and Instructional Technology

7.1 ENRICHING THE PRACTICES OF INSTRUCTIONAL TECHNOLOGY

The fundamental challenge of constructivism is in its changing the locus of control over learning from the teacher to the student. Educational technologists, with their foundations in behaviourism, have sought to design programmes in such a way that students would be enticed to achieve pre-specified objectives. Constructivists have said that this violates both what we know now about the nature of learning (situated interactive) and about the nature of knowledge (perspectival, conventional, tentative, and evolutionary). They have claimed that objectives should be negotiated with students based on their own felt needs that programmed activities should emerge from within the context of their lived worlds, that students should work together with peers in the social construction of personally significant meaning and that evaluation should be a personalized ongoing, shared analysis of progress (Hanckbarth, 1996).

The study of human cognition has many specific applications for educational practice and technology use. The following are the five general educational applications of constructivist theory that should be considered when designing instruction:

- First, if learning depends on how information is mentally processed, then students' cognitive processes should be major concern to educators. Students' learning difficulties can often be attributed to ineffective or inappropriate cognitive processes. Teachers must become aware of not only of what students learn, but also of how they attempt to learn it.

- Second, educators must consider students' level of cognitive development when planning topics and methods of instruction.
- Third, students organise the information they learn. Teachers can help students' learn by presenting organized information and by helping students see how one thing relates to another.
- Fourth, new information is most likely acquired when people can associate it with things they have already learned. Therefore, teachers should help students' learn by showing them how new ideas relate to old ones. When students are unable to relate new information to anything with which they are familiar, learning is likely to be slow and ineffective.
- Fifth, if students control their own cognitive process, it is ultimately the students themselves who decide what information will be learned.

Usually schools ensure that children have many opportunities to interact with their environment and are given plenty of concrete materials to develop their subject knowledge understanding. In using computers in education, Seymor Papert has argued that educational software should be designed to develop children's thinking.

There are some evidences that when working with computers, children are collaborating rather than just working alongside each other which is often the case in children's group working. Some evidences show that when children are working with computer, the interaction is related to the task and the children rely on each other for help rather than the teacher. But the success on a session depends on how the teacher has prepared the work and who is working together and what the task is (Jones, 1995).

Enrichment of the practices of Instructional Technology will depend on the following basic principles of constructivism such as:

- Authentic Learning Task.
- Interaction.
- Encourage Voice and Ownership in the Learning Process.
- Experience with the Knowledge Construction Process.
- Metacognition.

Authentic learning task: A central constructivism criticism of traditional formal teaching is that it is disembedded from the students' experience outside the classroom. The task lack meaning for the student. It is argued that learning tasks should be embedded in problem-solving contexts that are relevant in the real world. Learners must see the relevance of the knowledge and skill to their lives, and the leverage it provides in problems they see as important (Boyle, 2000). The tasks may be problem-based or case-based.

Interaction: Interaction is viewed as the primary source material for the cognitive constructions that people build to make sense of the world. Many constructivist theorists place particular emphasis on social interaction. Dialogue and the negotiation of meaning provide the basis for the individual to develop, test and refine their ideas. The traditional didactic mode of transmitting information in de-contextualised settings is rejected. There are two main strands for developing interactive, social contexts for learning. These strands focus on tutor-student relationships and peer group relationships respectively.

The first type of 'collaborative configuration' is thus between a mature partner and a learner. The mature partner provides the principles which the learner acquires through structured social interactions. One of the best examples is probably Cognitive Apprenticeship theory. Cognitive Apprenticeship emphasizes the active role of the teacher in supporting the learner. The learner acts as an apprentice to the master craftsperson in the domain, i.e., the teacher. The teacher first provides a model of expert performance in the task. The teacher may do this by talking through a problem solution in mathematics, or the processes involved in composing an essay. The learner observes the model to build up a conceptual picture of nature performance in the domain. The teacher actively coaches the learner in acquiring the target skills and knowledge. The teacher then gradually removes this support, forcing the learner to become increasingly independent in their application of skills and knowledge.

The second type of social collaboration is between peers in a group. The proposal is that individuals can often learn best the processes of knowledge construction, negotiation and refinement in a community of peers. Group discussion is encouraged to elicit multiple perspectives and encourage the negotiated construction of meaning.

Encourage voice and ownership in the learning process: The theme of student centred learning is continued with an argument that students should be allowed to choose the problems they will work on. Rather than the teacher acting as the taskmaster, the teacher should serve as a consultant to help students to generate problems which are relevant and interesting to them. It is argued that this is a vital part of solving problems in the real world.

Experience with the knowledge construction process: The emphasis is on authentic task and rich interaction provides a base for experience with the knowledge construction process. There is a basic question here of what the outcomes of the learning process should be. Conventionally these outcomes would be defined in terms of the knowledge and skills the students has acquired. Constructivists argue that experiencing and becoming proficient in the process of construction knowledge is more important. In other words, it is learning how to learn, how to construct and refine new meaning that is most important.

Metacognition: This is the ultimate goal of a constructivist approach. Problem-solving involves the processes of reflecting on problems and searching for solutions. Metacognition is the higher order process of reflecting on our own thinking about thinking and problem-solving processes. Metacognition has powerful problem-solving potential. If we are stuck with a problem we can reflect not just on the structure of the problem, but on the structuring of our approaches to the problem. We can then try to generate alternative, more productive strategies. However, this is viewed not just as a useful problem-solving ability, but the ultimate expression of education—the ability to reflect back on what has been created by the process of education. This opens up opportunities to transform our understanding and to 'liberate' ourselves from prior ways of thinking.

Thus, with all assertions we can say that any form of Instructional Technology must strive to have constructivist approaches to education. This is to provide rich resources to enable the construction of meaning by the learner. Built into this approach is the recognition of the need to support the learner in moving from their initial state of knowledge to more abstract levels of understanding.

Traditional designers first attempt to analyze content and prerequisites (Gagne & Briggs, 1979) to identify a course sequence. A constructivist course designer knows that content cannot be pre-specified. Although a certain amount of content may be available for students to use, they are encouraged to seek out as many alternate sources of knowledge as they can find which will deepen their perspective of the topic they are working on. And the notion of situated learning is important, where students are encouraged to consider what real life people in a particular environment would do. Traditional theory focused on the typical learner and what he would know when the course was completed. A constructivist learner is not described. Instead through metacognition, all learners are encouraged to reflect on how and what they are learning and how it fits into what they already know. Traditional theory specifies objectives for knowledge acquisition in advance. Constructivism attempts to identify the culture of a knowledge domain. For example, a constructivist learner would be encouraged to learn how to think like a historian, as opposed to learning dates in history.

The synthesis or design phase of traditional instruction would involve the design of a sequence and message which would achieve specified performance objectives. Pre-specified content and objectives are not congruent with the constructivist worldview. Substituted for these activities would be: learning based on situating cognition in real world contexts; cognitive apprenticeship and modelling; and negotiation of meaning through collaborative learning which emphasizes multiple perspectives of analysis. Another emphasis in constructivism is to make available an array of cognitive tools which can scaffold the learner within this rich, sometimes confusing, environment.

Constructivism has brought a new revolution in the field of instructional technology as it has given us the opportunity to re-examine the ways in which some aspects of traditional instruction can be re-conceived to operate effectively in the online asynchronous environment. This technological shift—from knowledge being fixed to a certain time and place, to knowledge being accessible at anytime and at anyplace—creates the potential for a change in the way learning is transacted from those who provide information (i.e. teachers or facilitators) to those who receive it (i.e. students) (Gold, 2001). There is still much debate over what exactly is and is not constructivism, but any constructivist instruction includes three principles:

1. Progress from the specific to the general, from the concrete to the abstract. Constructivist learning emphasizes the creation of rich, meaningful learning environments where learners can best induce the knowledge to be learned. The difficulty, frankly, is not the use of these environments when teaching new material, but incorporating the proper assessment activities that are derived from the content.
2. Actively build with and from prior assimilated structures. Only through knowing what types of learning failures and misconceptions students hold can learning be assimilated. This is done through reflection mediated by a teacher-facilitator. To achieve greater assimilation and accommodation, teachers must learn to recognize and understand the strategies students are using to perform tasks, ask questions to elicit better comprehension and reflection, and challenge the learners through facilitation procedures so students must defend their position.
3. Teach for conceptual understanding. Skills and strategies used by students are representative of some deeper, underlying understanding they possess. While

practice and reinforcement are used for skill mastery, constructivism is meant for deep understanding. So, while practice should not be neglected, teachers and course content should be less about a superficial review of knowledge and more about creating new experiences.

In sum, constructivist environments start with observations within a world of authentic artefacts rooted in authentic situations. Students, while accessing various materials, construct ongoing interpretations of their observations, and collaborate with their peers. Finally, students serve as coaches and teachers to each other to show their mastery of what they learned.

Constructivist online learning activities presuppose the purposeful and appropriate use of technology that enables online teachers to design quality learning environments. Although online technology provides opportunities for developing quality online learning, the use of advanced technology will not necessarily lead to quality learning if it is not matched with appropriate pedagogies. Therefore, the pedagogy associated with online learning is crucial. Also, the integration of collaborative technology tools and teaching/learning principles rooted in social constructivism can result in a quality online learning environment. The key elements of constructivist learning include collaboration, interaction and co-construction of knowledge (Maor & Hendriks, 2001). The challenge is to translate these theoretical principles into the online environment so that there is a fit or congruence between the technology and pedagogy used by the teachers.

The constructivists argue that the 'systematic' process offered by instructionists is a problem. According to constructivists, there is nothing systematic about how we learn or construct knowledge. Rather, constructivists believe that knowledge is constructed socially using language (Vygotsky, 1962) and everyone has different social experiences resulting in multiple realities (Jonassen, 1996). If we accept the assumptions that there are multiple realities of what the truth must be and learning is based on prior knowledge, educators will need to acknowledge that they cannot assume that all their learners will understand new information in the same way (as the instructionists assume). Based on this assumption, constructivists argue that educators will need to understand that learners will require a variety of different experiences to advance to different kinds and levels of understanding. Thus we must bring our learners' prior knowledge to the forefront if they are to apply their current understandings to new situations in order to construct new knowledge. To achieve this, educators need to spend time understanding learner's current perspectives and, based on this information, incorporate learning activities that have real world relevance for each learner. Only recently has it become feasible to consider constructivism principles within the context of technology-mediated higher education (Gunawardena, Lowe & Anderson, 1997; Blanchette & Kanuka, 1999). This is due primarily to advances in communication technologies resulting in an effective means to implement constructivism principles, which would be difficult to accomplish with other media (Driscoll, 1994). Specifically, communication technologies have the capacity to provide an interactive environment that can support instructional methods required to facilitate constructivist principles. For these reasons, constructivism has become a popular epistemological position for many educators who are using technology-mediated learning.

Instructional strategies should also include content sequences that progress from simple to complex with a variety of contexts. The progression from simple to complex learning should continue until there are realistic levels of complexity in the learning environment and the learner is functioning in the 'authentic' environment (Honebein, Duffy and Fishman, 1993; Strommen, 1995). Based on the assumption that there are multiple realities, Spiro, et al. (1991) argues that there is a need for "multiple dimensions of knowledge representation, for multiple interconnections across knowledge components". The emphasis on learning in this view capitalizes on the students' need to create interpretations and actively struggle with a variety of opposing understandings (Cunningham, 1991; Perkins, 1991). Although this may at first glance seem similar to the central concept in the cognitive constructivism view, it is not. Specifically, although both views would agree that opposing views should be presented as a social process, the cognitive constructivism view maintains that conflict should be encouraged and actively explored, whereas situated constructivism believes that conflict should be deferred. Situated constructivism invites learners "to 'bracket' their intuitive models for a while and just learn a new way of thinking and talking about the phenomena. When the new way has become somewhat familiar and consolidated, then the instruction turns back to the naive model and explores relationships between the two" (Perkins, 1991).

Instructional activities from this view are largely concerned with collaborative problem-solving skills resulting in "advanced knowledge acquisition in ill-structured domains" (Molenda, 1991). In an ill-structured world where there are multiple truths, learners must be able to use their knowledge flexibly, "to be able to find the most useful of the valid representations to fit the needs of a particular case, one must have available a diverse repertoire of ways of *constructing* situation-sensitive understandings" (Spiro, 1999). In agreement with the radical constructivist position, instructional strategies might include exploration of multiple and differing perspectives, general and content specific problem-solving processes, and—in particular—using a random access instruction strategy discussed by Spiro et al. (1990). Random access instructional strategies focus on explorations of multiple views (preferably, though not necessarily, contradictory views). An example that McManus (1996) provides of random access instruction is the use of the World Wide Web and cross-links that "take the learner through the same information several times and from several directions. This enables the learner to explore multiple routes through the same content thereby reinforcing cognitive construction". Small discussion groups following the presentation of each view on the topic would enable the learner to explore and understand multiple perspectives of the content. In the end, the goal of instruction is to help the learner understand multiple interpretations of reality, rather than to assure that the learner know 'the' reality (Cunningham, 1992).

Understanding occurs through interaction with the environment. What is learned cannot be separated from how it is learned, suggesting that knowledge is not just within the individual, but part of the entire context. Based on these assumptions, the emphasis in instruction is on the importance of helping learners engage in 'generative' rather than 'passive' learning activities (The Cognition and Technology Group at Vanderbilt, 1993; Jones et al., 1997). In agreement with the other positions, learning activities such as rote memorization are insufficient instructional methods. Co-constructivism claims that "students need to engage in argumentation [similar to the cognitive constructivist position] and reflection as they try to use and then refine their existing knowledge as they attempt to make sense of alternate points of view" (The Cognition and Technology Group at Vanderbilt). As knowledge is constructed through social negotiation, discussions with other individuals are a primary instructional methodology. Small discussion groups in a risk free environment, brainstorming and categorizing, Socratic dialogue, and debriefing are examples of instructional methods that can allow learners to examine their understandings through other individuals. Learners should also be encouraged to test their ideas against alternative views and alternative contexts. Consistent with cognitive construction, other people are considered to be the greatest source of conflict that stimulates new learning. In addition to providing generative learning activities, instruction should also include 'anchored instruction' where the instruction includes meaningful problem-solving contexts (The Cognition and Technology Group at Vanderbilt, 1993). Anchored instruction provides an opportunity to create shared environments that support learners with sustained exploration.

Finally, cooperative learning is also an instructional method that can provide opportunities for generative learning. Cooperative learning is a "learner-centred instructional process in which small, intentionally selected groups of 3-5 students work interdependently on a well-defined learning task; individual students are held accountable for their own performance and the instructor serves as a facilitator in the group learning process" (Cuseo, 1997). Cooperative learning creates an opportunity to form communities of inquiry that provide learning environments that encourage critical dialogue and, hence, understanding (Vygotsky, 1978; Cuseo, 1997).

There are three examples (Debate, Case method and Brainstorming, etc. already mentioned in the fourth chapter under the section 4.6 "Constructivist Teaching Strategies") of instructional methods that facilitate constructivism learning principles and translate well to technology-mediated learning environments.

7.2 INSTRUCTIONAL DESIGN REVISITED

Revisiting the Instructional Design raises two fundamental questions such as what basic assumptions/principles of constructivism are relevant to instructional design and how should instruction be structured to facilitate learning? In response to these questions it can be stated that under the theory of constructivism, educators focus on making connections between facts and fostering new understanding in students and teaching strategies should be tailored to student responses and encourage students to analyze, interpret and predict information. Teachers also rely heavily on open-ended questions and promote extensive dialogue among students.

Wilson (1993) provides some interesting insights into how instructional design (ID) must change in a constructivist environment:

Who does the design?: A key element in effective ID is the nature of the design team. Instead of a designer and subject expert working in relative isolation, constructive ID suggests that all major constituencies be represented on the design team, including teachers and students. These end users, the "consumers" of the instructional "product", should contribute directly to the project's design and development. Greenbaum & Kyang (1991) refer to this as participatory design and Clancey (1993) recommends "We must involve students, teachers, administrators, future employers, and the community as participants in design..., working with students and teachers in their setting not just calling them into the...lab to work with us."

Accommodating multiple perspectives: In a pluralistic world, more flexity must be built into the instruction; after all, even experts disagree on optimal solutions to problems. Not all students share the same learning goals; not all students' learning goals converge completely with instructional goals; students have different styles of learning, different background knowledge. Rather than ignoring these differences, instruction should acknowledge the evolving nature of knowledge and encourage students to engage in a continuing search for improved understanding. This plurality of content, strategies and perspectives typifies post-modern approaches to instruction. Such a pluralistic approach to instruction follows a clear trend toward accommodating multiple goals, styles and perspectives in instruction (Collins, 1991).

Guidelines for doing constructivist ID:

General methodology: There is a need to apply a holistic/systemic design model that considers instructional factors (learner, task, setting, etc.) in increasing detail throughout the development process. A number of key factors are systematically related in any instructional situation. Rather than doing a learner or task analysis once early in the process, return to these factors and their interactions continuously through the project cycle.

Using fast-track: There is a need to adapt ID methodology to the constraints of a given situation. A single generic ID model is not appropriate for all situations. Identify key principles underlying ID methods; such as consideration of the learning environment; then to use those principles in determining a procedures that fits the situation.

Including end users: There is a need to include the end users—both teachers and students—as part of the design team. Incorporate participatory design techniques, with design activity moving out of the "lab" and into the field. There is a need to use rapid prototyping techniques to model products at early stages. Rapid prototyping is particularly useful in testing out the feasibility of innovative methods or user interfaces.

Needs assessment: Consider solutions that are closer to the performance context (job aids, just-in-time training, performance support systems, etc.). This is consistent with situated models of cognition and with the notion of distributed cognition (Perkins, 1993). Make use of consensus and social oriented needs assessment strategies in addition to gap-oriented strategies. Not all instruction is designed to improve performance in a specific work setting. Resist the temptation to be driven by easily measured and manipulated content. Many important learning outcomes cannot be easily measured.

Goal/task analysis: There is a need to distinguish between educational and training situations and goals. Acknowledge that education and training goals arise in every setting. Schools train as well as educate, and students must be educated not just trained in skills to work effectively in job market. Discerning different learning goals in every setting provides a basis for appropriate instructional strategies. Use objectives as heuristics to guide design. Don't always insist on operational performance descriptions which may constrain the learner's goals and achievement. Pushing goal statements to behavioural specifications can often be wasted work. The "intent" of instruction can be made clear by examining goal statements, learning activities and assessment methods. Goals and objectives should be specific enough to serve as inputs to the design of assessments and instructional strategies. Allow for multiple layers of objectives clustering around learning experiences. Instruction need not be objectives-driven. A rich learning experience may embody a whole cluster of meaningful learning outcomes. Don't expect to capture the content in the goal or task analysis. Content on paper is not the expertise in a practitioner's head (even if you believed expertise resided in someone's head!). The best analysis always falls short of the mark. The only remedy is to design rich learning experiences where learners can pick up on their own the content missing between the gaps of analysis. Allow for instruction and learning goals to emerge during instruction. Just as content cannot be fully captured, learning goals cannot be fully pre-specified apart from the actual learning context. Instead of two levels expertise (Expert of proficient performance and novice or initial performance), a series of qualitative models of expertise may be needed for modelling student's progression in learning critical tasks (White & Frederiksen, 1986). There is a need to be prepared to confront learners' naive, intuitive theories and to scaffold their learning.

There is a need to give priority to problem-solving, meaning-constructing learning goals. Instead of rule-following, emphasize problem-solving (which incorporates rule-following but is not limited to it). Instead of simple recall tasks, ask learners to make sense out of material and demonstrate their understanding of it. Also, there is a need to look for authentic, information-rich methods for representing content and assessing performance (e.g., audio, video). High resolution methods for representing content can be useful throughout the ID process. Whereas we usually associate audio and video representations only with presentation of material to students, the same representation tools may be useful for documenting expertise and assessing student understanding.

Define content in multiple ways: Use cases, stories and patterns in addition to rules, principles and procedures. Rich cases, stories and patterns of performance can be alternative metaphors for finding and representing content. Appreciate the value-ladenness of all analysis. Defining content is a political, ideological enterprise. Valuing one perspective means that other perspectives will be given less value. One approach is given prominence; another is neglected. Somebody wins, and somebody loses. Be sensitive to the value implications of the decisions.

Instructional strategy development: Distinguish between instructional goals and learners' goals and support learners in pursuing their own goals. Bereiter (1991) distinguish among (i) task-completion goals or hoop jumping; (ii) instructional goals set by the system and (iii) personal knowledge-building goals set by the student. The three do not always converge. A student motivated by task-completion goals doesn't even consider learning, yet many students' behaviour in schools is driven by performance requirements. Constructivist instruction would nourish and encourage pursuit of personal knowledge building goals.

Allow for multiple goals for different learners: ID often includes the implicit assumption that instructional goals will be identical for all learners. This is sometimes necessary, but not always. Hypermedia learning environments almost by definition are designed to accommodate multiple learning goals. Even within traditional classrooms; technologies exist today for managing multiple learning goals (Collins, 1991). There is a need to appreciate the interdependency of content and method. Traditional design theory treats content and the method for teaching that contents as orthogonally independent factors. Postmodern ID says that we can't entirely separate the two. Also, there is a need to resist the temptation to cover material at shallow levels. Constructivist ID may throw away half the ostensive content and focus on deeper learning of less material. We should look for opportunities to give guided control to the learner, encouraging development of metacognitive knowledge. There is a need to encourage growth in students' metacognitive knowledge, what we often call "learning how to learn". Unnecessarily we should not assume that students know how to exercise effective learning control; instead, establish metacognitive skills as a learning goal for instruction to achieve.

There is a need to think in terms of designing learning environments rather than selecting instructional strategies. Grabinger, Dunlop & Heath (1993) provide design guidelines for what they call realistic environments for active learning (REAL); these guidelines reflect a constructivist orientation:

- Extend students' responsibility for their own learning.
- Allow students to determine what they need to learn.
- Enable students to manage their own learning activities.
- Enable students to contribute to each other's learning.
- Help students develop metacognitive awareness.
- Make maximum use of existing knowledge.
- Anchor instruction in realistic settings.
- Provide multiple ways to learn content.
- Promote active knowledge construction.
- Use activities to promote higher level thinking.
- Encourage the review of multiple perspectives.
- Encourage creative and flexible problem-solving.

- Provide a mechanism for students to resent their learning.

Instructional design must have provision for situated learning environments:

1. Provide *authentic contexts* that reflect the way the knowledge will be used in real life.
2. Provide *authentic activities.*
3. Provide access to *expert performances* and the modelling of processes.
4. Provide *multiple roles and perspectives.*
5. Support *collaborative construction of knowledge.*
6. Promote *reflection* to enable abstractions to be formed.
7. Promote *articulation* to enable tacit knowledge to be made explicit.
8. Provide *coaching* and *scaffolding* by the teacher at critical times.
9. Provide for *authentic assessment* of learning within the tasks.

These provide a checklist of guidelines for the instructional design of a learning environment which enables the situated elements to be operationalised, together with supporting authors, researchers and theorists.

Guidelines for Design and Implementation of Learning Environment

1. **Provide authentic context that reflect the way the knowledge will be used in real-life** (Brown et al., 1989b; Collins, 1988; Gabrys, Weiner, & Lesgold, 1993; Harley, 1993; Moore et al., 1994; Palincsar, 1989; Resnick, 1987; Winn, 1993; Young, 1993):

A situated learning environment should provide:

- A physical environment which reflects the way the knowledge will ultimately be used (Brown et al., 1989b; Collins, 1988).

- A design to preserve the complexity of the real-life setting with 'rich situational affordances' (Brown et al., 1989b; Collins, 1988; Young & McNeese, 1993).
- A large number of resources to enable sustained examination from a number of different perspectives (Brown et al., 1989b; Collins, 1988; Spiro, Vispoel, Schmitz, Samarapungavan, & Boeger, 1987; Young & McNeese, 1993).
- A design which makes no attempt to fragment or simplify the environment (Brown et al., 1989b; Honebein, Duffy, & Fishman, 1993; Spiro et al., 1987; Young & McNeese, 1993).

2. **Provide authentic activities** (Brown et al., 1989b; Cognition and Technology Group at Vanderbilt [CTGV], 1990a; Griffin, 1995; Harley, 1993; Resnick, 1987; Tripp, 1993; Winn, 1993; Young, 1993):

- Activities which have real-world relevance (Brown et al., 1989b; Cognition and Technology Group at Vanderbilt [CTGV], 1990a; Jonassen, 1991; Resnick, 1987; Winn, 1993; Young, 1993).
- Ill-defined activities (Brown et al., 1989b; CTGV, 1990a; Winn, 1993; Young, 1993).
- A single complex task to be investigated by students (Bransford, Vye et al., 1990; CTGV, 1990b; Jonassen, 1991).
- An opportunity for students to define the tasks and sub-tasks required to complete the activity (Bransford, Vye et al., 1990; CTGV, 1990b; Collins et al., 1989; Young, 1993).
- A sustained period of time for investigation (Bransford, Vye et al., 1990; CTGV, 1990).
- The opportunity to detect relevant versus irrelevant information (CTGV, 1990a; Young, 1993).
- The opportunity to collaborate (Young, 1993).

- Tasks which can be integrated across subject areas (Bransford, Sherwood et al., 1990; Bransford, Vye et al., 1990; Jonassen, 1991).

3. **Provide access to expert performances and the modelling of processes** (Collins, 1988; Collins et al., 1989; Lave & Wenger, 1991; Resnick, 1987):

- Access to expert thinking and modelling processes (Collins, 1988; Collins et al., 1989).
- Access to learners in various levels of expertise (Collins et al., 1989).
- Opportunity for the sharing of narratives and stories (Brown et al., 1989b; Brown & Duguid, 1993; Lave & Wenger, 1991).
- Access to the social periphery or the observation of real-life episodes as they occur (Brown et al., 1989b; Brown & Duguid, 1993; Lave & Wenger, 1991).

4. **Provide multiple roles and perspectives** (Bransford, Sherwood et al., 1990; Brown et al., 1989b; CTGV, 1990a; CTGV, 1993; Collins et al., 1989; Lave & Wenger, 1991; Spiro, Feltovich, Jacobson, & Coulson, 1991a; Spiro, Feltovich, Jacobson, & Coulson, 1991b; Young, 1993):

- Different perspectives on the topics from various points of view (Bransford, Sherwood et al., 1990; Brown et al., 1989b; CTGV, 1990a; CTGV, 1993; Collins et al., 1989; Lave & Wenger, 1991).
- The opportunity to express different points of view through collaboration (Honebein et al., 1993).
- The opportunity to criss-cross the learning environment by providing more than one investigation within a resource sufficiently rich to sustain repeated examination (Spiro et al., 1991a; Spiro et al., 1991b; Young, 1993).

5. **Support collaborative construction of knowledge** (Bransford, Sherwood et al., 1990; Brown et al., 1989b; CTGV, 1990a; Collins et al., 1989; Resnick, 1987; Young, 1993):

- Tasks which are addressed to a group rather than an individual (Alessi, 1996; Brown et al., 1989b; Collins et al., 1989; Hooper, 1992; Resnick, 1987; Young, 1993).
- Classroom organization into pairs or small groups (Hooper, 1992).
- Appropriate incentive structure for whole group achievement (Hooper, 1992).

6. **Promote reflection to enable abstractions to be formed** (Brown et al., 1989b; CTGV, 1990a; Collins, 1988; Collins et al., 1989; Resnick, 1987):

- Authentic context and task (Brown et al., 1989b; Norman, 1993).
- The facility for students to return to any element of the programme if desired, and to act upon reflection (Boud, Keogh, & Walker, 1985; Collins & Brown, 1988; Kemmis, 1985).
- The opportunity for learners to compare themselves with experts (Collins, 1988; Collins & Brown, 1988; Collins, Brown, & Holum, 1991).
- The opportunity for learners to compare themselves with other learners in varying stages of accomplishment (Collins et al., 1989).
- Collaborative groupings of students to enable reflection with aware attention (Kemmis, 1985; Knights, 1985; von Wright, 1992).

7. **Promote articulation to enable tacit knowledge to be made explicit** (Bransford, Sherwood et al., 1990; Collins, 1988; Collins et al., 1989):

- A complex task incorporating inherent, as opposed to constructed.
- Opportunities to articulate (Bransford , Sherwood et al., 1990; Collins, 1988; Collins et al., 1989; Edelson, Pea, & Gomez, 1996).

- Collaborative, groups to enable social than individual understanding (Mercer, 1996; Vygotsky, 1978).
- Public presentation of argument to enable articulation and defence of learning (Lave & Wenger, 1991; Pea, 1991).

8. **Provide coaching by the teacher at critical times, and scaffolding and fading of teacher support** (Collins, 1988; Collins et al., 1989; Griffin, 1995; Harley, 1993; Resnick, 1987; Young, 1993):

- A complex, open-ended learning environment (Collins, 1988; Collins et al., 1989; Resnick, 1987).
- No attempt to provide intrinsic scaffolding and coaching (Collins & Brown, 1988; Dreyfus & Dreyfus, 1989; Greenfield, 1984; Reeves, 1993b; Wilson & Welsh, 1991).
- Collaborative learning, where more able partners can assist with scaffolding and coaching (Collins, 1988; Collins et al., 1989; Young, 1993).
- Recommendations that the teacher implementing the programme is available for coaching and scaffolding assistance for a significant portion of the period of use (Collins, 1988; Griffin, 1995; Harley, 1993; Young, 1993).

9. **Provide for integrated assessment of learning within the tasks** (McLellan, 1993; Young, 1993; Young, 1995):

- Fidelity of context (Meyer, 1992; Reeves & Okey, 1996; Wiggins, 1993).
- The opportunity for students to be effective performers with acquired knowledge, and to craft polished, performances or products (Wiggins, 1989; Wiggins, 1990; Wiggins, 1993).
- Significant student time and effort in collaboration with others (Kroll, Masingila, & Mau, 1992; Linn, Baker, & Dunbar, 1991).

- Complex, ill structured challenges that require judgment, and a full array of tasks (Linn et al., 1991; Torrance, 1995; Wiggins, 1993).
- The assessment to be seamlessly integrated with the activity (Reeves & Okey, 1996; Young, 1995).
- Multiple indicators of learning (Lajoie, 1991; Linn et al., 1991)
- Validity and reliability with appropriate criteria for scoring varied products (Hooper, 1992; Lajoie, 1991; Resnick & Resnick, 1992; Wiggins, 1990; Young, 1995).

Provide authentic context that reflects the way the knowledge will be used in real-life:

- A physical environment reflecting real use.
- A non-linear design.
- A large number of resources.
- No attempt to simplify.
- The classroom interface and programme organized around the central context of mathematics classrooms.
- Non-linear navigation enabling ready access to any media element in a non-sequential order.
- Provide resources—classroom scenes, video interviews, text documents, and samples of work.
- No simplification of real-life resources.

Provide authentic activities:

- Activities which have real-world relevance.
- Ill-defined activities.
- A single complex task.
- An opportunity for students to define the tasks.
- A sustained period of time for investigation.
- The opportunity to detect relevant information.
- The opportunity to collaborate.
- Tasks which can be integrated across subject areas.

- Five investigations mirror the kind of tasks teachers face in real life.
- The problem is presented simply in the form of two letters or memos, there is no well-defined task.
- Each investigation presents a complex task with a single sustained context.
- When given the two documents for investigation, students determine a course of action including the presentations to class.
- Students work on the project for weeks rather than days.
- No attempt is made to edit out irrelevant material.
- Each investigation is addressed to a group, and students are advised to work in collaborative groups.
- Assessment strategies presented are relevant to other Disciplines.

Provide access to expert performances and the modelling of processes:

- Access to expert thinking and modelling processes.
- Access to learners in various levels of expertise.
- Sharing of stories.
- Access to the social periphery.
- Experienced teachers model assessment strategies in *Scenarios*, and experts give their views in *Interviews*.
- Preservice teachers give their advice in *Reflections*.
- Collaborative groups enable the sharing of stories.
- Scenes filmed in real classrooms to provide real-life episodes.

Provide multiple roles and perspectives:

- Different perspectives on the topics from various points of view.
- The opportunity to express different points of view.
- The opportunity to criss-cross.

- The learning environment.
- Each strategy can be seen from the perspective of the classroom teacher, a school student in the class, a mathematics education expert and a preservice teacher.
- Collaborative groups and the presentations to class.
- Enable the expression of different points of view.
- Five investigations are provided and the option of students creating their own investigations.

Support collaborative construction of knowledge:

- Tasks which are addressed to a group rather than an individual.
- Classroom organization into pairs or small groups.
- Appropriate incentive structure for whole group achievement.
- Each investigation is addressed to a group, e.g., the Mathematics Sub-committee.
- Lecturers are advised to divide students into small collaborative groups.
- Grades for class presentations and written reports are given for a group effort, not individually.

Element of situated learning Guidelines for implementation, manifestation in the learning environment and promote reflection:

- Authentic context and task.
- Non-linear navigation.
- Opportunity for learners to compare with experts.
- Opportunity for learners to compare with other learners.
- Collaborative groupings of students.
- Real classroom context and task.
- Non-linear navigation enabling ready access to any media element in a non-sequential order.

- Students can compare their thoughts to an experienced classroom teacher and mathematics education experts.
- Students can compare their thoughts to a preservice teacher in the end of their teacher training course.
- Collaborative groups recommended to enable reflection with aware attention.

7.3 TRADITIONAL INSTRUCTION VS. CONSTRUCTIVISM

Instruction includes planning, implementing and evaluating the curriculum or the material covered in scope and sequence (Morphew, 1994). The scope of curriculum includes the breadth and depth of what is taught, and the sequence is the order in which it will be taught. Together the scope and sequence of the curriculum steer the act of instruction, though practically speaking, curriculum and instruction are inseparable. Theoretically, the curriculum that is taught should equal the curriculum learnt (Passe, 1999). Unfortunately, in reality this seldom occurs. Instead, the difference in what is taught and learnt shows itself in poor test scores and gross misconceptions. To bring the taught and learnt curriculum closer together, the experiences made available to the learner must be amenable to what Dewey called "the flux" in learning. This attention to the experiences offered to learners helps ensure the act of co-construction of meaning.

In order for the learner to co-construct meaning, he or she must be open to the process of co-creation. To some degree instructors may influence the willingness of learners to learn, though much of this is intrinsically motivated. To a great extent, instructors may impact the learning experience. Thus, the question arises, what experiences should an instructor provide to help facilitate the act of co-construction?

In traditional classrooms, instructors have adopted various teaching practices that maximize the potential for this flow by creating dynamic learning experiences. A number of strategies are adopted which have proven effectives such as Concept Maps and

Semantic Webs; Venn Diagrams and Other Graphic Organizers; Models; Analogies and Metaphors; Hypothesis Making and Testing; Integrated Themes; Journaling; Portfolios; Dialogue and Cooperative Learning; Learning and Cycle Lessons, etc.

Concept maps and semantic webs: Concept maps are a visual representation diagramming concepts and relationships among concepts. Concepts are arranged hierarchically so that the most general concepts are located at the top of the diagram, and the most specific are located toward the bottom (Baker & Piburn, 1997). Semantic webs are also visual representations of concepts, yet they are not hierarchical in nature. Rather all concepts emanate from one overriding concept, showing relationships between the subordinate concepts and the main concept (Baker & Piburn, 1997). Concept maps and Semantic webs may be created by either the instructor, learner or both and may be introduced any time relationships among existing knowledge are made, or whenever new knowledge is constructed.

Venn diagrams and other graphic organizers: Venn diagrams, like concept maps and semantic webs, help show the connection between related concepts. They can be simple or complex and may be created by the instructor, learner, or both to accentuate connections between concepts or attributes of concepts. Venn diagrams are a type of graphic organizer: any visual representation used to help make the abstract concrete. A graphic organizer shows the patterns of inductive and deductive reasoning.

Models: Creation and utilization of models is another experience that provides learners with concrete examples of connections and relationships. For instance, relief maps help learners understand connections between flat topographic maps and changes in land elevation. A model of the solar system showing relative location and distance of the planets to the sun may be used to make the abstract concrete.

Analogies and metaphors: Analogies and metaphors are helpful in making connections between prior knowledge and new knowledge. For example, a learner may benefit from understanding that the transmission of messages in a computer system is like the transmission of nerve impulses in the human body.

Hypothesis making and testing: Hypothesis making and testing are experiences that help facilitate co-construction of meaning by requiring the learner to draw from a vast store of previously learned concepts to make inferences about new ones. Hypotheses are statements that show a cause and effect relationship between two or more factors. They are often written in the if-then format. "If temperature is increased, then pressure will increase." "If blue is added to red, then purple will result." These statements are meaning-building in their creation but also in their testing. In testing hypotheses, the learner must experiment to co-create new concept formation. This new knowledge will later be a part of future hypotheses making.

Integrated themes: The relevancy of connections becomes apparent to learners when themes and concepts are integrated holistically. For example, the learner who constructs meaning about the lifestyle of colonists during India's Freedom Struggle at the same time he/she learns about the science of that time and place has a better chance of building connections than if he/she were taught these concepts in isolation. Elementary instructors more often teach integrated thematic units than secondary instructors. Unfortunately, the traditional isolation of secondary teaching teachers doesn't allow for integrated planning and thus, presentation to learners.

Journaling: Journaling is the process of reflecting on a given statement or question to make sense of it in terms of the learner's past and current experiences. For example, learners may begin a journal at the beginning of a unit on space travel. Early in the journal learners may be asked to reflect and write on what it would be like to leave their familiar planet to journey for a new life wrought with uncertainties. As the learners progress through the unit, preferably thematically, they are asked to reflect on their travels as they journey farther and farther away from planet Earth. How are their survival needs being met? What kinds of hardships are they encountering? What improvements to their quality of life are they discovering? Like hypothesis testing, analogies, and metaphors, this type of experience forces the learner to reach back into her prior learning to co-construct meaning of the new.

Portfolios: Portfolios are a system of organizing various documents so that connections among the documents and their conceptual meaning may be made. Portfolios may contain paradigm statements or declarations of what students understand about a concept at that place and time in their life. For example, beginning teachers are often asked to document their educational philosophy early on in their careers and to revisit those statements as they grow up in the profession. By reflecting on where they have been, where they are, and where they might be going, connections can be made between prior, present, and future knowledge and experiences. Another example may be at the beginning of a unit on particle physics; learners might be asked to explain their current understanding of the atom. As new concepts are introduced in their learning experience, the students would record how these concepts measure up to new ones in the process of co-construction of meaning. Other instruments may be used to analyze current conceptions. Questionnaires, surveys and checklists may be periodically completed and updated as students move through the study of a concept. These documents may be added to the portfolio to help the learner understand how he/she constructs knowledge most fully. This act of self-observation and interpretation is called metacognition and is consistent with constructivist thought.

Dialogue and cooperative learning: Dialogue with others and cooperative learning provide students with experiences where the act of co-creation of meaning can occur simultaneously with other learners. When learners are asked to engage in dialogue, their prior knowledge is called up and constantly challenged as new concepts are introduced. In the cooperative learning experience, where groups of learners work together to construct meaning toward the solution of a given problem, similar connections are made. For example, a cooperative group of learners, given the task of building a better mousetrap, will exchange prior knowledge about the construction of typical mousetraps. Different learners will likely be familiar with different types of traps. Together, the exchange of dialogue helps learners share and build new meaning. Cooperatively, the learners will test possible prototypes of new mousetraps and modify their existing understanding of what a mousetrap means.

Learning cycle lesson: The learning cycle lesson is a process of presenting material so that the learner capitalizes on the constructive nature of learning. The learning cycle lesson has several phases to its delivery. The first phase is the exploration phase, where students are given an opportunity to explore components of the curriculum. In a science lesson, students may be given different shells to observe. The students will be asked to record their observations and begin to make inferences about their observations. The next phase is the explanation phase, where the instructor helps the student co-construct meaning of the observations and inferences. This phase, also known as the Term Invention phase, is where sense is made of the phenomenon. Here terminology, explanation and connections will make up the learning experience. In our example, perhaps the shells might be described in terms of their biological attributes. Connections to remains of other sea life would likely be addressed to connect former knowledge with new knowledge, and to help students discard any preconceived ideas that they now realize are incorrect. The expansion phase, also known as the Concept Application phase, is where students are given an opportunity to apply what they just learnt. Here students might develop a family tree of the shells and compare to the actual taxonomic relationship delineated by scientists. Learners would then have the opportunity to compare previous understanding with new and see how they measure up to one another. In some versions of the learning cycle, an additional phase is listed. This phase, the evaluation phase, is actually an ongoing act of assessing for the co-construction of meaning. Student responses, questions, records and actions are all considered when assessing learning.

Recommendations for web-based constructivist learning and instruction: The foregoing discussion on experiences used by constructivist instructors in the traditional classroom has numerous implications for distance learning education, too. With some creativity, much of the same experiences that stimulate thinking and facilitate the co-construction of meaning in traditional settings can be made available to the distance learner.

Web-based learning and instruction: A constructivist approach for example, as a distance learning educator plans for instruction, he/she must keep in mind that the experience is paramount in the constructivist learning process. But before the experiences can be selected, the scope and sequence of the curriculum must be decided. Questions such as, "What knowledge of this topic is worth knowing and significant to understanding other concepts?" and "What depth of understanding is essential for learners to make important connections?" will be helpful in narrowing down the plethora of material on a given topic. Next, the distance learning educator must decide what planning will be necessary to deliver the curriculum. Choices must be made regarding related web sites, CD-ROMs and other technology that will be used to help make the curriculum deliverable. Once the technology is selected, careful attention must be paid to the experiences that will be provided to learners to make meaning possible. The appropriateness of every experience described previously should be evaluated to determine the degree to which it would bring the taught curriculum closer to the learnt curriculum. Following this planning, the distance learning educator must orchestrate all the technologies and experiences for the implementation phase of instruction. During this phase, educators should closely monitor the growth in the learners and efficacy of the programme by keeping abreast of journal responses, paradigm statements, or whatever other experiences are being used as part of the distance learning education programme. Instructional plans should be modified based on this feedback to most fully ensure co-construction of meaning by the learners. This process of monitoring and modifying should be ongoing throughout the distance learning education programme. During the evaluation phase of instruction, the distance learning educator should review growth of the learners in terms of meaning construction and should assess how closely the curriculum taught and the curriculum learnt match. In this way, evaluation of the learner and programme can be accomplished simultaneously.

Jonassen, Peck, and Wilson (1999) propose a conceptual model of learning environments for technology. According to their model, Constructivist Learning Environments (CLEs) should engage students in investigation of the problem, critique of related cases, review of information resources, development of necessary skills, collaboration with others and use of social support in implementation of the learning experience. Perhaps merging of the conceptual model of constructivist distance learning education described in this chapter and that presented by Jonassen, et al. will better serve distance learning educators and learners alike? Learner and programme evaluation will testify to the efficacy of web-based constructivist learning and instruction. The degree to which this process will bring about the desired learning is a question for future study. Most web-based instruction today is based on behaviourism, viewing the learner as an empty vessel waiting to be filled.

7.4 WHAT ROLE CAN TECHNOLOGY PLAY IN A CONSTRUCTIVIST SETTING?

A complementary relationship exists between technology and constructivism, the implementation of each one benefiting the other. Constructivism is a doctrine stating that learning takes place in contexts, while technology refers to the designs and environments that engage learners. Recent attempts to integrate technology in the classroom have been within the context of a constructivist framework (e.g., Richards, 1998). Constructivist strategies include collaborative and cooperative learning methods, engaging in critical and reflective thinking, evaluation through electronic portfolios, and a critical look at emerging teacher roles within constructivist paradigms. Success has been reported in the development of constructivist course modules using technology as cognitive tools, benefiting both students and faculty. However, many teachers do not use constructivist practices, and those who do are not judicious in their selection of technology use (Rakes et al., 1999). Technology needs to be viewed in a three-dimensional perspective: semiotic, epistemic, and pragmatic, enabling the "construction of knowledge" by learners through a process of acculturation.

"Once knowing is no longer understood as the search for an iconic representation of ontological reality, but, instead, as a search for fitting ways of behaving and thinking, the traditional problem disappears. Knowledge can now be seen as something that the organism builds up in the attempt to order the as such amorphous flow of experience..." (von Glasersfeld, 1984). The use of computer technology to support learning has been difficult to document and quantify (Clark, 1994; Russell, 1999), leaving the role of computers in the classroom precarious. In the past decade, a sudden resurgence of interest was markedly observed in the classroom use of technological innovations, along with the increased use of the Internet and other digital technologies (Reiser, 2002). The field of Instructional Design and Technology, too, saw the evolution and emergence of alternative approaches, such as cognitive and constructivist theories, that deviated sharply from traditional practices, such as behavioural models. New emphases, like electronic performance support systems, web-based instruction, and knowledge management systems, not only shook the knowledge base of the field, but also widened its horizon across business and industry, the military, health care and education, worldwide (Reiser, 2002). Initiatives, such as situated learning theory and constructivism presented fresh approaches to bring about reforms in the domains of public education and higher education (Anderson, Reder & Simon, 1996; Brown, Collins & Duguid, 1989; Jonassen, 1999; Reiser, 2002).

To understand the potential of technology implementation in enhancing the teaching-learning process, the impact of constructivism on classroom practices has been studied by many researchers (e.g., Black & McClintock, 1995; Richards, 1998; Brush & Saye, 2000). Other researchers have suggested that constructivist strategies exploit technologies for greatest impact in learning (e.g., Duffy & Cunningham, 1996). A complementary relationship appears to exist between computer technologies and constructivism, the implementation of each one benefiting the other.

The focus of both constructivism and technology are then on the creation of learning environments. Likewise, Hannafin and Hill (2002) depict these learning environments as contexts:

"in which knowledge-building tools (affordances) and the means to create and manipulate artifacts of understanding are provided, not one in which concepts are explicitly taught a place where learners work together and support each other as they use a variety of tools and learning resources in their pursuit of learning goals and problem-solving activities".

In order to understand learning within a constructivist framework, as an activity in context, the whole learning environment must be examined. However, the wide diversity of constructivist views makes the task very complex and beyond the scope of this chapter. These views commonly emphasize the role of the teacher, the student, and the cultural embeddedness of learning (see e.g., Duffy & Cunningham, 1996; Honebein, Duffy, & Fishman, 1993; Simons, 1993). Using these commonalities as guidelines, this review outlines the relationship of constructivism with technology by looking at (a) technology as cognitive tools, (b) constructive view of the thinking process, and (c) the role of the teacher in technology enhanced environments.

Technology as cognitive tools: A central assumption of constructivism is that learning is mediated by tools and signs (Duffy & Cunningham, 1996; Ezell & O'Keeffe, 1994). "Culture creates the tool, but the tool changes the culture. Participants in the culture appropriate these tools from their culture to meet their goals, and thereby transform their participation in the culture" (Duffy & Cunningham, 1996, p. 180). The computer is an exemplar of mediational means that has aspects of both tool and sign. The computer's role in education has been largely viewed as an instructional tool and for providing a richer and more exciting learning environment (Duffy & Cunningham, 1996; Jonassen & Reeves, 1996; Taylor, 1980). However, by focusing on the learner, the role of technology can support new understandings and capabilities, thus, offering a cognitive tool to support cognitive and metacognitive processes. Further, clarifying the role of technology in learning, Duffy and Cunningham (1996) state:

> Technology is seen as an integral part of the cognitive activity.... This view of distributed cognition significantly impacts how we think of the role of technology in

> education and training, the focus is not on the individual in isolation and what he or she knows, but on the activity in the environment. It is the activity—focused and contextualized—that is central.... The process of construction is directed towards creating a world that makes sense to us, that is adequate for our everyday functioning.

Thus, the task of the learner is seen as dynamic, and the computer makes available new learning opportunities.

The view of technology as cognitive tools is also shared by other researchers (Jonassen, 1994; Jonassen & Reeves, 1996; Lajoie, 2000). The traditional view of instructional technologies of instruction as conveyors of information and communicators of knowledge is supplanted with active role the learner plays in learning with technology. Technologies, primarily computers, help build knowledge bases, which will "engage the learners more and result in more meaningful and transferable knowledge.... Learners function as designers using the technology as tools for analyzing the world, accessing information, interpreting and organizing their personal knowledge, and representing what they know to others" (Jonassen, 1994). Technological tools such as spreadsheets, databases, expert systems, video conferencing and others can be used by students to analyze subject matter, develop representative mental models, and then transcribe them into knowledge bases (Jonassen, 1994; Jonassen & Carr, 2000; Jonassen & Reeves, 1996).

According to Kafai and her colleagues (1997), the multimedia software proved to be a good context for students to learn through collaboration and project management. The interaction between team members, the flow of ideas and loud thinking encouraged the children to experiment and find alternative ways for designing and solving problems. For example, the students worked on different characters individually, but then worked together to integrate all the characters, and in debugging (Kafai et al., 1997).

Cognitive tools do not preclude the use of computers to increase productivity for learning. Off-loading repetitive tasks and lower order tasks to cognitive tools frees cognitive resources for deeper thinking (Duffy & Cunningham, 1996; Jonassen, 1999) and reduces errors. According to Swain and Pearson (2001), teachers and students must be educated to use the computer as a productivity tool, as well as a tool for learning, research, networking, collaboration, telecommunications, and problem-solving.

Constructivist view of "Thinking": The process of thinking in constructivist paradigms requires higher-order skills, delving deeper and harder into content and context (Black & McClintock, 1995; Jonassen, n.d.; Manzo, 1998; Swain & Pearson, 2001). Traditional schooling, according to Manzo (1998), actually discourages constructive thinking with goals of transmitting existing knowledge that conflicts with any real attempt to generate new understanding. "Constructivist thinking combines both the critical and creative intellectual processes. It can be practised by encouraging critical analysis in activities. Schools, teachers and students can be conditioned to veer away from traditional schooling regimen to encourage constructive thinking" (Manzo, 1998). Cognitive tools, along with constructivist learning environments, guide and activate cognitive learning strategies and critical thinking (Jonassen, 1994). Cognitive tools help in knowledge construction and not knowledge reproduction. The knowledge constructed by the learners reflects their comprehension and conception of the information. To illustrate, when students build knowledge bases with databases, they need to analyze the content domain and engage in critical thinking.

Black and McClintock (1999) stress the importance of interpretation as being central to cognition and learning. Their design of Study Supported Environments (SSEs) based on constructivist design principles called Interpretation Construction Design (ICON) focused mainly on the interpretive construction of authentic artefacts in the context of rich background materials, and spanning across different fields of study. Their study showed that in addition to learning specific content, students were able to acquire generalizable interpretation and argumentation skills.

Reflective thinking, that requires careful deliberation, is also encouraged by constructivists (Kafai et al., 1997;

Swain & Pearson, 2001; Walker, 2000). Metacognition, or the self-monitoring and self-control of the learning process, is emphasized. New knowledge which is composed is added to previous representations, modifying them in the process. This usually requires external scaffolding in the form of people, books, or technologies such as computers. Swain and Pearson (2001) advocate the practice of reflective thinking by teachers to evaluate their technology use. They stress the importance of documentation of reflective thoughts to determine the extent and quality of personal versus instructional uses of technology, organization and implementation of environments and activities. Jonassen (1994) describes technological tools as "intellectual partners" and "powerful catalysts" in the process of learning, "scaffolding the all-important processes of articulation and reflection, which are the foundations of knowledge construction".

The role of the teacher in technology enhanced environments: The role of the teacher as a facilitator is seen as most important in a constructivist context (Witfelt, 2000; Richards, 1998). Within a constructivist classroom, the teacher engenders social and intellectual climates, where collaborative and cooperative learning methods are supported. In parallel, technology-enhanced classrooms tap constructivist strategies (Jonassen, 1999), arranging problem-based projects where students actively construct knowledge, linking knew knowledge with previous knowledge.

In non-traditional classrooms such as the open/global classroom (Walker, 2000; Witfelt, 2000), the role and responsibilities of the teacher have changed. The teacher, as an agent, has to constantly update information and technology for making learning authentic and relevant. For example, while developing a course module for teachers and taxonomy for teacher competencies in the use of educational multimedia, Witfelt (2000) observed that it was important to combine several theories such as constructivism, postmodernism, situated intelligence and multiple intelligences. However, the theoretical framework would be constructivist in nature with the teacher assuming the role of the facilitator, providing an environment for spontaneous research, understanding the social and collaborative nature of learning, helping children construct knowledge and initiate problem-based, project-oriented work. With this transition in roles and responsibilities, Witfelt (2000) listed new teacher competencies in constructivist contexts that include supervisor qualifications, supporter and facilitator of students' work, advisor and subject-matter expert, inspirer and encourager, arbiter at group discussions, critic in mobilizing greater effort when objectives are not being met, and evaluator to improve general learning capacities of students.

In the area of teacher education, Kim and Sharp (2000) observed that the planning of teachers consistent with constructivist practices was highly variable with most preservice teachers knowing very little about the effective integration of technology in education. Since teachers tend to teach as they were taught, it is essential that both preservice and inservice teachers must be exposed to constructivist-based instruction, which would then facilitate the development of teaching strategies consistent with recent reform movements (Kim & Sharp, 2000). An exposure to constructivist teaching methods and simultaneous multimedia learning experiences influenced the planning of constructivist behaviours and infusion of technology (Kim & Sharp, 2000).

Technology may also influence teacher practice to incorporate constructivist principles. Rakes et al., (1999) report that as the amount of technology available, the level of technology skills of the teachers, and the use of technology increased, the use of constructivist strategies in the classroom also appeared to increase. "Technology can provide the vehicle for accomplishing constructivist teaching practices" (Rakes et al., 1999). So, increasing the skill levels of teachers with regard to computers and providing additional opportunities for teachers to integrate technology into lessons may encourage the use of constructivist behaviours.

Morrison, Lowther, and DeMeulle (1999) have aptly suggested, "Technology and a constructivist approach need not be at odds with each other. If we change our view of computers from merely a means to deliver instruction to one of a tool to solve problems, then the reform movement can influence the use of technology, and technology can influence the reform of education."

7.5 THE CONSTRUCTIVISM-COMPUTER CONNECTION

Many researchers have explored the role computers can play in constructivist teaching. Roger Schank, Seymour Papert and Marcia C. Linn among others have demonstrated that computers often can provide an appropriate creative medium for students to express themselves and demonstrate their construction of new knowledge. Online collaboration projects and web publishing have both proved to be an exciting new way for teachers to engage their students. But because constructivism can require extended periods of classroom time and individualized attention to students, some educators have resisted its adoption and continue to support a drill-and-practice approach to learning.

In 1999, Professor Hank Becker of the University of California at Irvine began publishing the results of his 1998 Teaching, Learning and Computing Study (TLC). TLC (1998) was one of the first major research studies to examine teachers and students who use Internet computers on a regular basis. Becker and his colleagues looked at schools with high technology use—in other words, schools where teachers and students had easy access to Internet computers. One thing they discovered is that constructivist teachers were more likely to have students use Internet computers than traditional teachers. Those teachers who were more comfortable with constructivist teaching style were much more likely to have students use computers. Constructivist English and Social Studies teachers turned out to be most likely to use computers. In contrast, those teachers who were much more traditional, who preferred to stand in front of the classroom and give a lecture and who didn't encourage their students to be creative thinkers were much less likely to have their students use Internet computers. Says Becker (1999): "This [computer/constructivist] relationship is perhaps due to the fact that technology provides students with almost unlimited access to information that they need in order to do research and test their ideas. It facilitates communication, allowing students to present their beliefs and products to broader audiences and also exposes them to the opinions of a more diverse group of people in the real world beyond the classroom, school and local community—all conditions optimal for constructivist learning."

Another interesting find in the TLC study has been the relationship between constructivist practice and professional development. As Hank Becker and Margaret Riel write in their third TLC snapshot, Teacher Role Orientation: Classroom Focus Collaborative Professional Practice: Teachers' instructional styles mirror their own interaction patterns.... Teachers who learn from their peers, lead their peers, and present their ideas and opinions to their peers are more likely to have their students do the same in the classroom. They conduct their classes in a manner similar to the way they conduct their professional activities.

What might this tell us about teachers? If teachers are uncomfortable with sharing their thoughts or interacting with their colleagues in a constructivist setting, they may be just as uncomfortable using constructivism with their students. If teachers want to make the best use of the e-Learning—utilize its interactivity, collaboration opportunities, creative opportunities—the teachers themselves must be open to interactivity, collaboration and creativity. Thus, there is an urgent need not only to integrate e-learning (not merely inclusion of e-Learning) with Teacher Education but also to make ourselves capable enough to use e-Learning in such a manner so that we can situate the hole gamut of teaching and learning in Constructive Paradigm which is the demand of the time.

Now the question arises how to do that? Keller (1979) has claimed that design needs to address more than practical issues and provide for the human spirit. There has been a widespread increase in the use of web-based instruction (Simbandumwe, Parson, 1997). However, Boshier (1997) examined 127 courses and expressed concern that some sites emulated "the worst of face-to-face courses where power relations are unproblematised and learners constructed as passive recipients of information". Many web-based subjects have not utilised the full capability of this technology, a trend in education that is not unfamiliar. In fact a shift in approaches to pedagogy is required by teachers as well as a way of supporting alternate frameworks for instruction within a web-based environment.

There are models, whilst applicable in a behaviourist environment, are not serving instructional designers well when the theoretical foundation for the subject outcomes is based on a constructivist approach to learning. The constructivist group of theories places less emphasis on the sequence of instruction and more emphasis on the design of the learning environment (Jonassen, 1994). In a web-based environment this proves to be even more challenging.

Constructive learning environment: Constructivism, with the focus on learning rather than instruction, challenges the instructional designer to look for new models, but it seems that by its very nature, constructivism defies the concept of a model. Jonassen suggests in fact that it is not possible to create one since "knowledge construction is context-specific" (Jonassen, 1994). The difference he asserts is that rather than designing instructional sequences, the emphasis is on the design of a learning environment (Jonassen, 1994).

Wilson takes this idea of a learning environment further: "Thinking of instruction as an environment gives emphasis to the 'place' or 'space' where learning occurs. At a minimum, a learning environmental contains: (a) the learner; (b) a 'setting' or 'space' wherein the learner acts, using tools and devices, collecting and interpreting information, interacting perhaps with others, etc." (Wilson, 1996). He defines a constructivist learning environment as "a place where learners may work together and support each other as they use a variety of tools and information resources in their guided pursuit of learning goals and problem-solving activities" (Wilson, 1996).

Development of design goals: Jonassen and Duffy have determined three common elements, context, collaboration and construction as being fundamental to the environment, which are key processes rather than products. Later he added the use of conversation to the common elements (Jonassen, 1995). From these processes they determined a set of heuristics for a design process, which indicate that such an environment should support:

- Knowledge construction which is:
- Founded on internal negotiation of meaning;
- Established as a social negotiation of reality;
- Assisted by exploring real world environments and the creation of new environments; and
- Developed into mental models.
- A context for learning which is meaningful and authentic and makes use of knowledge constructed, which should:
- Be supported by such things as case-based scenarios which are situated in the real world and based on authentic tasks;
- Require an understanding of both problem-solving methods and thinking processes in that specific context; and
- Be modelled by a performer who is skilled though not necessarily expert.
- Collaboration, both student/student and student/teacher, where the teacher becomes a coach or mentor rather than the holder of knowledge who:
- Employs and encourages social negotiation; and
- Supports an intellectual toolkit to encourage mental modelling through internal negotiation. (Jonassen, 1994).

Design Goals of a Constructivist Learning Environment (Duffy and Cunningham, 1996):

- All knowledge is constructed; all learning is a process of construction.
- Many worldsviews can be constructed: hence there will be multiple perspectives.
- Knowledge is context dependent, so learning should occur in contexts to which it is relevant.

- Learning is mediated by tolls and signs.
- Learning is an inherently social-dialogical activity.
- Learners are distributed, multidimensional participants in a socio-cultural process.
- Knowing how we know is the ultimate human accomplishment.

All knowledge is constructed; all learning is a process of construction: Through the provision of teaching activities for students to direct their own learning, the designer acknowledges the students' need for autonomy in the learning process in order to construct their own understanding.

Many worldviews can be constructed: hence there will be multiple perspectives: Designers need to provide learning experiences which encourages students to look beyond their own view, since in order to have a worldview one's own view needs to be compared to the alternatives. Multiple perspectives can be determined through engagement with text but are best created through engagement with others, through discussion and argument.

Knowledge is context dependent, so learning should occur in contexts to which it is relevant: The provision of realistic or authentic contexts for learning is the basis for many constructivist learning environments. The learning environment should "stimulate learners so that their thinking is related to actual practice".

Learning is mediated by tolls and signs: The idea of mediated action in which ample theory of higher mental processes is grounded is identified as the basis for constructivism as viewed by Cunningham and Duffy (1996). They support the view of Wertsch (1994) who suggest that the "essence of mediated action is that it involves the tension between the mediational means as provided in the socio-cultural setting, and the unique contextualised use of these means in carrying out particular, concrete actions (Wertsch, 1994).

Learning is an inherently social-dialogical activity: This goal is a component of goal 4, which emphasizes the importance of language as the mediational means. It has been separated from the previous goal because of its importance since group discussion is emphasized in constructivist learning environments as one of the keys to understanding. Duffy and Cunningham argue that the main way that "mental functions are altered by the mediation of language signs is that knowledge, and thereby learning, becomes a social, communicative and discursive process, inexorably grounded in talk" (Duffy and Cunningham, 1997).

Learners are distributed, multidimensional participants in a socio-cultural process: This concept moves away from the idea that learning is effective internalising of knowledge towards one that involves a connection with communities and a pattern of participation in community. It should not be a lonely act of a single person but a matter of being "initiated into the practices of a community, of moving from legitimate peripheral participation to centripetal participation in the actions of a learning community" (Duffy and Cunningham, 1997).

Knowing how we know is the ultimate human accomplishment: Duffy and Cunningham (1997) identify self-awareness of learning and knowing as the most important goal. They stress that rather than the ideas of metacognition (Flavell, 1997) which "stress the strategies for efficient processing" (Duffy and Cunningham, 1997), they use the term 'reflexivity' which they identify as meaning self-referential. They argue that the essence of reflexivity occurs when "we experience or are shown a situation where our existing beliefs are inadequate, so our awareness of our own state of knowing is enhanced" (Duffy and Cunningham, 1997).

Many web-based courses have already moved from the provision of lecture notes on the web to increasingly providing avenues for communication and interaction, through synchronous and asynchronous discussion. Therefore, socio-cultural processes and socio-dialogical aspects can be supported through these environments, where the students are separated by distance and time. Through the provision of real world contexts and opportunity for collaboration, the learning experience can be designed to provide opportunity for students to take control of their own learning.

Current instructional design models do not provide effective strategies for designing constructivist learning environments. However, good instructional designers have always moved beyond the models by adapting and manipulating them for a specific context. To my mind, the design goals identified by Duffy and Cunningham (1996) require further development if they are to be used by instructional designers. Currently they provide experienced instructional designers with a framework for designing web-based constructivist learning environments that are a useful starting point for design, opening up interesting new areas for research.

There is a need to go beyond the traditional instructional model of teaching and learning. Despite the large availability of educational technologies, educators and trainers have difficulties to go beyond the traditional 'delivery' model of teaching. Several so-called e-learning courses do not go beyond the publication of learning content made available in different formats. The emergent needs of the contemporary society demand people not only with wider skills in different disciplines, but also with adequate awareness and sensitivity to make the most of these skills according to the situation they are in at a specific moment.

The ACOT (Apple Classroom of Tomorrow) Programme Development Centre contrasts traditional instruction and constructivist learning in the following fashion (Apple Computer Inc., 1994): "Instruction, drill and practice—is a great way to introduce skills or concepts, or build awareness, or reinforce some set of actions that can be replayed habitually. When breadth is valued over depth in curriculum, instruction is one way to make sure you cover the necessary content in a given amount of time. When depth and understanding are the desired outcomes, however, knowledge construction is a better strategy to help learners personalize and deeply internalize ideas to create situations where skills and concepts can be applied in different contexts to solve problems; to explore or generate ideas; and to generalize and synthesize knowledge."

Below is a summary of Apple's perception of the difference between instruction and knowledge construction practice in the classroom:

Function	Instruction	Construction
Classroom Activity	Teacher-centred; didactic	Learner-centred; interactive
Teacher Role	Fact teller; expert	Collaborator; learner
Student Role	Listener; always the learner	Collaborator; sometimes the expert
Instructional Emphasis	Facts, memorization	Relationships; inquiry and invention
Concept of Knowledge	Accumulation of facts	Transformation of facts
Demonstration of Success	Quantity	Quality of understanding
Assessment	Norm-referenced; multiple-choice items	Criterion-referenced; portfolios and performances
Technology Use	Drill & practice	Communication, collaboration, information access and retrieval; expression

By providing opportunities for relevant, timely, self-directed study utilizing technology-based instruction, collaborative learning and alternative assessment techniques, the differences in classroom practices is substantial. Dwyer (1994), in discussing ACOT's approach to the development of critical thinking skills states: "In-depth study of a sample of students' thinking processes began to show significant change in the way they thought and worked.... A four-year longitudinal study showed the greatest difference to be the manner in which they organized for and accomplished their work. Routinely, they employed inquiry, collaborative, technological and problem-solving, skills uncommon to graduates of traditional programmes."

The positive effects of the programme have been far-reaching. As stated by Dwyer (1994), "We watched technology profoundly disturb the inertia of traditional classrooms." Benefits have been found with regard to both student and teacher behaviours. Regarding students, one benefit is the fundamental change seen in the way that children think about their personal learning processes, organize materials and engage in the learning process itself. This is directly analogous to Cunningham's (1992) description of reflexivity. According to Dwyer and his colleagues, these skills are a direct outgrowth of the integration constructivist learning principles coupled with the daily use of computer technology into the classroom. From their research, ACOT project coordinators have seen a marked increase in the development and application of student's critical thinking skills both in and outside the classroom.

With regard to teachers, ACOT—conducted research (Dwyer, 1994) has found that "teachers reported and were observed to interact differently with students—more as guides or mentors and less like lecturers. For many teachers, personal efforts to make technology an integral part of their classrooms opened them to the possibilities of redefining how they went about providing opportunities for students to learn.

The other challenge is how to account for the demonstrated proficiencies such as creative problem-solving, collaborative learning and alternative forms of communicating about one's knowledge. Traditional assessment systems do not allow for much deviation from quantitative, clearly defined measures, including those measurement rubrics employed at the state and national levels. As stated by Dwyer (1994), "teachers struggle with the new methods of evaluation that could capture the novel ways that students were demonstrating their mastery of skills and concepts". Even with the success that ACOT has been able to demonstrate, there are still barriers and challenges that make the transition between a traditional and constructivist classroom environment difficult.

CMC (Computer Mediated Communication) is another model that is able to engage each participant at length and in detail on the construction of common understanding. A model of the target system, roughly what the teacher expects as outcomes, must connect to a mental model in order to be internalized. In developing a conceptual model a teacher should take into account the kinds of things an expert considers. ".... When experiences are carefully facilitated which support the conceptual model of the target, learners are able to adapt and reshape internal mental models and construct knowledge for themselves" (Brandt, 1997). The teacher as facilitator initiates the class discussion by presenting the experts' mental model to the students and then steps out of the discussion to let mental models develop in the learners through interaction. The CMC discussion can include all members of the class and is nearly unlimited in time. Learners unsure of the 'correctness' of their own current mental model can read others' models and proffer their own for inspection by the class.

The teacher's role is to facilitate a learning environment that helps students create good schemas of understanding. By facilitating students working with others, the teacher creates a 'community of scholars'. Students communicate ideas and make sense of others' ideas. Four techniques suggested to facilitate the group discussion are to question students' answers whether right or wrong, insist that all students try a contribution to the group, stay in the discussion long enough to direct a positive tone, and have all students self-evaluate their own ideas (Gadinidis, 1994). Using the transcript of a CMC the teacher can monitor each student's progress and give structure to help students meet the goals.

An aspect of constructivism has to do with conflict. Within a context of growth and cooperation, conflict is the source of developmental progress. It is not the teacher's intent to avoid conflict. It is the facilitator/teacher's job to help students negotiate the frictions that inevitably surface and provoke them to challenge ideas (Brooks, 1990). The facilitator models higher-order thinking by asking questions that probe students' knowledge deeply. Interactions remain at the metacognitive level. The facilitator's role is to challenge the learner's thinking. The facilitator and students will constantly ask questions such as: What does this mean? What are the implications of that? The students gradually will take over the role in collaboration (Duffy and Cunningham, 1996).

The traditional class provides a lively interaction among students and teacher but it is too quickly over and may easily not include everyone. It is the asynchronous CMC that can extend the discussion at the discretion of the students and include all students at the instance of the instructor. The probe of shared meaning can extend until the CMC discussion group has reached agreement.

A social dimension to learning—what is sometimes called collaborative or cooperative learning—often, although not always, fosters learning (Perkins, 1999). CMC may allow the teacher to match the kinds of knowledge under consideration to the template. Each kind of knowledge may be acquired in a different structure of interactive discussion. The template selected by the teacher to organize the non-linear discussion can be tested for effectiveness and student satisfaction. Essentially the template allows students to pose 'questions', make statements and read the group's construction of common knowledge.

Constructivist teaching practices help learners internalize, or transform, new information. In this active, constructive process, the brain makes the best interpretation it can, according to its previous experiences and the limited information available. Assessment techniques must permit students to express their personal understanding of concepts that is uniquely theirs (Holloway, 1999). The ability to think—to be lifelong seeker and integrator of new knowledge—is based on the ability to ask and consider important questions. By learning question-based problem-solving strategies, students become more effective thinkers and learners (Richetti and Sheerin, 1999). CMC can be used effectively for this purpose.

The three kinds of knowledge are physical, social (conventional) and logico-mathematical knowledge. Piaget's distinction among the three is based on their ultimate sources and modes of structuring (Kamii and Ewing, 1996). Here it can be argued that in the context of asynchronous CMC teaching, it is the group that relates the conflict for each other. A mental model of the structure of the particular kind of knowledge is placed in play in the CMC discussion and the learner experiences reinforcement or reconstruction.

The individual student develops his/her own meaning while interacting with others. Learning, then, is a process acculturation.

In other words, learning is an inherently social-dialogical process. Hence, our reason for using groups is to promote the dialogical interchange and reflexivity. The richness of computer technology permits us to provide a richer and more exciting (entertaining?) learning environment that will better engage the student in learning the material being presented (Duffy and Cunningham, 1996). CMC seems the ideal context to engage students in the activity to the fullest extent possible. It is a mixture of asynchronous thoughtfulness and synchronous spontaneity.

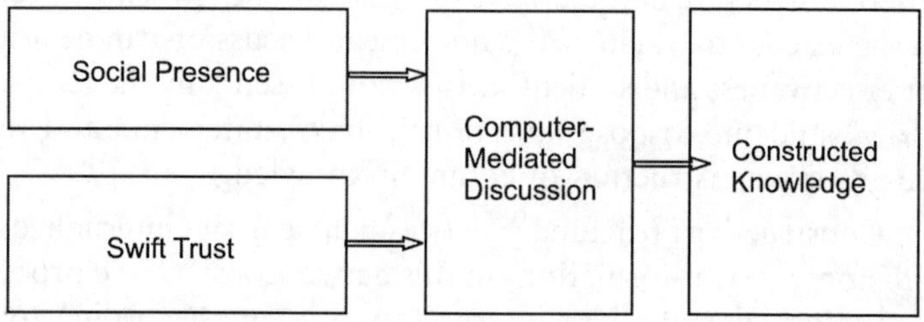

Instructional Model: CMC contribution to constructivist learning (Spencer, 2000)

Social presence and swift trust are the socio-contextual drivers that may lead to construction of knowledge. The model depicts the theory of social presence as contributing to the discussion as it predicts by encouraging the individual to perceive that interaction with fellow students as enjoyable and valuable. The persuasive and frank discussion of the subject studied enables students to exchange ideas and previous experiences to construct knowledge upon the common denominator of the group.

Research has shown that combining face-to-face meetings with asynchronous CMC discussions is more effective than decisions reached in just face-to-face meetings or in just synchronous CMC. The degree of satisfaction with the process was not found to be mode dependent but the combined mode participants were more satisfied with their resulting decisions (Ocker et at., 1998). It is found that larger groups using brainstorming techniques are more effective when they are using CMC.

8

Constructivism and Curriculum

As many other countries across the world, India is in a process of curriculum reform involving a change of paradigm of educational practices. The shift is from a rather "pure" behaviourist to an eclectic constructivist approach and this has wide-reaching implications throughout the educational system, but in each and every country where this is happening curriculum developers seem to be at a bit of a loss as to how to cast constructivist thinking in a national curriculum. The curriculum questions are deceptively simple: What should our children learn? How should they learn it? How do we know they have learnt it? Unfortunately there are no clear answers to these or how to develop curricula, because constructivism is not primarily about how to develop a curriculum (in the sense of the codification of intended learning). It is more like a conglomerate of understandings and research about knowledge, intelligence, learning and development. Out of this, and a belief that good learning is learner-centred, curriculum developers are struggling to provide statements of intended learning based on constructivist principles.

Most of the curriculum today is based on the encyclopaedic view of knowledge, a neatly categorised and prescribed quantity of unchanging information, learnable and containable. Education has become a narrow repertoire of ritualised classroom behaviours, and only two skills are developed: memorization and repetition. No more than that. Sufficiently and strongly repeated behavioural stimuli produces the result, assessed and certified through formalized examinations. The organization and management of the system is correspondingly authoritarian. If the learner did not succeed, the fault was with the learner, not with the system.

First, if one takes an absolute stance about knowledge being constructed and the approach being learner-centred, there is a fundamental contradiction in having a national curriculum at all: what becomes the curriculum should be neither prescribed nor described but negotiated and developed from scratch between teacher and learner. In real terms, however, the pragmatic dilemma is how to provide a national framework which is at the same time open for local content, and individualization in the classroom.

If a curriculum is to describe what knowledge it is intended to be transmitted, shared, acquired, and/or discovered, how should that knowledge be classified if it is to be experienced as holistic and integrated? Dewey recommended starting with an integrated project approach in the first few years of school, moving into given scientific disciplines from the middle years upwards. That model seems to have been widely used, although often given only lip service: some systems, even today, have subject teachers right down to class one, something which mitigates against integration.

Few systems depart from conventional subject classifications entirely, but the changing relationships between, and conceptualisation of, subject shows how reality is making curriculum developers unsure about how to classify knowledge today. Very many systems are struggling with content overload in the curriculum and this is related to how knowledge is classified. On the one hand is the legacy of the encyclopaedia versus the new demands of developing a wide range of skills. On the other hand is the conventional classification of subjects versus more and more cross-curricular themes such as environmental education, population education, education, life skills, entrepreneurial education, etc. The first dilemma is also a question of "less is more"—only by reducing the quantity of encyclopaedic content can time and space be created for skills content and thus better learning.

The second dilemma is one of a rapidly changing reality which needs new knowledge and new ways of knowing, in a more holistic way. If one drew up a matrix of subjects and cross-curricular themes, it could be turned on its side and knowledge classified as relevant themes, with subject disciplines as tools for understanding rather than ends in themselves. The early years and the middle years curriculum for the schools are enquiry rather than subject-based, which is an interesting move in this direction. Should one continue to modify existing classification, or is there a need for a clean start from new first principles to achieve a more holistic approach? Given that we live in the communication age, should communication be a new area of learning, involving all forms of communication: linguistic, visual, musical, kinaesthetic? Given the inseparability of science and moral challenges, should Natural Science become Nature, Life and Values? What would provide the closest integration and holistic understanding?

Assessment is another area where the strongest contradictions can occur between a constructivist learner-centred approach to teaching and learning and the need to know what learning has actually taken place. A constructivist understanding of learning recognizes the importance and value of different learning profiles and paces. If one takes an absolute stance, the organization of teaching and learning in formal education goes against this since all learners are expected to learn the same things at the same pace. Late developers, slow learners and those with learning disabilities are the ones who lose out. This dilemma is resolved either by resourcing the school to give adequate individual attention (support teaching, or materials), and/or by allowing learners with low or limited achievement to proceed to the next class. On the other hand, the technicist demand to measure system efficiency (completion rate, cycle time, etc.) and the need to ensure that all learners are learning what they should, has led to setting standards which all are expected to achieve. The lack of economy in being able to define and describe assessment is symptomatic of the fact that curriculum developers are still wrestling with the conceptualisation and practice of assessment in a constructivist and learner-centred approach, at the same time as they are under pressure from education authorities demanding tools to measure system accountability and efficiency, including using aggregated results of learner assessment. On top of that comes the problem of making assessment manageable in the classroom.

In some systems, it has not been found necessary to have elaborate specifications about assessment. It is integrated into the teaching/learning process and teachers are trained to do it. However, it has been found in major systems that there was a lack of clarity about what exactly the learners had achieved, and attention is now being given to how to define and assess expected learning outcomes more precisely. Some competency-based systems distinguish between two levels of competency, using terms such as basic and advanced competencies, or essential and desirable competencies, or minimum and extended. The idea here is to provide a range to cater for high and low achievers, and to fix a minimum which all learners should reach, but it complicates the manageability.

The dilemmas posed by assessment are heightened when the time for annual/public examinations comes. This is where the form of assessment limits what range of skills and competencies can be assessed and how, and because of the importance of examinations as a filter they have a powerful backwash effect. There is an increasing repertoire of assessment techniques to try and capture a wider range of nuances of learning. Self-assessment, peer-assessment, negotiating assessment criteria, developing portfolios of work, using a variety of assessment situations, are all part of these trends. For both formative and summative assessment, interesting work from a constructivist perspective has been done on authentic assessment/educative assessment but it has not been used on a national scale. It seems that time and cost factors play a decisive role in how far assessment and examinations can be consistent with a constructivist curriculum. We can note that the curriculum document is the coding of knowledge, and the textual and visual discourse of the curriculum has real and symbolic meaning.

Curriculum as the driving force of reform: The curriculum is the heart of education, the sharing of learning experiences between the teacher and learner. All else in the system should be derived from this: how learners should be assessed, how teachers should be trained and develop, what textbooks and other learning support materials should be like, how schools and the educational system should be organized and managed, and the allocation of resources necessary for the system to function.

The nature and degree of change which the shift to a constructivist paradigm entails is considerable. It involves a change of power-knowledge relationships at all levels (Foucault). The re-classification and re-framing of knowledge (Bernstein) is a shift from the vested interests of entrenched subject disciplines. The change to participatory, enquiry and discovery methods in the classroom and negotiated learning and assessment, is a change to the gradual sharing of power in the classroom instead of the authoritarian teacher and subservient learners. It is democratic learning processes which need a democratic school and managerial environment if they are to thrive. The constructivist approach also has implications for cultural capital and cultural reproduction. If the knowledge and experience of the learner and local community is valued and used, new cultural capital is accessed and the mechanism of cultural reproduction of the dominant elite is weakened.

If the term curriculum is taken broadly, it means the text and the trajectory from the agreed statement of intended learning to what the learner comes out with at the end of schooling. It is the teacher who is the most crucial actor in the field, and curriculum reforms of this nature across the world have to deal with how to develop teachers for a different understanding and approach to learning and assessment. Within the somewhat broad parameters of constructivism, the methodological approach is variously called active learning, participatory learning, co-operative learning, learning with understanding, child-centred education, learner-centred education, learning-centred education. The corresponding paradigm of teacher education and development is, however, more clearly conceptualised in the terms "the reflective practitioner" and "critical practitioner enquiry". In this paradigm of teacher education and development, the teacher constructs her/his understanding of how to improve teaching and learning in the class through continuous analysis of the learning processes and experiences of the learners, and of herself/himself as a teacher. The tools for reflection include i.e. reflective writing, keeping a logbook, action research, peer-peer support and development. As the teacher develops, he/she constructs him/herself as a professional person, gaining deeper understanding, empathy and professionality. In many reform processes, educating teachers in a constructivist approach has been reduced to classroom techniques and checklists only—how to organize group work, how to make locally produced materials, etc. Without a deeper understanding of knowledge, intelligence, and learning, teachers do not have the conceptual framework for reflection. A constructivist approach means that the teacher must learn and be able to decide when it is best to convey content directly or to let learners discover or explore information for themselves; when they need directed learning; reinforcement of learning; when the focus should be on skills more than content; when there are particular building blocks that are necessarily sequenced (phonics, mathematical operations); or when the learners can be allowed to find their own way through a topic of area of content. In addition, the teacher must have a good relation with the community and know how to organize learning experiences in and using the community. This sort of approach has wide-reaching implications for preservice as well as in-service teacher education and ongoing professional development. Only if the student-teacher has the same sort of learning experiences, approaches and assessment throughout their studies as he/she is expected to manage in the classroom, will he/she emerge as a reflective practitioner? The key to that change is to change the teacher-educators themselves.

The change of paradigm to a constructivist approach not only means a change of curriculum and assessment, and a change in the role of the teacher, but also a change in the role of the learner. Previously, the learner has been the more or less passive recipient of information conveyed by the teacher and/or textbook. Constructivism is premised on the fact that understanding is what we construct ourselves in co-operation with others, and in education, if we want to get children and young people to understand the world around them, we must help them to learn how to construct understanding. To do this, conditions have to be created by the teacher where the learner can learn actively. Active learning is not just outer activity: it is inner mental and emotional activity. It involves processes of guessing, hypothesizing, assuming, synthesizing, using intuition, being aware of feelings and responses, all part of trying to understand what they have found out, tried out, observed, and done. Constructivism is both an aspect of the globalization of knowledge and an approach which asserts the importance of local, collective, and individual context and understanding. It is a major paradigm shift with immediate consequences for teaching, assessment and examination, the education and development of teachers, and not least curriculum development. We should not forget that a curriculum might be very well designed and developed, consistent and coherent, but if it is not manageable by the ordinary teacher in the ordinary classroom, it is of no use. In evaluating curricula and syllabi, manageability has to be a key criterion or a lot of effort will be wasted.

Secondly, we envision a new sort of teacher, perhaps the teacher we all wanted to become but never knew how. The general approach of the reflective practitioner seems to be a way towards this. Yet, beneath the theoretical paradigm, and the methodologies, is the insurmountable fact that the good teachers are the teachers who care, and caring cannot be curricularized.

Arnold (1991) espouses a curriculum based reform effort, supporting knowledge construction: "The attempt to separate content and process, or to make one subservient to the other, belies a faulty epistemology. James (1974) tells us that knowledge involves both question (process) and answer (product or content). One of the major faults of schooling, and perhaps a reason why content tends to be denigrated, is that we are constantly giving students answers to questions that they have not asked." Regarding the value of content Arnold (1991) states that "an educated person knows how to learn, but also knows about significant issues and ideas". To develop a curriculum rich in meaning, she suggests that such a curriculum embodies three distinct yet interrelated principles:

- Material should be genuinely important and worth knowing.
- Meaningful curriculum deals directly with values and beliefs about the content area.
- Both content and methodology must relate directly to the needs and interests of the student populations; i.e. developmental appropriateness.

In addition to above stated facts, there are also the meta-cognitive and affective components to learning. According to Herman, Aschabacher, & Winters (1992), "meaningful learning is intrinsically motivating. By focusing on developing a "thinking curriculum", (Resnick & Klopter, 1989), both process and product are reinforced. In a thinking curriculum, the focus is on in-depth, thematic learning that relates to real-world issues, and exposes the utilization of holistic, alternative assessment procedures, providing a direct connection of content and process to the learner's background. In this manner, the essence of the content can be fully addressed in a manner that is directly accessible to the student.

Framework: Four principles have been developed that support the Teaching for Understanding framework (Unger, 1994). These principles are:

- Learning should be generative, and go beyond the subject matter covered. Students should be encouraged to apply their learning 'outside the box'.
- Clear educational goals should be established and shared with students, thereby empowering them to work towards, known and understood standards.
- Assessment should be performance-based, giving the students the opportunity to demonstrate their knowledge in a manner meaningful to them and accessible to others.
- Assessment should be ongoing and iterative.

Constructivism replaces the standard curriculum with solving problems within the context of a person's previous knowledge. The curriculum is the content from which and upon which reflections of understanding (i.e. ideas) are made.

Constructivist curriculum urges to have greater understanding of developmental psychology and learning models, group learning using cooperative learning strategies, active cognitive involvement (hands-on—heads-on), personal input from students regarding relevant information, student centred—not subject centred classroom environments, integration of subject matter to convey connections to the experiential world, interaction, discussion and reflection, and flexibility of teacher in both curriculum and pedagogical strategies.

Thomas (1989) described the students as "architects of their own learning" who can construct and organize their learning experiences. Glasersfeld (1983) contended that the change of notion in curriculum planning "will shift the emphasis from the student's correct replication of what the teacher does, to the student's successful organization of his or her own experiences". This "constructivist perspective" on the learners can no doubt encourage more student involvement and participation in the planning, structuring and organizing of their learning. The constructivist curriculum advocates that the aims of the curriculum should be to help the students to:

(a) obtain a broader picture of the society in which they live

(b) develop as well-educated individuals

(c) achieve a deeper understanding of the fellow students

(d) develop a group identity and a sense of belonging which will lead to team spirit

(e) improve their confidence, leadership, planning and organizational skills

There is growing consensus that education must extend its traditional goal of student mastery of subject-centred scholastic knowledge, to include the development of individuals who can prosper in complex and changing social, cultural and economic worlds. The 'inner intent' of reform efforts being made and advocated widely, could be characterised by these key principles: (1) emphasis on exit outcomes (prospering in the real world); (2) active learning for intellectual quality (constructivism); (3) personal responsibility for own learning and behaviour (genuine engagement); (4) individual meaning and relevance (not one-size-fits-all); (5) real-life purposes, roles and contexts (integrated curriculum); (6) links with community for mutual capacity building (productive partnerships in a learning community); and (7) extension of pedagogical repertoires (teachers moving from 'sage on the stage' to 'guide on the side'). However, teachers, schools and systems are having great difficulty resolving some of the contradictions between these principles and practices on the one hand, and pressures of accountability and traditional school culture on the other.

Thompson and Zeuli (1999), for example, observe that perhaps the most striking thing about teachers' efforts to learn and put into practice current reform ideas is that 'it is possible—indeed, fairly common—to get a great deal right and still miss the point...of the reforms'. After all, the effort to change teachers' mindsets and practices takes place within a set of cultural, structural and accountability constraints that often remain largely unchanged. The most crucial value determining the quality of relationships and the nature of learning environments (including policy environments) is the way in which power operates in them. Foucault (1977) explained that, 'The problem is not one of changing people's "consciousness" or what's in their heads; but the political, economic, institutional regime of the production of truth.' It should not surprise us, then, that the history of curriculum change is a history of little change (Glatthorn & Jailall, 2000), or, as Woodrow Wilson put it so nicely, 'It is easier to change the location of a cemetery, than to change the school curriculum' (quoted in Bailey, 2001). Attempts at curriculum reform that fail to make it possible for power to operate in fundamentally different ways in learning environments will fall victim to the inertia of the traditional, industrial age educational paradigm.

How are patterns of power currently determining the student's experience of schooling, and constructing the student's image of self, others, and the world? We know that many of the most potent messages students receive are not communicated through the explicit curriculum and its content. Rather, the messages are part of the hidden curriculum. They are part of the form that curriculum takes. Curricular form determines what students can and cannot experience, and the ways in which they can and cannot act, and in the words of Aristotle, 'It makes no small difference whether we form habits of one kind or another from our very youth; it makes a very great difference, or rather all the difference' (quoted in Hunt, 1990).

Teachers and schools are challenged to ask themselves, how can we reconcile the principles of the reform agenda with the constraints of formal systemic curriculum and assessment policies, and our traditional modes of instruction and interaction? We must bear in mind that, 'Those who want to influence the learning of others should try to create as much correspondence as possible between institutional goals and learners' goals.' When all epistemological authority remains with teachers, or with curriculum policy-makers, who decide what is worth knowing and doing, two of the most intractable educational problems remain—lack of student engagement and superficiality of learning, along with the myriad associated personal and social problems which flow from them.

The guidelines must emphasize the importance of creating a supportive community of learners, allowing children opportunities to make choices and construct their own understandings, providing children with engaging environments and meaningful activities that are tailored to their specific needs and interests, and creating curriculum that integrates subject areas and addresses children's physical, emotional, social, linguistic, aesthetic, and cognitive development (Bredekamp & Copple, 1997). Teaching practices based on these guidelines form a sharp contrast to more traditional ones, in which teachers strictly define what students need to learn and how they will learn it—often with "undue emphasis on rote learning and whole group instruction of narrowly defined academic skills" (Bredekamp & Copple, 1997). Although it is widely accepted that every classroom will have some didactic components (i.e., transmission of conventional knowledge), these components are found minimally in more developmentally appropriate curriculum.

Based on constructivist principles, *constructivist curriculum* advocates an approach to teaching and learning that is developmentally appropriate. Students in constructivist classrooms actively construct their own knowledge through "hands-on, minds-on" learning experiences (Murphy & Goffin, 1992). They participate in learning communities in which they work independently as well as collaboratively with others to solve problems that encompass a wide variety of content area curricula. The four developmental domains of *constructivist curriculum*—Sociomoral, Cognitive, Representational, and Physical Development—are encompassed in this process-oriented curriculum to address the developmental needs of the whole child. The literature reveals an ample array of studies suggesting that developmentally appropriate currriculum (child-centred, constructivist curriculum) helps children to learn and achieve more than didactic (teacher-directed, traditional curriculum) practices. Teachers must see themselves as playing a crucial role in children's learning and development. To accomplish this as a constructivist teacher, de Vries et al. (2002) identified seven principles of constructivist teaching. They are:

1. **Establishment of a cooperative, socio-moral atmosphere:** A cooperative, socio-moral atmosphere is one in which mutual respect is continually practiced. Every classroom has a socio-moral atmosphere that may be viewed along a continuum of coercive to cooperative. Cooperation occurs between students and their peers, as well as the students and the adults. Opportunities to work together in groups, share thoughts and feelings, discuss issues, and contribute to the workings of the classroom on an equal footing are some of the characteristics of a cooperative, socio-moral atmosphere. A constructivist teacher must create a community of learners in which autonomy rather than obedience is encouraged. All other principles rest on this first principle.
2. **Appeal to children's interests**: Curriculum that responds to the interests of children is one that will provide meaningful opportunities for construction of knowledge. A constructivist teacher must be able to

recognize, as well as stimulate, children's interests. This can be done in several ways observe what children do spontaneously, solicit children's ideas about what they want to learn, propose enticing activities, and provide ample opportunities for children to make choices.

3. **Teach in terms of the kind of knowledge involved:** Piaget's distinction among three kinds of knowledge is helpful to constructivist teachers. These types of knowledge are physical knowledge, logico-mathematical knowledge and conventional, or social knowledge. Different strategies of teaching are applied for the different types of knowledge. For example, conventional knowledge is arbitrary and children must be told or shown the information usually delivered through direct instruction, which is considered didactic. With physical knowledge, one assists children in finding opportunities to act on objects and find out their reactions. If the knowledge is logico-mathematical, one provides experiences through which children can reorganize their own knowledge.
4. **Choose content that challenges children:** Constructivist teachers create a culture of inquiry and develop curriculum that (1) focuses on "big ideas" that allow in-depth study, (2) provide activities and materials appropriate to a wide range of developmental levels, and (3) analyze activities in terms of regularities and relationships.
5. **Promote children's reasoning:** An important part of the role of a constructivist teacher is to use questions and other interventions that will move children's thinking forward. Sharing ideas and encouraging children to provide explanations are means for enhancing children's reasoning.
6. **Provide adequate time for children's investigation and in-depth engagement:** Adequate time refers to the amount of time during the day that is provided for children's investigations, as well as time over weeks and even months. Children cannot be expected to construct

complex relations when their exploration is limited to fifteen or thirty minutes a day.

7. **Link ongoing documentation and assessment with curriculum activities:** Assessment should be a part of teaching and not separate from it. In constructivist classrooms assessment has two forms—assessing children's performance and assessing the curriculum. Constructivist teachers strive to understand children's thinking by identifying the relationships they are constructing. Constructivist teachers must consider how to teach academics in ways that do not impede socio-moral development and that promotes both learning and intellectual development (de Vries & Edmiaston, 1998). "The challenge for the constructivist teacher in approaching any academic content is to distinguish what must be *constructed* and what must be *instructed.*" (de Vries & Edmiaston, 1998)

Concept maps and curriculum design: Concept maps can be used as excellent planning devices for instruction. Edmondson (1993) describes the importance of using concept maps to develop the curriculum for a veterinarian programme: "Concept maps are effective tools for making the structure of knowledge explicit, and our hope is that by using them in our planning... the material will be more accessible and more easily integrated by students." The type of curriculum described by Edmondson is based on constructivist principles. It is both problem-centred and student-centred. Extensive faculty planning using concept maps helps teachers to know what it is that they want students to be able to learn. Instead of asking, "what do I want to teach", the emphasis is on, "what do I want students to learn?"

Martin (1994) conducted a study in which he taught education majors to use concept maps to make lesson plans. The teachers in the study found the maps quite useful for the development of course plans. "Our students view concept mapping as giving teachers a more comprehensive understanding of what they are preparing to teach, eliminating sequencing errors, and enabling teachers to develop lessons that are truly interdisciplinary." The following list of advantages in using concept maps for curriculum design was composed from the work of Allen, Hoffman, Kompella, & Sticht (1992).

- By constructing a concept map, you can see areas that appear trivial, that you may want to drop from the course.
- You can discover the themes you want to emphasize.
- You can understand how students may see or organize knowledge differently from you, which will help you better relate to the students and to challenge their ways of thinking.
- The mapping process can help you identify concepts that are key to more than one discipline, which helps you move beyond traditional disciplinary boundaries.
- Concept maps help you select appropriate instructional materials. You can construct a map that incorporates teaching strategies as well as time and task allocations for various parts of the course.
- You can visually explain the conceptual relationships used for your objectives in any course.
- You can facilitate efforts to reconceptualize course content.
- Rather than being a traditional course plan that assumes students will integrate learning, concept maps depict the intentions of faculty—the integration you expect to occur.
- You can use concept maps to provide a basis for discussion among students and to summarize general course concepts.
- Concept maps support a holistic style of learning.
- Mapping concepts can increase your ability to provide meaningfulness to students by integrating concepts.
- Concept maps can increase your potential to see multiple ways of constructing meaning for students.

- Mapping the concepts can help you develop courses that are well-integrated, logically sequenced, and have continuity.
- Concept maps help "teachers design units of study that are meaningful, relevant, pedagogically sound, and interesting to students".
- Concept maps help "the teacher to explain why a particular concept is worth knowing and how it relates to theoretical and practical issues both within the discipline and without".

Steps in making a concept map

- Write down major terms or concepts about a topic.
- Identify the most general, intermediate, and specific concepts.
- Begin drawing the concept map:
  - Concepts are circled.
  - Place the most general concepts at the top.
  - Place intermediate concepts below general concepts.
  - Put specific concepts on bottom.
- Draw lines between related concepts.
- Label the lines with "linking words" to indicate how the concepts are related.
- Revise the map.

Like Concept Map there are other constructivist based methods which can be applied for curriculum designing and construction.

9

Constructivism in Mathematics and Science Education

9.1 CONSTRUCTIVIST MATHEMATICS EDUCATION

The most influential and widely accepted philosophical perspective in mathematics education today is constructivism which holds that individuals construct their own knowledge, it sees the learner as an active participant, not as a blank slate upon which we write or as an empty vessel which we fill. In this view, cognition is considered adaptive, in the sense that it tends to organize experiences so they "fit" with a person's previously constructed knowledge. As a consequence, both researchers and teachers ask, "What is going on in students' minds when...?", rather than speaking of behavioural outcomes and asking, "Which stimulus will elicit a desired response?"

Much of the old curriculum approach to Mathematics teaching is counter-productive. The instructivist approach has led to feelings of shame and inadequacy in learners (Peter de Lisle, 1997). The subject is feared and disliked, and produces a negative self-image in learners. Wilensky (1997) terms this pattern of "symptoms" epistemological anxiety. Basically learners do not have a way into the subject that enables them to access it meaningfully. Features of traditional Mathematics teaching contributing to this situation are:

- Unitary definitions of concepts.
- Lack of connection to previous knowledge.
- Focus on a single way to arrive at correct answer.
- Lack of a "personal voice", fear of expressing half-formed understandings, and resultant social isolation.

The "therapy" for this epistemological anxiety is Connected Mathematics (Peter de Lisle, 1997). This stresses the importance of multiple perspectives. It emphasizes the importance of messy, half-formed concepts for both novices and experts. Mathematical knowledge is seen as a field open to enquiry and discovery. It connects all concepts to concrete, intuitive knowledge. Above all, it foregrounds the affective side of mathematics learning, "...emphasizing the role of play, joy, wonder and curiosity".

Technology is an important part of Connected Mathematics. It is an agent of empowerment of the learner. It facilitates exploration through providing modelling tools. It becomes a means of personal expression on the road to concept formation.

A related new approach is Soft Mathematics (Devlin, 1996). This is based on the notion that mathematics is context-based, that different contexts require different depths of mathematical precision applied to the same information. Thus, a problem is approached in a layered manner, starting with fuzzy, non-formal methods, and proceeding to more formal ones as required. It is a non-threatening approach as it starts from the concrete, known situation and proceeds to more abstract levels only when necessary.

Humanistic Mathematics is another approach to the subject that attempts to overcome the stigma and anxiety generated by traditional methods. Students are encouraged to enjoy mathematics by connecting to it through projects, journals and any other channels that promote ingenuity and creativity and which link to their everyday experiences (Christensen, 1996; Mahdavi, 1996).

These alternative approaches to mathematics teaching are clearly very much in keeping with the constructivism, and they also are in opposition to the kind of teaching that characterizes the behaviouristic framework. With a strong emphasis on syllabus, teachers have felt that there is no time to waste on discovery, projects and the like. Setting high standards has often come to mean being overly harsh on learners and not attempting to enter their world of concepts. Basically there is no acceptance of the affective aspect of learning. By denying this in the interests of efficiency, the entire enterprise is doomed to failure.

On the objectivity and subjectivity of mathematics: The problem with mathematics and mathematics education is that if we mix the two then we will be placed in one of two camps: absolutism or fallibilism. Either we regard mathematics as a fixed and immutable body of objective knowledge that has certainty, and an existence that is independent of individual cognition or social acceptance, or we regard mathematics as a human creation, based on assumptions and conventions. In the former, mathematics is discovered; in the latter, mathematics is invented. The problem of mixing mathematics with mathematics education is that if reference is made to the teaching of mathematics as a body of knowledge then absolutism is seen to be implied. The confusion is the objectivity of mathematics confused with the acceptance by the academic community. It is easy to see how the error is made: if we were to regard mathematics as fallible and yet to have validity independent of individual cognition or social acceptance, then it would be very tempting to ask where that validity does come from and where does it exist? The error is made in the move from mathematics is fallible to it is the social that confers objectivity to mathematics. Consider the following statements by Ernest (1991):

- Objectivity itself will be understood to be social.
- Publication is necessary (but not sufficient) for subjective knowledge to become objective mathematical knowledge.
- To identify the immutable and enduring objectivity of the objects and truths of mathematics with something as mutable and arbitrary as socially accepted knowledge does, initially, seem problematic. However, we have already established that all mathematical knowledge is fallible and mutable. Thus many of the traditional attributes of objectivity, such as its enduring and immutable nature, are already dismissed. With them go many of the traditional arguments for objectivity as a superhuman ideal. Following David Bloor we shall adopt

a necessary condition for objectivity, social acceptance, to be its sufficient condition as well.

- It has been established that objectivity is understood to reside in public, intersubjective agreement, that is, it is social.
- According to the social constructivist view, mathematical knowledge is fallible, in that it is open to revision, and it is objective in that it is socially accepted and publicly available for scrutiny.

Mathematics is fallible, it is a human construct that has its origins in social and physical interaction. It is we who determine its axioms and its hypothetical/deductive logic. However, once its axioms and hypothetical/deductive system have been established then there exists an objective problem-situation. Following Chalmers (1978) argument that science is a process without a subject, mathematics is a process without a subject because its development creates objective problem situations whether or not mathematicians realize the problem situation. A particular community may or may not practise a legitimate mathematics, and different social set-ups have created different contributions to a single (albeit multifarious) mathematics (e.g. Pascal's France and the China that created Pascal's triangle centuries before).

This is an objectivist position because it implies the existence of mathematics as an autonomous practice, independent of individual or consensus opinion, that constitutes the activity involved in its development. Although its development is dependent on the participation of the individual mathematician and of the community, nevertheless, mathematical concepts bear a relationship to each other independently of whether or not the individual or community realizes it. Mathematical theory does not reside in Popper's third world of ideas (the world of the objective content of thought), nor does it reside in Plato's world of forms; it is, instead, constantly produced and developed as a result of mathematical practice. It is mathematical practice that determines the objectivity of mathematics, yet its objectivity consists precisely in having validity independently of individual cognition or social acceptance.

With behaviourism the ways that mathematics and other school subjects are viewed has changed. Curriculum documents written recently involve analysing the subject and topic into objectives. With the 'new maths' the ordering of these objectives was based on a logical analysis of the subject. More recently it has been based on a psychological analysis involving the order in which we believe students learn topics. In spite of the recent acceptance of constructivism both curriculum and assessment are still dominated by objectives. These layers involve moving from basic facts and procedures to merging this information with life experiences, and then with what we know more intuitively, this merging involving both analysis and synthesis. As we move on to understanding we need to add an emotional dimension, considering both heart and head, and see our world not only from the individual perspective but also from that of the community. Wisdom emerges when an ethical dimension is added to understanding and from this comes the possibility of personal and cultural transformation. For me, Hart's ideas resonate. Information is not the goal of education, and we ignore this merging of information with experience, intuition, synthesis, emotion and ethics at our peril. The challenge is to incorporate these ideas into education and mathematics.

Mathematics has traditionally been in the curriculum, this question of purpose has not always been asked or taken seriously, and mathematics has usually only addressed the academic area of growth. Every subject is taught to help each learner develop new ways of making sense of their world. With mathematics this means to be able to think of and make sense of aspects of their world quantitatively, spatially, symbolically, graphically, and in terms of relative certainty and of uncertainty. Making sense of one's world requires thinking so mathematics education involves thinking numerically, geometrically, algebraically and statistically, and this thinking in turn involves problem-solving, logical reasoning, communicating, making connections, and thinking creatively. With this in mind, it is believed that the emphasis in mathematics needs to shift from the current content orientation, to a thinking orientation in which the mathematical content will arise purposefully. And to a large extent, this is possible if this is constructivistic shift. Aspects of constructivist philosophy that can enhance mathematics teaching include the following:

A holistic, as opposed to reductionistic, view of knowledge. Traditionally-trained students are inclined to think of mathematics as the foundational basis of science: a timeless edifice to be mastered and from which to build other forms of knowledge. Social constructivism shifts the emphasis from mastery to interaction between students and disciplines, transforming mathematics from knowing to doing.

Motivation from physical context, rather than theoretical construct. Mathematics often emerges from empirical circumstances, rather than from theoretical concerns. This is particularly true for the curriculum in introductory courses. The order of presentation is reversed from the traditional theoretical discussion, followed by one or more applications.

Higher-level reasoning as opposed to skill mastery. The primary emphasis is on the ability to address a wide variety of problems, rather than those that fit simple templates. The advent of computer algebra systems will force this innovation upon us, to some extent. Nevertheless skill mastery must remain a concern, although secondary.

Quasi-empirical exploration leading toward abstraction, rather than axiomatic knowledge construction. This is one aspect of the Archimedean distinction between "analysis" and "synthesis". The former refers to the unpublished, less structured patterns of thought that produce the original path to the solution; the latter is the polished and published, yet often unmotivated formal proof. Constructivists propose to bring the analysis to light, de-emphasizing synthesis.

A continuous honing of native language skills, leading toward mathematical language. Mathematical thought remains an alien, separated skill in the public perception, partially because the synthesis discussed above does not often truly depict the thought process leading to a mathematical conclusion. The student's inherent mathematical ability must be brought forth from his/her existing reasoning and communication skills, not built from scratch in a new thought category.

The realization of these goals may occur in a number of ways, including (i) the lecture period (which becomes an interactive problem-solving time, leading to the development of theory), (ii) the assigned homework (emphasizing grasp of concepts already taught and skill acquisition), and (iii) the laboratories (which model mathematical behaviour in a variety of settings).

It's not surprising that constructivism has a strong voice in the current dialogue on mathematics education. Many are concerned about the success—or lack of success—of mathematics education. Constructivism cuts a nice path between the main ideas that have influenced how mathematics has been taught: the concept of mathematics as facts to be transmitted to the student, and the view that some people have it and some people don't, where the educator's task is to figure out how "smart" students are and choose the right tasks for them to perform. Questions remain, however, about whether these offer rich information for developing different ways of teaching. And what's to be done for the students who aren't succeeding?

In contrast, constructivism focuses our attention on how people learn. It suggests that mathematics knowledge results from people forming models in response to the questions and challenges that come from actively engaging mathematics problems and environments—not from simply taking in information, nor as merely the blossoming of an innate gift. The challenge in teaching is to create experiences that engage the student and support his or her own explanation, evaluation, communication, and application of the mathematical models needed to make sense of these experiences.

Given this view, there are many approaches to improving teaching: look for different ways to engage individual students, develop rich environments for exploration, prepare coherent problem sets and challenges that focus the model building effort, elicit and communicate student perceptions and interpretations, and so on.

It seems as though a belief in a constructivist approach to knowledge or learning is contrary to the fields of mathematics and science, where knowledge is viewed as true facts, principles, theorems, and laws. In literature, however, it makes sense that the reader constructs her own meaning of the works of Prem Chand or Anita Desai because he/she is interpreting the writings and intentions of the authors. But there is only one interpretation of 2+2, and it is 4. There is a danger in trying to apply that logic with mathematics and science because constructivism is not questioning the interpretation of simple arithmetic or the notion of gravity; rather it is saying that each person comes to construct their own conclusions and conceptions. These individually constructed conceptions are personally valued whether they are consistent with what the field deems acceptable or not. A belief that the world is flat is just one particular view. It was once accepted by society, but now is not. Bodies of knowledge including mathematics and science change, and what is claimed to be known in the fields is either a logical derivation from the available conventions, or "the best way of conceiving the situation because, at the moment, it is the most effective way of dealing with it" (von Glasersfeld, 1993). In fact, some constructivists do not acknowledge that there is a single truth to be known. Instead what is (traditionally) "true" can be thought of as what is viable (von Glasersfeld, 1993).

The shift of emphasis from the objective content to the subjective experience has serious implications for both the subject to be taught (e.g. mathematics) and the learning of that subject. These implications can already be seen in practice. Creating a teaching practice guided by constructivist principles requires a qualitative transformation of virtually every aspect of mathematics teaching (Schifter, 1996).

But it goes much further than that—the teaching practice itself would alter the very nature of the subject matter to be taught. If all knowledge is regarded as subjective, as in von Glasersfeld's (1984, 1995, 1996) claim that knowledge is a personal construct that makes sense of his or her experiential world, or inter-subjective, as in Ernest's (1991) claim that objectivity is conferred on the mathematical thought through its social acceptance, following publication, then the subject itself—as a body of knowledge—will be denied to many. Mathematics will be either reduced to the experience of the individual and his or her personal knowledge (the radical constructivist position), or to problem-solving that is related in its entirety to the narrow aspirations and social situation of the class (for example, the social constructivist position of Ernest 1991).

The emphasis on personal or collective knowledge has become so subjective that it has become fashionable to elevate student intuitive and idiosyncratic misconceptions of scientific concepts above scientific knowledge itself. Consider the following statement by Trumper (1990): One implication of a constructivist view of learning is that it is neither possible nor desirable to remove these intuitive ideas and to replace them with the accepted scientific concept.

"Mathematical knowledge cannot be reduced to a stock of retrievable 'facts' but concerns the ability to compute new results. To use Piaget's terms, it is operative rather than figurative. It is the product of reflection—and whereas reflection as such is not observable, its product may be inferred from observable responses" (Glasersfeld, 1987). Operative knowledge is constructive. "It is not the particular response that matters but the way in which it was arrived at" (Glasersfeld, 1987). But how is the student to attain such operative knowledge in mathematics, when the "structure of mathematical concepts is still largely obscure"? (Glasersfeld, 1987)

Most definitions in mathematics are formal rather than conceptual. In mathematics, definitions "merely substitute other signs or symbols for the definiendum. Rarely, if ever, is there a hint, let alone an indication, of what one must do in order to build up the conceptual structures that are to be associated with the symbols. Yet, that is of course what a student has to find out if he or she is to acquire a new concept" (Glasersfeld, 1987).

By rooting mathematics understanding in each student's individual sensory experiences, we are shifting the responsibility for success in mathematics from the students back to those who guide and lead the process of co-constructing knowledge. This, in turn, should radically change prevailing beliefs about who should be studying mathematics and who should be successful at it: everybody has access to understanding, not just those who possess the "math gene"—it should not be socially acceptable anymore to fail in mathematics.

Intertwined with these myths is the belief that constructivism is merely a rehash of past attempts at educational reform. Constructivism is not the only view that argues that children learn actively or that teachers attempt to understand students' thinking.

Constructivism is not the same as the "discovery" view promoted earlier in this century that, in one form, advised against telling students anything. Students can construct knowledge, even from lectures, if they listen to, and think about, what is appropriate for them. However, a difference exists between talking at and talking with students, both in giving students opportunities to invent mathematics and in encouraging positive beliefs about learning mathematics. One overarching goal should be that students become autonomous and self-motivated in their learning. Students should see their "job" not as finishing assigned tasks but as making sense of, and communicating about, mathematics (Clements and Battista, 1990). Constructivist views place more demands on teachers and children than do "unguided discovery" approaches.

Having students work with manipulatives and on projects is consistent with constructivism but not unique to it. Constructivist views emphasize understanding and building on students' thinking. Although accomplished in different ways, one main goal is for students to develop mathematical structures that are more complex, abstract, and powerful than the ones they currently possess (Clements and Battista, 1990; Cobb, 1988). No matter how ineffective or inefficient students' ideas and methods might seem, they must be the starting points for instruction (Steffe and Cobb, 1988). This idea implies that as teachers we need to learn from other teachers and researchers, and study our own students, to better understand how children think. We need to go beyond the general platitudes "children are active learners" and "start where the child is" when those merely mean where he or she is in the textbook. Instead, we need to study how children think about the particular mathematical topics we teach, and we need to work to understand our students' thinking at a level deeper than everyday communication. To paraphrase Papert (1980), you cannot learn much about learners unless you learn about learners' learning specific mathematics.

As teachers, we also need to reflect on the developmental progression of children's thinking to understand the wide range of thinking patterns of students in a class and to plan tasks for groups and individuals. In so doing, we move beyond traditional teaching and become curriculum builders (Steffe, 1991). Both teachers and students become more responsible for learning.

All these ideas culminate in the belief that mathematics is not "in" textbooks or manipulatives. People create and recreate mathematics. Constructivism emphasizes active, living systems, not passive empirical data. For constructivists, mathematics is the activity of constructing patterns and relationships (Wheatley 1991).

Role of teacher education programme: Commenting upon effective mathematics Hatfield (1995) says, "Effective mathematics is the result of a complex coordination of specific knowledge and specific beliefs. Too often, however, the emphasis within teacher education programmes is placed on the infusion of content knowledge, pedagogy, and pedagogical content knowledge, with only a cursory treatment of the beliefs that, for better or for worse, will govern the eventual application of what has been acquired within these programmes (Larry L. Hatfield, 1995). However, we need to remember that prospective teachers do not come to teacher education feeling unprepared for teaching (Feiman-Nemser et al., 1987). "Long before they enrol in their first education course or math methods course, they have developed a web of interconnected ideas about mathematics, about teaching and learning mathematics, and about schools" (Ball, 1988). These ideas are more than just feelings or fleeting notions about mathematics and mathematics teaching. During their time as students of mathematics they first formulated, and then concretized, deep-seated beliefs about mathematics and what it means to learn and teach mathematics. It is these beliefs that often form the foundation on which they will eventually build their own practice as teachers of mathematics (cf. Fosnot, 1989; Skott, 2001). As such, it is one of the roles of the teacher education programmes to reshape these beliefs and correct misconceptions that could impede effective teaching in mathematics (Green, 1971).

An individual's beliefs, along with attitudes and emotions, comprise the affective domain (McLeod, 1992). The affective domain is most simply described as feelings—how an individual feels about something. In the context of mathematics, the affective domain was introduced to explain why learners who possessed the cognitive resources to succeed at mathematical tasks still failed (Di Martino & Zan, 2001). In this context, the beliefs are what learners believe to be true about mathematics and are often based on an individual's own experiences as learner of mathematics. For example, beliefs that mathematics is "difficult", "useless", "all about one answer", or "all about memorizing formulas" stem from experiences that introduced these ideas and then reinforced them.

In the context of teaching mathematics, beliefs have more recently been involved in explaining the discordance between teachers' knowledge of mathematical subject matter and teacher practice. The researches have revealed that the formation of teachers' beliefs about mathematics teaching and learning come from their own experiences as a learner of mathematics (cf. Fosnot, 1989; Skott, 2001). So, a belief that learning mathematics is "all about learning algorithms" may manifest itself as a belief that teaching mathematics is "all about teaching algorithms", and an experience that "all problems have one solution" may manifest itself in the teaching that "all problems must have one solution".

Robust beliefs are difficult to change. However, an abundance of research purports to produce changes in preservice teachers of mathematics. Prominent in this research is an approach by which preservice teachers' beliefs are challenged (cf. Feiman-Nemser et al., 1987). Because beliefs that preservice teachers possess are often implicitly constructed from personal experiences as learners of mathematics, challenging these beliefs helps an individual make explicit the basis of their beliefs, thereby transforming beliefs from non-evidential to evidential (Green, 1971) and exposing them to the individual for critique and analysis.

Another prominent method for producing change in preservice teachers is by involving them as learners of mathematics (and mathematics pedagogy), usually submersed in a constructivist environment (cf. Ball, 1988; Feiman-Nemser & Featherstone, 1992). Theoretically, this approach serves two purposes. First it models for preservice teachers the ideas of constructivist learning, involving them in experiences which may be completely absent from prior learning encounters. Second, it uses a teaching methodology that repeatedly has been proven effective in promoting construction of new knowledge, new ideas, and new beliefs.

Some researches have shown that preservice teachers' experiences with mathematical discovery has a profound, and immediate, transformative effect on the beliefs regarding the nature of mathematics, as well as their beliefs regarding the teaching and learning of mathematics (Liljedahl, 2002). This approach combines the aforementioned methods by challenging preservice teachers to make explicit their ideas on teaching and learning mathematics in the face of their own experiences with mathematical problem-solving in group environments.

The teacher educators must make the pupil-teachers to realize that mathematics is that as something that one 'does' as opposed to something one 'learns'. These changes can be summarized as a change from seeing mathematics as a noun ('the rules we learn') to a verb ('to do, to struggle, to think').

- The meaningfulness of mathematics, not through its application to the real world, but through their own experiences with it.
- Importance of the group work to their experience of 'doing' mathematics.
- Through their own experiences with mathematics in a non-traditional setting they came to see, and to believe, in the value of teaching mathematics through 'doing', through 'talking', and through 'thinking'.

Apart from abovementioned facts we should note that socio-cultural theories, combined with elements of constructivist theory, have been a major trend in mathematics education research during the past decade (Cobb, 1994), capturing the interests of many researchers. The emergence of constructivism as a theory has increasingly been in the context of an emphasis on the socially and culturally situated nature of mental activity, with participation in social and cultural settings acting as a catalyst for cognitive development (Cobb, 1994b; Nunes, 1992; Lave & Wenger, 1991). Thus these theoretical perspectives suggest that different forms of knowledge emerge in different cultural settings in response to the needs and the problems faced by the people in a given place and time. Efforts have been made to incorporate the advantages of this viewpoint into teacher training programmes, with several recent examples of teacher preparation programmes modelled on constructivist and socio-cultural theories. Although still in the early stages of exploration, work by Lampert and Heaton (1993), for example, has combined research on learning and research on teaching by looking at both through a sociological lens. They advocate a new pedagogy of teacher education that includes field experiences in which preservice teachers have not only increased contact with teacher educators, but also the opportunity to grapple together with the deep and perplexing challenges of mathematics teaching. This approach to teacher education includes "a practice-centred process of learning to teach where the actual problems of practice are central, where the question of what it means to know and learn mathematics shapes the discourse, and where analysis and action are integrated in ongoing work with students" (Lampert & Heaton, 1993). Presmeg (1998) also reports on the need for a culture-inclusive course for both prospective and practising teachers, describing how such a course can stress the students' ownership of personally meaningful cultural mathematics.

A third example of socio-culturally based teacher preparation exists in the work of Cochran-Smith (1991). In programmes reflective of collaborative resonance, Cochran-Smith suggests that "reinventing student teaching is to link what students learn about teaching from their field-based school experiences through mutually constructed learning communities". The assumptions that guide programmes of this nature include more than simply teaching student teachers how to teach. Rather, it is teaching them how to continue learning in diverse school contexts by prolonging and intensifying the influences of university and school experiences. Programmes based on collaborative resonance simultaneously aim to capitalize on the potency of teaching culture to alter students' perspectives by creating or tapping into context that support student-teachers' ongoing learning in the company of experienced teachers who are actively engaged in efforts to reform, research or transform teaching. Thus, it is often recognised that educating the pupils mathematically is more difficult, challenging and complex than teaching them some mathematics (Bishop, 1988).

Also, the continuing debate over the epistemological nature of mathematics is relevant to teacher training too. Mathematics is still considered by many to be a neutral and value free discipline, but if it is socially constructed as a part of culture, as Frank (1990), Thomas (1997), d'Ambrosio (1997) and many others maintain, then the role of alternative cultures becomes a vital consideration. Some evidence for this view has emerged from word problems that have historically represented very concrete and complex cultural, social and economic relationships (Cohen, 1982; Swetz, 1987, 1992). Steinbring (1998) discusses the importance of epistemological knowledge of mathematics in social learning settings and his analysis suggests three important components that could be introduced into mathematics teacher education, namely: (a) the developmental nature of mathematical knowledge, (b) interactive social processes of mathematical communication, and (c) the interdependence of social and epistemological constraints in mathematical communication. D'Ambrosio (1997) maintains that multicultural opportunities for teachers are very common, "In the daily practice of the school teacher, opportunities for experiencing multiculturalism abound.... What can the teacher do in this situation? From the multicultural standpoint the teacher can learn from the student." This context, an increasing number of multicultural countries around the world (Gerdes, 1998), suggests a need to revisit teaching practice, and in particular teacher training programmes, in the light of society's multicultural context and ask whether teachers are being prepared to be active participants in the multicultural classroom. Bishop (1985) has provided a rich framework of ideas with which to explore this area, focusing on sharing and developing mathematical meaning between teacher and students and among students themselves. This, of course, involves language, which in turn is related to the social, linguistic and cultural background of the students.

Shulman (1987) stresses a necessity for teachers to have three knowledge domains: content knowledge, pedagogical content knowledge, and curriculum knowledge. That is, teachers need to be confident in understanding the content of mathematics, in their ability to teach mathematics content, as well as in understanding the curriculum if they are to meet the mathematical needs of their learners (Britt et al., 1993). However, many students enter their teacher education course being unconfident in their knowledge of mathematics. Teachers who are insecure about their mathematics knowledge lack confidence in encouraging the ideas of their learners (Thomas, 1999). Teachers with limited mathematics knowledge "will depend on the text for content, de-emphasise interactive discourse in favour of seatwork assignments, and in general, portray the subject as a collection of static factual knowledge" (Brophy, 1991). But even when beginning teachers are confident in teaching mathematics evidence suggests that they take on the teaching practices of their model mathematics teachers rather than the pedagogical approaches they are taught in their teacher education. Social cognitive learning theorists (McInerney & McInerney, 1998) allege that we learn through observation and modelling. It would, therefore, follow that student teachers would teach the way they learnt mathematics, what they observed and had modelled to them for many years rather than using a problem-solving or social constructivist approach. Thomas (1999) argues that a sustained level of professional development is needed if there is to be improvement in the teaching of mathematics because there is "as much to unlearn as to learn". However, there is evidence that teachers with limited subject knowledge are less likely to benefit from professional development (Britt et al., 1993). It is not enough to model for your students how we believe they ought to teach, expecting them to be active learners and problem-solvers (Thomas, 1999). What is necessary is to have our students reflect on these experiences so they do not merely imitate our practices.

Some concrete suggestions:

- Most of our student teachers entering teacher education are not confident in mathematics.
- As teacher-educators we need to consider how best we can increase students' confidence in both mathematical content and in pedagogical knowledge.
- Students and teachers need to be introduced to both theory and research in order to change their teaching practices.
- An effective understanding of both theory and research requires classroom teaching experience.
- Teachers need to be supported with ongoing professional development in order to improve their content and pedagogical knowledge in mathematics.
- Engaging in their own classroom based research is an effective way to bring about changes in teachers' pedagogical practices and understanding of mathematics.

9.2 CONSTRUCTIVIST SCIENCE EDUCATION

Constructivist learning is recognized as a valuable technique to increase the depth of understanding of scientific ideas through students building their own knowledge through inquiry-based exercises (Brooks and Brooks, 1993). There is also evidence that students taught by constructivist methods learn science concepts better than those taught even by talented lecturers (Hake, 1998). The constructivist approach differs from traditional laboratory exercises in that it is open-ended to some degree and is designed to make students confront a problem as a researcher does, looking at all angles, trying different hypotheses and tests, and using the power of collaborative thinking and their collected prior knowledge and problem-solving skills (Diggs & Kimbrough, 2002).

Scott (1987) defines a constructivist in science as one who "perceives students as active learners who come to science lessons already holding ideas about natural phenomena, which they use to make sense of everyday experiences.... Such a process is one in which learners actively make sense of the world by constructing meaning". Tobin and Tippins (1993) would add to the definition of the construction of knowledge in science education. They state that the constructed knowledge of science is "viewed as a set of socially negotiated understandings of the events and phenomena that comprise the experienced universe". They further explain that in order to have new knowledge, that "knowledge is accepted by the scientific community as viable because of its coherence with other understandings and its fit with experience". An interesting debate stems from this definition of how "new" knowledge then comes about. Tobin and Tippins (1993) continue to explain that "scientific knowledge continues to change over time because goals and problems of society change leading to new experiences; technology provides new ways of experiencing; what is known continues to increase at an exponential rate; and the individuals that comprise the scientific discipline continually change".

Science in constructivist paradigm may be explained by five Es such as Engage, Explore, Explain, Elaborate and Evaluate.

Engage: In the stage Engage, the students first encounter and identify the instructional task. Here they make connections between past and present learning experiences, lay the organizational groundwork for the activities ahead and stimulate their involvement in the anticipation of these activities. Asking a question, defining a problem, showing a surprising event and acting out a problematic situation are all ways to engage the students and focus them on the instructional tasks. If we were to make an analogy to the world of marketing a product, at first we need to grab the customer's attention. We won't have their attention unless they have a need to buy the product. They may be unaware of a need, and in this case we are motivated to create a need.

Explore: In the Exploration stage the students have the opportunity to get directly involved with phenomena and materials. Involving themselves in these activities they develop a grounding of experience with the phenomenon. As they work together in teams, students build a base of common experience which assists them in the process of sharing and communicating. The teacher acts as a facilitator, providing materials and guiding the students' focus. The students' inquiry process drives the instruction during an exploration.

Explain: The third stage, Explain, is the point at which the learner begins to put the abstract experience through which he/she has gone into a communicable form. Language provides motivation for sequencing events into a logical format. Communication occurs between peers, the facilitator, or within the learner himself. Working in groups, learners support each other's understanding as they articulate their observations, ideas, questions and hypotheses. Language provides a tool of communicable labels. These labels, applied to elements of abstract exploration, give the learner a means of sharing these explorations. Explanations from the facilitator can provide names that correspond to historical and standard language, for student findings and events. For example a child, through his/her exploration, may state they have noticed that a magnet has a tendency to "stick" to a certain metallic object. The facilitator, in her discussion with the child, might at this stage introduce terminology referring to "an attracting force". Introducing labels, after the child has had a direct experience, is far more meaningful than before that experience. The experiential base he/she has built offers the student an attachment place for the label. Common language enhances the sharing and communication between facilitator and students. The facilitator can determine levels of understanding and possible misconceptions. Created works such as writing, drawing, video, or tape recordings are communications that provide recorded evidence of the learner's development, progress and growth.

Elaborate: In stage four, Elaborate, the students expand on the concepts they have learned, make connections to other related concepts, and apply their understandings to the world around them. For example, while exploring light phenomena, a learner constructs an understanding of the path light travels through space. Examining a lamp post, she may notice that the shadow of the post changes its location as the day grows later. This observation can lead to further inquiry as to possible connections between the shadow's changing location and the changes in direction of the light source, the Sun. Applications to real world events, such as where to plant flowers so that they receive sunlight most of the day, or how to prop up a beach umbrella for shade from the Sun, are both extensions and applications of the concept that light travels in a straight path. These connections often lead to further inquiry and new understandings.

Evaluate: Evaluate, the fifth "E", is an ongoing diagnostic process that allows the teacher to determine if the learner has attained understanding of concepts and knowledge. Evaluation and assessment can occur at all points along the continuum of the instructional process. Some of the tools that assist in this diagnostic process are: rubrics (quantified and prioritized outcome expectations) determined hand-in-hand with the lesson design, teacher observation structured by checklists, student interviews, portfolios designed with specific purposes, project and problem-based learning products, and embedded assessments. Concrete evidence of the learning proceed is most valuable in communications between students, teachers, parents and administrators. Displays of attainment and progress enhance understanding for all parties involved in the educational process, and can become jumping off points for further enrichment of the students' education. These evidences of learning serve to guide the teacher in further lesson planning and may signal the need for modification and change of direction. For example, if a teacher perceives clear evidence of misconception, then he/she can revisit the concept to enhance clearer understanding. If the students show profound interest in a branching direction of inquiry, the teacher can consider refocusing the investigation to take advantage of this high level of interest.

Viewing the evaluation process as a continuous one gives the constructivistic philosophy a kind of cyclical structure. The learning process is open-ended and open to change. There is an ongoing loop where questions lead to answers but more questions and instruction is driven by both predetermined lesson design and the inquiry process.

Social constructivism and the epistemology of science: It seems that there are two senses in which the term "constructivism" has been used by the social constructivists in many of recent controversies on science and knowledge. One sense of constructivism is the moderate version that most scientists subscribe to. It holds that what we call "knowledge of the world" (including "facts" and "theories") is a set of beliefs that we have constructed by interpreting conscious sensory experiences (sensations and sensory perceptions), and that this construction is guided (but not determined) by biological, cognitive, and social (including historical) factors. Another sense of constructivism is the extreme version that many of the postmodern critics of science appear to subscribe to. It holds the view that there cannot be any universal criteria for the critical evaluation of knowledge, and hence all knowledge claims are equally good. The following statements are meant to flesh out the details of constructivism:

1. "Science" refers to a mode of inquiry, reserving the term "scientific knowledge" to refer to the product of the inquiry.
2. As many twentieth century scientists have repeatedly pointed out, science offers reliable knowledge, but not infallible or absolute knowledge. A belief that is accepted as "true" today can be rejected as false when fresh evidence becomes available tomorrow. We can provide reliable evidence to justify the belief that scientific theories are true, but we can never prove that any given scientific theory is true.
3. Science hopes to understand the Nature that exists independently of the human mind and society (where "Nature" includes the human mind and human society), but there is no guarantee that the "knowledge" that science offers is The Truth of Nature. Scientists grant that we will not discover the

Ultimate Truth of Nature. However, they believe that as the inquiry proceeds, we get closer and closer to Nature. Yet, there is no guarantee that even this belief is correct.

4. The term "objectivity" in the context of science refers to "independent corroboratability" or "convergence of evidence" from independent sources (what Edward Wilson calls "consilience"). Objectivity is a matter of degree and greater degree of objectivity does not guarantee infallible truth. Science does offer "objective" knowledge in this sense.
5. Science is guided by a set of critical criteria such as those of consistency with observations, prohibition against internal logical inconsistency, independent corroboratability, simplicity, and so on.
6. Scientists agree that all knowledge, including scientific knowledge, is a human construction. In this sense, the leaders of this century science are constructivists.
7. What is called "enlightenment science" constitutes at least the following critical criteria for admitting a knowledge claim as knowledge: (a) we should not accept as "knowledge" a proposition that is unsupported by evidence and reasoning; (b) disagreements are to be settled on the basis of reasoning and observations that people agree on, not on the basis of statements of authority; (c) reasoning is an extremely powerful means to knowledge; (d) no two propositions within a body of knowledge can be logically contradictory; (e) all else being equal, a simpler explanation is better than a less simple one; (f) corroboration from independent sources increases the strength of confidence in a knowledge proposition. During the early days of enlightenment, there was the belief that (g) when properly followed, reasoning can lead to totally certain knowledge of the world (e.g. Descartes). Postulate (g) is no longer present in twentieth century science. It is replaced by the following premises: (h) all human knowledge of the world contains some degree of

uncertainty (unlike mathematical theorems, claims about the world cannot be proved to be true, even though we can provide evidence for such knowledge claims); (i) given any finite body of information as evidence, there is always in principle many distinct interpretations (theories) which can explain it.

8. The epistemological postulates that characterize the mode of inquiry that we call "science" can be practiced not only in natural sciences, but also in humanities and social sciences.

What are implications of above stated facts for the science teaching and science teachers? As Bell and Pearson (1992) have pointed out, it is not possible to change what teachers usually do in the classroom (simple transmission of knowledge) without transforming their epistemology, their conceptions about how scientific knowledge is constructed, their views about science. Effectively, teachers' spontaneous epistemology includes many distortions and reductionisms acquired acritically by social impregnation that impedes a correct orientation of science teaching (Gil-Pérez, 1993; Hodson, 1993; Meichtry, 1993; Guilbert & Meloche, 1993; McComas, 1998). It is not a question, we believe, of engaging science teachers—not even science education researchers—in the nuances and subtleties of the epistemology of different authors. In spite of their differences, there is a common base in how authors such as Popper, Kuhn, Toulmin, Lakatos, Feyerabend, Laudan, Giere...conceive the nature of science, and it is this common base which must be enhanced, in our opinion, in order to facilitate a better understanding of the construction of scientific knowledge.

This common base can be expressed by the general rejection of an ensemble of distortions of the nature of science. This is not just a question of denouncing once again the well-known extreme inductivism of many science teachers' conceptions. We have to pay attention to an ensemble of distortions which support each other (Nersessian, 1995; Gil-Pérez, 1996; McComas, 1998) as, particularly: Extreme inductivism, enhancing 'free' observation and experimentation ('not subject to aprioristic ideas') and forgetting the essential role played by hypotheses making and by the construction of coherent bodies of knowledge (theories). On the other hand, in spite of the great importance verbally assigned to experimentation, science teaching remains quite frequently purely bookish, with very few practical works. For this reason, experimentation keeps the glamour of an 'unaccomplished revolution'. This inductivist vision underlies the orientation of learning as discovery and the reduction of science learning to the process of science.

Generally, the 'Scientific Method' is presented as a linear sequence of stages to be followed step by step. Quantitative treatments and control are enhanced, forgetting—or even rejecting—everything related to invention, creativity, tentative constructions.... Scientific knowledge is presented in its 'final' state, without any reference either to the problematic situations which are at its origin, its historical evolution, the difficulties overcome...or to the limitations of this knowledge, which appears as an absolute truth, not subject to change. The rejection of this rigid and dogmatic vision sometimes leads to an extreme relativism, close to the radical constructivist philosophical theses. A relativism both methodological ('anything works', scientific activity hasn't specific strategies) and conceptual (there isn't an objective reality which allows us to verify the validity of scientific constructions: the only base of scientific knowledge is the consensus of researchers).

An exclusively analytical vision which enhances the necessary fragmentation and simplification of the studies, but neglects unification efforts in order to construct wider bodies of knowledge, the treatment of 'border' problems between different domains. In the opposite direction there is a tendency today to present the unity of nature, not as the result of scientific development but as a starting point.

A merely accumulative vision: Scientific knowledge appears as the result of a linear development, ignoring crisis and deep restructurings.

A 'common-sense' view which presents scientific knowledge as clear and 'obvious', forgetting the essential differences between scientific strategies and common-sense reasoning (characterized by quick and very confident answers, based on 'common-sense evidences'; by the absence of doubts or consideration of possible alternative solutions; by the lack of consistency in the analysis of different situations; by reasoning which follows a linear causality sequence...).

A 'veiled' and elitist view: No special effort is made to make science meaningful and accessible; on the contrary, the meaning of scientific knowledge is hidden behind mathematical expressions. In this way, science is presented as a domain reserved for specially gifted minorities, transmitting poor expectations to most pupils and falling into ethnic, social and sexual discrimination.

An individualistic view: Science appears as the activity of isolated 'great scientists', ignoring the role of co-operative work and of interactions between different research teams.

A socially 'neutral' view: Science is presented as something elaborated in 'ivory towers', forgetting the complex STS relationships and the importance of collective decision-making on societal issues related to science and technology. In contrast to this vision of science out of context, there is currently an opposite tendency, in the Secondary School, towards a 'sociological reductionism', which limits the science curriculum to the treatment of STS problems and forgetting the search for coherence and other essential aspects of science. This spontaneous epistemology constitutes a serious obstacle to the renewal of science teaching in as much as it is accepted a critically as 'evident'. However, it is not at all difficult to generate a critical attitude towards these common-sense views if teachers are given the opportunity to discuss possible distortions to the nature of science, transmitted by science teaching; the real danger seems to be the lack of attention to what is acquired by impregnation, without conscious reflection. This reflection is absolutely necessary in order to overcome simplistic tendencies to accept 'what has always been done' or to look for a new and more successful 'recipe'. We connect here to another kind of criticism to the constructivist proposals in science education.

For all these reasons, the teaching strategy that seems to us more consistent with the characteristics of scientific reasoning is to organize learning as a treatment of problematic situations that pupils can identify as worth thinking about (Gil and Carrascosa, 1994; Cachapuz, Praia and Jorge, 2000).

This strategy aims basically to involve pupils in the construction of knowledge, approaching pupils' activity to the richness of a scientific treatment of problems, including, among others:

- The consideration of the possible interest and worthiness of the situations proposed, which gives meaning to their study and prevents students from becoming immersed in the treatment of a situation without having had the opportunity to form a first motivating idea about it.
- The qualitative study of problematic situations, taking decisions—with the help of the necessary bibliographic researches—to define and delimit concrete problems (an activity during which pupils begin to make their ideas explicit in a functional way).
- The invention of concepts and forming of hypotheses (occasion for using alternative conceptions to make predictions).
- The elaboration of possible strategies for solving problems, including, where appropriate, experimental designs to check hypotheses in the light of theory.
- The implementation of the strategies elaborated, and the analysis of the results—checking them with those obtained by other pupils and by the scientific community—that can produce cognitive conflicts between different conceptions (taking all of them as hypotheses), and requiring the formation of new hypotheses and the reorientation of the research.
- The application of the new knowledge in a variety of situations to deepen and consolidate it, putting special emphasis on the STS relationships which frame scientific development, and orienting all this work to show the nature of a coherent body of knowledge of any scientific domain.
- The conception of new problems.

The acceptance of a constructivist view of learning influences several aspects of science education, including curriculum, instruction, and assessment. In making decisions concerning science curriculum, educators must take into account what students already know and then attempt to modify and build upon this knowledge so that it agrees with currently accepted scientific explanations. In making decisions concerning instruction, teachers must first determine the prior knowledge of the students and then organize instruction to modify and build upon what the students already know. Constructivist teaching involves classroom interactions in which the teacher helps the students gain a deeper understanding of reality. Constructivist teachers provide structure and guidance for learning and constructing knowledge through their interactions with students. Five basic elements of constructivist teaching are: (1) activating prior knowledge, (2) acquiring knowledge, (3) understanding knowledge, (4) using knowledge, and (5) reflecting on knowledge (Tolman & Hardy, 1995). Each of these five elements is further described below:

1. *Activating prior knowledge:* In order to build on students' pre-existing understandings of a topic, teachers must become familiar with their prior knowledge. This can be done in many ways, including simply asking students what they know, brainstorming, administering surveys, and concept mapping.
2. *Acquiring knowledge:* Once prior knowledge is activated, students must interpret new information in the context of what they already know in order to effectively acquire new knowledge. In other words, students must determine the extent to which the new knowledge fits with what they already know.
3. *Understanding knowledge:* This involves students exploring and communicating their own interpretations of the new knowledge. Teachers must provide many ways for new knowledge can be shared. Oral reports, individual projects, group activities in which students express their ideas, demonstrations, and role-playing are all ways in which students can communicate understandings.

4. *Using knowledge:* Teachers must immediately encourage students to use their new knowledge in unique situations in order to make meaningful connections to their prior understandings. Problem-solving activities are particularly effective strategies for encouraging students to use their new knowledge because they allow students to express their understandings and receive immediate feedback. This is especially useful when students are asked to work in groups to solve problems.
5. *Reflecting on knowledge:* At this point, teachers must provide activities like journal writing and portfolios that ask students to look back at and analyze what they have learned.

It is important to note that these five elements should not be interpreted as sequential steps in the practice of constructivist science teaching. They are actually overlapping teaching practices that should be repeated and reused whenever necessary to ensure that students properly understand and retain science concepts.

In making decisions concerning assessment, constructivist teachers must embrace "alternative assessment" strategies in order to truly understand what students are thinking and to identify the steps they have taken to construct meaning out of their learning experiences. Alternative assessments strategies include observation, interviews, concept mapping, journals, performance assessment tasks, open-ended problems, drawings, and portfolios (Chiappeta, Koballa, & Collette, 1998). Alternative assessment complements the constructivist approach to teaching by providing ongoing assessment of learning and more accurate measures of actual student understanding. They allow teachers to examine the process of knowledge construction that takes place as students interact with new information. Alternative methods of assessment also provide teachers with more accurate representations of what students have actually learned about a particular topic. While paper-and-pencil exams may only measure what students are able to memorize for short periods of time, alternative assessments require students to demonstrate their knowledge to a much deeper extent.

In order to analyze and assess the changes that occur in students' cognitive structures as a result of instruction, the constructivist teacher could use the "concept mapping" strategy as described by Novak (1991). Concept maps are graphical, two-dimensional representations of a person's knowledge about a specific topic. They visually represent the relationships that exist between concepts within a person's cognitive structures. Concept maps are particularly useful as alternative assessments because they can be used to identify misconceptions held by a learner both prior to and after instruction (Roth, 1992). The observable changes evident in student-created concept maps represent the unseen changes that occur as the students assimilate and accommodate new information into their existing cognitive structures.

Because of the ways in which it can be used to demonstrate the process of knowledge construction, concept mapping is an assessment tool that reflects the basic tenets of constructivism. First, constructivist theory stresses the importance of considering what is already in the learner's mind as the place to initiate instruction. Teachers can do this by using concept maps before instruction on a particular topic (Roth, 1992). Also, constructivist theory views learning as a process of constructing personal meaning from interactions with the learning environment. In other words, students must show that they can make sense out of their learning experiences. Concept mapping is one way in which students can confirm their understandings by visually representing the relationships that they perceive to exist among important concepts.

The idea of constructivism has become popular among science educators as they have looked for ways to better understand the learning process. It is clearly evident that constructivist theory has influenced science curriculum, instruction, and assessment. Ultimately, the idea of constructivism can be used as a framework for creating a specific type of learning environment. A constructivist science classroom is a place where students are involved in scientific investigations that require them to ask questions, to find answers, and to incorporate these answers into their previous knowledge to develop deeper understandings of scientific concepts. In a constructivist science classroom, students are involved in hands-on interaction with scientific materials, and they are frequently encouraged to communicate their ideas. In a constructivist science classroom, teachers constantly assess student understandings and intervene with instruction when necessary. Teachers provide the necessary structure and guidance to ensure that students effectively incorporate new ideas into their cognitive structures. Learning in such an environment is a process of "uncovering rather than covering" information (Watson & Konicek, 1990).

For many students, trying to learn science is a downward spiral of confusion and failure. Classroom practices do not meet their needs, nor do practices seem to take into account their knowledge and skills. Every teacher has high expectations for their students. They want students not only to understand the material, but also to develop higher order thinking skills, such as analysis, reasoning, and problem-solving. Unfortunately, the day-to-day practices in most classrooms encourage students to learn only superficial ideas and low level skills. Without a strong conceptual foundation and without analysis, reasoning, and other skills, students will continue to adopt superficial and formulaic approaches to problem-solving. Analysis-based problem-solving addresses these issues. Taking into account students' prior notions enables them to distinguish scientific definitions of concepts from everyday definitions. Having them analyze physical situations helps them to relate concepts to each other, and improves their conceptual understanding even more. Having them reason about physical situations helps them to solve interesting problems. Encouraging them to reflect on prior activities helps them to structure their knowledge. This is the sequence of learning experiences by which students acquire the knowledge, the skills, and the opportunities to succeed. By using analysis and reasoning as a bridge between deep, conceptual understanding and proficient problem-solving, we can create a classroom environment where learning flourishes. This does not mean that equations are not important or useful. It means only that equations are not the most important or useful part of doing physics. Equations are needed, but only near the end of the problem-solving process, when principles, laws, and definitions are applied. It also does not mean that concepts are not important. Rather, it means that conceptual understanding alone is not sufficient to promote the problem-solving skills that we, as instructors and educational researchers, desire and value. Our image of effective classroom practice is very different from the images shown before. Communication is two-way, with the student communicating with the teacher as much, if not more, than the teacher is communicating with the student. The student is an active participant in the learning process—monitoring communication, evaluating his/her own learning, reflecting on what learning experiences are most effective for him/her and more. He/she is self-aware and aware of the thought patterns of his/her classmates. He/she has developed a variety of skills, including operational, procedural, strategic, analysis, and reasoning skills, and he/she knows when and how to use them. He/she has learned how to learn. Analysis-based problem-solving approach suggests an approach that removes the tendency to learn without understanding—a tendency that often leads to failure in science. It also brings back an enthusiasm for learning to everyone in the classroom.

Constructivist science teacher preparation programmes: Constructivist science teacher preparation programmes should be intentionally designed to be transformational, not just informational. Preservice teachers may constantly be given opportunities to make new connections in a setting focusing on personal empowerment and critical reflection. The programmes must challenge preservice teachers to move toward self-directed life-long learning (Osman & Plourde, 2003):

- Seek out and use student questions and ideas to guide lessons and instructional units.
- Encourage students to initiate ideas.
- Promote student leadership, collaboration, seeking of information and taking action as a result of the learning process.
- Use the thinking, the experiences, and the interests of students to drive the lesson.

- Encourage the use of alternative sources of information.
- Encourage students to test their own ideas, even predicting and speculating on outcomes.
- Use cooperative learning strategies that emphasize collaboration, respect of individuals, and encourage the division of labour.
- Provide adequate time for students to reflect and analyze information.
- Encourage and support the collection of real evidence to support ideas and the reformation of ideas in light of new evidence or experiences.

We can think of using technology too in teachers' training programme. Some of important measures based on Chicago Academy of Sciences (1998) are following which may be used by the teacher-educators themselves and also they can ask their pupil-teachers to practice these during practice teaching period:

- Adapt the online lessons based on students' own experiences and interests to better fit what they want to learn.
- Use the online lessons and information as a guide, not as an absolute rule.
- Focus discussion and brainstorming on students' prior knowledge.
- Encourage the students to have an open attitude about science and learning, and foster interest by acting as a facilitator in the understanding, rather than as an explainer.
- Use scientific models as often as possible.
- Leave time for reflection; students must have time to reflect on ideas and resolve conflicts when concepts do not fit their frameworks.
- Silence during discussion is not a bad thing.

- Allow students opportunities to have discussions among themselves; constructive dialogue is not a bad thing either!
- Ask open-ended questions and pose contradictions to student views to promote inquiry.
- Incorporate less structure in science instruction by using more cooperative group work instead.
- Teach the students to be aware of their thoughts and actions, and to feel comfortable with what is not yet known.
- Above all, enjoy yourself!

10

Constructivist Research

Many organizations have supported researchers in studying effective constructivist policies and practices, and in return, they have produced findings to help educationists, policy-makers, curriculum framers in general and schools, students, teachers and teacher-educators in particular to participate and progress in the general education curriculum. The number and percentage of research documents containing references to constructivism indicate that scholars are more interested in constructivist epistemology and pedagogy now than ever before.

Some researchers have urged the schools to take a fresh look at constructivism and its potential for engaging students and improving student performance in terms of understanding and knowing. So, what's appropriate? What benefits can be expected? What makes for good constructivist policies and practices? Research doesn't have all the answers, but a review of existing data yields some helpful observations and guidance.

The trend known as social constructivism—which has many followers amongst educational researches—takes phenomenology as a bases to state that research should consider the meanings and intentions held by the social actors and, in order to accomplish this goal, the researcher should approach the social groups putting "in parenthesis" his/her beliefs and values. This procedure is necessary because reality is multiple.

The research of social constructivism is much related to Discourse Analysis. Emphasis is often put on the role of language, on historical studies of our subject knowledge, and the often forgotten or suppressed role of power and institutions in forming that knowledge. Constructivist research may involve empirical case studies of scientific activities in order to learn how scientists do research and develop their theories. Constructivist research is mostly based on relativist and anti-rationalist assumptions and do not see science as guided by one particular method.

Sample of research outcomes:

- The largest study of constructivist versus non-constructivist education is by Pfannenstiel (1997) and Pfannenstiel and Schattgen (1997; Project Construct, 1998) who focus on Project Construct classrooms in Missouri where the state Department of Elementary and Secondary Education since 1986 has adopted constructivist education for statewide implementation (although it is not mandatory). Findings from this study show that children from constructivist classrooms were significantly more advanced than were children from traditional classrooms on performance tests of classification, writing, reading, and social behaviour. They were also significantly higher on standardized tests of mathematics and language. In constructivist classrooms, poverty did not predict children's learning except in the area of arbitrary conventional knowledge (such as the names of objects). In authoritarian teacher-directed classrooms, higher poverty was associated with lower achievement on standardized tests of mathematics and language while in constructivist child-centred classrooms, higher poverty was associated with higher achievement in these domains. The overall conclusion is that: Students whose teachers employ pedagogy based on constructivism attain higher levels of achievement than do students whose teachers use practices rooted in traditional beliefs about learning.
- The constructivist teachers reported greater use of integrated curriculum, active learning centers, encouragement of children's participation in making

classroom decisions, and an evaluation process shared by teachers and children (Morse, 1995).

- Children in the constructivist group had superior knowledge of the logic of commutativity (knowing, for example, not only that 8 + 2 = 10 but that 2 + 8 = 10) (Kamii, 2000).
- DeVries and her colleagues (de Vries, Haney, & Zan, 1991; de Vries, Reese-Learned, & Morgan, 1991) studied interpersonal understanding in three kindergarten classrooms differing in socio-moral atmosphere and academic programme and they found that the constructivist teacher provided the array of activities described earlier as typical.
- There is evidence that students taught by constructivist methods learn science concepts better than those taught even by talented lecturers (Hake, 1998).
- Piaget's (1932/1965) research and theory convinces constructivist educators that a particular type of adult-child relationship is necessary for children's optimal development and learning.
- Pfannenstiel (1997) summarized, stating "kindergarten children in constructivist classrooms are much more educationally advantaged than their peers in traditional classrooms".
- In an earlier study, de Vries and Goncu (1987) used the board-game format to compare interpersonal understanding between 4-year-old children from constructivist and Montessori classrooms. Constructivist children had a significantly higher proportion of Stage 2 strategies and resolved a significantly higher proportion of their conflicts.
- Results showed that children from Center A (the constructivist center) expressed higher personal autonomy in 1992 and 1995 than children from the authoritarian centers (Araujo, 2000).

- Analysis of children's activities showed that mean complexity score of children from the constructivist programme was significantly higher than that of children from the regular programme. Moderate or extraordinary complexity was found in a significantly higher percentage of constructivist children (Duckworth, 1978).
- Curriculum development occurs, not through imposition of new ideas on teachers, but through personal development (Andrey Grey, 1997).
- Student affairs professionals value holistic student development, active learning, collaboration, and acting over reflection (Love et al., 1993).
- de Vries and Zan (1994) propose that the teacher-child relation fostering autonomous morality is one in which the tPeacher cooperates with children by encouraging them to make classroom rules, develop strategies for resolving conflicts with others, and reflect on social and moral issues in literature and in the classroom.

Future direction for research:

- In addition to studying constructivist's overall effectiveness, researchers should examine how variation in constructivist approaches might influence their efficacy. One obvious question is whether constructivism is more effective for some subjects than for others.
- A comparative study of constructivist teaching practices of urban and rural teachers can be done.
- A comparative study of constructivist learning styles and assessments of urban and rural students can be done.
- A comparative study of perceptions of male and female students towards constructivist teaching practices can be done.
- A critical study of constructivist and traditional educational philosophies can be done.
- A study of constructivist epistemological belief system can be done.

- A study to modify and validate an actual and prefered version of the Constructivist Learning Environment for the use at the secondary and senior secondary phases of schooling in India can be done.
- A study to describe the learning environment of individual classrooms using the Constructivist Learning Environment in India can be done.
- A study to find whether teachers are able to make use of learners' responses to the Constructivist Learning Environment to develop and implement action research strategies to improve learners perceptions of the constructivist learning environment can be done.
- A study to underline how successful is the use of journals as a means of encouraging teachers to reflect on their teaching strategies and to improve their learning environments can be done.
- A study to find that the learners who have been exposed to NCF-2005 perceive a different learning environment from those who have not can be done.
- A study to find the perceptions of the actual and preferred learning environments differ for:
  1. Teachers and learners?
  2. Male and female learners?
  3. Learners of different ethnic backgrounds, etc. can be done.
- A study into the impact of constructivism on teachers' and learners' attitude can be done.

Sample of Questionnaires, which may be helpful for the researchers going to conduct the research in the area of Constructivist Teaching and Learning:

Classroom Observation Comments for Teacher Quality Measure

School__________________ Observer__________________ Time in _________
Teacher Code_____________ Observation Date __________ Time out ________
Subject/Activity overview____

Directions: Comment on whether the following items are present or not during your observation.

Tools of Inquiry	Noted	Comments
Employs constructivist techniques	______	__________________
Concept attainment/formation	______	__________________
Cooperative learning	______	__________________
Discussions/debates	______	__________________
Inquiry	______	__________________
Learning centers	______	__________________
Problem-solving	______	__________________
Projects/research	______	__________________
Role play/simulations	______	__________________
Other	______	__________________
Links new learning to prior understanding	______	__________________
Uses authentic examples and materials	______	__________________

Learning Outcomes	Noted	Comments
Engages all students	______	__________________
Uses effective feedback and probes	______	__________________

Instructional Opportunities	Noted	Comments
Engages students in active learning	______	__________________
Uses differentiated learning	______	__________________
Accommodations	______	__________________
Adaptive technology	______	__________________
Alternative activities	______	__________________
Inclusive instruction	______	__________________
Independent study	______	__________________
Learning contracts	______	__________________
One on one	______	__________________
Peer support	______	__________________
Small groups	______	__________________

Varied activities	_____	_____
Varied assignments	_____	_____
Varied texts	_____	_____
Other	_____	_____
Draws from students' prior knowledge	_____	_____
Models respectful communication	_____	_____
Listens closely	_____	_____
Makes eye contact	_____	_____
Pleasant vocal tone	_____	_____
Pleasing facial expression	_____	_____
Uses students' names	_____	_____
Other	_____	_____
Instructional strategies	Noted	Comments
Uses higher order questioning strategies	_____	_____
Varies role (teacher, coach, facilitator)	_____	_____
Motivation	Noted	Comments
Enforces classroom behaviour rules	_____	_____
Allow students to make some decisions	_____	_____
Uses cooperative/collaborative techniques	_____	_____
Employs encouraging feedback	_____	_____
Compliments sincerely	_____	_____
Praise for accomplishment/achievement	_____	_____
Other	_____	_____
Uses two or more motivational strategies		
Appropriately challenges	_____	_____
Creates curiosity	_____	_____
Meaningfulness	_____	_____
Relevance to students	_____	_____
Gives students limited control	_____	_____
Students involved	_____	_____
Other	_____	_____
Verbal, nonverbal, media communications	Noted	Comments
Uses appropriate oral/written communication	_____	_____
Provides media-rich environment	_____	_____
Books	_____	_____
Posters/pictures	_____	_____
Computers/software	_____	_____
Videos	_____	_____
Other	_____	_____

Employs active listening	Noted	Comments
Models appropriate nonverbal communication	______	____________________
Exhibits positive body language	______	____________________
Makes eye contact	______	____________________
Nods	______	____________________
Pleasing facial expression	______	____________________
Other	______	____________________

Planning instruction	Noted	Comments
References units of study or projects	______	____________________
Announces changes in lesson plan	______	____________________
Plans lessons with colleagues	______	____________________

Assessment strategies	Noted	Comments
Uses 2 or more formal assessment strategies	______	____________________
Learning logs	______	____________________
Performances	______	____________________
Portfolio/work samples	______	____________________
Post-test	______	____________________
Pretest	______	____________________
Other	______	____________________
Uses informal assessment strategies	______	____________________

Opinionaire for Teachers' Responses

Name: ____.

Qualification: ____________________________________

Designation: ________________

Teaching Experience: ________________

Classes taught: ________________

Teaching subject: ____________________________________

Name of School: ____________________________________

School Address: ____________________________________

Phone and E-mail: __________________________________

Residential Address:

____

____

____

E. Mail Address (if any) ______________________________

Notes:

- Please read all the questions carefully.
- Answer all the questions, as all questions are compulsory.
- Feel free to answer.
- Your response will not be revealed to any body.
- Take sufficient time before answering a question.
- Please answer the following questions on your own.
- These questions are not to test your knowledge rather to find out the general trend prevalent.

1. As classrooms are cognitive theatres. So, teachers should use manipulative material and handsome activities to discover relationship in classroom.

   (a) Strongly agree (b) Agree (c) Disagree

   (d) Strongly disagree

2. As teacher is responsible for teaching, so I direct classroom as per my desires and should not employ whole classroom discussions on topic.
   (a) Strongly agree (b) Agree (c) Disagree
   (d) Strongly disagree
3. Interaction is necessary for learning. Students learn better when they are engaged in dialogues with other students and teacher.
   (a) Strongly agree (b) Agree (c) Disagree
   (d) Strongly disagree
4. Learners have predispositions, in which modification for an individual is not possible due to shortage of time. So, I don't consider the beliefs and attitudes of learners.
   (a) Strongly agree (b) Agree (c) Disagree
   (d) Strongly disagree
5. As learner learns most from his environment by passing maximum time in community, so, I acknowledge the critical role of experience in learning.
   (a) Strongly agree (b) Agree (c) Disagree
   (d) Strongly disagree
6. I teach what students want to learn and not what I want to impart irrespective of boundaries of curriculum.
   (a) Strongly agree (b) Agree (c) Disagree
   (d) Strongly disagree
7. Teacher is transmitter of knowledge not facilitator.
   (a) Strongly agree (b) Agree (c) Disagree
   (d) Strongly disagree
8. Teacher is a guide in cognitive learning classroom and should help students to construct their own concepts.
   (a) Strongly agree (b) Agree (c) Disagree
   (d) Strongly disagree

9. I know more than students, so I impart my informant on students.
   (a) Strongly agree (b) Agree (c) Disagree
   (d) Strongly disagree
10. Personal conferences are good tools for evaluation than unit tests.
   (a) Strongly agree (b) Agree (c) Disagree
   (d) Strongly disagree
11. Modelling and concept mapping should be used as evaluation tool at the place of traditional homework.
   (a) Strongly agree (b) Agree (c) Disagree
   (d) Strongly disagree
12. Yearly evaluation is more necessary than continuous evaluation for students to promote in next classes.
   (a) Strongly agree (b) Agree (c) Disagree
   (d) Strongly disagree
13. Completion of curriculum in fixed time limit is necessary.
   (a) Strongly agree (b) Agree (c) Disagree
   (d) Strongly disagree
14. As learning is individual, social activities should be avoided for better learning.
   (a) Strongly agree (b) Agree (c) Disagree
   (d) Strongly disagree
15. Learning is not contextual and is predetermined.
   (a) Strongly agree (b) Agree (c) Disagree
   (d) Strongly disagree
16. Content should be spirally arranged rather than traditional branching arrangement.
   (a) Strongly agree (b) Agree (c) Disagree
   (d) Strongly disagree

17. Curriculum should reveal social issues as school itself is a miniature society.
    (a) Strongly agree (b) Agree (c) Disagree
    (d) Strongly disagree
18. I first enquire about own understanding of concepts before sharing students' understanding of those concepts.
    (a) Strongly agree (b) Agree (c) Disagree
    (d) Strongly disagree
19. It is better when students themselves decide what activities are to be done in classes.
    (a) Strongly agree (b) Agree (c) Disagree
    (d) Strongly disagree
20. Content is primary for a teacher and should be preferred over experiential learning.
    (a) Strongly agree (b) Agree (c) Disagree
    (d) Strongly disagree
21. As every learner is different but teacher has to choose a path for teaching by considering average mental abilities. So, I don't consider learners' mental model into consideration.
    (a) Strongly agree (b) Agree (c) Disagree
    (d) Strongly disagree
22. It is teacher's job to provide resources and assistance to construct concepts but not to state concepts.
    (a) Strongly agree (b) Agree (c) Disagree
    (d) Strongly disagree
23. Content is the focus and should be completed in specified time favouring over learner.
    (a) Strongly agree (b) Agree (c) Disagree
    (d) Strongly disagree

24. Understanding and performance should be favoured over information.
    (a) Strongly agree (b) Agree (c) Disagree
    (d) Strongly disagree
25. Teacher is cognitive supporter to challenge creativity and encourage independent learning.
    (a) Strongly agree (b) Agree (c) Disagree
    (d) Strongly disagree
26. Learning is better without active involvement of learner as they cause disciplinary problems by providing wrong answer. So, I avoid students' engagement in dialogue with others on topic.
    (a) Strongly agree (b) Agree (c) Disagree
    (d) Strongly disagree

Opinionative for Teachers' Responses

Student's name:____________________

Roll No.: ___________________

Class: ___________________________ Section: ______________

Name of the School: ____________________________________

Residential address: _____________________________________

Contact No.: ____

Email: ____

Notes:

- Please read all the questions carefully.
- Answer all the questions, as all questions are compulsory.
- Feel free to answer.
- Your response will not be revealed to anybody.
- Take sufficient time before answering a question.
- Please answer the following questions honestly on your own.

- These questions are not to test your knowledge rather to find out the general trends prevalent.

1. It is more important for me to think independently and generalize the concepts than merely accepting as teachers' statements.

   (a) Strongly agree (b) Agree (c) Disagree
   (d) Strongly disagree

2. Every class member learns in the same classroom but has different meanings for the same concept and also learns differently.

   (a) Strongly agree (b) Agree (c) Disagree
   (d) Strongly disagree

3. As I am special from others in my mental abilities, so, I need special assignments from others.

   (a) Strongly agree (b) Agree (c) Disagree
   (d) Strongly disagree

4. As I am learning throughout year. So, continuous evaluations should be introduced at the place of yearly exams.

   (a) Strongly agree (b) Agree (c) Disagree
   (d) Strongly disagree

5. As learner learns better when they are directly associated with the problem. So, I learn better when I am directly linked with the context of learning.

   (a) Strongly agree (b) Agree (c) Disagree
   (d) Strongly disagree

6. As learning is for me and my understanding of concept is necessary. So, project work is better for me than exercising the questions of the book.

   (a) Strongly agree (b) Agree (c) Disagree
   (d) Strongly disagree

7. We learn better when we are engaged in dialogue with other students and the teacher.

   (a) Strongly agree (b) Agree (c) Disagree
   (d) Strongly disagree

8. As every concept requires previous knowledge of content. So, rote memory of content is better for understanding the next concept.

   (a) Strongly agree (b) Agree (c) Disagree
   (d) Strongly disagree

9. Teacher is our guide to frame concepts for individual. Teacher is not an authority to pose as he/she wants to pose.

   (a) Strongly agree (b) Agree (c) Disagree
   (d) Strongly disagree

10. Content should be rigid and structured uniformly not flexible to meet as per the need of the classroom.

    (a) Strongly agree (b) Agree (c) Disagree
    (d) Strongly disagree

11. I learn better when I am directly associated with teacher's statement. So, fixed steps should be provided to resolve the problem.

    (a) Strongly agree (b) Agree (c) Disagree
    (d) Strongly disagree

12. It is necessary to teach what teacher wants to teach and not students want to learn.

    (a) Strongly agree (b) Agree (c) Disagree
    (d) Strongly disagree

13. Completion of curriculum in fixed time limit is necessary as I will be examined.

    (a) Strongly agree (b) Agree (c) Disagree
    (d) Strongly disagree

14. Learning is better without active involvement of learner as they cause disciplinary problems by providing wrong

answers. So, I feel disturbed when student engages in dialogue with others on topic.

(a) Strongly agree (b) Agree (c) Disagree
(d) Strongly disagree

15. It is necessary to state first what we are going to learn.

(a) Strongly agree (b) Agree (c) Disagree
(d) Strongly disagree

16. Content should not be the primary aspect for learning as I can gather more information than the teacher.

(a) Strongly agree (b) Agree (c) Disagree
(d) Strongly disagree

17. Classroom learning activities should be decided by the teacher and not by the learner as he/she know more than the learner.

(a) Strongly agree (b) Agree (c) Disagree
(d) Strongly disagree

18. I learn better when teacher first inquire about his/her own understanding of concepts before sharing students understanding of that concept.

(a) Strongly agree (b) Agree (c) Disagree
(d) Strongly disagree

19. I learn better when I know that on which aspects I will be evaluated.

(a) Strongly agree (b) Agree (c) Disagree
(d) Strongly disagree

20. Syllabus should be completed as per demands of examinations.

(a) Strongly agree (b) Agree (c) Disagree
(d) Strongly disagree

21. I am living in society. So, my learning should be associated with social activities.

(a) Strongly agree (b) Agree (c) Disagree
(d) Strongly disagree

22. Learning is due to combined effect of formal and non-formal agencies. So, teacher is responsible to associate both agencies with learning.

    (a) Strongly agree (b) Agree (c) Disagree

    (d) Strongly disagree

11

Constructivism: Potentials and Problems

For, Hein (1991), Constructivism, although it appears radical on an everyday level, is a position which has been frequently adopted ever since people began to ponder epistemology. According to him if we align ourselves with constructivist theory, which means we are willing to follow in the footsteps of Dewey, Piaget, and Vygotsky, among others, then we have to run counter to Platonic views of epistemology. We have to recognize that knowledge is not "out there"; independent of the knower, but knowledge is what we construct for ourselves as we learn. Besides, we have to conçede that learning is not tantamount to understanding the 'true' nature of things, nor is it (as Plato suggested) akin to remembering perfect ideas, 'but rather a personal and social construction of meaning out of bewildering array of sensations which have no order or structure besides the explanations...which are fabricated to them'.

Critiques of constructivism have made an unsheathing attack and said that unrealistic claims have been made by the advocates of constructivism. One such claim has been made by none other than Glasersfeld himself when he stated that "If the theory of knowing that constructivism build...were adopted as a working hypothesis, it could bring about some rather profound changes in the general practice of education" (Glasersfeld, 1989).

No doubt, there is much that is laudable, insightful, and progressive about constructivist theory and practice. It is far superior to the wooden and limiting behaviourist theory. The pedagogical implications of constructivist epistemology stresses on pupil engagement in learning, and the importance of understanding students' current conceptual schemes in order to teach fruitfully, are progressive; as is its stress on dialogue, conversation, argument and the justification of student and teacher opinions in a social setting. Importantly, constructivist's stress on understanding as the purpose of education is a major advance over the rote learning and mantra-like repetition of formulae that characterizes so many science and mathematics classrooms where pupils memorise everything, but they don't know what anything meant.

The main criticism is that constructivism maintains the widespread, commonsensical, subject-centred, Aristotelian-empiricist epistemological paradigm, and by correctly pointing to a major error in empiricist assumptions, it then swings to a relativist epistemology without abandoning the paradigm itself. The relativist conclusion only follows within the empiricist paradigm, if this paradigm is rejected—and there are good reasons for so doing—no such relativist epistemological conclusions follow, and certainly no idealist ontological conclusions follow. Due to this reason, Michael R. Matthews (1992) has labelled the constructivism as the empiricist wine, so criticised by constructivists, served up in new bottles.

Some extracts from constructivist's writings indicate the range of epistemological and ontological positions:

- Such (constructivist) approaches view knowledge as personally and socially constructed, rather than 'objective' and revealed; theories as provisional, not absolute (R. Miller and R. Driver, 1987; quoted by Matthews, 1992).
- Science as knowledge is an intellectual construct, and what are referred to as the laws of nature are merely the result of this human activity. Nature as such does not have laws (R. Nadeau and J. Destautels, 1984; quoted by Matthews, 1992).
- The fact that scientific knowledge enables us to cope does not justify the belief that scientific knowledge

provides a picture of the world that corresponds to an absolute reality (Glasersfeld, 1989; quoted by Matthews; 1992).

- Although we may assume the existence of an external world we do not have direct access to it; science as public knowledge is not so much a discovery as a carefully checked construction. (R. Driver and Oldham, 1986; quoted by Matthews, 1992).
- Put into simple terms, constructivism can be described as essentially a theory about the limits of human knowledge, a belief that all knowledge is necessary a product of our own cognitive acts.
- We can have no direct or unmediated knowledge of any external or objective reality. We construct our understanding through our experiences, and the character of our experience is influenced profoundly by our cognitive lens (J. Confrey; quoted by Matthews, 1992). Scientific knowledge is invented in order to make sense of observations which are themselves theory-laden. There is no great book of nature that can be consulted in order to check if the models or theories correspond to an ontological reality (J. Desautels and M. Larochell, 1990; quoted by Matthews, 1992).
- Constructivism is, logically, a post-epistemological position. The standard questions of epistemology cannot be answered—or even reasonably asked—from this perspective. Its premises suggest, rather, abandonment of traditional epistemological language (N. Noddings, quoted by Matthews, 1992).

Although most constructivists are ontological realists—the world although unknowable does actually exist apart from our thinking about it, some "radical constructivists" are idealists—the world is created by human thought and dependent upon such thought. Ernst von Glasersfeld's radical constructivism is perhaps the best known. He says: "The realist believes his constructs to be a replica of reflection of independently existing structures, while the constructivist remains aware of the experiencer's role as originator of all structures...for the constructivist there are no structures other than those which the knower constitutes by his very own activity of coordination of experiential particles" (Glasersfeld, 1989).

Although there are variations in constructivist epistemology, the common thread is that it is subject-centred, experience-based and relativist. But, its relativism needs to be distinguished from other relativisms in which the goal of science as a search for truth about the world is accepted and it is then asserted that we cannot know of different accounts which one is actually true or better. In contrast for most constructivists our knowledge does not tell us about the world at all, it tells us about our experiences and how they are best organized.

Lerman (1989), following Kilpatrick, suggests that the core epistemological theses of constructivism are:

1. Knowledge is actively constructed by the cognizing subject, not passively received form the environment.
2. Coming to know is an adaptive process that organizes one's experiential world; it does not discover an independent, pre-existing world outside the mind of the knower.

Michael R. Matthews (1992) says that the first thesis is a psychological claim; the second is an epistemological claim. Lerman believes in the first but implies the second. Wheatley (1991) offers a nearly identical summation of the epistemological core of constructivism. He says: "The theory of constructivism rests on two main principles.... Principle one states that knowledge is not passively received, but is actively built up by the cognizing subject.... Principle two states that the function of cognition is adaptive and serves the organisation of the experiential world, not the discovery of ontological reality.... Thus we do not find truth but construct viable explanations of our experiences."

Constructivism is correct in stressing the inventive, humane, culturally and historically dependent aspects of creating the theoretical objects of science—but none of this bears, of itself, upon truth. Further although constructivists stress this creative aspect of knowledge production, they seldom extend the analysis: their model of creation is a sort of personal model; it is the personal model of knowledge construction that leaves aside the necessary social and communitarian dimensions of cognition—the dimensions that inclined Freire, following Hegel, to say that "it is the 'we think' that determines the 'I think' and not the other way around" (Matthews, 1992).

Nowhere is this challenge more evident and therefore more problematic than in the application of constructivist teaching to the classroom. Employing constructivist teaching practices is problematic at two levels: (1) there is an absence of empirical evidence of effectiveness; and (2) employing this approach for which there is a lack of evidential support, means not employing instructional practices for which there is empirical support.

Whether stated explicitly, or as more often the case, implicitly, the implications of an epistemological view that contends there is no objective reality has a profound effect on how the process of education in the classroom is approached. An important and necessary question in the educational process must be, "How does one establish and evaluate knowledge?" In order to answer this question, we inherently assume that: (1) there is some correspondence between language and reality; (2) our propositions about our observations are logically coherent; and (3) there is a reliable and systematic method of testing our observations. If there is no reality other than that constructed by language and our narrative lacks internal coherence then the two criteria for verifying any observation have been eliminated and one is left with a relativistic nihilism.

This relativism makes no distinction between objective (i.e., verifiable) knowledge (e.g., astronomy) and superstition (e.g., astrology). As such, the merits of a given perspective are resolved through discourse (the methods of science being one form of discourse) within a particular community (i.e., the scientific or astrological) (Gross & Levitt, 1994). In the absence of a verifiable reality not only are the tenets of science reduced to a relativistic narrative, so is, for example, history. The anti-realism of constructivism allows for historical revisionism independent of verifiable historical data (since such data are merely constructed).

Von Glasersfeld defines radical constructivism in the form of two propositions (Glasersfeld, 1995), which may be summarized as follows:

1. Knowledge is not passively received, but is actively built up by the cognizing subject.
2. The function of cognition is adaptive, and serves the subject's organization of the experiential world, not the discovery of an objective ontological reality.

For the argument which follows below, it is important to note that these two propositions make explicit reference to cognitive knowledge, and to cognition as the procedure for gaining such knowledge. First proposition is perhaps not too startling. But second is problematic, and indeed somewhat provocative: at first glance, it seems to say that learning cannot give us knowledge of the real world! Does not this contradict the very basis of natural science? In fact, the epistemic position of radical constructivism has become the center of bitter controversy within the philosophy of science community, with critics charging that it denies the existence of physical reality.

Second proposition, makes a sharp distinction between issues of epistemology (dealing with the nature of human knowledge) and ontology (dealing with existence, or being—for instance, the question of whether there exists an objective reality, which is independent of our perception). And here it is important to note that radical constructivism does not claim that such a reality does not exist; rather, it asserts that this issue is a matter of preferred belief, and as such not within the scope of cognition. Thus, the theory does not deny the possibility of an objective reality, existing independently of all subjects; but it does assert that it is in principle not possible to obtain cognitive knowledge of such an entity, and hence it is irrelevant in the context of cognitive learning.

One of the charges most often directed against radical constructivism is that it is a "relativist" theory. And this assertion is, of course, quite literally true: radical constructivism does feature an epistemic relativism, in the sense that it rejects the idea that cognitive knowledge can have an ontological underpinning—

i.e. that it can be knowledge of an objective reality of some kind. In the academic discourse, however, the word "relativism" is often used with strongly negative qualifications: thus, critics will accuse the theory of featuring an "insidious relativism" (implying a crafty and treacherous attack on rationality), or even a "hopeless relativism" (suggesting that it is beyond salvage by reason). Quale says that the opposing epistemic positions of realism and relativism may, for present purposes, be described roughly as follows:

- Realism asserts that there exists an objective physical reality, which is independent of human observers, and that it is possible for science to attain true (correct) knowledge of this reality. In other words: it is in principle possible to discover an objectively true representation of this reality—for instance, in a scientific context, to find the Final Theory of physics...!
- Relativism asserts that it is not cognitively meaningful to speak of such an objective reality. Any piece of knowledge is (and must be) constructed by individuals, for some specific purpose and in some particular context; and its "truth value" can then only be determined in relation to this purpose and context.

The relativity of knowledge that is inherent in radical constructivism is claimed, by many of the critics, to imply that one must assume all knowledge to be "equally true". In fact, the radical-constructivist assertion that all knowledge is made (i.e. constructed by the individual learner), and not found (i.e. discovered, as a more or less correct representation of reality), is often taken to imply the extreme epistemic position of solipsism: the notion that we are all free as individuals to invent our own knowledge of the world, in any way we may fancy. In particular, this would then also apply to the generation of scientific knowledge—a claim that indeed is easily ridiculed!

Quale says that "this kind of criticism does not hold, for the following reasons: First, it is almost trivial (as has been remarked by many) to repudiate the position of solipsism, simply by pointing out that the world clearly does not always conform to our desires—a fact that is amply experienced by every one of us, every day! In other words: Life is not always happy days; and wishful thinking about "how things ought to be" will generally get us nowhere. Second (and on a deeper level), it may be remarked that the solipsist position is also epistemically self-defeating. The question we must address is this: If all knowledge is constructed by the individual learner, and resides in his own mind, how can he know that there is anyone else out there, with whom he can communicate and share his knowledge? Indeed, how can he even know that there is a world outside him—how can he exclude the possibility that he is entirely alone, locked up in his own skull and hallucinating all his experiences?" The answer, as given by radical constructivism, is that: (i) he cannot, but (ii) for him, this is beside the point! The fact is that for the individual learner such a solipsist stance may well be logically irrefutable (i.e. he can never have a hundred per cent watertight guarantee that the world he perceives around him is not just a hallucination in his own mind); but it is also existentially irrelevant for him (i.e. he will choose to disregard this possibility, in the way he conducts his life). It is in our nature to assume that the world that each of us experiences is in fact there to be experienced. In other words: we all accept as a given ontological assumption that we share an experiential world with other people, and that it is accessible for us to act on this world, and to interact with each other in it—indeed, for a learner to call this assumption into question would generally be considered a sign of mental aberration on his part...! Hence we may reject the "solipsism fallacy". Briefly, then, radical constructivism accepts that we share our experiential world with other individual learners. In fact, this is a fundamental premise for the manner in which we choose to conduct our lives—an integral part of the human condition, so to speak! However, the knowledge that we can gain of this experiential world is not just "lying out there" somewhere, for us to discover, register and store—it must be constructed by each one of us individually.

Radical constructivism has asserted that any knowledge must, in order to be accepted as valid, be constructed in such a way as to be viable for the knowers (i.e. the individuals who are in possession of the said knowledge). This requirement of viability means, first of all, that the knowledge must agree with the constraints that are imposed by experience—in other words, it must not be in conflict with accepted observational data. However, it is important to note that such agreement with experience is not in itself enough; viable knowledge must also respect the "rules of the game"—i.e. the rules defining the kind of knowledge that is being sought. Radical constructivism has also asserted that we are not free to dream up any world model that we may fancy—or rather, we are perfectly free to do so, but we cannot then claim that the resulting model represents valid scientific knowledge, unless it is viable for us in the context of science. Note carefully the last qualifying phrase here: it is important to recognise that viability of knowledge is something that is experienced by the individual knower, in a particular setting. Thus, the notion of viable scientific knowledge may be defined (somewhat tautologically) as: knowledge that is viable for scientists, i.e. for individuals working within the accepted demarcation of science...! It should be emphasized that there is no conception here of proclaiming this as the universally "correct" definition of viability: a supporter of creationism would presumably be able to claim in all honesty that his knowledge, as established within the guidelines of this theory, is viable (and hence valid) for him, even though it is in conflict with the corresponding scientific knowledge.

It is a basic premise of radical constructivism that we construct our own past. In other words: the question of "what really happened" is, from the point of view of cognition, a meaningless one! All we can do is construct our cognitive knowledge of the past to be viable—that is to say, to be as compatible as possible with present-day experience (which may include personal memory, hearsay, records, artefacts, fossil evidence,...), and with whatever theory and other assumptions we may subscribe to. The stance of radical constructivism is one of epistemic relativism: here it is cognitively meaningless to speak of "what really happened", and we have to be content with constructing the past, in a way that is viable. At this point we are likely to meet the accusation that so often appears, when discussing relativist epistemic positions: the charge of "denying reality". Does radical constructivism, then, claim that the past did not happen. The answer is no! We all have an intuitive experience of the notion of Time, and that includes the conception of past and future events, as seen from the moment Now. In other words, we all agree that "the past has happened". However, the issue is: what kind of knowledge can we have of the past? In general terms, the goal of learning here is to tell a story—or, equivalently, draw a picture—which describes past events, using (i) present-day observations and (ii) some theory which can be used to interpret these observations. In this way, we will (hopefully) arrive at some viable knowledge about the events under consideration. The story that constitutes this knowledge will in general have both cognitive and non-cognitive elements: in other words, some of it will be such that we can share it (i.e. demonstrate it, teach it), while some will be non-shareable (consisting of belief, personal wishes or preferences, etc.). Note that it is the cognitive (shareable) part of our knowledge about the past that is of chief interest for scientific research. The point is that it is not possible to decide who is right here; within the framework of cognitive knowledge, it is not possible to ascertain and demonstrate which of the two is "the closer to reality"! This is because the differences are of a non-cognitive character. Thus, the charge of the critics, that the relativism of radical constructivism must necessarily destroy the idea of valid knowledge, does not hold—that is, unless one wants to insist that knowledge must necessarily refer to an objective reality, as required by the epistemic position of realism. Elsewhere (Quale, 2002) it has been suggested that much of the misinterpretation of radical constructivism that may be found in the literature stems from the injudicious use of metaphors associated with 'truth' and related notions. These metaphors are very powerful, and they condition their users strongly to favour (consciously or unconsciously) a realist epistemic position: indeed, such a position is then often perceived as being "rational" and "obviously true", while an alternative relativist epistemic position is similarly seen as "absurd" and "against common sense". However, it should be realised that the metaphors do not in themselves constitute a reason to embrace the position of epistemic realism. Rather, it is the other way around: it is the adherence to realism that underlies and justifies the use of these metaphors. Summing up, then: We have here two epistemologies that are mutually antagonistic: an adherent of realism will in general reject relativism, and *vice versa*. However, it should be noted that the antagonism is not quite symmetric. Thus, on the one side, the realist would tend to argue that the relativist position is wrong, and that his position of epistemic realism is right; while, on the other side, the relativist would say that the categories of right and wrong do not apply here—both these epistemic positions are in principle tenable, but as it happens, he prefers relativism...!

As part of the criticism of relativism, we note that radical constructivism is sometimes accused of being logically inconsistent. The inconsistency arises (it is claimed) from one of the classical paradoxes associated with self-reference. In a simplified formulation, it may be described something like this: Consider the statement "there is no such thing as true knowledge". If this statement is true, then it expresses true knowledge, which contradicts the content of the statement; hence, it must be false. Or, in the present context: The basic claim of radical constructivism—that there is no true knowledge—reflects back on and undermines the theory itself, since it denies that the theory can be right! However, this criticism misses the point—that radical constructivism makes no claim to represent "truth", neither in a logical nor an ontological sense! In other words: it is not a logical proposition, to be deduced from an axiomatic base; and it does not claim to give a true (correct) representation of "the way the world is". On the contrary, it would be more correct to say that radical constructivism offers itself to the individual knower, as a possible epistemic position that he/she may find to be useful for him/her in his/her quest for knowledge. However, the actual adoption of this position is then up to him/her: he/she may choose to do so, if he/she feels that it resonates well with his/her own thinking. This freedom of the individual learner, to choose his/her own epistemic position, is fundamental to the relativism that lies at the heart of radical constructivism. And note that this kind of choice is an instance of non-cognitive learning—a matter of personal preference on the part of the learner. Relativism is not the monstrous delusion that many critics have charged. It lies at the heart of radical constructivism, as an epistemic position of great explanatory power, clarifying the scope and limitations of knowledge. It definitely does not lead to solipsism, epistemic anarchy or the devaluation of knowledge.

In the end, constructivism is a philosophy of learning that offers a perspective on how people—all people—learn, all the time and thus we can say that it is a powerful paradigm of teaching and learning but confusion about what constructivism does and does not mean has engendered a number of myths which has diluted and polluted it. Thus, we need to demystify such myths to have better insights.

Myth 1: Students should always be actively and reflectively constructing. One powerful way to construct knowledge is through conscious, reflective construction. As educators, we too seldom give students appropriate time, tasks, and encouragement to think deeply and to talk about mathematical ideas.

Not all constructions are of that type, however, nor should they be. Our minds actively construct ideas without our "working at it" or even being conscious of it. Even when we are consciously working on a problem, we are not fully aware of all that we are learning. There is a time for many different types of constructing: time for "experiencing"; for "intuitive" learning; for learning by listening; for practice; and for conscious, reflective thinking. During all these activities, students construct valuable, but different kinds of, knowledge. We need to balance these times to meet our goals for students.

Myth 2: Manipulatives make learners active. A related myth is that when students are using manipulatives, then they are "actively learning". Manipulatives can help students actively construct knowledge (Clements and McMillen, 1996); however, teachers can also use manipulatives to impose prescribed procedures for routine problem types. Students then learn to use manipulatives only in a rote manner (Clements and McMillen 1996). So teaching with manipulatives is not necessarily "teaching constructively".

Myth 3: Constructivist learners are lonely voyagers. "Constructing their own knowledge" does not imply that students build their ideas in isolation. Rather, the phrase means that one person cannot simply and directly transmit knowledge by means of words into the mind of another person. One can say words with intended meaning, but active listeners have to create their own meanings for the words they hear (Steffe, personal communication).

So students do not construct knowledge alone, even though each has to modify his or her own ways of thinking and acting. Further, although inventing mathematical ideas together is important, so is learning to better communicate these ideas to others. We must rethink social relations among students and between student and teacher. For example, constructivist-oriented teachers must be skilled in structuring the social climate of the classroom so that students discuss, reflect on, and make sense of mathematics tasks.

Myth 4: Cooperative learning is constructivist. Students can work in groups in many different ways, many of which are consistent with constructivist views of learning. Some approaches to cooperative learning, however, are based on an absorption view. The way students think and interact is more important than the size of the group in which they work. Just using cooperative groups does not necessarily make teaching more "constructivist".

Myth 5: Everybody's right! When we encourage diversity in students' thinking, it is easy to go overboard. After receiving several estimates of the sum of 17 and 21, one teacher said, "What's the right answer? Eight is right and thirty-six is right. Everybody's right!" Every student may have valid reasons for his or her solution, but the goal should be building solutions that make sense within the system of mathematics that is socially constructed by the class and the wider community. Thus, everybody's effort can be respected without abandoning the notion that some solutions are better than others and that some just do not make sense.

Myth 6: There is no focus for learning, no clear goal in constructivist-based instruction: Is it possible to create a purposeful learning environment under the knowledge construction assumptions of constructivist learning? The answer is an unqualified yes. Constructivism maintains that learning is purposeful, intentional and collaborative (Scardamalia & Bereiter, 1994), and that learners will actively strive to achieve a cognitive objective. However, constructivism does not prescribe a particular set of activities and thought processes in which the learner must engage in order to achieve intended learning. Nor does it offer clear guidelines for establishing a particular sequence of instruction. By no means does this imply that no learning outcomes are identified for learners as a group or that instruction cannot be planned in any systematic way. Rather, it emphasizes the design of learning environments that focus on knowledge construction, instead of reproduction (Duffy & Jonassen, 1993). Such environments, as Jonassen (1991) put it, "are not unregulated, anarchic, sink-or-swim, open-discovery learning cesspools that many fear". Constructivist learning environments are carefully designed for a knowledge construction task. Designing such a constructivist learning environment is admittedly a difficult task because there is a certain degree of unpredictability of outcome and complexity in knowledge construction process.

Myth 7: Constructivist based instruction is not thoroughly planned; careful preparation is less important than in traditional instruction: It is learnt that to design a constructivist learning environment, a teacher must first define a learning focus, some challenge, case or problem. What constitutes a problem is any relatively complex task (for the given learner), and ideally, one that is an authentic activity (i.e., design and construct a parallel and a series circuit). He/she also has to define a set of instructional goals and objectives, that is, specify what the learner must know to meet the task/challenge (how to construct a simple circuit, how to design and construct a parallel and a series circuit, identify the differences between a parallel and a series circuit). The learning strategies (where and how the learner will obtain those skills and knowledge) and the tools that can be used to better understand the problem/task/case must be identified as well. However, all of these design decisions are negotiated and refined through a collaborative process between the teacher and learners. Once students are presented with a learning focus or challenge, the teacher and learners negotiate and refine what the learners have to learn (based on individual prior learning histories and predilections), where and how they are to acquire the knowledge and skills, and how they are to demonstrate the intended learning (performance criteria). Among the more important aspects of the teacher-student negotiation is reaching agreement on how the learner will demonstrate the desired learning performance. Without question, then, there is concern for validating the quality of students' achievement (i.e., assessing students' learning).

Myth 8: There is an absence of structure for learning in a constructivist learning environment: Structure also exists in a constructivist learning environment. It emerges in two ways. On the one hand, a curriculum or a lesson has an organizing topic, task or question (design and construct a parallel and a series circuit) that sets the initial direction of the classroom conversation (Applebee, 1996). This overall focus provides direction for decisions for creating a seminal learning experience and key essential learning materials, as well as what will be peripheral to the principal topic or task. The judgment of which potentially related topics will be relevant to the learning of the broader instructional goal, however, will continue to evolve in response to the interests and knowledge of each group of students.

The second aspect of structure involves the relationships among the various parts of a learning experience. For example, when presented with a problem to be solved, the teacher and learners search for its causes, note similarities and differences with tasks with which the learners are familiar, and classify it hierarchically or taxonomically as part of a larger system. Thus, a constructivist teacher engages in a complex planning process although one that is different from what is prescribed in typical instructional theories.

Myth 9: As long as learners are involved in discussion and other forms of social interaction, learning will take place: In a constructivist learning environment, teachers must monitor discussions carefully to see if students get off track or develop misunderstandings about the topic, or if there is a need to intervene and redirect the discussion (Brown & Campione, 1994). It is imperative that the teacher carefully monitor group work and whole-class discussion and intervene as necessary to keep students on track, to stimulate consideration of key issues and perspectives, and to lead students to correct their misunderstandings. This calls for highly sophisticated teaching, requiring careful teacher judgment, essential aspects of the constructivist teacher's role.

Myth 10: Since teachers are not primarily engaged in delivering instruction (lecturing and explaining), their role in the classroom is less important: In a constructivist learning environment, the teacher is certainly no less important; but the role of the teacher changes so that the focus is on guiding rather than telling the learner. Indeed, an argument can be made that teachers' roles are both more important and more difficult when teaching based on constuctivist views of learning. Guiding students to genuine understanding is a sophisticated process; no rules tell us when to intervene or how extensive the intervention should be. Teachers must make these decisions on their own, based on their knowledge of subject matter, learners, and learners' past experiences. Moreover, the number of on-the-spot decisions that teachers must make in a constructivist learning environment requires skilful, reflective and spontaneous teachers who are capable of mentoring, coaching and facilitating students' learning.

Bibliography

Alfonso J. Damico (1978). Individuality and Community: The Social and Political Thought of John Dewey. Gainesville, FL: University Presses of Florida.

Allen, B.S., Hoffman, R.P., Kompella, J., & Sticht, T.G. (1993). *Computer-based mapping for curriculum development.* In: Proceedings of selected Research and Development Presentations Technology sponsored by the Research and Theory Division. New Orleans, LA (Eric Document Reproduction Services No. ED 362 145).

Anderson, J.R., Reder, L.M. & Simon, H.A. (2000, Summer). Applications and Misapplications of Cognitive Psychology to Mathematics Education. *Texas Educational Review.*

Atherton, J.S. (2005). Learning and Teaching: Assimilation and Accommodation [On-line] UK: Available: http://www.learningandteaching.info/learning/assimacc.htm.

Bendar, A.K., Cunningham, D., Duffy, T.M. & Perry, J.D. (1992). Theory into Practice: How do we Link? In T. M. Duffy, & D.H. Jonassen (Eds.), *Constructivism and the Technology of Instruction: A Conversation.* Hillsdale, NJ: Lawrence Erlbaum Associates, Publishers.

Berger, Kathleen S. (1978). *The Developing Person.* New York, NY: Worth Publishers.

Blanchette, J. & Kanuka, H. (1999). Applying constructivist learning principles in the virtual classroom. *Proceedings of Ed-Media/Ed-Telecom 99 World Conference*, June, 1999, Seattle, WA.

Bredekamp, S. & Copple, C. (Eds.) (1997). *Developmentally appropriate practice in early childhood programs* (Rev. ed). Washington, DC: National Association for the Education of Young Children.

Brooks, J. & Brooks, M. (1993). *In search of understanding: The case for constructivist classrooms.* Alexandria, VA: Association for Supervision and Curriculum Development.

Brooks, J. & Brooks, M. (1993). *The Case for a Constructivist Classroom.* Alexandria, VA. ASCD.

Brown, J.S., Collins, A. & Duguid, P. (1989). Situated cognition and the culture of learning. *Educational Researcher, 18*, 32-42.

Bruner, J. (1966). *Toward a Theory of Instruction.* Cambridge, MA: Harvard University Press.

Bruner, J. (1971). *The Relevance of Education.* N.Y.: Norton.

Bruner, J. (1986). *Actual Minds, Possible Worlds.* Cambridge, MA: Harvard University Press.

Bruner, J. (1990). *Acts of Meaning.* Cambridge, MA: Harvard University Press.

Bruner, J. (1996). *The Culture of Education.* Cambridge, MA: Harvard University Press.

Cobb, P. (1996). Constructivism and learning. In E. De Corte and F.E. Weinert (Eds). *International Encyclopaedia of Developmental and Instructional Psychology*, pp. 338-41, Pergamon Press.

Cobb, P. (1996). *Where is the Mind? A Co-ordination of Socio-cultural and Cognitive Constructivist Perspectives.* Constructivism: Theory, Perspectives and Practice, C.T. Fosnot (ed.), Teachers College Press, New York.

Cobb, Paul (1994). Constructivism in math and science education. *Educational Researcher.* 23(7). 13-20.

Cobern, W. (1993). Contextual constructivism in Tobin, K. (Ed). *The Practice of Constructivism in Science Education.* Washington DC. AAAS. pp. 51-69.

Cobern, W.W. (1991). *Contextual constructivism: The impact of culture on the learning and teaching of science.* Paper presented at the annual meeting of the National Association for Research in Science Teaching. Lake Geneva, WI. April 7-10.

Cochran-Smith, M. & Lytle, S. (eds) (1993). Inside/outside: teacher research and knowledge. New York: Teachers College Press.

Cochran-Smith, M. (2003). Learning and unlearning: the education of teacher educators, Teaching and Teacher Education, No. 19, pp. 5–28.

Cunningham, D.J. (1991). Assessing constructions and constructing assessments: A dialogue. *Educational Technology, (31) 5*, 13-17.

Cunningham, D.J. (1992). Assessing constructions and constructing assessments: A dialogue. In T.M. Duffy & D.H. Jonassen (Eds). *Constructivism and the technology of instruction: A conversation.* Hillsdale, NJ: Lawrence Erlbaum Associates, Publishers.

de Vries, R., Zan, B., Hildebrandt, C., Edmiaston, R. & Sales, C. (2002). *Developing Constructivist Early Childhood Curricula.* New York: Teacher's College Press.

Dewey, J. (1916). *Democracy and Education: An Introduction to the Philosophy of Education*, Macmillan Company. Also at [http://www.ilt.columbia.edu/publications/dewey.html]

Dewey, J. (1938). *Experience and Education.* New York: Macmillan.

Dewey, J. (1933). How we think: a restatement of the relation of reflective thinking to the educative process. Chicago: Henry Regnery.

Duffy, T.M. & Bednar, A.K. (1991). Attempting to come to grips with alternative perspectives. *Educational Technology, (31)* 10, 12-15.

Duffy, T.M. & Jonassen, D.H. (1991). *Constructivism: New Implications for Instructional Technology?, (30)* 10, 7-12.

Duffy, T.M. & Jonassen, D.H. (1992). *Constructivism and the Technology of Instruction: A conversation.* Hillsdale, NJ: Lawrence Erlbaum Associates, Publishers.

Duffy, T.M., Lowych, J., Jonassen, D.H. & Welsh, T. M. (1993). *Designing Environments for Constructive Learning.* New York, NY: NATO Scientific Affairs Division.

Edmondson, K.M. (1993). *Concept mapping for the development of medical curricula.* Paper presented at the Annual Conference of the American Educational Research Association, Atlanta, GA (Eric Document Reproduction Services No. ED 360 322).

Eisner, E. (1991). *The Enlightened Eye: Qualitative Inquiry and the Enhancement of Educational Practice*, Macmillan, New York.

Ernest, P. (1991). *The Philosophy of Mathematics*, The Falmer Press, London.

Ernest, P. (1994). 'Social Constructivism and the Psychology of Mathematics Education' in P. Ernest (Ed.) *Constructing Mathematical Knowledge: Epistemology and Mathematical Education*, The Falmer Press, London, pp. 62-72.

Evans, R. (1973). *Jean Piaget: The Man and His Ideas.* New York: E.P. Dutton & Co., Inc.

Fosnot, C. (1989). *Enquiring teachers, enquiring learners: a constructivist approach for teaching.* New York: Teachers College Press.

Fosnot, C.T. (1996). 'Constructivism: A Psychological Theory of Learning', in C.T. Fosnot (ed.). *Constructivism: Theory, Perspectives and Practice*, Teachers College Press, New York.

Fosnot, C.T. (1996). Constructivism: A psychological theory of learning. In C.T. Fosnot (Ed.), *Constructivism: Theory, Perspectives, and Practice.* New York, NY: Teachers College Press.

Foucault, M. (1977). 'The political function of the intellectual', *Radical Philosophy, 17.*

Gallimore, R. & Tharp, R. (1990). Teaching mind in society: teaching, schooling and literate discourse. · In L. Moll (ed.) *Vygotsky and Education: Instructional Implications and Applications of Sociohistorical Psychology.* Cambridge, UK: Cambridge University Press, pp. 175–205.

Gergen, K.J. (1991). *The Saturated Self.* New York: Basic Books.

Gergen, K.J. (2001). *An Invitation to Social Construction.* London: Sage Publications.

Glaserfeld, E.von (1996). Introduction: Aspects of Constructivism. In C.T. Fosnot (ed.) *Constructivism: Theory, Perspectives, and Practice.* New York, NY: Teachers College Press.

Glasersfeld, E. von (1984). 'An Introduction to Radical Constructivism', in P. Watzlawick (ed.) *The Invented Reality*, London, W.W. Norton and Co.

Glasersfeld, E. von (1987). Learning as a constructive activity. In: Janvier, C. (ed.) *Problems of Representation in the Teaching and Learning of Mathematics.* Lawrence Erlbaum: Hillsdale, NJ, pp. 3–18.

Glasersfeld, E. von (1990). An exposition of constructivism: Why some like it radical. In R.B. Davis, C.A. Maher and N. Noddings (Eds.) *Constructivist View on the Teaching and Learning of Mathematics* (pp. 19-29). Reston, Virginia: Council of Teachers of Mathematics.

Glasersfeld, E. von (1995). *Radical Constructivism: A Way of Knowing and Learning,* The Falmer Press, London.

Glasersfeld, E. von (2004a). *Learning, Cybernetics, holograms.* Karl Jasper Forum TA73 R8. http://www.kjf.ca/.

Glasersfeld, E. von (2004b). *Representation and Communication.* Karl Jasper Forum TA73 R10. http://www.kjf.ca/.

Goodlad, J.I. (1979). *Curriculum Inquiry. The Study of Curriculum Practice,* New York: McGraw-Hill.

Hannafin, M.J. and Peck, K.L. (1988). *The Design, Development and Evaluation of Instructional Software.* New York: Macmillan.

Herman, W.E. (1995). *Humanistic influences on a constructivist approach to teaching and learning.* Paper presented at the Annual Meeting of the American Educational Research Association, San Francisco, CA (Eric Document Reproduction Services No. ED 393 814).

Hunt, J. (1990), 'Philosophy of adventure education', in J. Miles and S. Priest (eds.) *Adventure Education*, Venture Publishing, Passedina.

Jaworski, B. (1994). *Investigating Mathematics Teaching: A Constructivist Enquiry*. London, The Falmer Press.

Johnson, D. & Johnson, R. (1987). *Learning Together & Alone: Cooperative, competitive, & individualistic learning*. Englewood Cliffs, NJ. Prentice-Hall.

Jonassen, D. and Mayes, J.T. (1993). A Manifesto for a Constructivist Approach to Technology in Higher Education. Available online: http://www.icbl.hw.ac.uk/ctl/msc/ceejw1/paper11.html.

Jonassen, D.H. & Welsh, T. (1993). *Designing Environments for Constructive Learning* (eds.). New York, NY: NATO Scientific Affairs Division.

Jonassen, D.H. (1988). *Instructional Designs for Microcomputer Courseware*. Hillsdale, NJ: Lawrence Erlbaum.

Jonassen, D.H. (1990). Thinking technology: Toward a constructivist view of instructional design. *Educational Technology, 30*(9), 32-34.

Jonassen, D.H. (1993). *Computers in the Classroom: Mindtools for Critical Thinking*. Englewood Cliffs, NJ: Prentice Hall.

Jonassen, D.H. (1997). Instructional design models for well-structured and ill-structured problem-solving learning outcomes. *ETR&D (45)* 1, 65-94.

Jonassen, D.H. Evaluating constructivist learning. In T.M. Duffy & D.H. Jonassen, *Constructivism and the Technology of Instruction*, New Jersey, Educational Technology Publications, 1992, pp. 137-48.

Jonassen, D.H., Peck, K.L. & Wilson, B.G. (1999). *Learning with Technology: A Constructivist Perspective*. Upper Saddle River, NJ: Prentice-Hall, Inc.

Kant, Immanuel, Werner S. Pluhar, tr. 1996 [1781, 1787]. *Critique of Pure Reason*. Indianapolis: Hackett Publishing Company.

Kelly, G.A. (1955). *The Psychology of Personal Constructs* (2 vols.). New York, NY: Norton.

Kovalik, S. (1994). *ITI: The Model Integrated Thematic Instruction*. Kent, WA: Books for Educators.

Kozmetsky, G. (1980). The significant role of problem-solving in education. In O. Tuma & Reif (Eds.) *Problem-solving and Education: Issues in teaching and research*. Hillsdale , NJ. Laurence Erlbaum Press.

Kuhn, T.S. (1962). *The Structure of Scientific Revolutions*. Chicago: University of Chicago Press.

Lacey, C.A. & Merseth, K.K. (1993). Cases, hypermedia and computer networks: 3 curricular innovations for teacher education. *Journal of Curricular Studies, 25*(6), 543-51.

Lakatos, I. (1976). Proofs and Refutations. The logic of mathematical discovery. Cambridge University Press: Cambridge, MA.

Lanzing, J.W.A. (1997). *The concept mapping homepage.* [On-line]. Available HTTP: http://users.edte.edte.utwente.nl/lanzing/cm_home.htm.

Lerman, S. (1994). 'Articulating Theories of Mathematics Learning', in P. Ernest (ed.) *Constructing Mathematical Knowledge: Epistemology and Mathematics Education*, London, The Falmer Press.

Machlup, Fritz (1962). The Production and Distribution of Knowledge in the United States. Princeton, NJ: Princeton University Press.

Mahdavi, K. (1996). Humanistic Mathematics. Available online: http://www.forum.swarthmore.edu/orlando/mahdavi.orlando.html.

Martin, D.J. (1994). Concept Mapping as an aid to lesson planning: A longitudinal study. *Journal of Elementary Science Education, 6(2),* 11-30.

Math Forum (1996). Constructivism. Available online: http://www.forum.swarthmore.edu/mathed/constructivism.html

Matthews, M.R. (1998). Introductory comments on philosophy and constructivism in science education. In: Matthews, M. *Constructivism in Science Education.* Kluwer Academic Publishers: Norwell.

Matthews, M.R. (2000). Appraising constructivism in science and mathematics education. In: Phillips, D.C. (ed.) *Constructivism in Education: Opinions and Second Opinions on Controversial Issues.* National Society for the Study of Education: Chicago.

Maturana, Humberto and Varela, Francisco (1987). *The Tree of Knowledge: The biological roots of human understanding.* Boston MA: Shambhala Press.

McManus, T. (1996). Special considerations for designing Internet based instruction. [Online]. Available: http://ccwf.cc.utexas.edu/~mcmanus/special.html.

Millar, R. (Ed.) (1989). *Doing Science: Images of Science in Science Education.* Philadelphia, PA, Falmer Press.

Moore, M.G. & Kearsely, G. (1996). *Distance Education: A systems view.* New York: Wadsworth Publishing Company.

Murphy, D. & Goffin, S.G. (1992). *Project Construct a Curriculum Guide: Understanding the Possibilities.* Jefferson City: MO Department of Elementary and Secondary Education.

NCTM (National Council of Teachers of Mathematics) (2000). Principles and Standards for School Mathematics. http://standards. nctm.org/protoFINAL/.

Noddings, H. (1990). "Constructivism in Mathematics Education." *Journal for Research in Mathematics Education #4*. Reston, Va.: NCTM.

Novak, J. (1977). *A Theory of Education*. Ithaca, NY, Cornell University Press.

Papert, S. (1988). "The Conservation of Piaget: The Computer as Grist to the Constructivist Mill." In *Constructivism in the Computer Age*, edited by G. Forman and P.B. Pufall. Hillsdale, N.J.: Lawrence Erlbaum Associates.

Perkins, D. (1996). Preface: Minds in the "hood", in B. Wilson (ed.) *Constructivist Learning Environments: Case Studies in Instructional Design*, Educational Technology Publication, Englewood Cliffs, NJ.

Perkins, D.N. (1991). Technology meets constructivism: Do they make a marriage? *Educational Technology, (31)* 5, 18-23.

Perkins, D.N. (1991). What constructivism demands of the learner. *Educational Technology, (31)* 10, 19-21.

Perkins, D.N. (1992). Technology meets constructivism: Do they make a marriage? In Duffy, T.M. & Jonassen, D.H. (eds.) *Constructivism and the Technology of Instruction: A Conversation*. Hillsdale, NJ: Lawrence Erlbaum Associates, Publishers.

Piaget, J. & Inhelder, B. (1973). *Memory and Intelligence*. NY: Basic Books. Reigeluth, C.M. (1991). Reflections on the implications of constructivism for educational technology. *Educational Technology, (31)* 10, 34-37.

Piaget, J. (1965). *The Child's Conception of Number*. Norton & Co.

Piaget, J. (1969). *The Mechanisms of Perception*. London: Routledge & Kegan Paul.

Piaget, J. (1970). *The Science of Education and the Psychology of the Child*. NY: Grossman.

Piaget, J. (1972). *To Understand Is To Invent*. New York: The Viking Press, Inc.

Piaget, J. (1983). *The Origin of Intelligence in the Child*. Penguin Books.

Piaget, J. (1987). *Possibility and Necessity*. Volume 1. University of Minnesota Press.

Piaget, J. (1987). *Possibility and Necessity: The Role of Necessity in Cognitive Development*. Volume 2. University of Minnesota Press.

Piaget, J. and B. Inhelder (1971). *Psychology of the Child*. New York: Basic Books.

Piaget, J. *The Development of Thought: Equilibration of Cognitive Structures*. New York, Viking Press, 1977.

Resnick, L. & Resnick, D. (1989). *Assessing the Thinking Curriculum: New Tools for Educational Reform*, National Commission on Testing and Public Policy, Washington, DC.

Roth, M.W. (1994). Student views of collaborative concept mapping: An emancipatory research project. *Science Education, 78(1),* 1-34.

Russo, T.J., Scheurman, G., Harred, L.D. & Leubke, S.R. (1995). *Thinking About Thinking: A Constructivist Approach to Critical Thinking in the College Curriculum.* River Falls, WI: Wisconsin University.

Saunders, W. (1992). The constructivist perspective: Implications and teaching strategies for science. *School Science and Mathematics*, 92(3), 136-41.

Savery, J.R. & Duffy, T.M. (1996). Problem based learning: An instructional model and its constructivist framework. In Brent G. Wilson (Ed.) *Constructivist Learning Environments: Case Studies in Instructional Design.* Englewood Cliffs, NJ: Educational Technology Publication.

Schifter, D. (1996). 'A Constructivist Perspective on Teaching and Learning Mathematics', in C.T. Fosnot (ed.) *Constructivism: Theory, Perspectives and Practice*, New York, Teachers College Press.

Schmidt, S.J. (2000). Ernst von Glasersfeld's philosophy of language: Roots, concepts, perspectives. In: Steffe, L.P. & Thompson, P.W. (eds.) *Radical Constructivism in Action.* Building on the pioneering work of Ernst von Glasersfeld. Routledge Falmer: London.

Schoenfeld, A. (1988). "When Good Teaching Leads to Bad Results: The Disasters of 'Well Taught' Mathematics Courses." *Educational Psychologist* 23, 2: 145–66.

Schön, D. (1987). *Educating the Reflective Practitioner.* San Francisco, CA: Jossey-Bass, Publishers.

Schuurman, G. (1997). Can we pull up South Africa's poor Maths Rating? *Educator's Link.* 1(6), 23-24.

Seltman, M.M. & Seltman, P. (1985). *Piaget's Logic: A Critique of Genetic Epistemology.* Unwin Hyman.

Smith, M.K. (2002). Jerome S. Bruner and the Process of Education, the Encyclopaedia of Informal Education (http://www.infed.org/thinkers/bruner.htm).

Soloman, J. (1987). Social influences on the construction of pupil's understanding of science. *Studies in Science Education,* 14, 63-82.

Spiro, R., Feltovich, P., Jacobson, M. & Coulson, R. 1992, 'Cognitive flexibility, constructivism, and hypertext: Random access for advanced knowledge acquisition in ill-structured domains', in T. Duffy & D. Jonassen (eds.), *Constructivism and the Technology of Instruction: A Conversation*, Lawrence Erlbaum Associates, Hillsdale, NJ.

Spiro, R.J. & Jehng, J.C. (1990). Cognitive Flexibility and Hypertext: Theory and Technology for the Nonlinear and Multidimensional Traversal of Complex Subject Matter. In D. Nix & R.J. Spiro (Eds.) *Cognition, Education, and Multimedia: Exploring Ideas in High Technology.* Hillsdale, N.J: Lawrence Erlbaum Assoc.

Spiro, R.J., Feltovich, P.J., Jacobson, M.J. and Coulson, R.L. (1991). Cognitive Flexibility, Constructivism, and Hypertext: Random Access Instruction for Advanced Knowledge Acquisition in Ill-Structured Domains. In T. Duffy & D. Jonassen (Eds.) *Constructivism and the Technology of Instruction.* Hillsdale, N.J.: Lawrence Erlbaum Assoc., Publishers.

Steffe, L.P. and Tzur, R. (1994). Interaction and Children's Mathematics, in P. Ernest (ed.) *Constructing Mathematical Knowledge: Epistemology and Mathematics Education*, London, The Falmer Press.

Streibel, M. (1993). Instructional Design and Human Practice: What can we learn from Grundy's Interpretation of Habermas' Theory of Technical and Human Interests? In R. Muffoletto and N.M. Knupfer (Eds). *Computers in Education: Social, Political and Historical Perspectives.* Cresskill, N.J.: Hampton Press.

Strolovich, H.D. & Keeps, E. (1991). Selecting and writing case studies for improving human performance. *Performance Improvement Quarterly,* 4(1), 43-54.

The Cognition and Technology Group at Vanderbilt (1993). Designing learning environments that support thinking: The Jasper series as a case study. In T.M. Duffy, J. Lowyck, D.H. Jonassen & T. Welsh (Eds.) *Designing Environments for Constructive Learning.* New York, NY: NATO Scientific Affairs Division.

The Cognition and Technology Group at Vanderbilt (CTGV)2 (1991). Some thoughts about constructivism and instructional design. *Educational Technology, (31)* 10, 16-18.

Thomson, C. & Zeuli, J. (1999). 'The frame and the tapestry: Standards-based reform and professional development', in L. Darling-Hammond & G. Sykes (eds.) *Teaching as the Learning Profession: Handbook of Policy and Practice*, Jossey-Bass Publishers, San Francisco, pp. 341-75.

Tobin, K. & Tippins, D. (1993). *Constructivism as a referent for teaching and learning.* In Tobin, K. (Ed). (1993) *The Practice of constructivism in science education.* Washington DC. AAAS.

Veer, R.V.D. & Valsiner, J. (1991). *Understanding Vygotsky: A Quest for Synthesis.* UK: Blackwell.

von Glasersfeld, E. (1980). *Adaptation and Viability, American Psychologist,* 35(11), 970-74.

von Glasersfeld, E. (1981). The concepts of adaption and viability in a radical theory of knowledge. In I.E. Siegel, D.M. Brodinski, R.M. Golinkoff (eds.) *New Directions in Piagetiean Theory and Practice.* Hillsdale, Erlbaum.

von Glasersfeld, E. (1984). Radical Constructivism. In P. Watzlawick (eds.) *The Invented Reality*. Cambridge, MA: Harvard University Press.

von Glasersfeld, E. (1985). Reconstructing the Concept of Knowledge, *Archives de Psychologie,* 53, 91-101.

von Glasersfeld, E. (1987). *Constructivism as a Scientific Method*. Pergmon Press.

von Glasersfeld, E. (1989). Abstraction, representation, and reflection. In L.P. Steffe (Ed.) *Epistemological Foundations of Mathematical Experience*. New York: Springer. In press.

von Glasersfeld, E. (1989). Cognition, construction of knowledge, and teaching. *Synthese*, 80(1), 121-40.

von Glasersfeld, E. (1990). Environment and Communication. In L. Steffe & T. Wood (Eds). *Transforming Early Childhood Mathematics Education: An International Perspective*. Hillsdale, Erlbaum.

Vygotsky, L.S. (1962). *Thought and Language*. Cambridge, MA: MIT Press.

Vygotsky, L.S. (1978). *Mind in Society.* Cambridge, MA: Harvard University Press.

Wertsch, J.V. (1985). *Cultural, Communication, and Cognition: Vygotskian Perspectives*. Cambridge University Press.

Wheatley, G.H. (1991). Constructivist perspectives on science and mathematics learning. *Science Education* 75 (1), 9-21.

Wiggins, G. *Educative Assessment: Designing Assessments to Inform and Improve Student Performance.* (San Franciso: Jossey-Bass, 1998).

Wilson, B. (1996). *Constructivist Learning Environments*. Englewood Cliffs, NJ: Educational Technology.

Wilson, B.G. (Ed.) (1996). *Constructivist Learning Environments: Case Studies in Instructional Design.* Englewood Cliffs, NJ: Educational Technology Publication.

Zeichner, K. & Liston, D. *Reflective Teaching: An Introduction* (New Jersey: Lawrence Erlbaum Associates, 1996).

http://www.siu.edu/-deweyctr/index2.html

www.newfoundations.com/GALLERY/Dewey.html

www.bu.edu/wcp/Papers/Amer/AmerVand.htm

www.oikos.org/Piagethom.htm

www.oikos.org/vonen.htm

http://www.piaget.org/

http://www.ship.edu/~cgboeree/piaget.html

http://hubcap.clemson.edu/~campber/piaget.html

www.brainconnection.com/topics/?main=fa/piaget

www.nndb.com/people/359/000094077/

http://raven.cc.ukans.edu/~kupsych/dennisk/Cog_Inf.htm

http://www.piaget.org

http://www.psych.ualberta.ca/~mike/Pearl_Street/Dictionary/contents/E/equilibration.htm

http://www.learningandteaching.info/learning/assimacc.htm

http://www.nwlink.com/~donclark/hrd/history/history.html

http://www.kolar.org/vygotsky

http://www.marxists.org/archive/vygotsky

http://mathforum.org/mathed/vygotsky.html

http://www.infed.org/thinkers/bruner.htm

Index

A

Accomodation, 46; 51-52
Adaptation, 19; 54
Alternate assessment, 232; 236; 241
Analytic proposition, 30
Assessment, 231
Assimilation, 46; 51-52
Asynchronus instruction, 315
Authentic assessment, 235

B

Beliefs, 36
Brainstorming, 230

C

Cognition, 31; 84
Cognitive, 36
Cognitive apprenticeship, 215; 331
Cognitive Constructivism, 16
Cognitive development, 59; 64
Cognitive power, 31
Cognitive structure, 57
Conceptual growth, 163
Consciousness, 39; 63-64
Conscious reflection, 56
Co-operative learning, 10
Constructivism, 6-7; 15-17; 19-20; 28; 69; 85; 91; 99-104; 106; 108; 110- 111; 126; 133; 155; 193
Constructivist classroom, 186-188; 192; 194; 196-197; 199
Constructivist curriculum, 393
Constructivist education, 6
Constructivist epistemology, 3; 133; 142
Constructivist teacher, 182-185; 189; 196; 202-205; 209-211; 282
Constructivist teaching, 172; 174-175; 177; 181
Constructivist learning, 144; 149; 152-153; 156
Constructivist research, 435
Constructivist theory, 17-19
Curriculum, 76; 79

D

Developmental constructivism, 116-117
Distance learning: 314-317
Dialectical constructivism, 120; 122
Distributed cognition, 213

E

Education, 39; 42; 46; 79-80; 87
Endogenous, 111; 119
Epistemology, 2-3; 48
Epistemic agents, 21
Epistemic enquiry, 133

Epistemological belief, 105; 167
Epistemological constructivism, 116
Epistemological enquiry, 133
Equilibrium, 46
Exogenous, 111; 119

F

Figurative knowledge, 50

G

Genetic constructivism, 115-116
Growth, 40

H

Human knowledge, 12; 37
Human mind, 26

I

Inference, 32
Inert knowledge, 16
Intelligence, 19
Instructional strategies, 344
Intellectual development, 59; 265
Intelligent enquiry, 36
Intuition, 29

J

Journalling, 362

K

Knower, 4; 138
Knowing, 15; 37; 48; 58; 60; 75
Knowledge, 1; 3; 5; 13; 20; 24; 29-30; 36-37; 40; 49; 54-55; 57; 62; 67; 69; 80-81; 83-84; 87-88; 90-92; 99. 102-104; 106; 110; 133; 135-139; 141-145; 151; 155; 161; 165; 178.

L

Language, 25; 39; 62-63; 71; 82; 179
Learner, 157; 158; 161
Learning, 16; 23-24; 66; 80; 87; 102-104; 107; 109; 145-147; 151; 155-156; 167; 178; 222
Learning Journal, 277
Learning to teach, 264-265
Logical analysis, 19

M

Mathematical knowledge, 409
Meaning, 82; 102; 105
Metacognition, 216; 340
Metaphysical constructivism, 116
Mind, 38-39; 73; 80

N

Non-gradedness, 302

O

Objectivist view, 3-4.
Online environment, 324

P

Perception, 31; 63
Personal theory, 300
Problem-based learning, 213
Professional development, 260-261
Professional preparation, 256
Pure cognition, 31

R

Radical constructivism, 80; 113
Reality, 48; 69
Reason, 25; 43; 81
Reflection, 160
Reflecting teaching, 270
Reflective abstraction, 59
Reliability, 3; 43
Rote learning, 19

S

Scaffolding, 218; 219
Schemas, 50; 53
Self, 45
Service learning, 270
Situated cognition, 215
Situated constructivism, 119; 345
Soft-mathematics, 402
Synthetic proposition, 30

T

Teaching, 127
Teaching strategies, 130
Teacher, 72
Teacher education, 250; 254
Teacher educators, 288
Team-teaching, 305
Theory, 17-18
Think, 37
Thinking, 38; 80
Thought, 68

V

Valid knowledge, 2
Valid study, 3
Validity, 3
Viability, 4

W

Web-based environment, 326

Z

Zone of proximal development, 64-65; 327.